CIVIL ENGINEERING

HOUSING IN TRANSITION

Mildred Deyo Roske

California Polytechnic State University

Holt, Rinehart and Winston

New York   Chicago   San Francisco   Philadelphia
Montreal   Toronto   London   Sydney
Tokyo   Mexico City   Rio de Janeiro   Madrid

Cover and text design by Gloria Gentile

Library of Congress Cataloging in Publication Data

Roske, Mildred Deyo.
Housing in transition.

Includes bibliographies and index.
1.   Housing—United States.   2.   Housing policy—United States.
3.   Home ownership—United States.   4.   Real property—United States.
I.   Title.
HD7293.R75   363.5′0973   82-911
ISBN 0-03-051256-5   AACR2

Address correspondence to:
383 Madison Avenue
New York, N.Y. 10017
All rights reserved
Printed in the United States of America
Published simultaneously in Canada
3 4 5 6   016   9 8 7 6 5 4 3 2 1

CBS COLLEGE PUBLISHING
Holt, Rinehart and Winston
The Dryden Press
Saunders College Publishing

Preface

American housing is changing. This text examines the transition process already well underway. Existing housing is not going to disappear, nor will the ideas that have generated it. Nevertheless, housing in the next twenty years will have somewhat different characteristics. It will in part be produced differently, financed differently, and located in areas not yet developed. Above all, it will shelter individuals and families whose housing needs may differ from those of individuals and families in the past.

The major theme of *Housing in Transition* is composed of seven sub-themes. They are these: (1) a growing and shifting population will create much new housing in some areas of the United States, whereas other areas will meet their housing demand largely with existing housing; (2) families will increasingly consist of singles, single-parent families, elderly, and women employed outside the home, all of which are factors that will alter housing needs; (3) traditional housing values will find expression in alternative forms of housing at the same time that emerging housing values will take on more importance in family housing decisions; (4) inflation may continue to be a major factor in rising costs of new and existing housing and its related costs; (5) housing consumers will help create housing alternatives and financing alternatives; (6) urban decay, the inability of moderate-income families to own their housing, and declining rental housing may spur the creation of new approaches toward solutions of these problems at all levels of government; and finally (7) the housing industry can provide needed leadership to produce well-planned housing for all income levels. These seven themes recur throughout the diverse subjects covered in fourteen chapters.

The organization of this text is designed to introduce the student in a college level housing course to a broad range of topics. The breadth of material is also of value to students in sociology, planning, and real estate.

The text begins with a look at the overall influences on the kinds of housing we have. The history of housing is largely a history of residential land use in the development of towns and cities. The demographic forces that create demand for housing should be understood along with problems of housing production. Stage in the life cycle, lifestyle, social class, and values are interrelated concepts affecting the personal choice of suitable housing. Then, home ownership is explored with emphasis on the process of first-time buying and selling. The experience housing consumers have with housing law through home ownership, renting, codes, and fair housing is covered. This leads into planning concepts because they have become part of the housing laws directly affecting housing trends. The nation's housing problems are the focus of four chapters, the first two dealing with governmental actions, past and present, intended to solve problems. The next chapter deals with the special problems and solutions of housing for the elderly. It is followed by the problems and solutions associated with housing and energy. The final chapter reiterates the main themes of the book by pointing out where changes in housing are likely to occur and ways in which housing consumers can affect desirable changes.

Both the chapter introductions and chapter summaries have been written to help college students comprehend complex material. Each chapter is introduced with a clear outline of the topics covered therein and with an explanation of their logical connection. Summaries are written so that every major point made in each chapter is restated. Both introductions and summaries should facilitate review for examinations.

An extensive glossary, consisting of key words necessary to a housing vocabulary, appears at the end of the book. The first time each glossary term appears in the text it is printed in boldface type for easy identification. Words are often defined in context as well so that the student is provided a definition pertinent to the discussion.

The list of suggested readings at the end of each chapter is provided to give a diverse, up-to-date list of resources a student can use to further research any chapter topic. The readings listed have been selected because they are readable as well as authoritative. The notes for each chapter may provide additional resource material for the serious student.

Boxed inserts are a unique feature of this text. They are separate, short, and interesting pieces that relate to the topics within the text without being tied to them. These shorter pieces can be read or not without losing the cohesive meaning of the chapter. They were selected because of their entertainment value as well as their embellishment on the text material. Illustrations are also used to enrich the text material. They are used extensively in all chapters to provide a visual story of *Housing in Transition* to accompany the written one.

Many persons provided thoughtful comments throughout the process of developing this text. For the care with which critical reviews were done, I wish to thank Marie Anderson, North Texas State University; Jackie Bell, University of Georgia; Jeanette Brandt, Oregon State University; Charles E. Bryant, Southern University; Harold W. Fitzner, Jr., Michigan State University; E. Thomas Garman, Virginia Polytechnic Institute; Marjorie Keiser, Montana State University; James Montgomery, University of Georgia; Roberta Null, Purdue University; Robert Rice, University of Arizona; Peggy Schomaker, University of Maine; and Betty Jo White, Colorado State University.

Two persons were especially helpful and close at hand. Evelyn Lew helped me meet deadlines with flawless typing of moutains of material at a time. Linda Hensley helped me research and organize illustrations and copyright permissions. Two persons were helpful for just being there, my children, Peter and Emily.

Contents

4

THE BASICS OF HOUSING CHOICE   75

5

INFLUENCES ON HOUSING CHOICE   97

6

THE PSYCHOLOGY OF HOUSING   117

7

BUYING AND SELLING YOUR FIRST HOME   140

8

HOME OWNERSHIP IN OTHER FORMS   168

9

HOUSING LAW AND YOU   192

10

PLANNING CONCEPTS AND HOUSING TRENDS 219

11

FEDERAL HOUSING PROGRAMS BEFORE 1974 247

12

GOVERNMENT SOLUTIONS TO CURRENT HOUSING PROBLEMS 267

13

HOUSING FOR THE ELDERLY   288

14

HOUSING AND ENERGY   313

15

HOUSING IN TRANSITION   333

Boxed Inserts

6

7

8

9

10

11

12

13

14

15

Housing in Historical Perspective

1

It is the perspective of this text that housing is currently undergoing dramatic change. The many aspects of that change are the substance of the chapters that follow. Before the focus can be on the transition from one national housing picture to another, an obvious question should be asked: what is the present situation of American housing? The second chapter, Housing Today, attempts to answer that question. This first chapter answers a related question: how did American housing evolve into what it is today?

American housing has always been in transition. The essential factor in colonial settlement was the establishment of communities in an undeveloped land. Primitive housing gave way to permanent and often architecturally interesting structures. Villages grew into towns, and some into cities. Industrialization changed the character of the economy, of cities, and of housing. The great expanses of land to the west evolved into farms and towns and cities. All through American history, the population was growing, the economy was changing, and the characteristics of housing were keeping pace with changing needs.

This introductory chapter examines some of the major trends in American housing history. The primary one of these is the tradition of land settlement. Beginning with the **land-use** pattern in the establishment of New England towns, the section on land settlement also includes early western ex-

Brick row housing replaced wooden "three deckers" built in Boston to house many persons. This Boston row housing shown is similar to that found in Philadelphia, Baltimore, and Washington, D.C. Photo courtesy of U.S. Department of Housing and Urban Development.

pansion, with emphasis on the importance of the **gridiron method of subdivision** in the development of the Midwest. The roles played by the railroads and **speculation** in the tradition of land settlement are also covered in the first chapter section.

The focus then shifts to the problems of urban housing that developed in New York and other major cities. The responses of these rapidly growing industrial cities to the housing needs of thousands of immigrants set in motion a series of housing related events. Distinctly urban forms of housing, as well as government regulation of housing, are the enduring heritage from this era.

The housing trend that has dominated housing in transition in the past hundred years is that of suburbia, and the third chapter section deals with the suburban housing ideal. The chapter concludes with the important historical trend of **prefabrication**, which has evolved recently into the complete production of housing in factories.

THE TRADITION OF LAND SETTLEMENT

The land-use pattern of New England towns has not survived intact in present planning practices, yet it combines elements that have importance in contemporary planning theory. The ideals of sharing common space, building with respect for natural elements, and using land for the community's benefit have currency in today's planning goals.

New England Towns

The most striking characteristic of land use in New England towns was that land was thought of in terms of what it could do best for the community rather than in terms of what it could do as individual property. The

town was a self-sufficient economy in which the family unit was the basic component of labor. Each family was granted a home lot and was obligated to erect a house and barn, plant fruit trees and a garden, and care for family animal stock. The land allocations varied from one-half acre for a bachelor to 20 acres for a larger or wealthy family. The services of millers, blacksmiths, and ministers were acquired by granting these townspeople extra allotments of land. All in all these allocations were the most equitable in American history.[1]

Each family also had a farm plot of about 120 acres, part of which was cultivated and most of which was used for cattle grazing and firewood. Cattle also grazed on the fenced common ground left open by the basic town layout along two streets. The cattle were later removed from this central strip of land, and with relandscaping these common town greens have become, as Warner says, "the envy of most suburban subdivisions ever since."[2]

Houses were lined up along the two town streets. Their building pattern was not so rigid as our present-day practice of house placement. Instead the pattern was irregular because houses were sited to block the wind or to take advantage of exposure or view.[3]

The freedom of opportunity in group instead of individual terms lay at the base of the township system of land use. Individuals could not break away from the basic economic and religious pattern. In succeeding generations, however, the system began to erode. Religious consensus gave way and the cohesive village could not accommodate population growth. Sons and grandsons of the first villagers were given outlying farmlands. "By such inheritance practices, the old New England towns came to resemble the speculator-managed eighteenth-century farm settlements and thus New England fell in with common American ways."[4] Ultimately the New England system of land use

The allocation of land in New England towns resulted in an irregular cluster of houses surrounded by family farmland. Photo courtesy of H. Armstrong Roberts.

was destroyed because it failed to account for change—**demographic change**, economic change, and social change.

Early Expansion

Western expansion began with pioneer settlement west of the Appalachians. One of the first cities to be planned west of these formidable mountains was Pittsburgh. At the junction of two rivers, it was a logical place to settle a town to be used as a place of departure for development of the Ohio Valley. The original plan for Pittsburgh was made up of rectangular lots and parallel streets, but the entire town is divided in its orientation to one of two rivers which joined at the site.

Many earlier settlements evolved into towns. Often settler families built their houses close together for defense purposes. In Kentucky, a stockaded quadrangle form of "town planning" was used for settlements along the Kentucky River. Virginia encouraged western settlement by promising 200-acre land plots to each family in groups of twenty or more families to settle in land-grant territory. The houses were to be clustered together on half-acre sites, but the overall arrangement was to be rectangular.[5]

Louisville had the benefit of the visionary scheme of an early town planner. Open public space was planned along the river front, and at intervals throughout the rectangular street pattern. Later, these public lands were sold and the open space they might have provided a later urban area was lost.[6]

The Giant Gridiron. With the growing interest in western settlement following the Revolution, there was a need for a national land policy. In 1785, the Land Ordinance attempted to solve the problem by dividing up unsettled land and selling it to willing pioneers.

Land was to be laid out in townships, each one six miles square. Each township consisted of thirty-six squares, one mile each. Some of the squares were to be sold at auction as sections, some as townships, and the minimum price was one dollar per acre, in cash. The first surveyed land sold slowly because no credit was available and because the threat of Indian violence had not passed.

Thus the gridiron pattern already used in cities became the dominant framework for planning (and for housing) for the rest of the nation. Reps explains this phenomenon:

> The survey system adopted by the Continental Congress and the policies for disposal of western lands established in 1785 governed the settlement of America during the next century until the closing of the frontier. Today as one flies over the last mountain ridges from the east one sees stretching ahead to the horizon a vast checkerboard of fields and roads. With military precision, modified only on occasion for some severe topographical break, or some earlier system of land distribution, this rectangular grid persists to the shores of the Pacific. America thus lives on a giant gridiron imposed on the natural landscape by the early surveyors carrying out the mandate of the Continental Congress expressed in the Land Ordinance of 1785.[7]

The effect of the Federal Land Survey's grid pattern on housing is also evident today. The original township allocation of squares six miles on a side subdivided into thirty-six even squares (640 acres) has evolved into thousands of towns with main streets one mile apart, and housing set in rigid rectangular patterns in between. The pattern of rectangular houses set back evenly from straight, parallel streets, is our visual heritage, and we repeat it over and over in our **suburbs.** It has not only become an American tradition, it is so much a part of our housing culture that we question any alternative.

Settlement of the Midwest. One theory about the settlement of the Midwest holds that a crossroads provided an attractive position for pioneer home building. A handful of houses evolved into a village, it into a town, and eventually perhaps the towns into the major cities of today. This process no doubt can be found to be historically accurate in some cases. But another more recent theory about settlement in the Midwest holds that many, if not most, of the towns of the Midwest were planned communities. What were to become urban centers were originally the sites selected by individuals, churches, railroads, or governmental agencies. The undeveloped sites were surveyed and laid out into streets, lots, blocks and open spaces. Only then were houses, shops, mills, churches, stores, and public buildings erected at predetermined locations.[8]

The farming potential of the Midwest brought many easterners into the plains to live in very primitive circumstances, not in towns completely planned, if not completely built. The pioneer farmers of the Midwest often erected crude sod huts as initial dwellings before they established farms for their livelihood. By 1850, farm machinery made it possible for the pioneer family to survive. It was the construction of railroads, however, that made it possible for farm families to sell their surplus at urban markets, and to get the goods they needed.

The permanent effect of the Federal Land Survey grid pattern is seen in this map where evenly spaced north-south and east-west streets ignore natural elements. Map reproduced by permission of the American Automobile Association, copyright owner.

Railroads

The development of many towns in the Midwest was largely influenced by the growth of railroads. The formation of a town was determined by the choice of a station stop by the railroad. Once decided, the town was laid out in grid fashion—all streets equidistantly laid due north and south or due east and west. The pattern was inflexible, and according to Jackson, the grid "destroyed or hid all topographical beauty, produced inaccessible building sites, and often made easy communication and assembly impossible."[9]

By 1850, railroads were being built west of Chicago, so that single-family prairie farms could send their produce to eastern markets. The problem of lack of forests in the Midwest was solved by the railroads because lumber could be shipped to the new settlements. Beyer described the process:

Boxlike structures began to appear over the prairie—simple, square or rectangular structures, consisting of one or two rooms, with single slope roofs. Interiors were papered with newspapers. As lumber was raw, cracks developed between boards, and the spaces often were covered over with strips of cloth.[10]

In the post-Civil War period, the further development of railroad towns increased. The Illinois Central railroad, for instance, laid out towns at regular intervals. Thirty-three towns, identical in grid plan, and street nomenclature (based on Philadelphia) were begun along its westward line.[11] The origins of these towns might be obliterated by time and prosperous growth, but the system used in this kind of land development remains a permanent part of the American landscape today.

Factory towns depended on railroads as well. In the factory town, it was the factory management, rather than the railroad, that determined the town form and provided housing for its workers. New factory towns lured workers by providing comfortable houses (or so they were advertised) and community **amenities.** The typical factory town, however, was a grim place dominated by a huge mill and its accompanying piles of raw material. The checkerboard pattern of small frame or brick houses was interspersed with churches, schools, and an occasional library. The main streets were reserved for commerce, and/or saloons.[12]

Speculation

Speculation, within the housing frame of reference, is often accused of contributing to the current problem of rapidly rising housing costs. Yet the practice of buying undeveloped land in the expectation that a large profit would be made with its development has a central role in the tradition of land settlement.

In 1862, the Homestead Act was passed by the U.S. Congress. It allowed the settlement of 160-acre parcels of land for nominal payment, providing the land was used for residence. The consequence of this fed-

eral policy of land disposal was "to deliver up the development of the West—farms, plantations, villages, towns and cities—to private speculator control."[13] It was people with capital, or access to capital, who could buy up many parcels and pay for land clearing, home and barn building, and farm development. The agents of eastern banks had an enormous advantage over individual families. They could purchase a whole valley or townsite and then in turn sell it to settlers. The speculator often became the local money lender as well so that the true homesteaders were dependent on them for farm development.

Speculators also played an important role in the location of key features of development—canals, railroads, county seats, colleges, or hospitals. Many railroads were fought over by competing speculators, and illogical transportation lines resulted. Many colleges, hospitals, and other federal and state institutions are poorly located due to the speculators' power in legislative chambers.[14]

Speculation continued into the twentieth century, indeed into our own time; it witnessed its most successful period after World War I. The growth of existing cities became the setting for enormous speculative landholdings. Detroit with its growing auto industry and Los Angeles with its fledgling movie industry (and desirable climate) were both attracting huge influxes of population. Florida was, and is, an area attractive to tourists and retirees. The speculators' work is easy when the lure of jobs and/or climate is certain to create a demand for housing.

URBAN HOUSING

Immigration in the United States in the nineteenth century was largely a housing problem of eastern cities. The eastern ports

_____ Kansas City and the Railroads _____

At the close of the Civil War in 1865, during which Kansas City, in common with all the border towns of Missouri and Kansas, was disturbed by the conflict, a tremendous immigration began to flow westward through the city. Railroad enterprises in Kansas and beyond were opening up the country for settlement, and the families of those who had lately been engaged in war rushed westward to take up the vacant lands offered them.

Railroad building in the country immediately tributary to Kansas City became active at the close of the Civil War, and has continued until the present time (1901), when two new main lines are under construction

towards the city. The railway companies with lines entering Kansas City now are the Chicago, Burlington & Quincy, the Chicago, Rock Island & Pacific, the Atchison, Topeka & Santa Fé, the Chicago, Milwaukee & St. Paul, the Wabash, the Chicago & Alton, the Missouri Pacific, the Missouri, Kansas & Texas, the St. Louis & San Francisco, the St. Joseph & Grand Island, the Kansas City, Fort Scott & Memphis, the Kansas City Southern, the Chicago & Great Western, the Kansas City & Northern, the Union Pacific, the Suburban Belt, and the Kansas City Belt.

Nowhere in the United States can be seen a better demonstration of

the wonderful development of the transportation system of the country. Besides its trunk-line railroads the city has two belt railway systems and numerous private tracks, so that its equipment for industrial work is unexcelled. Its street-railway system of nearly two hundred miles is one of the finest in America. The tracks and the equipment are thoroughly modern in every respect.

Excerpted from: Gleed, C. S. Kansas City: The Central City. In L. P. Powell Historic Towns of the Western States. *New York: G. P. Putnam's Sons, 1901, pp. 386–389.*

were not only the point of entry for thousands, even millions, of destitute Europeans, they became the permanent places of work and ultimately places of social opportunity. The rapid development of housing to accommodate this population influx resulted in urban housing patterns that are a permanent part of our housing heritage.

New York

Between the War of 1812 and the Civil War, the population of New York expanded eightfold.[15] By the 1840s, the housing form known as the **tenement house** had developed. These were built without governmental regulation to house immigrant families. One early and famous tenement is

described as housing 116 two-room apartments in five floors. The long and narrow building had access to it through very narrow alleys, but each unit was without much light or air as the two small windows in each opened onto the stench of open sewers and doorless privies below. When inspected in 1864 for public health problems, sixty-seven cases of diseases such as smallpox, typhus, and consumption were discovered in what was then considered normal tenement housing for that part of the city.[16]

Most tenements by the 1850s were built on 25 by 100 foot city lots, the result of a grid pattern layout for New York done in 1811. A 25 by 50 foot five-story house was erected at the street side of the lot, and a

25 by 25 foot house was erected at the rear.[17] The little plot of land left in between served as the only access to open air, and it soon became an open sewer as slop from individual apartment windows joined overflowing privy cesspools. At the same time, there was some public concern regarding the crowding, filth, and immorality (it was considered outrageous to observers that young girls slept in the same rooms as the rest of the family and boarders). But new construction of tenements rose to sixteen per week.

Tenement house reforms began to occur in the 1860s. In spite of them, what next evolved was a longer narrow building known as the railroad tenement. It had twelve to sixteen dark rooms on each floor, since only the front two rooms and rear two rooms had light and air. Over the next few decades, improvements in tenement design were more often discussed by health officials than supported by restrictive legislation. Nevertheless, by the 1890s, a tenement form evolved based on city requirements for light, safety, and sanitation. Jackson describes the typical dumbbell tenement of the 1890s period:

> The solution for a standard five-story, fourteen-room-per-floor building was to pinch in the 25 by 85 foot plan at the staircase-toilet center, to increase the length of the slot formed by the party wall indentation to service five rooms on each side, and thus to produce the typical "improved" dumbbell silhouette.[18]

Since each room had a window, the air shaft thus formed was larger than any preceding; stairs were lighted and ventilated;

This present day slum housing in New York City is reminiscent of the tenement houses built 150 years ago. Photo courtesy of U.S. Department of Housing and Urban Development.

water closets were on every floor but removed from living rooms; and each apartment had water and a kitchen sink. The dumbbell tenement was considered to be the ideal way to house poor immigrants. "A tenement acceptable to enlightened opinion had been achieved through evolutionary legislation."[19]

The dumbbell tenement was soon to become the "worst type of housing in New York City."[20] The Tenement House Act of 1901 set up a regulatory department to correct the "evils" of those tenements already constructed. New tenements built thereafter provided more space, light, and ventilation and "were the forerunners of today's better apartment-type structures."[21]

Not all housing in New York built in the 1800s and early 1900s was for the huge numbers of immigrants. The period also saw the construction of "brownstones," so called because of the color of the building material used, which were narrow (20 to 30 feet wide), three-story, single family, and expensive. The narrow width was due to the original lot allocation for the whole city. Originally intended for the building of small single-family houses, with ample garden space in the rear, the long narrow lot was adapted to tenements, brownstones, and later, apartment houses.

The first large-scale apartment building in New York was the Stuyvesant. In 1880, when it was built, New York was not ready for this type of "French flat" as apartments were then called, and it was believed it would lead to the breakdown of the American family.[22] The project was successful. By 1890, hundreds of apartments were being built in New York. Usually, early apartments were built on narrow lots and used narrow deep shafts between building for light and ventilation into interior rooms just as the tenements did. In fact, plans for early apartments were not very different from tenement plans. The difference was in middle-class living habits and in lack of crowding.

Apartments built in the early 1900s ranged from two-room "bed-in-a-door" and "dinette" types, to five-room standard middle-class apartments.[23] Some apartment buildings were especially designed for affluent residents. In these, whole mansions, consisting of libraries, servants' quarters, suites of rooms, vestibules, and so on, were accommodated on one or two floors of very large buildings.[24]

Other City Housing Patterns

With its inflow of population, Boston produced tenements similar to New York's, only there were seldom more than four floors to a building. More typical of Boston housing in the nineteenth century was the "three-decker." It was invented to meet the problem of an average thirty-seven persons per house living in single-family housing in the 1840s. The three-deckers were constructed of wood, and as such, began to disappear after a 1912 fireproofing law took effect in Massachusetts.[25] As late as 1930, however, tenements and three-deckers housed half of Boston's population.[26]

Philadelphia is still distinguished by its row houses built during the last century. They were made smaller to house poor immigrants, and the standard sixteen-foot width, and two stories, might have housed as many as six families.[27] Working people in nineteenth century Philadelphia generally had individual homes.

Baltimore and Washington, D.C. also developed a pattern of narrow brick row housing. Originally designed for single familes, much of this attractive housing was converted to multifamily use, thereby overcrowding it. This practice, however, prevented the building of New York style tenements in these cities.[28]

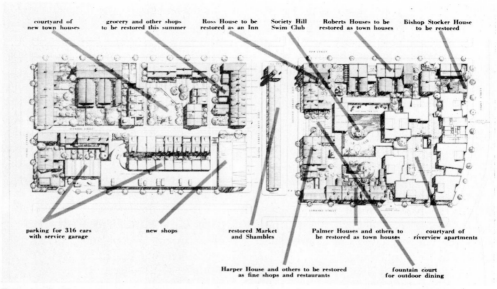

courtyard of
new town houses

grocery and other shops
to be restored this summer

Ross House to be
restored as an Inn

Society Hill
Swim Club

Roberts Houses to be
restored as town houses

Bishop Stocker House
to be restored

parking for 316 cars
with service garage

new shops

restored Market
and Shambles

Palmer Houses and others to
be restored as town houses

courtyard of
riverview apartments

Harper House and others to be restored
as fine shops and restaurants

fountain court
for outdoor dining

This plan for the restoration of Head House Square in Philadelphia indicates the early urban pattern of narrow lots laid out on a grid. Photo courtesy of U.S. Department of Housing and Urban Development.

A Philadelphia style row house was adopted for use in St. Louis, but it was without common walls. It evolved there from 1890 to 1930 from a one-family house to a two-family, then a double two-family, and finally a double three-family type of structure. More and more people were thus accommodated on the same narrow lots.

Chicago, Detroit, and Cleveland all housed growing numbers of working people, but mostly in one and two-story houses. Tenements of the type known in New York, or even in Boston, were almost unknown in these cities.

THE SUBURBAN IDEAL

Perhaps the most important development in our residential heritage was that of suburbs. Suburbs are communities, largely residential, at the outskirts of major cities. Most of the people who live there have traditionally relied on the city itself for jobs, goods and services. In recent times, suburbs have gained in economic and political independence. Indeed, it is possible to live in, work in, shop in, and be entertained in a suburb without ever visiting a city center.

Suburbs began as places to live away from the noise, dirt, commerce, and density of eighteenth century cities. Philadelphia, Boston and New York all had suburbs for those rich residents who could escape to quiet clean air and more room. Brooklyn is cited as the first suburb, but so is Lewellen Park in East Orange, New Jersey.[29] Regardless, the important fact about early suburbs is that the idea of an appropriate style of life had been planted and had taken hold. With the creation of "the tree-planted, landscaped lawn and the invention of the lawnmower, . . . the pattern of the suburban plot, open and fenceless, became established."[30]

Early suburbs were populated only by

Cities and Sanitation

The matter of sanitation has been one of the most serious problems related to American housing throughout its history. Any widespread improvement in sanitaton required water supplies and sewers. Boston was the first city to install a sewer system, in 1652, but it was inadequate almost from the start. It took more than two hundred years before municipal sewerage systems were no longer novelties. In fact, when a system was to be designed for Brooklyn, in 1857, there still was little knowledge on which to draw.

The first water closet had been invented in England in the sixteenth century, but it was an extremely primitive design. Later and more advanced models were patented in that country in the 1770's, one patented in 1778 having a valve at the bottom. Little progress was made during the next half century, but the first American patent for a water closet was entered in 1833.

However, water closets were still relatively scarce by 1860, partly because of the lack of municipal supplies and sewerage and the great burden they placed on already overstrained cesspools. It was 1900 before they were installed in most houses in cities. Rural housing improvement was slower and many farm houses even today still have outdoor privies.

Most cities made little progress in supplying residences with continuous and dependable water supplies until about 1850. Before that time, central pumps and wells were the chief sources of supply. In smaller communities without a municipal water supply, individual householders found it necessary to provide their own wells. In the West, artesian water supplies were developed in some areas. For washing, rain water was collected from the roof and piped into cisterns, which usually were underground but in some instances were on the roof or inside the house, high enough to provide pressure. A small force pump was used to bring the water to the location where it was required.

Water was, of course, unheated at first. Some water was available in reservoirs attached to kitchen ranges, but by the 1840s, boilers had become a chief source of hot water and remained so for many families until central heating had become an established part of the house.

For most people, at least in the nineteenth century, early bathing and washing facilities consisted of a pitcher and basin. The weekly bath was becoming an established practice, but since the water frequently had to be carried in from wells, it was sometimes used by several people. In small houses, bathing, having no place of its own, was a disruptive process. It usually took place in front of the fire or near the stove, in the kitchen or sitting room, and the privacy of the bather was protected by a screen; the rest of the family was relegated to whatever other space they might find while the activity was in process.

There is some question concerning when the first bathtub was introduced into this country. Official government records from 1834 indicate that bathtubs with plumbing had been installed in the White House and were in use at the time of Andrew Jackson's administration. It took some time for this facility to gain popular acceptance, as it was initially denounced by the clergy and even claimed by some doctors to be unhealthful. The first bathtubs were wooden boxes (usually oak or pine) lined with copper, lead, or zinc. Even when cast-iron tubs were put on the market in the 1850's, they were encased in wood. There were some shower baths at this early date, but their numbers were apparently limited by both the scarcity of running water and their general unpopularity.

the wealthy, as they relied on their own carriages to carry them to and from the city. Railways and trolleys were then run into outlying areas, so more and more people could afford to make the move out of the city. As the nation changed from a predominantly **rural** to a predominantly **urban** way of living, between 1910 and 1920, suburban growth around sixty-two of the largest cities was greater than growth within them.[31] In the 1920s, the nation's prosperity, along with available credit, allowed many middle-class city workers to move out into new developments alongside their wealthier predecessors. One form of twentieth century speculation was to develop land with sewers and streets, so that individual lots could be sold to these inner-city escapees.

By the 1930s, governmental action encouraged movement to the suburbs. The **Federal Housing Administration** (FHA), born in the Depression, encouraged suburban growth in several ways. The **FHA mortgage** system allowed, for the first time, low **down payments** and long-term payback periods so that home ownership was available to many families not previously financially qualified. At the same time, FHA bulletins encouraged suburban land development with subdivision layouts, house plans, and standards for minimum lot sizes. One such FHA bulletin stated that the further out the development, the more likely, and economically, large plots of land would be provided for the detached single-family house.[32]

The expanding economy in the prosper-

ous years following World War II allowed even more families, especially young families, to join the move to suburbia. Veterans Administration loans gave returning war veterans even better terms for home buying than FHA. To meet the need for thousands of new housing units at the same time, in the same place, building technology improved. The first mass-produced suburbs began to appear at the outskirts of major cities.

The interdependence of suburban living and automobile transportation cannot be overlooked. It is only when individual families can and will commute to their jobs every day that suburban living is a desirable and affordable alternative to city living. The development of freeway systems in and around most major cities was the result of the pressure of millions of Americans needing to get to work.

FACTORY PRODUCTION OF HOUSING

Lumber mills in settlement areas of the nineteenth century are an example of early prefabrication. Even in the 1820s, canal boats hauled lumber that was framed in Philadelphia to be transported to developing coal towns. As Tunnard and Reed described it, "a city was brought along the canal in sawed off lengths of wood—an early example of prefabrication methods applied to building."[33]

The western plains were settled because of railroad extensions, but also because of

Many middle-class persons moved out of the cities into suburbs during the 1920s and 1930s. Photo by author.

"**portablehouses**" built and shipped from Chicago. One builder in the 1870s built all forms of small buildings—schools, churches, taverns, and houses—to provide instant towns wherever needed.[34] Prefabrication was also part of the early settlements in California in the 1860s. The gingerbread exuberance of San Francisco was an outgrowth of the use of prefabricated gables, bay windows, porches, door and window trims ordered from catalogs and used to embellish an otherwise mass-produced house.

By 1924, the architectural critic, Louis Mumford, was to assess the mechanization of house building. He wrote, "The great mass of modern houses are no longer framed for some definite site and some definite occupants: they are manufactured for a blind market."[35] He bemoaned the cutting of boards in standard lengths, the fabrication of roofing in a roofing plant, the standardization of window frames, and the factory production of everything from china closets to balustrades. "The business of the building worker is reduced to a mere assemblage of parts; and except for the more expensive grades of work, the architect is all but eliminated."[36]

By the 1930s, the trend toward prefabrication was sanctioned by an FHA bulletin. It acknowledged the experimental nature of many prefabrication efforts of that era; nevertheless, it was promoting these efforts by distributing the names of fifty-seven such manufacturers with information about their products.[37]

Of particular interest is the fact that Sears and Roebuck sold 110,000 mail-order houses, "packaged down to the key and house numbers," in a period of forty years. A lesser known company, located in Michigan, had sold 100,000 packaged houses by 1906.[38] Wood prefabrication was widespread during World War I house building.

A retrospective survey of major home builders in America during the period from 1930 to 1960 cites a great many prefabrication innovations during this period. A "stressed skin" **plywood** panel system was adopted by a housing research firm in 1934. Other research foundations experimented with "house systems in frame, steel, panels and **modular** design." Standardized elements for sectional houses such as modular kitchens and baths were explored.[39]

Industrialized methods did not take hold

This aerial photograph illustrates the interdependence of freeway systems and suburban development since 1950. Suburban living for millions of Americans has meant commuting to work. Photo courtesy of U.S. Department of Housing and Urban Development.

in a large scale until the 1940s. The World War II period saw a revolutionized housing industry meeting the demands for thousands of new housing units as well as other types of wartime building. The stimulus in home building during this period resulted in the erection of many so-called temporary housing units. In the public mind, particularly those military personnel who lived in them, the association between prefabricated housing and temporary was permanently made. The stigma lasts to this day.

In the postwar period, a housing shortage was met in part through prefabrication in housing. By then, there were government efforts to sponsor large-scale housing production. The Veterans Emergency Housing Program hoped to offer incentives to build hundreds of thousands of prefabricated houses in 1946 and 1947. The actual construction of prefabricated houses in these years fell far short of those goals (about 37,000 in each year) in spite of the fact that some companies were experimenting with all-steel or all-aluminum manufactured housing.[40]

Of more importance in the postwar period was the adaption of industrialized methods to large-scale development such as the building of Levittown, a suburb of more than 17,000 homes built between 1948 and 1952. Levitt used "mass produc-

Suburbia as Wasteland

The massive, monotonous ugliness of most of our Surburbia must be blamed, in part, on those architects and planners who used to advocate a kind of garden-city development in which each family would have its own plot of land and its own house smack in the center of that plot. One of the leading advocates of this ideal was Frank Lloyd Wright, whose "Broadacre City" concept envisaged one-acre plots per family for most Americans. Wright was, of course, greatly influenced by the agrarian traditions of eighteenth- and nineteenth-century America; and while his proposals reflected those traditions and ideals, they hardly faced up to the desperate problems created by recent population growth in this country (an increase of 350 per cent in Wright's lifetime alone) and in the rest of the world.

What happened to *Broadacre City* (with one-family-per-acre), of course, was that it became Suburbia (with about five-families-per-acre). Yet, despite this rather basic change in density, those who proceeded to practice what they thought Wright had preached made no changes in concept; so that Suburbia today is what Wright himself called, in his later years, "a series of anonymous boxes that go into a row on row upon row," and what others have called "the great suburban sprawl."

Suburbia got that way for two simple reasons: first, because the developers who built it are, fundamentally, no different from manufacturers of any other mass-produced product: they standardize the product, package it, arrange for rapid distribution and easy financing, and sell it off the shelf as fast as they can. And, second, because the federal government, through FHA and other agencies set up to cope with the serious housing shortages that arose after World War II, has imposed a bureaucratic strait jacket on the design of most new houses, on the placement of these houses on individual lots, on landscaping, on street-planning, and on just about everything else that gives Suburbia its "wasteland" appearance.

Excerted from: Blake, P., God's Own Junkyard (New York: Holt, Rinehart and Winston, 1964), p. 17.

tion, planning, purchasing, and community development techniques. Precutting, prefabrication, shop-built components and preassembled plumbing units contributed to his fast site erection system."[41] Another builder of this period used walls fabricated on the site, roofs made of large sheets of plywood, a trussed roof system, and a prefabrication cutting shop. These, along with the use of engineering techniques, power tools and heavy equipment, distinguished him as a "leader in housing research" at that time.[42]

The **mobile home** is the most fully factory prefabricated house. The nearly nonmobile mobile homes of today grew out of the automobile factory methods of producing travel trailers. The housing experimentation of the 1930s, 1940s, and 1950s, never fully resulted in the completeness of prefabrication that the mobile home industry has. In the 1960s, the typical mobile home was 50 feet long and 10 feet wide. Since then, maximum widths have been allowed by state highway laws to expand to 12 feet in most states and 14 or 16 feet in

The prefabrication methods introduced in the postwar period set the pattern for large scale subdivisions built ever since. This contemporary subdivision has incorporated such methods as precutting, shop-built components, and a trussed roof system. Photo by author.

some. Pull-out rooms add additional space and plan variation to these narrow single-width mobile homes. Double-width mobile homes, of course, combine two standard-width units to achieve a house of equivalent square footage to the average three bedroom suburban home. Triple-width mobile homes also have been designed.

Mobile homes have in turn given birth to **modular homes.** These are completed housing units, built similarly to mobile homes and often in the same factories. Without the wheels underneath, they are attached to permanent foundations. Thus a complete factory produced house is delivered to a site, set up on a foundation in a few days, and financed and taxed in the same way as a conventional site-built home.

SUMMARY

The New England town set a pattern of community development still considered a planning ideal. The town was politically, socially and economically cohesive in a way that has never since been achieved. Yet the match of physical layout to the goals of the community has been admired and emulated into our own time.

Early expansion depended on both the willingness of pioneers to settle in strange

territories and the foresight of early planners. The theme of rectangular clustering of houses was evident in early stockaded settlements as well as in planned communities such as Pittsburgh. This early rectangularity in planning took hold on an enormous scale when the entire undeveloped land in the West was surveyed and divided by the Land Ordinance of 1785.

The Midwest was settled in two ways.

Towns were planned with street layouts, open space and designated residential areas before any building began. At the same time, pioneers were individually forging a farming livelihood on the open plains.

The expansion of railroads hastened the development of the Midwest by encouraging town development. They also improved the economic status of the pioneer farmers. Railroad towns and factory towns were laid out so that the pattern of streets and location of facilities were part of the community attributes used to attract potential residents. The grid pattern dominated in these towns, as well as in most development west of the eastern seaboard.

Speculation was aided by the Homestead Act because speculators could and did buy up large tracts of desirable land to be developed and sold at great profits. The practice of speculation not only helped determine the form of towns, and housing in them, throughout the nation, but also affected the expansion of existing cities.

Tenement housing in New York fostered the first efforts at urban housing reform. As tenement building gradually improved, cities came to understand the scale and dilemmas of urban housing. Cities such as Boston, Philadelphia, and St. Louis developed different patterns of urban housing, but also experienced the need to house more and more people in the same space within a relatively short period of time.

No other aspect of housing has shaped the American housing environment as greatly as the suburban ideal. Suburbs began to develop around major cities two centuries ago, but their major impetus came from the development of cheap transportation. This century witnessed government encouragement of suburban growth.

The trend toward standardizing housing components and toward the factory production of major housing parts has been slowly

Modular housing is an outgrowth of the mobile home industry. It is the culmination of more than a century of factory production of housing. Photo courtesy of U.S. Department of Housing and Urban Development.

revolutionizing the housing industry for more than a century. Most of the prefabrication experimentation of the 1930–1970 period has not been widely adapted. Nevertheless, the large-scale building of the postwar period did incorporate many small prefabrication ideas.

The production of mobile homes is truly factory production of housing. The travel trailer has evolved into a full-scale, well-constructed, and nearly immobile mobile home. The same industry that produces double- and triple-width mobile homes also produces modular housing.

American housing, then, is composed of many different types. The surviving New England colonial houses share importance with log cabins, row houses, urban tenements, Midwestern farmhouses, suburban tract houses and mobile homes in filling in the picture of housing today. The differences from region to region and over time form the housing history that has given shape to the housing environment presently in transition.

Notes

1. Warner, S. B., Jr., *The Urban Wilderness* (New York: Harper & Row, 1972), pp. 10–11.
2. Ibid., p. 10.
3. Mumford, L., *Sticks and Stones* (New York: Dover, 1924), p. 22.
4. Warner, *The Urban Wilderness*, p. 13.
5. Reps, J. W., *The Making of Urban America* (Princeton, N.J.: Princeton University Press, 1965), p. 212.
6. Ibid., p. 214.
7. Ibid., pp. 216–17.
8. Reps, J. W., *Cities of the American West: A History of Frontier Urban Planning* (Princeton, N.J.: Princeton University Press, 1979), p. x.
9. Jackson, J. B., *American Space* (New York: W. W. Norton, 1972), p. 31.
10. Beyer, G. H., *Housing and Society* (New York: Macmillan Co., 1965), p. 31.
11. Jackson, *American Space*, pp. 67–68.
12. Tunnard, C., and H. H. Reed, *American Skyline* (New York: Mentor Books, 1956), p. 128.
13. Warner, *The Urban Wilderness*, p. 19.
14. Ibid., p. 20.
15. Jackson, A. J., *A Place Called Home* (Cambridge, Mass.: MIT Press, 1976), p. 5.
16. Ibid., p. 7.
17. Ibid., p. 17.
18. Ibid., p. 72.
19. Ibid., p. 74.
20. Beyer, *Housing and Society*, p. 35.
21. Ibid., p. 36.
22. Tunnard and Reed, *American Skyline*, pp. 122–23.
23. Bemis, A. F., *The Evolving House* (Cambridge, Mass.: MIT Press, 1934), p. 394.
24. Alpern, A., *Apartments for the Affluent: A Historical Survey of Buildings in New York* (New York: McGraw Hill, 1975).
25. Tunnard and Reed, *American Skyline*, p. 101.
26. Beyer, *Housing and Society*, p. 36.
27. Tunnard and Reed, *American Skyline*, p. 100.
28. Beyer, *Housing and Society*, p. 36.
29. Fitch, J. M., *Architecture and the Esthetics of Plenty* (New York: Columbia University Press, 1961), p. 180; and Tunnard and Reed, *American Skyline*, p. 88.
30. Ibid.
31. Beyer, *Housing and Society*, p. 360.
32. Federal Housing Administration, *Planning Neighborhoods for Small Houses*. Technical bulletin No. 5 (Washington, D. C.: U.S. Government Printing Office, 1936), p. 78.

33. Tunnard and Reed, *American Skyline*, p. 70.
34. Jackson, J. B., *American Space*, p. 83.
35. Mumford, *Sticks and Stones*, p. 184.
36. Ibid.
37. Federal Housing Administration, *Recent Developments in Dwelling Construction*. Technical bulletin No. 1 (Washington, D. C.: U.S. Government Printing Office, 1936).
38. Bruce, A. and H. Sanback, *A History of Prefabrication* (New York: John B. Pierce Foundation, 1944), pp. 56–57.
39. Mason, J. B., "Builders of America: 1930–1960," *Builder* Part I (May 1978): p. 51.
40. Beyer, *Housing and Society*, p. 222.
41. Mason, J. B., "Builders of America: 1930–1960," *Builder* Part II (June 1978): p. 56.
42. Ibid.

Suggested Readings

Andrachek, S. E. "Housing the United States: 1890–1929." In G. S. Fish, (ed.). *The Story of Housing*. New York: Macmillan Co., 1979.

Beyer, G. H. *Housing and society*. New York: Macmillan Co., 1965, (chapter 1, "History of American Housing").

Fish, G. S. "Housing Policy during the Great Depression." In *The Story of Housing*. New York: Macmillan, Co., 1979.

Handlin, D. P. *The American Home: Architecture and Society—1815–1915*. Boston: Little, Brown and Co., 1979.

Jackson, K. T. "The Crabgrass Frontier: 150 Years of Suburban Growth in America." In R. A. Mohl and J. F. Richardson, eds. *The Urban Experience: Themes in American History*. Belmont, Cal.: Wadsworth, 1973.

Mason, J. B. "Builders of America: 1930–1960." *Builder*, Part I, May 11, 1978, pp. 43–58; Part II, June 5, 1978, pp. 55–60.

Muessig, P. "Industrialization in Housing." In C. S. Wedin and L. G. Nygren, eds. *Housing Perspectives* (2nd ed.). Minneapolis: Burgess, 1979.

Nenno, M. K. "Housing the Decade of the 1940s—The War and Post-war Periods Leave Their Marks." In G. S. Fish, ed. *The Story of Housing*. New York: Macmillan Co., 1979.

Reps, J. W. *Cities of the American West: A History of Frontier Urban Planning*. Princeton, N.J.: Princeton University Press, 1979.

Wedin, C. S. "A Historical Perspective of Major Forms in American Housing." In C. S. Wedin and L. G. Nygren, eds. *Housing Perspectives* (2nd ed.). Minneapolis: Burgess, 1979.

Woods, M. E. "Housing and Cities, 1790 to 1890." In G. S. Fish, ed. *The Story of Housing*. New York: Macmillan Co., 1979.

Housing Today

2

It is very difficult to assess American housing at any given time. It would be desirable to know exactly what kinds of housing exist, who lives in what types of housing, and what condition all housing is in. Furthermore, the housing industry should know exactly what types of housing to produce, who are the prospective buyers, in what locations they desire the housing, and at what price it should be available. Knowing good answers to these questions, of course, would not lead to the easy provision of housing to satisfy these demands. The nature of the housing industry prevents builders from quickly and accurately providing the amounts and types of housing when and where it is desired. The complex picture of the housing industry is the subject of the next chapter.

Census data, gathered every ten years, is the most complete and accurate infor-mation about the American population and housing characteristics. By comparing the census picture of one time to that of a decade before or after, long range trends in housing can be determined. Even though annual housing surveys are an attempt to keep up with trends, the only time housing specialists have a complete and comprehensive picture of American housing is at the beginning of each decade (1960, 1970, 1980, and so on).

The first section of this chapter covers the broad subject of demography and housing demand by examining four specific

Renovated urban housing has attracted many families back to the city. Inner city condominiums provide the achievement of two goals—ownership and city-center convenience. Photo courtesy of U.S. Department of Housing and Urban Development.

areas: household formation, declining fertility, the baby boom and housing demand, and aging America. The second major chapter section answers the question of "how well are we housed?" The answers are given in both a general framework regarding the nation's housing as a whole, and in a segmented framework in which specific groups are considered. Mobility and migration are the subjects of the third chapter section.

DEMOGRAPHY AND HOUSING DEMAND

The study of the distribution of population throughout all areas of the United States is critical to the study of housing. In the broadest sense, population is related to housing demand because a large number of housing units is needed to shelter a growing population. However, this simple relationship is not precise enough to be useful.

The important concept in analyzing housing demand is **household.** A household is defined by the **Bureau of the Census** as a residential group that occupies a single housing unit. This household can be made up of a single person living alone, a family of related individuals, or a group of unrelated individuals, such as college students. The household may **rent** or own its housing unit, but to be counted as a household, the unit must be its only residence. Traditionally, one person was designated as the head of the household, even in unrelated person arrangements, but there was no requirement that the person share any more than the front door. The 1980 census omitted the term "head of household" and used "householder" instead.

New household formations require individual housing units. Herein lies the essence of housing demand. New housing construction is largely attributable to the

Many different types of households may live in the same type of housing. This apartment building may accommodate single persons, couples, families with children, and unrelated persons living together. Photo courtesy of U.S. Department of Housing and Urban Development.

formation of new households. In recent decades, new households have accounted for two-thirds of new construction.[1] It is difficult to predict what a future rate of household formation will be, but the trend has been toward higher rates of household formation. The American population has been tending to live in smaller, and therefore more numerous, households.

Household Formation

Generally, it can be assumed that as the population of an area, or a nation, increases, then the number of households increases. If, as can happen, the population does not increase, but the number of households forming within the population does increase, this is referred to as the increase in incidence of households.[2] In the period from 1960 to 1975, the incidence of households did increase.

The Joint Center of Urban Studies of MIT and Harvard University outlined six basic factors that affect the household formation behavior of individuals and families.[3] The six major factors in combination affected this increase. At the present time, these six major factors are having fewer positive effects, and may reverse the trend by 1985. The trends in household formation have been identified as they relate to these six factors.[4]

Marital Status. Married couples are more likely to have their own households than are individuals. This is due to the greater wealth and earning power of couples as compared to individuals. Larger households are more likely to absorb a single person than they are a married couple.

The adult age group under 25 form many more households if they are married than if they are not. Since the trend is for more and more people to delay marriage, young adults have had a decrease in the formation of households. Divorce has the opposite effect; one household becomes two. Late marriages and more divorces will probably continue, and the number of nonmarrying young adults staying with their parents will be slightly outnumbered by the increase in households caused by divorces.

Family Size. Large families are unlikely to take in extra related or unrelated persons into what may be an already crowded household situation. Single people, who might move in with a smaller family (fewer children), are unwilling to do so with large families. Large families will be less common in the 1980s than they were in the 1960s. Compared to larger families, the older children of smaller families are less likely to move out and form their own households.

Availability of Relatives. Elderly who live with their grown children are an example of forming a common household with available relatives. A nonelderly single adult could also live with his or her parents, siblings, or children. The closer the family tie, the more likely the sharing of a household will occur, and conversely the fewer close relatives available to an individual, the more likely he or she will form a separate household.

Actually, the parents of the babies born in the 1940s and 1950s, when they become elderly in the 1980s and 1990s, will have more children with whom they may share a household. On the other hand, many of the elderly living today bore children in the 1920s and 1930s, when birth rates were low. So when the whole assessment is made regarding elderly living with children, the young elderly may have a lower incidence of household formation compared to the old elderly incidence of household formation.

Income and Wealth. The greater the capacity to afford the costs of housing, whether renting or buying, the higher the incidence of household formation. A very large house would cost less than two houses, each half the size of the larger house, with individual kitchen, plumbing, and heating facilities. But given the financial resources, two households would generally prefer to live in the two smaller units rather than doubling up in the less costly larger one.

Incomes grew rapidly in the 1960s, and even low-income and elderly groups were better able to afford suitable housing. The rate of growth in incomes is presently slowing down, and the incidence of households due to this factor is slowing down. It is unlikely that there will be substantial changes in redistribution of wealth to benefit low-income or elderly people. Income increases will be smaller, and the effect on household formation weaker than in the past.

Rising Costs of Household Formation.
When the costs of forming a separate household are high, the incidence of doing so will be low. If small apartments are renting at a relatively low cost, an individual wishing to live separately will likely do so. On the other hand, if very large houses are available for a price only slightly more than medium-sized houses, then households will move to larger housing space to keep from overcrowding.

While it was relatively inexpensive to form an individual household in the 1960s and early 1970s, it is becoming increasingly more expensive at the present time. The rate of construction of rental housing has declined. As a consequence, the rents on available multifamily housing will continue to rise.

Household-Housing Match.
The balance between housing demand and housing supply can affect the formation of households. Large households find it difficult to form or stay intact if large housing units are not available. Households then tend to separate into two or more smaller households. If there are more large housing units available than small ones, doubling up of households can occur.

In the recent past, construction has tended toward large single-family housing, accommodating the large families of the 1960s, and toward multifamily housing, accommodating singles, low-income families, and elderly. The present trend is an oversupply of large housing, when family size is decreasing, and an undersupply of middle-sized houses better suited for smaller families. These families then take up multifamily housing that might be better suited for singles. The resulting trend is toward a lower incidence in household formation due to the mismatch of available housing and household formation.

The production of large houses in the 1960s and 1970s was stimulated by the earlier trend towards larger households. The present trend toward smaller households may lead to an oversupply of large houses. Photo by author.

Even though some of the six factors will have a positive effect on household incidence in the 1980s, the effect will be less strong than in the past. Other factors, such as family size, matching households to housing, and housing cost, may have a negative effect.[5] While all six factors worked together to produce an increase in the incidence of household formation in the 1960s and early 1970s, the reverse is true today. It is reasonable to project an actual decline in the incidence of households. Nevertheless, there will likely be an increase in the actual number of households due to an increase in population.[6]

A study of the nation's families from 1960 through 1990 has identified types of households and their expected percentage changes by 1990.[7] Married couples will likely decline from 65.4 percent in 1975 to 54.9 percent by 1990. Households headed by males may double in that time span whereas female-headed households will increase to 29 percent of total households. It is interesting to note on Table 2–1 that the largest proportion of female-headed households will continue to be "widowed," but

TABLE 2-1   Types of Households in 1960 and 1975 and Projected for 1990
(Percentages)

HOUSEHOLD TYPE	YEAR		
	1960	1975	1990
Married Couples	74.8	65.4	54.9
No Children under 15 Present	33.3	34.0	27.2
Children under 15 Present	41.5	31.4	27.7
Other Male Head	8.1	10.9	16.0
Never-Married	3.2	4.7	6.8
Previously Married	4.9	6.2	9.2
No Children under 15 Present	4.4	5.6	8.3
Children under 15 Present	0.5	0.6	0.9
Other Female Head	17.2	23.6	29.0
Never-Married	2.8	4.4	6.3
No Children under 15 Present	2.6	3.7	5.0
Children under 15 Present	0.2	0.7	1.3
Divorced/Separated	4.7	8.2	10.8
No Children under 15 Present	2.6	4.2	5.8
Children under 15 Present	2.1	4.0	5.0
Widowed	9.7	11.0	11.9
No Children under 15 Present	8.6	10.2	11.2
Children under 15 Present	1.1	0.8	0.7

SOURCE: Masnick, G., and M. J. Bane, The Nation's Families: 1960–1990 (Cambridge, Mass.: Joint Center for Urban Studies of MIT and Harvard University, 1980), p. 57.

that the "never-married" and "divorced/separated" will each more than double their 1960 percentages of total households.

Declining Fertility

The national fertility rate has declined since the 1960s. With a fertility rate of 2.1 births per woman, the national population will increase annually by 2.2 million persons throughout the 1980s. The Census Bureau has projected this trend into the 1990s, at which time the population increase will decline.[8] The Census Bureau has also projected national population assuming a greater fertility rate and a much lower fertility rate. If the fertility rate were 2.7 births per woman, the annual population increase would rise sharply in the 1980s, and continue to rise into the next century. A 1.7 births per woman fertility rate would result

in a gradually declining population increase that would fall below **zero population growth** before the year 2025.[9]

The Reasons for Decline. Fertility rates have declined for three reasons. One is the increase in use of contraceptives. By 1975, three out of four married couples were using reliable methods of contraception (the pill, IUDs, or sterilization). A decade earlier, this proportion of married couples using reliable contraception was only one-third.[10] A second reason is that the norm for family size has decreased. Where four or five children per family was normal in the 1950s, two children per family was all that were expected by the 1970s. Some couples prefer to have no children, and even though this is not the norm, it is more and more acceptable family behavior. The third reason is that married couples wishing to have children postpone having them. Women's careers enter into this third reason, as does a desire for economic well-being before childbearing.

Employed Wives. The demographic fact of two-paycheck families relates to the trend toward smaller families. Women are starting working at an earlier age than in the past, but, more importantly, they are continuing work after they bear children. Women may consider their jobs a permanent part of their lives even if they also choose motherhood. Some women have higher paying jobs than in the past, and they are making headway in some traditional male-dominated high-paying professions, particularly medicine and law.

One view of employed wives accounts for varying degrees of attachment to jobs and contributions to family income.[11] Women have increased in their number in the labor force, but mere participation does not reflect accurately career commitment nor increase in family income. The low pay, part-time employment, and impermanent nature of many women's jobs account for surprisingly low levels of commitment to careers in the 1970s, if full-time employment is a measure of commitment to careers. In other words, the fact that 51.1 percent of women 16 and over were labor force participants in 1979 does not account for wide differences in participation, attachment and contributions to family income.[12]

The Baby Boom and Housing Demand

The children of the **baby boom,** that is the extraordinarily large increase in population

---

The baby boom of the 1950s and 1960s has resulted in potential homebuyers in the 1970s and 1980s. This population wave usually seeks smaller rental housing before it seeks the homebuying stage of life at about age 35. Photo courtesy of U.S. Department of Housing and Urban Development.

Housing and the Two-Worker Family

Theoretically at least, two-worker families would be more likely than one-worker families to move to better housing, reflecting their increased income. They might also be more likely to move to ease the time-constraint problems of two workers in getting to work, shopping, chauffeuring children, purchasing services and having access to recreational activities. At the same time, long-distance moves would be less likely because of the difficulties in finding jobs for two people in the same area.

These decisions about where to live are likely to be much more important for wives with strong labor force commitments. Women with part-time or intermittent jobs would not feel the same degree of time pressure. Nor are they likely to consider their own career or job prospects an obstacle to job-related moves by their husbands. Strongly attached working wives, on the other hand, are more likely to favor residential moves that would decrease commuting, shopping and other traveling time. At the same time, career women would be less likely to favor long-distance moves that would jeopardize their marriages or their own spouse's prospects of having a satisfying job.

As women become increasingly attached to the labor force, we expect that two-worker families will develop life styles that reflect their having relatively more money and relatively less time than one-worker families. They might be expected to look for more convenient housing, to invest in time-saving goods and to purchase more services. They might be more interested in leisure activities that can be done at home, or in housing convenient to recreational facilities—especially when they are childless. They may, in sum, demand different kinds of houses, goods and services than one-worker families.

Source: Masnick, G., and M.J. Bane, The Nation's Families: 1960–1990 (Cambridge, Mass.: Joint Center for Urban Studies of MIT and Harvard University, 1980), pp. 120–121.

during the period following World War II, have reached the household forming stage of life. Between 1970 and 1975, when the first half of the babies had turned into 18- to 28-year-olds, four of every nine additional households was headed by a person under 30. By the early 1980s, this wave of the baby boom is reaching the home buying stage of life, the 35 to 44 age group.[13] Following right behind are the children of the rest of the baby boom who will predictably form households, and then move into the home buying stage. Many became home buyers before reaching 35. Morrison describes the sequence well:

The most apparent feature of the population's age distribution today is the baby-boom bulge moving through the successive age boundaries. The bumper crop of babies after the Second World War crowded the schools during the next decade, and began forming their own households in the latter 1960s. From birth to maturity, they have exerted their pressure on the capacity of maternity wards, then schools, and then, the housing market.[14]

One might add that the same pressure already experienced will apply to other areas as well—health care, social security, housing for the elderly, and finally cemeteries.

The housing demand first for rental housing of modest cost, and then single-family housing for young families could have been predicted when the first sign of population increase was apparent. As it is, the supply of appropriate housing has never kept up with the demand. And what about thirty to forty years from now? Will there be an oversupply of single-family housing because the children of the baby-boom bulge have moved into the later years of their lives? They will probably have returned to the smaller housing units they left when they made their first single-family home purchase. Their children, however may replace them in creating a demand for the single-family houses that served their parents in the 1970s and 1980s.

This age group does have elements of unpredictability that should be recognized. They are not marrying and having children as early as their predecessors. Some choose not to marry, and some not to have children after marriage. Nonfamily housing situations are more difficult to categorize into standard housing types. Certainly freer attitudes about lifestyle choices affect housing demand.

Aging America

The baby boom is also critical in analyzing the growing number of older persons in the American population. The twenty-five to thirty million elderly of the 1980s are the parents of the baby boom. The "base of support" is both a psychological and a financial benefit to the increasing number of elderly. "If you could know how the 'baby boom' children will treat their parents—both as offspring and as voters—and how their children will treat them, you could unravel much of the mystery surrounding this impending population upheaval."[15] In about forty years, the number of persons over 65 will probably have doubled, yet the number of middle-aged and younger persons stabilized. Demographers expect the median age, because of this shift in population, to rise from 29 in 1977 to 37 in 2020.[16]

Not only is the number of people falling into the category of elderly growing, once there, they can expect to live longer. Life expectancy itself is increasing, and, therefore, increasing the number of elderly. A 65-year-old man who now expects to live on the average to age 78 will be followed by a 65-year-old man in year 2000 who will have a life expectancy 2 to 5 years longer. Women have the benefit of longer life expectancy (now 4 more years), and it too will increase by the year 2000.[17]

The elderly of the next twenty years will not resemble the present elderly. They will

In about 40 years, the number of persons aged 65 and older will have doubled and they will live longer. Aging America will have different housing needs than the present population. Photo courtesy of U.S. Department of Housing and Urban Development.

Elderly on the Rise

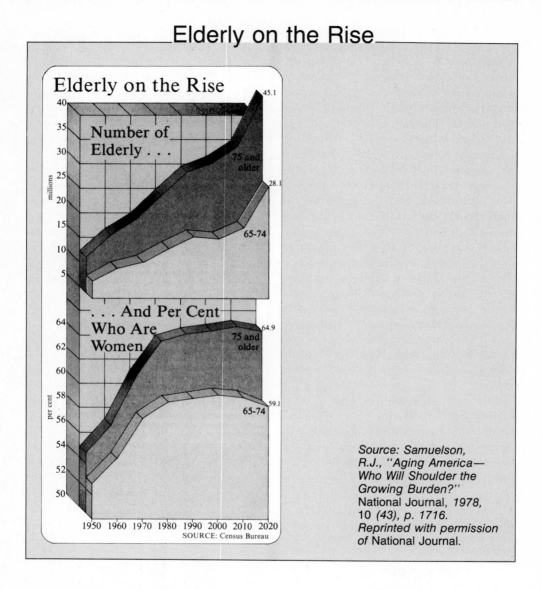

Elderly on the Rise

Number of Elderly . . .

75 and older

65-74

. . . And Per Cent Who Are Women

75 and older

65-74

SOURCE: Census Bureau

Source: Samuelson, R.J., "Aging America— Who Will Shoulder the Growing Burden?" National Journal, *1978, 10 (43), p. 1716. Reprinted with permission of* National Journal.

be better educated, and they will be comprised of a group in which many women worked. The concept of retirement is being challenged, as many older persons seek and find rewarding work, as well as delay official retirement from their major employment. Social security benefits which now assist 90 percent of elderly, will increase in dollars, from an average of $5,643 in 1983 to an average of $17,870 in 2000. The maximum annual benefits for 2000 is expected to be $21,427, but that would be based on a maximum previous year's earnings of $83,400. In 2000, the benefits would range from 53 percent of the previous income, to about 25 percent of the previous income, lower-income persons receiving the greater percent of previous income.[18]

HOW WELL ARE WE HOUSED?

In answering the question of how well we are housed, it is helpful to use a concept related to census information. It is the concept of **Standard Metropolitan Statistical Area (SMSA).** A SMSA is a county that contains at least one city (or twin cities) with a population of 50,000 or more persons. Counties next to each other may constitute a SMSA if there is a city of at least that population. In New England states, towns (townships) and cities are used instead of counties. The name used to identify the SMSA is the name of the city or cities qualifying it for this classification.

Annual Housing Surveys are taken to identify changes in housing characteristics in between **decennial** (complete) census years. The Annual Housing Survey was begun in 1973. Sixty SMSAs (Standard Metropolitan Statistical Areas) are used as a representative sample for all of them. Some Annual Housing Surveys have used twenty of these selected SMSAs, rotating three groups every three years. Beginning in 1978 the sixty SMSAs were divided into four groups of fifteen each.

The Nation's Housing

Comparing the 1978 Annual Housing Survey with the 1970 census, the following information can be derived.[19]

1. The total number of housing units increased from 68,672,000 units to 84,618,000 units, an increase of over 23 percent.
2. The percent of owner-occupied units

also increased, from 62.9 percent in 1970 to 65.2 percent in 1978.
3. The percentage of owner-occupied units was greater outside of SMSAs than inside SMSAs in 1978 as well as in 1970.
4. The rate of increase in owner-occupied units was greater outside SMSAs than inside SMSAs.
5. The rental vacancy rate (the number of year-round units as a percent of the total rental inventory) declined between 1970 and 1978.

In analyzing the numbers of housing units that fall into the Annual Housing Survey structure categories, the data from 1970 compared with data from 1978 provide some interesting changes. Table 2–2 compares density of the structure (as expressed in number of units per structure), renter-occupied and owner-occupied, in both 1970 and 1978.

That we are a nation of home owners is a well-known fact, but we can see in this comparison that both renters and home owners have increased since 1970. In 1978, owner-occupied units comprised over 65 percent of all occupied housing units. Single-family detached units accounted for a sizable increase of owner-occupied units (more than 7.8 million) but the number of rented single-family units decreased. Looking at the 2 to 4 unit category, there was an increase of renter-occupied and owner-occupied.

Even though there may be owner-occupied units in high-rise condominium developments of 20 or more units (even 50 or more units), they are lumped into the single figure for 5 or more units. Ownership in 5 or more units is relatively small.

If all the higher-density categories of renter-occupied units were listed simply as 5 or more units, they would account for the greatest proportion of all rental units, more

TABLE 2–2 Units in Structure, Renter-Occupied and Owner-Occupied, 1970 and 1978
(numbers in thousands)

UNITS IN STRUCTURE	OWNER-OCCUPIED UNITS		RENTER-OCCUPIED UNITS	
	1970	1978	1970	1978
1, detached	34,397	42,198	7,736	7,196
1, attached	1,113	1,799	794	1,101
2 to 4	2,161	2,317	6,218	7,426
5 or more	464	937	NA	NA
5 to 9	NA	NA	2,284	3,302
10 to 19	NA	NA	2,219	2,691
20 to 49	NA	NA	1,873	2,039
50 or more	NA	NA	2,115	2,491
Mobile home or trailer	1,752	3,032	321	639
Total	39,886	50,283	23,560	26,884

Source: U.S. Department of Commerce, Bureau of the Census. Annual Housing Survey: 1978; General housing characteristics for the United States and regions; Current Housing Reports, Series H-150-78, Part A (Washington, D.C.: U.S. Government Printing Office, 1980), p. 1.

than 10 million. But the majority of renters live in low-density units (fewer than 5 in the structure) expressed in the first three categories on Table 2–2 which total 15,723,000 units.

The size of individual housing units has increased since 1970. The median number of rooms per unit of all year-round housing units went up from 5.0 in 1970 to 5.1 in 1978.[20] The increase was due mainly to the increase in the number of rooms of owner-occupied units which had a median size in 1978 of 5.8 rooms per unit. Renter-occupied units stayed the same between 1970 and 1978 with a median of 4.0.

By tabulating the number of owner-occupied units according to the number of rooms in each (1, 2, 3, 4, 5, 6, 7, or more), an interesting comparison occurs between 1970 and 1978.[21] The number of units falling into the 5-room category was greater than any other in 1970, but in 1978, the number of units falling in the 7-rooms or more category was greater than any other. Renter-occupied units, on the other hand, did not show an increase in size. Both in 1970 and 1978, the greatest number of units fell into the 4-room category.

The information about the number of bedrooms also supports the fact that owner-occupied houses have become larger. Half of all owner-occupied units have 3 bedrooms, and a sizable proportion have 4 or more bedrooms (9 million out of 48 million units). More renter-occupied units have 2 bedrooms than have none, 1, 3, 4, or more. The greatest increase in rental units falls into the 2-bedroom category as well.[22]

The distribution of housing units is tabulated according to age.[23] By 1978, more than 16.4 million of the nation's housing stock of year-round housing units were rel-

The housing stock is tabulated according to age. Houses built before 1939 comprise a large portion of the present housing stock whereas housing produced since then is categorized by decade. The apartment units in this illustration are typical of multifamily housing built in the 1960s. Photo by author.

atively new; they had been built between 1970 and 1978. Older houses, those built in 1939 or earlier, comprised a very large portion of the total number of units, nearly 27 million. Looking at the decades between 1940 and 1970, the numbers of housing units fall into these categories: almost 8 million in the 1940 to 1949 period; almost 14 million in the 1950 to 1959 period and more than 17 million in the 1960 to 1969 period.

Plumbing facilities have been used as a measure of housing adequacy. In the 1978 Annual Housing Survey, the data for "lacking some or all plumbing facilities" is 2.5 million units.[24] Of these, 718,000 are owner-occupied and many more, 1,073,000 are renter-occupied. Owner-occupied units also have more bathrooms than do renter-occupied. Slightly more than half of owner-occupied units have one and one-half baths or more, but the great majority of renters (82 percent) live in units with one bathroom.[25]

The nation's housing is largely outfitted with individual kitchens. More than 392,000 units of owner-occupied housing have no kitchen facilities (8,000 households share kitchens with other households). The rental situation is not as good as this. Renter-occupied units have more than 762,000 units with no complete kitchen facilities.[26]

As might be expected, there are larger households living in owner-occupied units than in renter-occupied units. But from 1970 to 1978, the median size of household for owner-occupied units fell slightly, from 3.0 persons to 2.7 persons. Renter-occupied households also fell—from a median of 2.3 persons per household in 1970 to 2.0 in 1978. Renter-occupied households were generally larger outside of SMSAs than in SMSAs in both 1970 and 1978.[27]

Crowding is measured by the number of persons per room. The number of persons in the household is divided by the number of rooms used for living purposes. Even though this measure does not take into account the size of the rooms (or the ages of the persons), it has been a consistent method of assessing the reduction of crowding over the years. For instance, in 1970 the number of both renter-occupied and owner-occupied units with severe overcrowding (1.51 persons per room or more) was greatly reduced. The number of such units in central cities was reduced by one-third; the number of such units outside SMSAs was reduced by only 17 percent.[28]

Of the over 50 million owner-occupied units in 1978, over 30 million had a persons per room ratio of .5 or less (61 percent). This is an improvement from 1970 when 53 percent of owner-occupied units were at this lowest tabulated measure of crowding.[29] But this 8 percent improvement in numbers of units at this low persons-per-room ratio is overshadowed by the comparison of renter-occupied units. They increased in the .5 person-per-room ratio by category 11 percent, from 45 percent in 1970 to 56 percent in 1978.[30]

Rural Housing

To answer the question of how well we are housed, the focus on this section is on **rural housing**. Rural housing is defined as households living on farms, living in open country but not on farms, and in very small communities (under 2,500 population).[31] Some of these households are within Standard Metropolitan Statistical Areas. In 1976, about 28 percent of all households in the nation were rural but a very large majority of them do not farm the land.[32]

"Rural household" as used here is an abstraction of all rural households—from the very affluent to the very poor. More rural households own their own homes than do urban households—78 percent compared to 65 percent. Most of the rural home owners, however, live on less than ten acres.

Many own their homes free and clear.[33]

The contrast of rural housing characteristics is reflected in several ways. Generally it is of lower value than urban housing. Rural housing is more likely to have flaws; the estimate in 1976 for the national housing picture was 9.7 percent, but the estimate for rural housing was 12.4 percent.[34] Rural housing is more often defective in plumbing, sewage and kitchen facilities whereas the nation's housing as a whole is more likely to have problems with maintenance. In addition, rural households more frequently spend a larger portion of their incomes for housing than the general population. "Only 74 percent of rural households can be expected to find unflawed, uncrowded housing for the traditional 25 percent of income, and only about 79 percent can find it for 30 percent of income."[35]

Elderly Housing

How well are the **elderly** housed? The question is answered with several facts based on the 1976 housing survey. Households consisting of two people, with the husband at least sixty-five years old, account for slightly less than half of the elderly population (excluding persons in nursing homes, hospitals, and other group quarters). Of the elderly households in which the head of the household is sixty-five or older, 10 percent are single men and 33 percent are single women.[36]

Most elderly people live inside of SMSAs (63 percent). This is a slightly lower percentage than for the general population. Most are home owners (71 percent), and for elderly couples, the percentage is very high (83 percent).[37] The elderly and the general population live in multifamily houses and mobile homes in about equal proportions in spite of the fact that there are more elderly home owners than in the gen-

There is a higher percentage of homeowners among rural residents than urban residents, but most live on less than ten acres of land. Many older rural homeowners own their houses free and clear. Photo courtesy of U.S. Deprtment of Housing and Urban Development.

eral population. But the elderly live in older housing than the general population. And the housing has a higher proportion of some inadequacies than the general housing stock; for instance, inadequacies of plumbing, kitchen, sewage, maintenance and toilet access.[38]

Even though one can conclude that most of the elderly are adequately housed, there are housing problems for about one million elderly households. Apparently elderly males have a greater chance than elderly females to be inadequately housed, and elderly minorities have a greater chance to be inadequately housed than elderly whites. A **Hispanic** male over sixty-five has a 50 percent chance of being ill-housed.[39]

The rule of thumb that 25 percent of income is the proper amount to spend on housing can be applied to elderly housing. "Barely 59 percent of elderly households can be expected to find adequate housing for 25 percent of income, and only 66.5 percent can find adequate housing for 30 percent of income."[40] This compares with 80 percent and 84 percent respectively for the general population.

Elderly renters are especially disadvantaged. "Housing absorbs an extraordinarily large proportion of the cash incomes of at least the 3.9 million elderly households that rent their dwelling units."[41] In contrast, a high proportion of elderly home owners (84 percent) have paid off their **mortgages,** so their monthly costs of housing are greatly reduced. Nevertheless, they could not afford to buy equivalent housing.

Female-Headed Households

Almost a quarter of all households in 1976 were headed by women. More than 14 percent of all families were headed by women, and one-third of them were in the poverty-income category. But half of the women who head families work outside the home. The women who live alone are largely widows (elderly women are included in this as well as in other data in this section). Of the women living alone, there were more singles than divorced and a small percent of married with "absent" husbands.[42]

Compared with the general population, women who head households are more likely to have these housing characteristics:

(1) live in an urban area; (2) rent rather than own (53 percent); (3) live in multifamily dwellings; (4) live in older housing units; and (5) have maintenance and plumbing problems with their housing.[43] Large families headed by women are more likely to be ill-housed than smaller families headed by women or single women.

Female-headed households have even less chance than the elderly to find adequate housing within the 25 percent of income guideline—53 percent compared to 59 percent (the whole nation's percentage is 80). However, the measures of inadequacy show that these women live in adequate housing only in slightly lower proportions than those of the general population whereas their ability to pay for adequate housing is considerably lower.[44]

Housing for Blacks and Hispanics

The 11 percent of the American population which is black is generally housed very badly. The housing is flawed twice as often as the nation's housing, it is often aging, and it is very likely in urban areas, especially central cities.

> Almost everywhere in the country their neighborhood choices remain more restricted than whites. Some observers believe that historical factors may discourage some blacks, particularly women, from purchasing homes when they could afford to do so. Finally, and perhaps primarily, the availability of adequate housing for

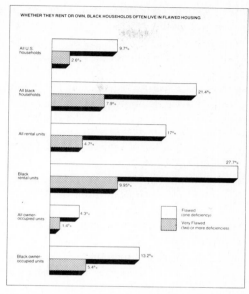

Figure 2–1. Whether They Rent or Own, Black Households Often Live in Flawed Housing

Source: U.S. Department of Housing and Urban Development, How Well Are We Housed? 3. Blacks (Washington, D.C.: Author, 1979), p. 10.

blacks is limited by their income, which is very considerably lower than that of the total population.[45]

Blacks as a group cannot afford adequate uncrowded housing in the same proportions as the whole population. Income is a determining factor in how well or how poorly blacks are housed. Maintenance is the leading physical flaw for rental housing, but plumbing and maintenance are the major flaws of owner-occupied housing. Both renters and owners who are blacks live in housing that has deficiencies in a higher proportion than the housing of the total population. These comparisons are made on Figure 2–1.

Hispanics also live in urban areas and in

One-third of elderly households are single women. Most elderly live inside Standard Metropolitan Statistical Areas (SMSAs) and women in this group have a greater chance of being adequately housed than men in this group. Photo courtesy of U.S. Department of Housing and Urban Development.

older, often inadequate housing when compared to the general population. Economically, Hispanics are better able to afford adequate housing than are blacks. The Cuban population in 1976 could afford housing to a greater extent than the population as a whole, but Puerto Ricans were much worse off. There are wider disparities in the housing of Hispanic groups than between Hispanics and the general public.[46]

The housing deficiencies for Hispanics have generally improved as they have for the other focus groups discussed. There are, however, interesting variations between the subgroups included in the Hispanic population. Table 2–3 shows the improvement of each subgroup.

To summarize, blacks and Hispanics have generally poorer housing and spend a higher portion of their income for it. Blacks as a group are more likely to live in inadequate housing than Hispanics. But Puerto Ricans are much worse off than blacks. The sex of the head of household seems to make a difference on the chances of having adequate housing. "A very poor Hispanic male over 65 years of age is the likeliest of his ethnic group to live in bad housing. A very poor Hispanic woman, on the other hand, is least likely to live in a unit with housing flaws."[47] The male would have a 50 percent chance, and the female an 80 percent chance of having good housing.

MOBILITY AND MIGRATION

At least as important as how many of us there are is the question of where do we want to live. We are a nation of movers. We move anywhere from a few blocks to a few states. The general trends in mobility and migration are the subject of this section.

Mobility

A short-distance move is residential mobility. If one changes residence within the same labor and housing market, however large, then the move is classified as mobility rather than migration. The actual distances can vary greatly. For instance, mobility in the Los Angeles urban region could involve a move of as much as sixty miles, whereas a move from one small cohesive community to another thirty miles away would constitute migration.

There are many more movers who are moving locally than to another region or state. Two-thirds of the nation's movers are changing residences and not changing jobs (at least at the same time). The primary motivation is improvement in housing. Even if the move is into another county, it is considered mobility if the labor and housing markets remain the same.

Why do so many of us move (20 percent every year)? The obvious answer is that we don't like where we are living. Clearly an increase in income can affect moving by allowing higher rent or home purchase, or a larger house, or more bedrooms or a better neighborhood, and so on.[48] Any one of these things, especially a poor neighborhood, can motivate a family to move. As a

TABLE 2–3   Percentage of Housing Units with Housing Flaws, 1975 and 1976

	1975	1976
Total population	10.1%	9.7%
Hispanic population	20.0%	18.5%
Mexican Americans	20.2%	18.9%
Cubans	7.1%	9.8%
Puerto Ricans	32.7%	27.1%
Central or South		
Americans	21.5%	16.4%

Source: U.S. Department of Housing and Urban Development, How Well Are We Housed? 1. Hispanics (Washington, D.C.: Author, 1980), p. 15.

couple forms a family and as the family grows, a need for more housing space will motivate a move. Having too much space, too many bedrooms, or too high maintenance costs can also provide motivation for late middle-age or elderly persons.

Traditionally, the movement of couples and families from rental units to owned single-family housing, a change in both type of housing and **tenure,** has also meant a move from the center or near center of the city to its outskirts. Even though there is no indication that the trend from renting to owning a home is subsiding, the moves involved may not be as unidirectional as in the past. There are many more rental units in the suburbs than twenty years ago. A young family can now achieve its desired tenure change by moving only a few blocks, or at most, a few miles into a neighboring suburb. As more and more **inner-city** apartments are converted into **condominiums,** ownership can be achieved by moving from a suburban rental apartment to an inner-city dwelling. For some, ownership is achieved by not moving at all.

The back-to-the-city movement is one small part of mobility trends. In a move counter to the general trend of leaving the city for the suburbs, some **middle-class** families have moved back into city-center houses. For the most part, these have been old houses in disrepair, but worth restoring because of their architectural merit and because of their convenient locations. Economy and personal achievement are also part of the motivation. Some cities which have experienced such back-to-the-city mobility are Boston, Philadelphia, San Francisco, Washington, D.C., Detroit, and New York.

Whether or not the rejuvenation of some older neighborhoods in some cities marks a general trend to move back into the city remains to be seen. Well-paying white-collar jobs are at the basis of this mobility as well as the suitability of inner-city housing to some stages in the life cycle and some life-styles. At least one demographer predicts that the general trend toward city abandonment ("downward spiral") will not be offset by the numbers of families who have moved back.[49]

Migration Patterns

Migration involves the long-range moves from one housing and labor market to another. The primary cause of migration is job improvement; a company may transfer an employee, or the employee may seek new job opportunities. Improved housing may result from the migration, but it is not the primary factor involved in it. The migration patterns of the nation as a whole can help determine housing demands in some areas, and explain oversupplies in others.

A useful concept in analyzing migration patterns is the regional divisions used by the Bureau of the Census. The whole of the United States mainland (excluding Alaska and Hawaii) is divided into four regions. The Northeast is the smallest, containing the New England and Mid-Atlantic states. The South is the region stretching from the Atlantic to Texas. The West is the largest region with Pacific and Mountain states included. And the North Central region includes thirteen states surrounded by the other three regions and Canada.

The number of SMSAs has increased since the 1970 census when 243 were used for data collection. By 1978, there were 259 SMSAs. About 16 percent of them (42) did not show population growth during the 1970s. What is significant is that most (75 percent) of these nongrowing SMSAs are in the northeastern part of the country. Migration away from the major northeastern cities is the major reason for this pattern.[50]

Another regional migration pattern is the

Both Florida and Arizona have attracted retirees from the Northeast and other colder regions. These residents of Sun City, Arizona are among the Sunbelt population growth phenomenon. Photo courtesy of Del E. Webb Development Co.

migration to the South will probably continue, and it has been predicted that the population growth there will be as large as that of the other three regions combined. (Northeast, North Central, and West).[51]

The pattern of migration to the West, particularly to California, continues. The Southwest has attracted retirees, along with Florida. California's climate and expanding economy have attracted job seekers for decades. Even though Los Angelinos have been known to move to Montana to get out of the "rat-race," the overall trend is still for population inflow into California, especially San Diego and San Jose. The trend of migration into both the South and the West has inspired the term **"Sunbelt"** to describe these growing regions.

Another dramatic migration pattern is

Migration to the South and the West may result in a disproportionate amount of deteriorated housing in older Northeastern urban areas. There will be fewer residents to share the burden of the problems these cities will have in maintaining its housing, providing services, and rejuvenating public facilities. Photo courtesy of U.S. Department of Housing and Urban Development.

growth in the South. There is a slight decline in the natural growth in the population of this region, but the overall population has increased. The reason is migration. Because migrants tend to be job seekers, that is voting-age adults, the political, economic, and cultural dynamics of the South will respond to this population shift. The

The Sunbelt Growth Phenomenon

No simple generalizations can be made about the economic bases of Sunbelt growth. It is probably true that many Americans want a better climate and a new way of life, but except for those who are retired or of independent means, jobs and businesses are needed (and to enjoy the climate, air-conditioning is often needed, and it is becoming expensive). Retirement living on transfer payments is part of the economic base in Florida, together with the dynamic influx of the Cuban refugee population. Oil and gas, both as industries and as forms of wealth, are part of the base in Texas. Military establishments and procurement are an important element in California, Washington, and much of the South. Regional functions and services are important to certain Southern metropolises that are situated in areas of rapid economic growth, just as they are to metropolises in California's Central Valley and parts of Texas, which are suffering decline.

Some shifts are visible within the growth patterns of the Sunbelt. The Pacific coast still has fast-growing areas, such as San Diego and San Jose, but its overall growth has been blunted, with the Los Angeles, San Francisco, and Seattle areas losing population in 1970–75. The Mountain States are growing rapidly, and so are areas in Appalachia and the Ozarks, which had been economic backwaters.

No comprehensive analysis of the components of Sunbelt growth has come to my attention, although a variety of partial studies is available. It appears that the expansion is broadly based on manufacturing and services, resulting in part from competitive shifts of economic activities formerly based in older areas, and in part from specialization in economic activities that are themselves growing rapidly.

In a very general way, part of the Sunbelt phenomenon rests on the shift to the "service," "post-industrial," or "information" economy, which complements the increased preference for the climate and life style of the Sunbelt. Try, for instance, asking the operator who answers an 800 area code for an airline, hotel, or car-rental company where she is located. From the point of view of the economics of communications cost, she could be anywhere, but in fact she is likely to be in a Sunbelt city like Denver. The extraordinary advances in the standardization, routine handling, and transmission of information, which render it subject to economies of scale and the use of semi-skilled labor (such as that telephone operator), make it possible to locate an increasing number of economic activities where they are wanted, rather than where they are forced to be. (On the other hand, it must be noted that Sunbelt metropolises are more than holding their own in manufacturing employment, as compared to older urban centers.)

Are there then different factors for Florida, the South, the Central States, and the Pacific States that coincide to create the Sunbelt phenomenon? What appears to be going on is a very long-run equalization of the national distribution of urban centers, restoring the South to national parity from the century-old effects of the Civil War, and filling in the country westward to rectify the original mistake of the first British settlers, who landed on the right-hand corner of our nation's map. It is worth repeating that the growth of many Sunbelt centers is not a recent phenomenon, but one that goes back almost to the turn of the century.

It was not noticed earlier because high rates of natural increase everywhere masked the differential growth based on inter-metropolitan migration.

Excerpted from: Alonso, W., "Metropolis without Growth." The Public Interest, 1978, 53, 80–81. Reprinted with permission of the author.

the move to **nonmetropolitan areas.** As recently as the 1960s, the flow of migration was into the cities, but that reversed by the early 1970s. "Nearly two-thirds of all nonmetropolitan counties have gained migrants in the 1970s, compared with only one-fourth in the 1960s, and one-tenth in the 1950s."[52]

The trend to small towns, and truly rural living, will affect those regions with less spectacular growth from migration than the South. When people decide to move to the country, they may do so within the same region. The Northeast and North Central regions will have a relatively small increase in population in the 1980s, nevertheless, there will be a demand for new housing in smaller cities and towns. The South, by comparison, will probably experience a growth of population in its rural areas as well as in its **metropolitan areas.**

Two major problems occur with the urban to rural migration pattern. The first, and familiar one, is the problem of decaying cities. As affluent whites leave for better jobs, and the implied better living environment, the city is left housing blacks, elderly and poor in disproportionate numbers. As overall population decreases in a metropolitan area, there is at the same time a huge demand for social services, while there are fewer residents to bear the tax burden of them. The shrinking city also shows decline through its underused schools, outmoded public facilities, aging factories, stores, and offices, and, most pertinently, abandoned housing. Much of the occupied housing is obsolete and deteriorated. These

"shrinking pains" are evidenced nationwide, not just in the Northeast where population declines are most dramatic.

The migration trend causes problems for the small towns and cities to which the urban migrants move. Seemingly overnight small communities, used to a stable or shrinking population, feel the pressures of growth. Immigration means the need for more schools, more social services, more houses. Congestion, sprawl and high support costs can result. Some communities have attempted to block the tide with policies that limit their rate of growth.

The 1980 Census. The migration patterns clearly established in the 1970s resulted in some dramatic changes in numbers of housing units. Comparing the 1980 Census to the previous census in 1970, the highest percentages of increase by region was achieved in the West and the South. The Mountain area of the West had the highest increase, 63.9 percent, while maintaining the smallest number of units for a division. Contrasting to this change, the middle Atlantic division of the Northeast had the lowest percent of increase, 12.8 percent.[53] Table 2–4 lists the comparative numbers of housing units and the percentages of change since 1970.

Individual states have experienced a wide range of growth changes. An extremely high growth pattern was experienced by Nevada which nearly doubled its housing units in ten years. Nearly all the top ten states regarding increases in housing units experienced over 50 percent increase. The nine

TABLE 2–4   Housing Unit Counts by Regions and Divisions: 1980 and 1970

REGION AND DIVISIONS	HOUSING UNITS		PERCENTAGE OF CHANGE
	1980	1970	1970 to 1980
Northeast	19,086,412	16,648,626	14.6
New England	4,850,375	4,033,047	20.2
Middle Atlantic	14,236,037	12,615,579	12.8
North Central	22,819,109	18,978,658	20.0
East North Central	15,970,364	13,329,258	19.6
West North Central	6,848,745	5,649,400	21.0
South	29,409,566	21,037,211	39.6
South Atlantic	14,682,883	10,255,253	42.9
East South Central	5,494,897	4,185,733	31.2
West South Central	9,231,786	6,596,225	39.8
West	17,079,487	12,039,820	41.7
Mountain	4,531,863	2,765,566	63.7
Pacific	12,547,624	9,274,254	35.1

Source: U.S. Department of Commerce, Bureau of the Census.1980 Census of Population and Housing: United States Summary Advance Report. (Washington, D.C.: Author, 1981), p. 4.

lowest growth states and the District of Columbia all experienced a change of under 20 percent. It is interesting to note the differences in increases in housing units compared to increases in population, also expressed in percentages. There are many states with markedly different rates of growth for population and housing units. For instance, Montana had a population increase of 13.3 percent, but in the same ten-year period, the housing units increased by 33.2 percent. Maryland is another example with 7.5 percent increase in population accompanied by a 25.7 percent increase in housing units.[54] Table 2–5 lists the ten fastest growing states during the 1970s decade as well as the nine slowest growing states including the two that lost population, Rhode Island and New York. The District of Columbia, with its loss of 16 percent in population experienced the only decrease in housing units (-0.6%). Without exception, every state had a larger percentage of increase in housing units than it did in population.

_____ SUMMARY _____

Demographic information as it relates to housing is most pertinent when it is translated into predictions of household information. Households are formed according to demographic trends in marriage, family size, and income levels. Housing costs also affect household formation. The trends of the past will give way to new trends empha-

TABLE 2–5   Highest and Lowest Population and Housing Unit Percent of Change: 1980

STATES	POPULATION PERCENT OF CHANGE 1970 TO 1980	HOUSING UNIT PERCENT OF CHANGE 1970 TO 1980
1. Nevada	63.5	96.8
2. Arizona	53.1	89.5
3. Florida	43.4	73.1
4. Wyoming	41.6	62.2
5. Utah	37.9	55.2
6. Alaska	32.4	78.8
7. Idaho	32.4	53.3
8. Colorado	30.7	57.5
9. New Mexico	27.8	55.3
10. Texas	27.1	44.9
42. Iowa	3.1	17.3
43. New Jersey	2.7	16.0
44. Illinois	2.8	16.6
45. Connecticut	2.5	18.1
46. Ohio	1.3	18.5
47. Massachusetts	0.8	16.8
48. Pennsylvania	0.6	17.1
49. Rhode Island	− 0.3	17.3
50. New York	− 3.8	9.0
51. District of Columbia	− 15.7	− 0.6

Source: U.S. Department of Commerce, Bureau of the Census. 1980 Census of Population and Housing: United States Summary Advance Report. (Washington, D.C.: Author, 1981), p. 4.

sizing the increase of single person households, male and female, each with and without children.

The nation's fertility rate is falling. Housing demand will depend on the size of future families and later the households future adults will form. One important aspect related to declining fertility is the trend of women working outside of the home. The employment data of women, however, must be balanced by other information regarding their career attachment and their contribution to family income. The single most dramatic demographic fact for the 1980s is the effect of the baby boom on the housing market.

The growing numbers of elderly in America increases the median age. The elderly to be housed with and by the children of the baby boom will be relatively better off financially and better educated than elderly in the past.

To answer the question of "how well are we housed?" several answers were given. The first was the general picture of the nation's high proportion of home ownership. Houses that are owned tend to be getting larger, to have more bathrooms and bedrooms, and to house fewer persons. Rental units have improved in size and facilities, but they are not comparable to owner-occupied units. Rural housing is not as new, as large, or in as good condition as the housing of the nation as a whole. Elderly housing appears to be generally good, with that of elderly home owners being very good. Elderly renters often have inadequacies in their housing units and also find it difficult to pay for housing.

The housing of women heads of households, blacks and Hispanics all share some common characteristics. It is difficult for many members of these groups to pay a reasonable amount of their incomes on housing. The housing often has inadequacies,

and it tends to be in urban areas. Hispanics have startling differences among subgroups, with Puerto Ricans being housed much more poorly than Cubans.

Mobility, moving within a housing or employment region, is very often motivated by a higher income, a desire for a better neighborhood, and a need for more space to accommodate an expanding family. Renters will move in order to achieve home ownership. A recent trend in mobility is the move back to the city.

Migration has been most evident in patterns of declining population in the Northeast and increasing population in the South and West—the Sunbelt. There has also been a migration pattern out of metropolitan areas, which may cause problems for both the cities that have been left behind as well as for the smaller communities which absorb large numbers of newcomers. The 1980 preliminary census revealed large differences in rates of increase for population and housing units by region and by state, with some areas showing a decrease in population and all areas showing from .2 percent to 96.8 percent increase in units.

Notes

1. Frieden, B. J., and A. P. Solomon, *The Nation's Housing: 1975 to 1985* (Cambridge, Mass.: Joint Center for Urban Studies of MIT and Harvard University, 1977), p. 3.
2. Ibid., p. 18.
3. Ibid., pp. 25–28.
4. Ibid., pp 31–37.
5. Ibid., p. 37.
6. Ibid., p. 31.
7. Masnick, G., and M. J. Bane, *The Nation's Families: 1960–1990* (Cambridge, Mass.: Joint Center for Urban Studies of MIT and Harvard University, 1980), p. 57.
8. Morrison, P. A., "Overview of Demographic Trends Shaping the Nation's Future," *Illinois Business Review*, 1978, 35(8), p. 7.
9. Ibid.
10. Ibid., p. 6.
11. Masnick and Bane, *The Nation's Families*, pp. 62–63.
12. Ibid., p. 66.
13. Morrison, P. A., "Demographic Trends That Will Shape Future Housing Demand," *Policy Sciences*, 1977, 8, p. 204.
14. Ibid., p. 206.
15. Samuelson, R. J., "Aging America—Who

Will Shoulder the Growing Burden?"
National Journal, 1978, *10*(43), p. 1712.

16. Ibid.

17. U.S. Department of Health, Education, and Welfare, *Our Future Selves: Report of the Panel on Behavioral and Social Sciences Research* (Washington, D.C.: U.S. Government Printing Office, 1978), p. 1.

18. Samuelson, "Aging America," p. 1714.

19. U.S. Department of Commerce, Bureau of the Census, *Annual Housing Survey: 1978; General Housing Characteristics, United States and Regions*, (Current Housing Reports, Series H–150–77, Part A (Washington, D.C.: U.S. Government Printing Office, 1980), p. 1.

20. Ibid., p. 2.

21. Ibid., p. 3.

22. Ibid.

23. Ibid., pp. 1–2.

24. Ibid., p. 2.

25. Ibid.

26. Ibid.

27. Ibid., p. 5.

28. Ibid.

29. Ibid.

30. Ibid.

31. U.S. Department of Housing and Urban Development, *How Well Are We Housed? 5. Rural* (Washington, D.C.: Author, 1979), p. 3.

32. Ibid., p. 4.

33. Ibid.

34. Ibid., p. 8.

35. Ibid., p. 16.

36. U.S. Department of Housing and Urban Development, *How Well Are We Housed? 4. The Elderly* (Washington, D.C.: Author, 1979), p. 3.

37. Ibid., p. 7.

38. Ibid., p. 9.

39. Ibid., pp. 14–15.

40. Ibid., p. 16.

41. Ibid., p. 18.

42. U.S. Department of Housing and Urban Development, *How Well Are We Housed? 2. Female-Headed Households* (Washington, D.C.: Author, 1980), p. 4.

43. Ibid., p. 7.

44. Ibid., p. 17.

45. U.S. Department of Housing and Urban Development, *How Well Are We Housed? 3. Blacks* (Washington, D.C.: Author, 1979), p. 3.

46. U.S. Department of Housing and Urban Development, *How Well Are We Housed? 1. Hispanics* (Washington, D.C.: Author, 1980), p. 21.

47. Ibid., p. 21.

48. Morris, E. W., and M. Winter, *Housing Family and Society* (New York: Wiley, 1978), p. 188.

49. Morrison, P. A., "Overview of Demographic Trends," p. 9.

50. Ibid., pp. 8–9.

51. Frieden and Solomon, *The Nation's Housing*, p. 67.

52. Morrison, P.A., "Overview of demographic trends," p. 9.

53. U.S. Department of Commerce, Bureau of the Census, *1980 Census of Population and Housing: United States Summary Advance Report* (Washington, D.C.: Author, 1981), p. 4.

54. Ibid.

Suggested Readings

Butler, K. "Up and Coming amid the Down and Out." *Mother Jones*, 1980, *5*(8) p. 52–54; 58–62.

"First-time Market." *Professional Builder*, 1981, *46*(1) 198–221.

Frieden, B. J., and Solomon, A. P. *The*

Nation's Housing: 1975–1985. Cambridge, Mass.: Joint Center for Urban Studies of MIT and Harvard University, 1977.

Holleb, D. B. "A Decent Home and Suitable Living Environment." *Annals*, AAPSS, 1978, *435*, 102–116.

Masnick, G., and Bane, M. J. *The Nation's Families: 1960–1990*. Cambridge, Mass.: Joint Center for Urban Studies of MIT and Harvard University, 1980.

Morris, E. W., and Winter, M. *Housing, Family, and Society*. New York: Wiley, 1978. (chap. 9, "Residential Mobility").

Morrison, P. A. "Demographic Trends That Will Shape Future Housing Demand." *Policy Sciences*, 1977 8(2) 203–215.

Schafer, R. "Metropolitan Form and Demographic Change." *Urban Studies*, 1978, *15*, 23–33.

U.S. Department of Commerce, Bureau of the Census. *1980 Census of Population and Housing: United States Summary Advance Report*. Washington, D.C.: Author, 1981.

U.S. Department of Housing and Urban Development. *How Well Are We Housed?* 1. *Hispanics*, 1980; 2. *Female-headed Households*, 1980; 3. *Blacks*, 1979; 4. *The Elderly*, 1979; 5. *Rural*, 1979. Washington, D.C.: Author.

The Housing Industry

3

The housing industry is referred to by economic analysts in the same way the automobile industry or the oil industry is referred to. Yet the comparisons between them are limited to one characteristic—impact on the national economy. The housing industry is a large part of the nation's goods and services, and it accounts directly and indirectly for a large part of national employment. On the other hand, the housing industry is hardly an industry at all. It is the fragmented association of many thousands of small companies each operating independently, and often unpredictably, from one another.

At the center of the housing industry is the developer-builder, the person primarily interested in producing housing. Some developer-builders specialize in other forms of building—shopping centers, hospitals, hotels, or schools. The focus here is on housing production. The business of building housing depends on the availability of money to be lent for the construction, then for the purchase, of housing units. The savings and loan institutions and other money lenders then are an appendage of the housing industry. The industry also depends on architects, engineers, surveyors, realtors, planners, subcontractors, lawyers, and public officials, to name just a few of the specialized supporting personnel.

Even though some materials have increased in recent years, the proportional cost of materials has dropped. Further savings could be achieved with less stringent building code requirements. For instance, studs placed 24 inches on center rather than 16 inches on center as shown could cut construction costs. Photo by author.

The housing materials suppliers are part of this industry. The wood, cement, bricks, heaters, paint, carpeting, toilets, in fact everything down to the doorknobs, that go into a housing unit are manufactured. And they are manufactured by hundreds of different companies in hundreds of different places. No one manufacturer makes all or even a large part of the products that go into the process of home building. The employees of these manufacturers are part of the housing industry just as much as those directly involved in on-site home construction. Housing construction itself depends on many different types of highly skilled and highly paid labor.

The housing industry is important to the national economy for reasons other than its far-reaching effects on banking, manufacturing and overall employment. It is sensitive to and can influence business cycles. A reduction in family income will affect housing production more dramatically than it will other forms of industry. In the Depression of the 1930s, lower incomes reduced manufacturing generally from 20 percent to 50 percent, but they reduced housing production by 80 percent.[1] Since housing is built in response to consumer demand that is fairly immediate and localized, its production can have "wide and violent fluctuations."[2] Housing production tends to accompany a general pattern of prosperity or economic decline, but the peaks are higher and the depressions are deeper than those of other industries.

The first section of this chapter examines fluctuations in housing production, and housing production needs. The process of home building of both **single-family** and **multifamily housing,** is explained. Constraints of housing production can be related to nearly every phase of the process of home building. The rising costs of housing are of current concern to professional build-ers, government housing officials and, of course, the home-buying public. The section on rising costs attempts to identify the areas where housing costs could be reduced. Mobile homes and modular housing have become a major part of the housing industry in recent decades. The last section will therefore explain manufactured housing production.

HOUSING PRODUCTION

Housing production is measured by the number of housing starts in a given period of time, usually the calendar year. A **housing start** is counted when the site is prepared for construction to begin. If an excavation is made on a piece of land for a 20-unit apartment building, then 20 housing starts would be added to the existing tally. The actual completion date does not figure into housing production measurement.

The Fluctuations of Production

The past five decades have witnessed widely fluctuating rates of housing production. In contrast to the building boom following World War I, the Depression saw housing production fall to a low of 100,000 new homes. It climbed back up to a high of 600,000 units per year by 1941, but the World War II building and housing needs took priority, and housing starts fell again to 139,000 by 1944. The pent-up demand for new housing was met by the postwar production of over a million new units, reaching 1,352,000 in 1950.[3] The 1950s and 1960s experienced fluctuations of as much as 500,000 units from one year to the next. The national production goal of 2.6 million housing units per year was established in 1968, to last ideally for ten years. Actual housing production never

Housing production is dependent on available land, supporting local government, available skilled labor, and favorable credit situation. Housing production varies widely from place to place and from time to time. Photo by author.

reached that goal in any one year, and peaked at about 2.4 million units in 1972. Then a production slump of six years was relieved in 1978 with over 2 million housing starts. Housing production is predicted to continue to fluctuate but generally to increase in the next decade.[4]

The housing production picture at the national level tells prospective home buyers nothing about the new or existing housing availability within their housing market. One location might have no new housing at all whereas another location might have an oversupply in new housing, and both could occur in what appears to be an average year nationally for housing production.

A great many factors affect the production of housing. In a given location, suitable and available land, supportive governmental regulations and review processes, a skilled labor pool, and favorable credit situation can together encourage high housing production if the demand exists. If any one of these factors is not favorable to home building, housing production in that area will be thwarted.

Developer-builders own small businesses for the most part. A builder might produce only a few houses a year. Anyone producing more than 100 houses a year is considered a large operator. The majority (about 60 percent in 1976) produce less.[5]

Because housing production depends on the business operations of many small companies, the housing industry has often been accused of being the most primitive large industry in modern America. Home building is still largely a one-by-one process, tied to the site and dependent upon localized conditions. Compared to the production of

TABLE 3–1   Where Will Construction Be Needed? 1975 to 1985
(numbers of housing units and mobile home shipments)

HOUSING REQUIRED	NORTHEAST	NORTH CENTRAL	SOUTH	WEST
Additional Vacancies	—	—	318,000	122,000
Replacement of Accidental Losses	493,000	525,000	661,000	434,000
Second Homes	538,000	410,000	418,000	144,000
Upgrading Demand	492,000	793,000	1,059,000	513,000
Replacement of Mobile Homes	404,000	319,000	521,000	201,000
Additional Households	1,074,000	1,998,000	5,788,000	3,040,000
TOTAL: Low Estimate	3,001,000	4,045,000	8,765,000	4,454,000
TOTAL: High Estimate	3,308,000	4,506,000	9,780,000	5,017,000

Source: Frieden, B. J., and A. P. Solomon, The Nation's Housing: 1975–1985 *(Cambridge, Mass.: Joint Center for Urban Studies of MIT and Harvard University, 1977), p. 78.*

automobiles, the housing industry does not enjoy the economic benefits of largeness of scale, efficiency in factory production, centralized management, and so on. Even though some prefabricated components have made mass-produced housing possible, there is not now a dominant movement toward factory-built housing. Manufactured housing does have a substantial role to play in meeting the nation's needs for new housing. Nevertheless, site-built housing done by small-scale developer-builders will continue to account for the great bulk of new housing production in the foreseeable future.

Housing Production Needs

What are our new housing production needs? Any answer is highly speculative, and will change from year to year because it has to take into account recent production. The most comprehensive answer

available at the time of this writing is a report done by the Joint Center for Urban Studies of MIT and Harvard University. The authors state that even if we adopt a strong conservationist policy of preserving and rehabilitating existing housing—and there are signs that this is a growing trend— we still have a need to maintain high production of new housing. As was reviewed in the last chapter, migration is carrying many thousands of families from northeastern cities into the so-called Sunbelt, and there is, consequently, less demand for older existing housing in the Northeast. At the same time, there is a strong demand for new housing in the South and Southwest. In all regions, the trend is to move out of larger metropolitan areas. ". . . In the smaller and newer communities, builders will have to work fast to keep up with the demand created by population growth and the lack of available housing."[6]

The Joint Center report projects a need for 20.2 to 22.6 million additional housing units between 1975 and 1985.[7] These figures take into account the need for second homes, the need to replace accidental losses, the need to replace obsolete homes (including mobile homes), the demand to upgrade living standards, as well as the demand created for new housing by household formation.

THE SINGLE-FAMILY HOME BUILDING PROCESS

It is useful to distinguish between **land developers, home builders,** and **developer-builders.** Land developers buy raw land, and go through the process of getting it ready for housing construction. This involves planning, plan approval, provisions for the **infrastructure** of a neighborhood— utility lines, sewers, water supply, streets, lighting, and so on—and subdivision into individual **lots.** Very few firms participate in only this stage of housing production.

Home builders are contractors who build on an already existing lot, such as those provided by land developers, or a lot already owned by a future resident. So-called **custom building** occurs when the owners work with a contractor to build a house to their specifications. An architect may be involved; more often a plan is chosen from a supply of stock plans provided by the builder. Custom building accounts for a very small part of housing production. There is a growing trend in owner-builder produced houses. In this case, the owner of the lot becomes his own contractor and may also do much of the labor instead of **subcontracting** for it.

Neither land developers nor home builders account for the bulk of housing starts generated by the method used by developer-builders (hereafter called developers). They buy raw land, develop it, and build the houses "**on-spec,**" that is, the house is designed and built in the expectation it will be sold to an unknown buyer. In this method, identifying the prospective housing market is a key factor in the success of the development. The wise developer will not only know the income level, stage in the life cycle, family size, and lifestyle of prospective buyers, the developer will know how to appeal to the taste preferences of this target group. This becomes important in exterior design, choice of materials, interior and exterior color schemes, furnishings used in models, types and quality of installed equipment, and landscaping.

The steps that are taken from initial purchase of raw land to selling all of the finished houses are briefly described here. They will help in identifying the constraints to home building discussed in the next section and the section on high costs of housing following that.

Land

Finding suitable land is the first major step. It has to be a size that can provide enough buildable lots to make the endeavor worthwhile. Its location in relation to schools, shopping, and recreation is a consideration in its marketability. It should provide buildable sites without unduly expensive alteration. If all of these desirable conditions are met in an area where housing demand exists, the land will be purchased, usually through a loan made for this purpose. The initial step involves not only the landowner, the developer, and the money lender, it involves a **real estate broker,** a **title company,** and possibly a lawyer.

Planning the **subdivision** is the next phase. If the land is to be divided into single-family lots, the streets and infrastructure must be planned to accommodate enough

building sites to develop profitably. A **zoning** change may also be required. In every case, the plan must be made and it must be approved by controlling governmental agencies. The planning review process may involve several levels and different agencies. Professional architects, engineers, surveyors, and planners may be involved in this stage.

Construction

Preparing the site for construction involves surveying, earth moving, laying out of streets, and digging trenches for water, sewer and **utility** lines. Individual house locations are marked on each lot, and construction begins. Prior to this, carefully coordinated materials orders have been placed so that everything needed in housing construction is available at the site in sequence.

Labor is subcontracted for each construction phase. **Masonry** and cement work would be handled by one subcontractor. Carpentry, roofing, plumbing, electrical, cabinetry, lighting, flooring, painting, and so on, each have their own subcontractors. Work is scheduled so that each subcontractor is available with a team of skilled laborers at the right time for that job to be done. Each step in the construction process is inspected to see if it complies with applicable **building code** requirements. These differ from one place to another, but plumbing and electrical work is inspected in nearly every area.

Selling

The job of selling the houses usually begins before construction is finished. Advertising may be done through newspapers, billboards, radio and television. If one or more model homes are to be furnished and landscaped for selling purposes, an interior designer must have complete furnishings and accessories ready to install when the first

Preparation of the site for housing construction involves surveying, earth moving, laying out of streets, and providing for utilities. Photo by author.

houses are completed. A display room might include scale models of the entire development, color selection display boards, and other selling aids. Colorful brochures are usually available for prospective buyers. Selling is usually handled by real estate salespersons.

Time

Time becomes one of the most important factors in housing production. Each of the stages can take from a few weeks to many months. If subdivision plans are not initially approved, they may have to be revised not once but several times to gain full acceptance in the review process. If materials are held up, whether because of a factory delay or shipping delay (either can be caused by strikes or bad weather), work schedules have to be rearranged to accommodate the change. Subcontractors may agree to one work schedule but may not be able to adjust to another one. Each inspection may take more time than expected. Finally, house sales may not be completed as rapidly, and profitably, as the developer would like. All the while, the developer is operating on borrowed money, and the longer the time period before sales are completed, the higher the total interest paid. Ultimately, there must be a profit to make this process a viable business enterprise. Since so many unforeseeable events can affect the time involved, the selling price of the house may well turn out to be several thousand dollars higher than was intended at the outset.

MULTIFAMILY HOUSING PRODUCTION

What has been briefly described above is the typical process of producing single-family houses. In producing multifamily housing, whether for a rental or a condominium market, construction shares the same basic steps of land acquisition, plan approval, materials delivery, subcontracting, and selling or renting, but the entire process is more complex.

Matching the site to a type of housing, allowable **density,** and desirable location for an identifiable housing market is difficult. Site design considerations are more complex, including needed parking, recreation and open space, orientation to view and adjacent streets, among other things. **Midrise** and **highrise** multifamily housing involves many structural design decisions. Locations of hallways, stairs, elevators, laundry rooms, and utility equipment become determinants of the livability in multifamily housing as much as the size and arrangement of each housing unit. All of the components of building design— heating and air conditioning, electrical, plumbing, ventilation—have to be designed with fire safety, long-term reliability, and cost effectiveness in mind.[8] None of these multifamily housing construction problems has simple, standard solutions

such as those used in single-family house construction.

One of the serious concerns of the housing industry and other housing experts is that rental multifamily housing is not being produced in adequate supply. The rental housing market has lost favor with developers for a number of reasons. Investors no longer have the income tax advantages that they did ten years ago, the costs of maintenance have risen dramatically, but at the same time, rents have not risen in relation to these costs. To add to the problem, many existing multifamily structures have been converted to condominium units. The ownership aspect has attracted a housing market that previously was limited to single-family home ownership. But as units are converted to condominiums, renters who want to remain renters are forced into a depleted and often deteriorating rental supply. In some communities, the response to the situation has been to enact both condominium conversion "freezes" and rent control laws. Both regulations discourage further the building of new rental multifamily units.

CONSTRAINTS TO HOUSING PRODUCTION

The foremost constraint to housing production is the cost of borrowing money and its availability. If interest rates rise, then both the developer and the housing consumer are affected. A *Forbes* analysis explains it this way:

> In recent decades construction in all its forms has been the economy's swing industry. When the Federal Reserve tightened money, the immediate impact was on building. The reason is obvious: You

The End of the Rental Housing Market

We are probably presiding over the end of the classic rental housing as we have known it in this country over the past hundred years. There are several reasons for this. Aside from the obvious tax advantages, these reasons may be grouped under the single heading of *the decline of the rights and benefits of ownership*.

The forms of holding and managing real property have varied very little in the past century, despite some development of cooperatives or limited dividend housing corporations and the like. The latter are relatively trivial in number and certainly for this country publicly owned housing makes up less than 2 percent of the total housing stock. However, the bundle of rights and privileges which we call property has been reduced very, very substantially. The privilege of renting to whomever one wants as a tenant, for example, is quite properly a victim of the civil rights and equal opportunities activity of the last 20 years. With it, *de facto* if not *de jure,* has gone much of the ability to evict tenantry pretty much at will, particularly in certain jurisdictions.

The standards at which housing is to be maintained—and much of the potential variation in the expense side of the operation statement—similarly has been shifted beyond the belief of the makers of the first tenement housing code in New York in the 1880's. In a considerable number of jurisdictions the top-side of the operating statement has similarly been affected by the various forms of rent control, rent stabilization, fair-rent legislation, and the like. New York City's Temporary Rent Control Act of 1943, which once presided over the field like the last of the dinosaurs, has now been joined by communities across the country; more than 30 towns in New Jersey, for example, have some form of rent stabilization or equalization and the number is growing.

But there are other factors involved in the flight from rental residential property. Not least of these is the reality that much of the life style of the middle and upper income renter was made possible at relatively inexpensive rents because of the availability of very low-paid service workers. Classically, the janitor or superintendent lived in the basement at a low salary over and above whatever "gifts" he could secure from the tenantry. In return he and other members of his family worked hours without end. Contrast this with the present situation where increasing unionization, as in local 32B in New York City, demands starting salaries of $700 or $800 a month for a 40-hour week, with no fringe work from the new professional's family.

The construction or operating procedures of rental facilities is as labor intensive as it was a generation or two ago. Labor saving devices really have had little significance. The answer, therefore, is either a reduction of service or very, very high rentals, and neither of these is completely marketable or for that matter completely without political repercussion.

The third factor is the limited availability of cash, the high cost associated with raising capital reflected not merely in interest but also increasingly in the level of equity which the developer or second-hand purchaser must advance . . . in order to make sales possible. The answer is very simple, "Avoid investment in rental facilities!" And so we have the condominium. And we have the condominium without any really broad analysis of its repercussions in a society in which the vagaries of employment location demands increasing flexibility; in which the price of being tied down may be very high indeed.

Excerpted from: Sternlieb, G., R. W. Burchell, and J. W. Hughes, "The Future of Housing and Urban Development." In R. W. Burchell and D. Listoken (eds.), Future Land Use, (New Brunswick, N.J.: Rutgers Center for Urban Policy Research, 1975), pp. 11–12.

can't build a house or a hotel or office building out of current income; you need to borrow. And if money is hard to get, the first thing hit is building.[9]

Housing consumers seem to be willing to pay the higher-than-ever interest rates and the higher-than-ever house prices, which reflect in part the cost of borrowed money to the developer. Savings and loan institutions have to attract savings deposits, by means of high interest rates, in order to have the money to lend for home builders.

Another major constraint to home build-

Multifamily housing construction process includes design considerations different from single-family housing. Parking, open space, shared facilities as well as hallways, stairs, and elevators, must be incorporated. Photo courtesy of U.S. Department of Housing and Urban Development.

TABLE 3–2 Government Regulations Affecting the Cost of Housing

HOUSING COST COMPONENT AFFECTED

LEVEL, TYPE OF REGULATION	UNIMPROVED LOT	LAND DEVELOPMENT	LAND DEVELOPMENT FINANCING	STRUCTURAL MATERIALS AND LABOR	CONSTRUCTION FINANCING	MORTGAGE FINANCING AND SETTLEMENT COSTS
Federal Government						
Clean Air Act	X					
Coastal Zone Management Act	X	X	X			
Consumer Product Safety Act				X	X	
Federal Noise Control Act				X		
Federal Water Pollution Control Act	X	X	X			
FHA and VA Mortgage Programs				X	X	X
National Flood Insurance Programs	X	X	X	X	X	
Occupational Health and Safety Act				X	X	
Real Estate Settlement Procedures Act				X	X	X
State Government						
Building Codes				X	X	
Coastal Zone Management	X	X	X			
Critical Areas Restrictions	X	X	X			
Land Development Acts	X	X	X			
Sewer Moratoria	X	X	X			
Local Government						
Bonding Requirements			X			
Building Codes				X	X	
Energy Codes				X	X	
Engineering Inspection		X	X	X		
Environmental Impact Review	X	X	X			
Mechanical Codes				X	X	
Plat Review		X	X			
Sewer Connection Approval and Fee		X	X			
Shade Tree Permits		X	X			
Site Plan Review		X	X			
Soil Disturbance Testing		X	X			
Utility Connection Fees		X	X			
Water Connection Approval and Fee		X	X			
Zoning	X	X	X			

Source: Seidel, S. R., Housing Costs and Government Regulations: Confronting the Regulatory Maze (New Brunswick, N.J.: Rutgers Center for Urban Policy Research, 1978), p. 20.

Developers of multifamily housing have preferred building condominiums to rental housing. The unfavorable investment aspects of rental housing have led to the dominance of condominums in the multifamily housing market. Photo by author.

ing is environmental protection regulation. Some communities have adopted outright **no-growth policies,** and others have used other tactics, particularly well-developed in California, to discourage home building. Frieden says, "The local politics of no-growth has reached a stage of maturity there."[10] Local governments have put land into agricultural preserves, declared moratoria on water and sewer connections, established service boundaries, and charged enormous fees for hooking up to existing utilities. The ultimate strategy is to limit the number of new housing units that can be built in any one year.

Delay in the review process can inhibit housing production. The importance of time in the production process has been explained above, and clearly an undue

amount of time can make the business of home building unprofitable.

The whole scope of home building requirements referred to in the general term of "government regulations" can be a deterrent to home building, and certainly affect the cost of new housing. Government regulation can be at the federal, state or local level, and can affect every stage of the housing production process. Table 3–2 (page 55) identifies the housing costs affected by government regulations of different types at different levels.

In an "objective inquiry into the relationship between government regulations and the costs of housing," Seidel identified direct costs of regulations (administrative costs), indirect administrative costs (delays and uncertainty), and the monetary costs of unnecessary or excessive regulations. Four case studies from three states were used for illustration. Seidel concluded:

> Costs were being shifted both from the public sector and from other private parties to the developer, and from the future to the present. The net result of these shifts has been to dramatically increase the initial price of housing and thereby severely limit the number of families able to afford these units. Regulations are supposed to have the effect of increasing the quality of new housing, and of reducing any burden on the municipality, but these same regulations also significantly increase the cost of housing to the consumer.[11]

Subdivision regulations along with growth controls, zoning ordinances, and environmental regulations can complicate the housing construction process. They determine the size, placement, and quality of housing and neighborhoods, but they add to the high costs of housing production. Photo by author.

Selling the First-Time Buyer: With Duplexes for Young Families in Las Vegas . . .

Pardee Construction has sold 418 duplexes in three years at its Spring Valley community by offering an attached home that looks and feels like a detached house.

"We're selling mostly to young families who have been priced out of detached houses," says Lee Antonello, Pardee's sales vice president. "They all want the benefits of homeownership, but they're turned off by the prospect of living in attached housing."

Prices and density. The duplexes represent an ideal compromise.

First, the siting has reduced prices 16% below comparably-sized detached houses that Pardee is also building at Spring Valley. (The duplex plans, sized 903 and 1,010 sq. ft., opened from $27,500 to $30,000 in 1975 and now sell from $44,000 to $47,000.)

"We're putting up seven duplexes per acre," explains Antonello. "Our conventionally-sited, detached houses never exceed 4.5 per acre."

Second, the duplex buildings look like large detached houses. And Pardee has reinforced the single-family feeling by including front, rear and side yards in the fee-simple ownership package; by building privacy walls on the lot lines; and by offering ten elevations.

"Our streetscapes have more diversity than most of the neighboring single-family projects" says Antonello.

Image problem. While the duplexes, called Colony Homes, have sold well at Spring Valley, the Las Vegas zoning authorities were far from enthusiastic when the concept was presented. The reason: Some duplexes had previously been built as rental units in the area and it was feared that Pardee's homes would attract a transient market.

"So we flew the county commissioners to southern California to look at duplex projects there."

Exterior diversity is provided by ten elevations. (Shown above is contemporary style.) Each unit has an attached garage and a covered carport.

Typical duplex lot *(below)* has features that give homes a strong single-family feeling. Each fee-simple purchase includes 760-sq.-ft. rear yard *(A)* and 160-sq.-ft. side yard *(B)*. Privacy walls divide rear yards *(C)* and run along rear and side lot lines *(D)*. Deeply recessed entries *(E)* and front-yard landscaping *(F)* offer extra privacy.

Conversion options are strong sales points of project's two duplex plans. Bedroom in 903-sq.-ft. home *(below)* can be turned into family room or den that is open to kitchen/dining area. Bedroom in 1,010-sq.-ft. layout *(below right)* becomes den open to living room. Plans opened from $27,500 to $30,000 and now sell from $44,000 to $47,000.

says Antonello."When were attracting, they gave
they saw the kinds of us the green light." *Source:* Housing. 55 *(1),*
buyers that these homes —J. G. C. *1979, p. 68.*

Seidel reached a good many specific conclusions and recommendations. Since they summarize some of the constraints in housing production, several are paraphrased here briefly to conclude this section.[12]

1. *Growth controls.* Growth controls often limit the amount of available land for development. Houses that are built may carry unnecessarily high prices. The use of growth controls should be limited to those situations in which clear planning objectives are being sought. A specific crisis, such as a water shortage, might justify growth controls.

2. *Environmental regulations.* An **environmental impact statement** (EIS, also called environmental impact report, EIR) is often required in the planning review process. If required, it can delay construction. An EIS for a specific housing development may not consider overall planning for the area. Neither does it always specify with factual certainty what the impact of a housing development will be on the local environment. "It is important that the magnitude of the projected damage be weighed against the benefits of the project and that both be placed in the context of the local and regional settings."[13]

3. *Subdivision controls.* The number of applications required, and the number of agencies involved, and the number of approvals required in the subdivision review process have all rapidly increased. Sometimes developers are required to make excessive improvements in order to gain subdivision approval. In the past, these requirements were often paid for by the government municipality, but they are increasingly paid for by the developer.

4. *Zoning regulations.* Zoning regulations may include provisions that prohibit the construction of moderately priced housing. Zoning exclusion of mobile homes and multifamily housing affects housing options for consumers. When a zoning change is required to develop land, the conditions and delays involved add to the cost of the housing eventually built.

5. *Building codes.* The housing consumer's best interests are not always well represented in building code specifications. Some code requirements are written in because of safety, yet some such items could remain optional. There are thousands of diverse local building codes. The setting of minimum standards for safety and quality could be similar throughout the country.

THE RISING COSTS OF HOUSING

Housing costs have risen dramatically in recent years (Table 3–3, page 62). While existing homeowners have benefitted, at least psychologically, from the inflationary increase in the value of their houses to double, triple, even quadruple what they paid for them, nonhomeowners planning to buy have been bewildered as house prices become increasingly out of reach. First-time buyers are most critically affected, whereas families living in high-priced houses can

Attached, Expensive and Selling in Volume

When the site is right and the designs are luxurious, builders can score high volume sales with attached houses that carry custom-sized price tags of $300,000.

That's what is happening at The Ridge at MountainGate, a townhouse development in a prestigious section of the Los Angeles area. Within three months 59 units were sold. Sales began about a month before models opened in January. Prices range between $240,000 and $500,000 for units with 3000 to 4200 square feet of space.

The Ridge is built on the ridges of the Santa Monica Mountains in Brentwood, just across the San Diego Freeway from Bel Air.

It's part of the 870-acre MountainGate planned community which is being built by Southwest Environments Inc., for Barclay Hollander Corp., a subsidiary of Castle & Cooke Inc.

Barclay Hollander has been in various stages of planning the development since the early '60s and has weathered landfill operations and environmental impact red tape.

The first section of The Ridge, an adult condominium community, will include 72 units on a 16-acre parcel. That is 4.4 units per acre. Children under 13 years of age are not allowed as permanent residents.

The entire MountainGate community plan calls for 870 houses plus a 27-hole golf course and a private tennis club. The cluster arrangement of the individual neighborhoods will leave about 75 percent of the total acreage as open space.

The traditionally styled two-story townhouses were designed by Carl McLarand & Associates, Santa Ana.

Varied roof lines have either high pitched wood shingle or red tile. Large eaves, use of custom masonry, exterior moldings and brick facing provide variety in the exterior treatment.

Large dramatic entryways with lush landscaping enhance the double doors surrounded by first- and second-story windows. Landscape architect Don Brinkerhoff of Lifescapes Inc. of Santa Ana has enhanced the natural beauty of the surrounding mountains by using full grown trees of many varieties, as well as native plants and flowers.

More than $1.5 million is being invested in special hardscaping and landscaping for just The Ridge section of the overall development. That includes ornate street lighting fixtures as well as sidewalks and driveways of decorative, stamped concrete in brick tones.

Matching the impressive entryways are interiors with formal foyers with ceiling heights of 18 feet or more. Other features include galleries bridging two-story living rooms, formal staircases, skylights, large master baths, private patio gardens and sweeping expanses of glass.

The four models provide two- and three-bedroom plans with dens, formal living rooms and dining rooms. Model interiors were designed by Yeiser/Garland & Associates.

The site, just north of Sunset Boulevard, had been assembled by Barclay Hollander Corp. in the early 1960s. Castle & Cooke acquired Barclay Hollander in 1969. This gave the development the kind of financial staying power needed to see the project through a planning process frought with environmental impact problems and the time-consuming process of landfill. Several million tons of refuse raised canyon levels as much as 240 feet. The golf course and other recreational spaces are now on top of the landfill.

Source: Professional Builder. *1979, 46 (5), pp. 78—79. Reprinted with permission.*

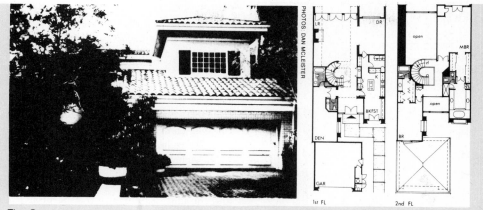

The Conventry model features an expansive den with private bath (see floor plan). Priced from $280,000 to $380,000 it has 3459 square feet. The house has extensive landscaping and stamped concrete in brick pattern.

use their equity to buy another, more expensive house.

New houses and existing houses have both gone up in price in the last few years. The phenomenon is a national one, but there are some regional variations as seen in Table 3–4 (page 63). It is interesting to compare the increase in the South (second lowest) to the increase in the West (the highest) since both are rapidly growing areas in the nation.

The prices of existing houses, even if smaller and with fewer amenities, have kept pace with new houses, but they typically are lower by a few thousand dollars. Nevertheless, between 1967 and 1976, the median sales price for new single-family houses rose over 94 percent while the median price of existing single-family houses rose more, 97.5 percent. Operating expenses, affecting all homeowners alike, went up even more drastically in the same period—118.7 percent.[14]

In the 1960s, incomes increased along with home prices and the slowly rising rates of rents. By the 1970s, the picture changed.

Incomes began to lag behind as house prices escalated. The consumer price index, measuring the prices of all standard consumer expenditures, rose throughout the decades of the 1960s and the 1970s but housing costs rose faster, and incomes rose more slowly. Rents have not risen as fast as incomes, and are relatively less inflationary than owned homes. Nevertheless, after 1972, they rose twice as fast as they had during the previous decade.[15]

One way to gauge loss of purchasing power is to determine what percentage of families are able to afford the cost of buying a median-priced house. A conventional income-to-housing cost relationship is that a family can only afford 25 percent of its gross income on housing. As recently as 1970, 45 percent of all families could afford the ownership cost of new or existing housing in this country. By 1976, that percentage had shrunk to 27 percent for the cost of a new home, and 36 percent for the cost of an existing home. By 1976, only 12 percent of new homes sold for less than $30,000.[16] As Frieden summarizes the

TABLE 3–3   Average Sales Price of New
One-Family Houses Sold 1964–1980

ANNUAL PERIOD	PRICE	PERIOD TO PERIOD PERCENTAGE CHANGE
1964	$20,500	+ 6.2
1965	21,500	+ 4.9
1966	23,300	+ 8.4
1967	24,600	+ 5.6
1968	26,600	+ 8.1
1969	27,900	+ 4.9
1970	26,600	− 4.7
1971	28,300	+ 6.4
1972	30,500	+ 7.8
1973	35,500	+ 16.4
1974	38,900	+ 9.6
1975	42,600	+ 9.5
1976	48,000	+ 12.7
1977	54,200	+ 12.9
1978	62,500	+ 15.3
1979	71,800	+ 14.9
1980	76,300	+ 6.3

Source: U.S. Bureau of the Census, Construction reports: Price Index of New One-Family Houses Sold *(Washington, D.C.: Author, March 1981), p.3.*

problem, "Whether measured by price trends relative to income, by the proportion of families able to afford the median-priced home, or by surveys of who actually bought new houses, the market for single-family homes has changed since 1970, to the disadvantage of the average family."[17]

Why Do Houses Cost So Much?

All of the constraints to housing production listed above are also factors in increasing costs of new homes. These factors have

varying degrees of influence on the final selling price. Two factors are little influenced by the attitudes and decisions made by housing consumers. One is the overhead and profit costs of the developer. The other is the cost of borrowing money. Both have risen in the last thirty years (Table 3–5, page 64). The discussion that follows focuses on two categories of housing costs which could be reduced with changed consumer attitudes: (1) land, and (2) material and labor.

Land. The cost of undeveloped land and the cost of preparing it appropriately for new-house development are the first component of the final housing cost. In 1950, these costs were only 10 percent to 12 percent of the price of a new house. By 1978, they represented 20 percent to 25 percent.[18] Limited land availability has driven up the price of developable land. When zoning restrictions or no-growth policies limit building, the land that is purchased for home building is high priced. Where there are strict land-use regulations, the cost of land may be as high as 30 percent of the price of the house.[19]

Site development is also very costly. Past experience and local preferences guide most regulations for street requirements, sidewalks, driveways, and water and sewer systems. The American Society of Civil Engineers has established standards for residential street widths. One study found a majority of communities had standards in excess of the recommendations, and if the recommended widths were used, the cost savings per house would be from $40 to $550.[20] The width and thickness of pavement used could be reduced to cut housing costs.

Sidewalks, too, could have less generous requirements for width and thickness. The reduction of one foot in width, from five feet required in many communities, to four

TABLE 3–4 Price Index of New One-Family Houses Sold, Including Value of the Lot,
United States and by Regions 1964–1980
(Price index based on average house price 1972 = 100;
Index based on kinds of houses sold in 1974)[1]

YEAR	UNITED STATES	NORTH-EAST	NORTH CENTRAL	SOUTH	WEST
1964	69.6	59.7	68.3	70.0	74.6
1966	74.2	66.8	74.7	74.3	78.2
1968	80.3	75.8	82.4	79.0	81.7
1970	89.1	88.2	90.7	87.5	90.3
1972	100.0	100.0	100.0	100.0	100.0
1974	119.1	118.3	115.8	115.2	126.3
1976	142.0	133.5	138.1	134.6	157.3
1978	182.1	157.3	175.8	165.3	221.6
1980	230.1	195.6	204.8	213.8	287.9

[1]*Kinds of houses sold in 1974 refers to adjustment of actual sales prices of houses to compare with the average house and lot sold in 1974 (size and amenities—10 characteristics are used).*
Source: U.S. Bureau of the Census, Construction Reports: Price Index of New One-Family Houses Sold *(Washington, D.C.: Author, March 1981), p. 2.*

feet, HUD's minimum requirement, could save as much as $60 per house.[21] If sidewalks were eliminated from the building requirements, there would be a savings of several hundred dollars per house. Similar savings could be found regarding the size and material for driveways, and for the type and materials for sewer and water lines.

Large lot requirements (one or one-half acre) affect housing prices in two ways: (1) the land itself costs more per house, and (2) the site development costs per house are greater because each requires more street utilities, sewer, and water installation. A lot size requirement of one-quarter acre is very common, whereas under 5,000 square feet per site is allowed in very few communities. The great majority of communities have minimum lot size requirements between 5,000 square feet and one-quarter acre (11,000 square feet). A lot that is only

50 feet wide had development costs of about $2,000 (1978 prices), but a lot 100 feet wide had double those costs.[22]

There might be as many as twenty-five different local review groups in one community with which the developer must deal, and the average is more than six.[23] The number of groups reviewing development plans can be reduced, as well as the length of time needed for approval in each. Different agencies can streamline and coordinate their efforts to reduce overall costs of housing.

Two more land-related costs affect selling prices of new houses. Developers are often required to dedicate land for parks, schools, recreational areas, and other municipal facilities. In the past, when communities wanted to attract home building, and consequent new residents, these costs were borne by the community through local taxes. The situation is now reversed, so that home buyers carry the cost of these new community facilities in the price of their homes. Secondly, fees charged for development, utility, and building have risen sharply. Fees can be charged for zoning and rezoning, reviews and inspections, permits for grading, clearing and other land alterations, water, sewer, storm drains; electric and gas utility lines have hook-up charges. Building fees include building permit fees, filing fees, occupancy fees, and so on. All of these add to the cost of the house, and ultimately, the new home buyer pays for them.

Materials and Labor Costs. The proportional cost of material has dropped since the 1940s, even though some materials have skyrocketed in recent years. Plywood, brick, brass and fittings have all led the price increase trend, with concrete, millwork, and asphalt roofing following. Plumbing, heating equipment, paint, and clay tiles have all increased as well, but at a slower rate.

On-site labor costs are about 16 percent of construction costs, roughly half of what they were forty years ago.[24] The inclusion

TABLE 3–5   Cost Components of a Typical
New Single-Family House
(National Association of Homebuilders)

	1949	1978
Land	11%	25%
Labor and materials	69%	47%
Finance	5%	11%
Overhead & profits	15%	17%
	100%	100%

SOURCE: *Montgomery, R. and Mandelker, D. R., Housing in America: Problems and Perspectives (Minneapolis: 1979). Reprinted with the permission of the Bobbs Merrill Company.*

in the housing production process of many prefabricated components has helped reduce labor costs.

Savings in both materials and labor can be gained, but often conventional building codes do not allow less expensive methods and materials. Building codes have also raised quality standards. In fact many building codes have been modernized, but the local building practices have not. Potential savings can be great—as much as $7,300 per house.[25] Consumer demand is also part of the problem. If potential home buyers believe only tried-and-true methods and materials to be desirable, and are willing to pay the higher price associated with them, then new methods are slow to be adopted.

There are some cost-saving methods and materials that have not been widely accepted in local building codes. The following is a list of such savings, with the average potential savings per house in 1978 dollars:[26]

1. 3 inch rather than 4 inch concrete basement floor ($141).
2. 2 inch by 4 inch studs spaced 24 inches rather than 16 inches on center (exterior wall) ($119).
3. No exterior sheathing ($225).
4. Plastic plumbing in hot/cold water supply rather than copper ($130).
5. Wood foundation instead of concrete ($323).
6. 1/2 inch thick single-layer subfloor and underlayment rather than thicker floor ($112).

Some construction requirements add a great deal to the cost of the house. The requirement for a garage, for brick exterior finish, and for all interior rooms to be finished, each carry a price tag of one or two thousand dollars. Table 3–6 shows eleven large cost-saving items, the average poten-

TABLE 3–6   Large Cost-Saving Items Not Allowed by Some Communities

LESS EXPENSIVE MATERIAL OR METHOD	AVERAGE POTENTIAL SAVINGS PER HOUSE	PERCENT OF 87 REPRESENTATIVE COMMUNITIES NOT ALLOWING THE ITEM
1. No garage or carport	$2,160	11
2. Exterior finish other than brick	1,499	1
3. One or more unfinished rooms (e.g., family room and extra bath)	1,100	32
4. Asphalt shingles	865	5
5. Drywall instead of plaster	700	2
6. Romex wiring	564	13
7. Exposed foundation instead of brick above grade	411	5
8. No fire sprinkler system	291	1
9. Prehung doors and windows	286	2
10. Poured concrete instead of block walls	254	3
11. Manufactured roof trusses	218	1

  Significantly, none of the 87 communities prohibited all of the above large cost-saving items. As can be seen, except for item number 3—one or more unfinished rooms—all of the other cost-saving items are allowed by about 90 percent of the communities.

Source: Controller General of the United States, Why Are New House Prices So High, How Are They Influenced by Government Regulations, and Can Prices Be Reduced? (Washington, D.C.: General Accounting Office, 1978), p. 36.

tial savings per house of each, and the small number of communities in a government survey whose building codes did not allow the item.

The Affluent Home Market

There are buyers for very expensive houses. At the same time that a current outcry for **"affordable housing"** is finding its way into every manner of public communication, the "nonaffordable" housing is selling. To the family who buys it, a $300,000 house is "affordable." The professionals involved

with housing production are not deaf to the outcry for affordable housing; it simply does not make sense to them when they have a well-defined housing market for the product they profitably produce.

The average new house in the 1950s contained less than 1,000 square feet, partly because FHA had been sponsoring efforts in small home building for years. By the 1960s, the average size of new houses had increased, and the trend continued steadily into the 1970s. By 1976, the average size of a new house had grown to 1,700

The new home of the 1950s was much smaller than the new home of the 1970s. Consumers have demanded extra bathrooms and bedrooms, fireplaces, and built-in appliances, all adding to the cost of the average house. Photos by author.

square feet.[27] A government report on high costs of housing summarizes the situation this way:

The trend toward larger, more expensive houses since 1950 was influenced by home buyers' desires for extra features. Some popular extras are additional bathrooms and bedrooms, two eating areas, and family rooms. Besides additional rooms, many of today's houses include items not generally popular in the past, such as air conditioning, built-in appliances, and fireplaces. While these latter items do not increase the size of a house, they do increase the price.[28]

MANUFACTURED HOUSING

Mobile homes have become a satisfying housing alternative to millions of housing consumers. With a desire for single-family home ownership, but denied access to the single-family suburban home, young families can achieve a reasonable compromise with mobile home ownership. Generally, mobile homes are parked more or less permanently (only 1 percent are moved) in a mobile home park, especially designed for mobile home residences. When mobile homes are parked on privately owned land, they may be subject to a minimum lot requirement, such as ten acres. Ten acres of rural property in many areas of the country is a sizable investment for young home buyers. Mobile home purchasing, renting and maintenance costs are discussed in Chapter 8.

The mobile home grew out of the production of travel trailers. When manufacturers realized travel trailers were being used for permanent housing, they focused their efforts on producing a sound and completely habitable housing unit. The single-wide mobile home grew from 8, to 10, to 12, then 14 feet wide. Nowadays, some 16-foot and 18-foot wide mobile homes are produced in states where units of these widths may be trucked on highways. Some units are as long as 85 feet, whereas a decade ago, typical lengths were 45 feet, 54 feet, and 60 feet.

When double-wides were introduced in the late 1960s, they offered housing units competitive in space and interior design to conventional single-family homes. By 1977, they accounted for 31 percent of the national market, with radical differences in some regions (70 percent in Florida, 6 percent in Wisconsin).[29] Triple-wides have been introduced by some manufacturers. These multi-sectional units are subject to the highway dimension restrictions of single-wides. Sections are trucked to the site and then they are attached as well as anchored and hooked up to utilities.

The Components of the Industry

Manufactured housing depends on three components. One is the factory production of the housing units. Whatever the width and number of sections, the housing unit is completely finished within a factory. This includes the plumbing, heating, air conditioning, and electrical systems. Many, if not most, mobile homes are sold with complete furnishings as well.

The "product" that comes out of the factory must be distributed and sold. The second component of the manufactured housing industry, then, is the dealer who sells a variety of mobile home models from several manufacturers. Accessories to mobile homes, as well as used mobile homes, are standard products also available on the dealer's lot. Dealers are responsible for sales to consumers, and for delivering, setting up, and servicing the mobile homes they sell.

The third component is the mobile home park. Since a majority of mobile homes are located in parks, the development and location of parks, and their amenities, become critical in providing the kind of housing that satisfies consumer needs. Without adequate parks, mobile homes sales will fall. Yet the manufacturer does not control this component of the industry. Critical to the success of the park for its residents is the manager or owner manager. The screening of tenants, maintenance of grounds and facilities, compliance with park regulations, and the creation of a desirable physical and social environment depends on good management. It is the final element in "the total housing service provided by the mobile home industry."[30]

Mobile Home Construction

Mobile home production depends on mass-production techniques, economies of scale in the supplying of materials, and year-round use of unskilled and semiskilled labor. Early mobile homes were often criticized for inferior construction and poor safety standards. But the industry set about regulating itself in the 1950s. By 1969, it adopted a performance building code designed specifically for mobile home production by the American National Standards Institute (ANSI). A majority of states adopted this code which preempted local building codes that often disallowed the materials and techniques common in factory production. The ANSI standards formed the basis for the Federal Mobile Home Construction and Safety Standards enacted in 1976.

The chassis is the frame on which the mobile home is constructed. It is made of steel and designed to carry the weight of the entire unit, as well as to support it evenly when parked. The "floor assembly" is made up of the appropriately sized floor joists, pipes and duct work, insulation, and plywood surface. Often the flooring material—

vinyl, carpeting, or tile—is applied in one piece over the floor.

Interior wall sections are placed according to the plan of the unit before side walls are put into place. Walls are preassembled before they are attached to the chassis and floor component. Walls are constructed typically of 2 by 4 inch studs, however, 2 by 3 inch studs are satisfactory. Prefinished wood paneling is often used throughout the walls for structural strength and to simplify finishing. However, some manufacturers have switched to dry wall for appearance and reduced fire hazard. Walls are insulated before the exterior siding is attached. The aluminum siding typically used on the exterior walls also adds to the structural strength of the mobile home by distributing the load of the roof diagonally. Some manufacturers are incorporating shingles, battens, plywood, and some masonry, as well as imitation masonry, into their exterior designs.

The roof is also preassembled. It is light-weight compared to conventionally built roofs. The interior structure makes use of plywood "scraps" from within the factory, one of the several ways factory production reduces waste. An insulating subroof forms the basis for the roofing material, often galvanized steel or aluminum decking. **Fiberglass blanket insulation** is the most common type used for roofs.

The manufacturing process succeeds in saving time and materials. The basic elements of the chassis, floor, walls and roof are preassembled. When joined, they form one structurally continuous unit.

Mobile home production fluctuates just as conventional housing production fluctuates, but not necessarily in a parallel pattern. For instance, in 1972, mobile home production was proportionally large in relation to standard home construction (575,940 mobile homes to 1.3 million conventional homes). While this was a sizable proportion of the total single-family home market, about 33 percent, five years

Floor, wall, and roof sections are preassembled in this triple-wide mobile home. When completely installed, the skirting will disguise the chassis and supports visible in this photograph. Photo by author.

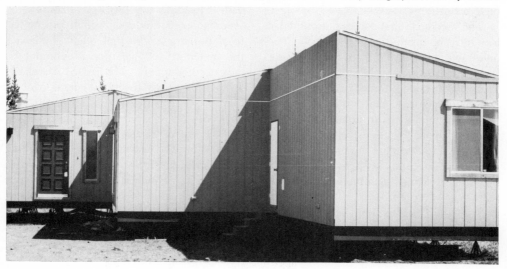

Mobile Home Construction and Safety Standards

Federal standards to protect the safety and health of mobile homeowners.

Nature of Program: In consultation with the Consumer Product Safety Commission, HUD issues Federal mobile home construction and safety standards to improve the quality and durability of mobile homes. The standards take into consideration existing State and local laws but preempt those which are not identical to the Federal standards. They apply to all mobile homes manufactured after June 15, 1976. Standards may be enforced by HUD through the Attorney General or the State. HUD may inspect factories and obtain records needed to enforce such standards. If a mobile home does not conform to Federal standards, the manufacturer must repurchase the home or bring it up to standards.

Modular homes manufactured in a factory, transported to a building site, and placed on a permanent site-built foundation may, through a certification process, be exempted from Federal mobile home construction and safety standards if the homes meet other specified equivalent codes.

The law prohibits use of the mails and interstate commerce to sell or lease mobile homes that do not meet safety standards. Civil and criminal penalties also are provided where violation of such prohibitions occur.

Manufacturers must notify consumers, dealers and HUD of hazardous defects. The manufacturer must correct the defect if it presents an unreasonable risk of injury or death.

Applicant Eligibility: Not applicable.

Legal Authority: Title VI, Housing and Community Development Act of 1974 (P.L. 93-383); Housing and Community Development Act of 1977 (P.L. 95-128).

Administering Office: Assistant Secretary for Neighborhoods, Voluntary Associations and Consumer Affairs, Department of Housing and Urban Development, Washington, D.C. 20410.

Information Source: See administering office.

Current Status: Active.

Scope of Program: The standards apply to mobile homes eight or more feet wide and 32 or more feet long built on a permanent chassis manufactured after June 15, 1976.

Source: U.S. Department of Housing and Urban Development, Programs of HUD, *(Washington, D.C.: Author, 1978),* p. 94.

later, the percentage had fallen to 16 percent.[31]

Mobile home markets are strong in California and Texas, but mobile homes are sold throughout the United States. Alaska has met its rapidly growing housing needs with mobile homes shipped from the mainland. One of the major costs to the mobile home consumer is shipping. The trucking distance from a factory can be as far as 300 miles, but most factories consider a 150-mile radius to define their best potential sales area.

Modular Housing

Many mobile home manufacturers are expanding their markets to include modular houses. These are produced in a similar

Modular housing units produced in a factory can be stacked to form townhouses. Photo courtesy of U.S. Department of Housing and Urban Development.

Manufactured housing is being used for conventionally developed subdivisions. These modular houses on small individual lots are sold at a lower price than site-built single-family houses in the same area. Photo by author.

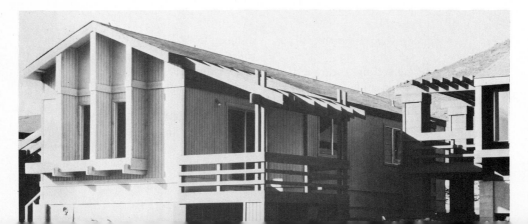

method to double-wide mobile homes, but are permanently attached to the site, and usually financed as conventional housing. Modular housing must meet state building code standards whereas, mobile homes are constructed under federal standards. Manufacturers might produce both, or convert exclusively to modular houses. The term manufactured housing aptly applies to both mobile and modular homes.

Several new markets have been identified by mobile home manufacturers. Modular units have been designed for **townhouses** and duplexes. Condominiums in townhouse and midrise form are a potential use for manufactured housing. One manufacturer produced units for 250 apartment developments in 125 cities in Ohio, and 30 apartment developments in 25 cities in Florida in 1978.[32] Other manufacturers see a potential for modular housing units in the back-to-the-city movement. One trend is the placement of "granny houses" at the rear of existing houses in older urban neighborhoods. The mobile home or modular house is hoisted over the existing house and placed in the rear yard. The process takes only a few hours. "This market is never going to be big enough to make any modular manufacturer's fortune."[33] But it is an application of manufactured housing

into existing neighborhoods.

Mobile home manufacturers still see their greatest marketing potential in the provision of modular units for suburban tract developments. Some manufacturers contract with developers to provide the house structures in otherwise conventionally developed housing subdivisions. These modular houses then are sold in the traditional manner. As construction methods have been upgraded, and as designs have more and more approximated the appearance of conventional houses, "the two forms of housing will be competing more directly over a larger segment of the single-family housing market."[34] The advantage of lower production costs then could enter into the production of traditional suburban development. It could develop also that conventional builders would adopt manufactured housing techniques for the benefit of a less costly house, and a savings to housing consumers. Perhaps the key to incorporating the cost savings of factory-produced housing into the mainstream of the housing market is acceptance by the house-consuming public.

SUMMARY

Even though the housing industry is of primary importance in the American national economy, it is made up of fragmented and uncoordinated manufacturing of housing materials and products and the production of housing units by small-scale developers. Housing production is drastically affected by business cycles and by federal economic policies.

The picture of annual housing starts in the United States is an uneven one. Production levels vary widely by locale. Developers operate within the limitations of local suppliers, government controls, and financing, and in response to local housing demand.

The single-family home-building process involves acquiring land, and preparing it for the development. Subdivision designs must meet many local requirements, and be approved by many local agencies. Efficient housing construction depends on subcontracted skilled labor and materials dependably delivered to the site. Inspections of each construction phase are part of the process.

The selling of the housing thus produced is like the selling of any other product. It involves packaging, in the form of well-furnished models, and advertising. Time becomes the most important factor in the process of home building because any delays in plan approval, construction, or in selling, will cut into the developer's planned profit. Multifamily housing production is based on the same steps, but it is far more complex and includes far more design decisions. The construction of multifamily rental units has declined, and many existing units have been converted to condominiums.

Constraints on housing production include limited available financing, and high interest rates. Government regulations have made the planning approval process more difficult. Various no-growth strategies have been used to the detriment of housing production. Growth controls, environmental regulations, subdivision controls, zoning, and building codes, all could be improved for the benefit of the housing consumer.

House prices have gone up because of the increasing costs of developable land, site development, and construction. Many savings, both large and small, could be gained in changed specifications for roads, sidewalks, driveways, sewers and utilities. While materials and labor account for less of the total cost of housing production than twenty years ago, both have gone up in cost in recent years. Nevertheless, new materials and streamlined methods of construction could lower the price of housing if widely accepted by the housing industry, and the housing public. Homes have become larger and better equipped in recent years. If housing consumers were willing to accept less space and fewer luxuries, new house prices would be lower.

Manufactured housing has become a large but fluctuating part of the nation's housing production. The factory methods differ in sequence and construction techniques from conventional stick-built housing. Modular homes, produced in the same manner as mobile homes, are making lower-cost housing available in the form of duplexes, townhouses, and midrise apartments. Whether or not manufacturer housing will become an increasing means of achieving lower-cost housing production depends on its acceptance by the housing consumer.

Notes

1. Meyerson, M., B. Terrett, and W. L. C. Wheaton, *Housing, People, and Cities* (New York: McGraw-Hill, 1962), p. 20.
2. Ibid.
3. Ibid., p. 22.
4. Breckenfeld, G., "A Decade of Catch-up for Housing," *Fortune*, 1980, *10* (7), pp. 96–97.
5. Seidel, S. R., *Housing Costs & Government Regulations: Confronting the Regulatory Maze* (New Brunswick, N.J.: Center for Urban Policy Research, 1978), p. 26.
6. Frieden, B. and A. P. Solomon, *The Nation's Housing: 1975–1985* (Cambridge, Mass.: Joint Center for Urban Studies of

MIT and Harvard University, 1977), p. 132.
7. Ibid.
8. Macsai, J. et al., *Housing* (New York: Wiley, 1976), chaps. 4–6.
9. "Construction," *Forbes*, Jan. 8, 1979, p. 62.
10. Frieden, B. J., *The Environmental Protection Hustle* (Cambridge, Mass.: MIT Press, 1979), p. 4.
11. Seidel, *Housing Costs*, p. 68.
12. Ibid., pp. 305–313.
13. Ibid., p. 313.
14. U.S. Department of Housing and Urban Development, *Final Report of the Task Force on Housing Costs* (Washington, D.C.: Author, 1978), p. 3.
15. Ibid., p. 2.
16. Frieden, B. J., "The New Housing-Cost Problem," *The Public Interest*, 1977, 49, p. 73.
17. Ibid., p. 74.
18. Controller General of the United States, *Why Are New House Prices So High, How Are They Influenced by Government Regulations and Can Prices Be Reduced?* (Gaithersburg, Md.: General Accounting Office, 1978), p. 15.
19. U.S. Department of Housing and Urban Development, *Task Force on Housing Costs*, p. 13.
20. Controller General, *Why Are New House Prices So High*, p. 16.
21. Ibid., p. 17.
22. Ibid., p. 22.
23. Ibid., p. 23.
24. U.S. Department of Housing and Urban Development, *Task Force on Housing Costs*, p. 47.
25. Controller General, *Why Are New House Price So High*, p. 29.
26. Ibid., p. 35.
27. Ibid., p. 9.
28. Ibid.
29. Bernhardt, A. D., *Building Tomorrow: The Mobile/Manufactured Housing Industry* (Cambridge, Mass.: MIT Press, 1980), p. 42.
30. Ibid., p. 17.
31. Walush, C. N., "Mobile Homes—Declining Share Of Single-family Homes," *Voice of the Federal Reserve Bank of Dallas*, June 1978, p. 21.
32. "Mod Builder Launches Condo Design," *Industrialized building*, Dec. 1978, p. 140.
33. Robinson, S., "Specialized Niche for Manufactured House in Back-to-the-City Movement," *Industrialized building*, Dec. 1978, p. 141.
34. Walush, "Mobile Homes," p. 23.

Suggested Readings

Barlowe, R. "Land for Housing." In C. S. Wedin and L. G. Nygren, eds. *Housing Perspectives* (2nd ed.). Minneapolis: Burgess, 1979.

Bernhardt, A. D. *Building Tomorrow: The Mobile/Manufactured Housing Industry.* Cambridge, Mass: MIT Press, 1980.

Frieden, B. J. *The Environmental Protection Hustle.* Cambridge, Mass: MIT Press, 1979.

Frieden, B. J., and Solomon, A. P. *The Nation's Housing: 1975–1985.* Cambridge, Mass: Joint Center for Urban Studies of MIT and Harvard University, 1977.

"Is Factory-built Housing Ready to Deliver?" *Housing.* 1981, 59 (3) 49–63.

Maisel, S. J. "Housing, Economic Aspects." In *International Encyclopedia of Social Sciences.* New York: Macmillan and Free Press, 1968.

Montgomery, R., and Mandelker, D. R. *Housing in America: Problems and Perspective* (2nd ed.). Indianapolis: Bobbs-Merrill, 1979 (chapters 1, 2, 3 and 4).

Rogg, N. H. "Housing Costs: What Can Be Done?" In C. S. Wedin and L. G. Nygren, eds. *Housing Perspectives* (2nd ed.). Minneapolis: Burgess, 1979.

Seidel, S. R. *Housing Costs & Government Regulations: Confronting the Regulatory Maze*. New Brunswick, N.J.: Rutgers Center for Urban Policy Research, 1978.

U.S. Department of Housing and Urban Development. *Final Report of the Task Force on Housing Costs*. Washington, D.C.: Author, 1978.

The Basics of Housing Choice

4

College students often find themselves in an interesting period of their lives regarding stage in the life cycle, one of the two basics of housing choice. They are seeking independence from their families and might be maintaining households separate from their parents for the first time. At the same time, they are often perplexed that their parents, responding to a change in life cycle, are changing their own residence; they would rather their parents maintain the homes of their childhood even though they are making the first steps towards not needing them.

Rented apartments, whether townhouses or high rise such as these in San Francisco, provide housing that meets the norms for space, tenure and location of many single persons. Photo courtesy of U.S. Department of Housing and Urban Development.

Typical housing requirements related to the traditional adult stage of the life cycle are explained in the first chapter section. Nontraditional stages of the life cycle are examined in the second section: "Changing Family, Changing Housing Needs."

During their college years students begin defining lifestyles for themselves independent of their families'. **Lifestyle** is the second basic of housing choice to be discussed in this chapter. It, too, has two sections, one from the traditional perspective and one from a nontraditional perspective. Two other concepts central to understanding individual differences in housing choice are **social class** and **values.** They are the subjects of Chapter 5. All of these concepts—stage in the life cycle, lifestyle, social class and values—interrelate in the effects they have on housing choice. For purposes of clarity, they will be analyzed separately in these two chapters before their interrelationship is explained at the end of Chapter 5.

HOUSING AND THE TRADITIONAL STAGES OF THE LIFE CYCLE

Most of the readers of this text will already have three traditional stages of the life cycle behind them—infancy, childhood, and adolescence. Even though each of those could be described in terms of the housing appropriate to each, the focus in this section will be on housing that meets the requirements of adult stages in the life cycle.

Norms are rules of behavior that we share as a society. Housing norms are aspects of housing we commonly expect to be right and proper. They can be more precise than housing values because they can direct what should be done in a given circumstance. For instance, a family with children should own a three-bedroom, single-family detached home, everyone should have indoor plumbing, and houses should be set back from the street in suburban neighborhoods. The norms for tenure, space, housing structure type, neighborhood, quality, and expenditure have been related to stage in the life cycle, social class, and other demographic characteristics.[1]

Typically, a single adult, whether or not a college student, will seek an independent living situation. Should this person marry, then another stage is established, that of the young couple. The birth of a child creates a **nuclear family** which can expand with more children. As the children grow older, and require more activity and storage space, the housing requirement for this stage changes. When teenagers begin to leave home, the couple is faced with new requirements again. Retirement, death of a

spouse, or divorce can cause changes that again alter housing needs. Finally, the elderly stage has characteristics that translate into unique forms of housing. Chapter 13 is devoted entirely to the housing of persons over sixty, therefore the stages of the life cycle preceding that one are dealt with here. Each stage is analyzed in terms of the tenure preferences, housing types, space needs and location desired for each. These preferences represent the housing norms within each stage, and needless to say, do not represent all persons within each group discussed. Since most of us follow the pattern of housing norms related to each stage in the life cycle, it is worthwhile to look at those patterns in detail.

Young Single Adults

Tenure and Housing Type. Most young single adults prefer to live alone in rented apartments. Many exceptions to this generality are obvious. Single adults pair up with members of their own or the opposite sex and share the costs of rent and utilities. Some own condominiums or mobile homes. Single-family homes, probably smaller than those preferred by families, might be rented or owned, and shared with other single adults.

Some apartment complexes have been designed with this housing market especially in mind. Usually these complexes have recreational facilities such as swimming pools, tennis courts, saunas, game rooms, and so on, so that residents may conveniently socialize with each other. These facilities may also provide entertainment opportunities for residents' guests.

Space Needs. The studio or one-bedroom apartment may be suitable for a young single adult; however, more affluent singles might prefer two-bedroom apartments in which they can comfortably accommodate overnight guests, prepare and serve meals for company and host small parties. Traditionally, young singles might not have the furnishings and equipment associated with these activities, but as more and more singles delay marriage and achieve at least moderate income levels, the picture is changing. Some singles might have storage needs for clothing, recreational equipment, and household belongings exceeding those of a young nuclear family.

Location. Distance to work and convenience of recreational and cultural activities may be of primary importance in choosing a desirable location for young singles.[2] In some urban areas, access to public transportation might be a strong criterion for housing location. Some smaller communities might accommodate bikers and walkers especially well. Some urban and surburban area residents depend entirely on private cars. The single adult has to weigh the advantages of a location close to desired social

activities, which might carry a high price tag, against the costs of travel (time and money) that often result from a lower-rent, further-out location.

Young Childless Couples

Tenure and Housing Type. When young singles marry, they might choose to stay in the housing one or the other already has. A spacious well-located apartment with reasonable rent might suit their housing needs very well, at least for a while. Young couples anticipating having children, however, may very likely be planning home ownership as well. Many will buy a condominium, a duplex, a small house, or a mobile home in this anticipation.[3] Their choice here is difficult, because what is suitable for the couple stage might not be suitable for the family with young children. Some mobile home parks and apartment complexes force the young couple to move when they have a baby. If a couple invests in a prop-

Duplex housing units are a preferred housing type for young childless couples. Whether rented or owned, they provide suitable space to meet their needs. Photo by author.

erty in order to use their equity for "trading up," their choices can be made suitable for each of these stages of the life cycle. Two-income families may have an advantage in managing the financial burden involved in this scheme. On the other hand, many couples prefer to continue to rent and use their double incomes for recreation, entertaining, travel, savings and investments.

Space Needs. Two adults do not need twice as much room as one adult. On the contrary, a two-bedroom housing unit that provided adequate space for sleeping, food preparation and eating, social interacting, and storage for a single adult might well provide enough for two. Most young couples would want at least enough room in their dining space to accommodate one or two other couples, and they might want an extra bedroom for an at-home office, guests, hobbies, and storage. These needs might justify the use of a three-bedroom dwelling.

Location. If both partners are employed outside the home, a mutually convenient location regarding their places of work is of primary importance. In a large urban area, both may have to commute great distances from a residence more or less midway between both work places. The couple may also desire convenient shopping, entertainment, and recreational facilities.

Nuclear Families— Young Children

Tenure and Housing Type. Once a child enters into the life cycle picture, housing needs change. The young family usually desires to own a home, and if the first home purchase has not already occurred, the birth of a child may prompt this decision. The association of home ownership with family life is a strong one in our

society. Perin describes this climb up the ladder as a " 'natural progression' through the stages of the life cycle—from renting an apartment or townhouse, duplex, or attached row house, to owning, as still another step, any one of those, along the way to the ultimate rung, that of owning a single-family-detached [sic] house."[4] The young family could find itself in any of these housing circumstances, but might be planning the next step as soon as financially possible.

Space Needs. A second bedroom in any housing unit could be converted from a study-hobby-guest room into a child's room. A second child could be accommodated in the same bedroom as the first until there is pressure for adequate play and storage space for two active children. The family may seek the standard three-bedroom, single-family detached house. The household functions of meal preparation, eating, laundry, and adult entertaining become more complex with the presence of one or more small children, and the space requirements would increase accordingly.

Adult supervision of children's outdoor activities may motivate the family to move to housing with a private yard. Even if multifamily housing is designed with children's play space, the parents often prefer supervision while remaining in their own housing unit. A feeling that children and parents are better off without the constant concern of bothering the neighbors with necessary noise from normal activities also motivates some families to move into a house without shared walls, but with spatial separation from neighbors, and access to the outside.[5]

Location. A young family often chooses to live in a suburban neighborhood with a local park and local shopping available, as well as close commuting distance to health care, major shopping, and suitable forms of recreation. Day care centers are increasingly needed or desired by families with young children. As soon as children enter school, the ease with which they can get to to school becomes a dominant factor in a desirable location. In communities with school bussing practiced, this requirement may be difficult to satisfy.

Nuclear Families— Teenagers

Tenure and Housing Type. A fully formed family frequently will want to own its single-family, detached home in the suburbs. This stage of the life cycle has the strongest tie to the norms of both ownership and single-family dwellings.

Space Needs. The space needs peak in this stage of the life cycle. Whatever doubling up of children that occurred while they were small will be thought undesirable when they are teenagers. Not every American child needs or has a bedroom of his or her own, but children of different sexes or of drastically different ages of the same sex are usually provided private bedrooms. Affluent families may also seek to separate teenage social space from adult social space in the form of a separate family room, recreation room, or den. Storage needs are great at this stage also, as each child develops individual interests and hobbies.

Location. The suburban neighborhood is the American ideal for this stage in the

Nuclear families with teenage children have need for more space than families in any other stage in the life cycle. A large well-located house provides the physical and social environment needed by these families. Photo by author.

life cycle for several reasons. The importance of schools has been mentioned, but for teenagers they need not be within a few blocks. More important is a social environment thought to be desirable for the maturing child. Parents like their children to meet, become friends with, and eventually marry the children of people very much like themselves, consequently they seek homogeneous neighborhoods that provide a built-in social pattern of this sort. It is a curious thing that persons who criticize tract housing because of its sameness in design character, overlook the social advantage, not so easily articulated, of families of similar size, ages, income level, and socioeconomic characteristics attracted to the same type and price of house.

Preretirement Childless Couples

Tenure and Housing Type. The family whose children have left home has much in common with the young childless couple, however, the existence of older children means the family's requirements are not identical. If they have owned a home, they may want to continue to own a home. Many condominium developments are designed for this housing market, called "empty-nesters," keeping in mind the needs of privacy, convenience, low maintenance, and luxury a couple may have when their responsibilities as parents have waned. Some families choose mobile homes at this stage of their lives, while many maintain their single-family home many more years. Oddly enough, it is not unusual for a family at this stage in the life cycle to acquire their dream home, in the location they have aspired to, and with the space and equipment they needed five to ten years before. It is because their children no longer consume most of their resources

that such couples can fulfill long-sustained wants at a time when that fulfillment may not make sound economic sense.

Space Needs. In a strict sense, space needs are reduced at this stage of the life cycle. But the picture is not as simple as that. Children move out in degrees, often leaving personal belongings in the care of their parents while they live in different housing situations. While the teenagers' activities may be eliminated from the space, the parents may substitute other activities. Generally, if housing space is decreased, it is not decreased to the size similar to that of the young childless couple.

Location. There may be a strong motivation for the couple to stay in the neighborhood of the previous stage in the life cycle because ties to neighbors, friends, church and community provide a satisfying social network. On the other hand, many couples may move out of the suburban environment and into a more central location to be near cultural activities, shopping, and entertainment. As long as one or two places of employment have to be considered, location may be limited.

CHANGING FAMILIES— CHANGING HOUSING NEEDS

A recent study explored the willingness of college students to participate in alternative marital and family forms.[6] Surprisingly, long-term cohabitation and five year evaluation and renewal of marriage was ranked highly by both men and women along with traditional and equalitarian marriage. Some of the other choices rating lower in preferences were childfree marriages, rural commune—shared sex, group marriage and spouse swapping, and remaining single.

Many condominimum developments have been designed to appeal to the "empty nester" stage in the life cycle. Pre-retirement couples enjoy the freedom from maintenance and at the same time benefit from the ownership of individual space and pleasant surroundings. Photo by author.

The study therefore focuses on the range of unusual and, until recently, deviant forms of families. It is the purpose of this section to examine a few of these alternatives as nontraditional stages in the life cycle.

Middle-aged Single Adults

It is difficult to draw a line between the group described in the traditional stages of the life cycle as "young single adults" and this group. A difference of age is implied, and often age thirty-five is considered the cross-over point. In any case, what is meant is a group of persons settled into a single-person form of life. One imagines a person who has chosen to remain single, whose income level is adequate to support travel and recreation envied by the family with children. What kind of housing do these persons need? There is no simple answer.

The National Association of Home Builders' marketing department reported in 1978 that singles accounted for a quarter of sales in some condominium developments in various parts of the country, and, more significantly, singles are a discerning and growing segment of the market.[7] Single people also buy single-family dwellings. The space needs are the same for either type of housing—at least one extra bedroom for guests, a well-equipped kitchen, entertaining space in living and dining areas, and storage space to accommodate a lot of clothes, sports equipment, supplies for hobbies and crafts, and built-in space to allow for work without intrusion into dining and kitchen areas.

Middle-aged singles who rent probably have the same space needs as young singles described above, but in all likelihood they would have the income level to allow for desired amounts of space, location and amenities. The amenities may become especially important when a person makes a rental housing choice that is not considered temporary. Available pools, saunas, tennis courts, and even jogging paths, may be as important as a view and desirable location.

Divorced Singles

Divorced singles over thirty-five, either without children or at least without children in custody, have a surprising number of housing options including remaining in the home of the marriage. Location, however, may be dictated by where children *are* located, and choice limited by constraints of child support and alimony. There is evidence that more men than women "go home to mother" even though the older a person is, the less likely this is.[8] Moving into a house with someone else is another option and older singles might move in with a child or sibling. If the divorced person is also seeking a different kind of life, a drastic change of job, location, or even geographical area can take place.

Single-Parent Families

A widowed or divorced person with children to care for has housing problems unlike the divorced person described in the previous section. Even though more and more fathers are gaining custody of their children, by and large it is women who keep the children. Either way, the parent generally prefers to keep the predivorce housing. The household routines, school associations, and community ties can remain intact if staying put is financially and emotionally possible. The actual space needs of the family are not drastically altered with the absence of one adult.

If the single-parent family must seek new housing, it faces the problem of fulfilling the requirements for space, location and ownership common to nuclear families with children. This may be difficult for a family whose income level is altered by divorce or

Single parents in need of rental housing have a difficult time finding units that accept children. Very few rental complexes are designed to accommodate the play space needed by young children. Photo by author.

widowhood. Many women in these circumstances seek employment and are caught with conflicting needs: to have housing more convenient to a job location, easier to care for, and lower in cost; at the same time to maintain a stable housing environment for the psychological well-being of themselves and their children.

Unrelated Adults

Cohabitation. Most people associate the practice of cohabitation with young singles, especially college students, as a prelude to marriage and the traditional stages of the life cycle. Cohabitation can also occur among single never-marrieds as a permanent marriage alternative, and among divorced persons as an interim arrangement. It is not unheard of that some elderly people cohabitate, often to their financial advantage.

It is easy to suppose that the housing suitable for this nontraditional stage in the life cycle, then, has more to do with the ages of the persons than their unmarried status. Young cohabiting couples would have the requirements of housing type, space and location matching those of a young married couple. They might prefer to rent. However, it should be recognized that cohabiting couples do own homes. That singles are "living and buying together" is one of four basic reasons given for the lively single home buying market identified by the NAHB.[9] If both partners are employed, they might be in a financial position to purchase housing of their choice. One can guess that their choice would probably be the luxury townhouse condominium over the standard suburban single-family dwelling.

Shared Households. Shared households consist of persons who have committed themselves to more than one other adult for purposes of living together. Most communes of the 1960s, at least the well-publicized ones, have a great many more characteristics than that, such as a quasi-religious leader, social goal, economic self-reliance, and so on. Contemporary communes more often have a goal of creating an "alternative family" or "intentional community."[10] Obviously, the choice of communal living is also a choice of lifestyle. Nevertheless, since communes have appealed to thousands of young single adults, and not a few middle-aged and elderly adults, the kinds of housing chosen by these groups are worth noting.

Many different forms of shared households have emerged in recent years. Their variety evolved from the diverse needs of the individuals and families who formed them. Raimy discusses some of this diversity as reflected in housing:

> Some communal households are formed by two or more nuclear families, or by a collection of single parents. In these groups childrearing is likely to be an important purpose. But other households have no kids and are built around a shared interest or a diversity of interests. A cluster community isn't a shared household, but rather an apartment building or a grouping of single-family homes whose residents want to create an extended family feeling. The cluster community is included here because successful clusters achieve the same goals that shared households do. There are households for older people, for women only, and for men only. Some households are an attempt to pool resources and live in luxury. Others are formed by people interested in personal growth. And there are still more types.[11]

Unrelated adults can also share housing for temporary periods and without a commitment to each other or to a binding ideal.

Unrelated adults of any age might double up in rental or owned housing units such as these. The arrangement may be temporary or permanent, but the advantage of shared costs is a benefit to both parties. Photo by author.

Middle-aged and elderly singles will move into a house or apartment together with the same casualness that college students and other young singles do, primarily to share costs for a time mutually convenient to both. Doubling up of nuclear families and single-parent families also occurs. However transient these arrangements are, they are very real stages in the life cycle for the participants even though they do not fit traditional classifications.

LIFESTYLE AND HOUSING

A recent public television program described the "lifestyle of California" as one of "energy, optimism and affluence."[12] This statement raises a few questions about lifestyle differences. Are these qualities unique to Californians? Do all or most residents of a state have a lifestyle that could be described with so few words? Where do the common denominators of lifestyles leave off, if that is what these qualities are, and individual or family differences begin? By taking a careful look at lifestyles, one will be able to find answers to these questions.

Definition of Lifestyle

There are several aspects of lifestyle that should be taken into account in a solid definition. These are discussed separately, even though a comprehensive understanding of lifestlye includes them all.

Role Emphasis.[13] We each have a multitude of roles that determine our behavior. At the same time, a person can be a student, a roommate, a girlfriend, a daughter, a sister, a waitress, and a friend. Each of these roles has a pattern of behavior expectations which are normally carried out. Roles imply relationships with people close to each individual, and each person's par-

ticipation in a variety of social groups— family, classes, dorm residents, and so on. Lifestyle is determined by the one or more roles that stand out or dominate the others. Most students would say that being a student is central to their self-images, so that role is basic in defining their lifestyles.

Central Life Interest.[14] Work and children are two of the more common central life interests that determine lifestyles. Others which could be very important to the individual are: ethnic heritage, politics, lineage, avocational pursuits, and religion. A central life interest is one which pervades other aspects of life beyond the associated activities directly related to it. If, for instance, people's ethnic heritage or religion determined where they worked, how they spend their income, with whom they spend their leisure time, and their everyday patterns of family life, it would be quite clear these are central life interests, and dominant factors in their lifestyles. Most of us do not have quite so clear-cut a central life interest, but we live according to the dominance of two or three central life interests.

Sociological Variables.[15] It is a common misconception that lifestyle is a matter only of income level; if you are rich you have one kind of lifestyle, and if you are poor you have another. Other considerations negate this simplistic relationship of money to lifestyle, even though it is true that a higher level of income might allow more lifestyle choices for a given individual. Besides income level, education and ethnic background will influence lifestyles. So will age, sex, and religion. Region is another important factor.

Some writers refer to an American lifestyle. It is possible to identify common consumer habits among many Americans such as fast food, shopping centers, television preferences, even house styles. But to focus on the sameness of American culture, based mostly on middle-class tastes and consumer patterns, is to overlook important individual differences. It is the differences in lifestyle that are critical to understanding the relationship of lifestyle to housing choice.

Traditional Types of Lifestyles

In a society as complex as ours, where there is much diversity in the way we live, it is difficult to categorize all of us into the traditional lifestyles of familism, careerism, and consumerism.[16] We are familiar enough with these types through personal experience to recognize them, but lifestyle has many dimensions besides these main three. The traditional types of lifestyle are discussed here in relation to the tenure and housing types associated with them, the probable housing space suitable to them and location factors to be taken into account.

Familism. The familism lifestyle has children as a central life interest and the mother and father roles as dominant. One can picture the kind of family that spends most of its leisure time together in family pursuits. These might be geared to education (a trip to a museum), to sports (little league games) or fun (a picnic, beach trip, Disneyland). One imagines individual pursuits along these same lines. The father might also be a Boy Scout Leader; the mother bakes cookies for the Halloween carnival at school.

To continue the stereotype, they live in a comfortable three-bedroom, single-family dwelling in a suburban neighborhood. They own their home, and they will move into a larger house if it will provide more space for privacy, family activities, and self-improvement of the children. It is likely that

this home base will remain intact even after the children have moved out on their own.

There are ethnic variations on the familism theme. One study of an area in Boston destined for urban renewal, the West End, uncovered a pattern of Italian-American family relationships based on the extended family.[17] Most persons had close relatives living in the same building or within a block or two, thus providing a network of familial relationships that was an integral part of their daily lives. Howard describes a family of Greek origin in *Families*.[18] Its familism lifestyle extended to the homeland an encompassed a wide geographic area in the United States with all members of the family intimately involved in each other's well-being. Familism takes on a different character if the family is, say, inner-city black, Midwestern rural Scandinavian, or Southwestern barrio Chicano.

Consumerism. This lifestyle is centered on personal pleasure. Most of the family's decisions about use of money and time are made on the basis of what will provide entertainment and self-enrichment. A social calendar crowded with eating out in fashionable restaurants, going to concerts and plays, especially the "in" ones, attending parties with the "right" people, would be typical of this family. The family may have children, but they play a secondary role.

The housing for this family would have to fit their image of themselves. It would probably be in a "good" part of town: "good" because it was an established address; "good" because it was a well-designed new development; or "good" because it was a charming older part of town being individually rehabilitated. The type of housing would not matter so long as admiration from others in the same social circle was an outcome of the choice. The interior would very likely be done every few years so as not to appear to be out of style. The monthly shelter magazines give us a lavish picture of this lifestyle, carried out to perfection.

There might be more renters in this lifestyle category than in familism. Since a fashionable location, with its available social activities, is more important than a quiet neighborhood with good schools, the suburban home ownership prototype does not fit. Many condominiums are designed to suit this lifestyle, however, and highrise inner-city condominiums and **cooperatives** are probably mainly occupied by people subscribing in part to this lifestyle.

Careerism. Traditionally, when the father's job was the basic determinant in where the family lived, whom they entertained, and how they spent leisure time, it could be said the lifestyle was careerism. A military family comes to mind, because relocation, the quality of the housing, the friendships formed, schools attended, everything, related to the father's military position. Striving executives might be in a similar lifestyle pattern. Many young people feel the need to work extra hours, attend professional meetings away from home, and otherwise prove their dedication to career goals. It may be that the wife and mother in these cases creates a familism lifestyle without the help of her husband. In recent times, in some role reversal marriages, it may be the father left to be primarily concerned with the wellbeing of the children while the mother is totally absorbed in her work.

Location would be chosen with regard to work as well as suitability of having business associates visit. The space requirements would have to include space and equipment for entertaining, again for business purposes. Career people are probably home owners due to income level and pressures for conformity. No doubt some people prefer to rent, especially if a move to another

A charming older part of a community might appeal to a family fitting the consumerism traditional lifestyle. This housing choice would reflect the family's interest in being in a good location near sources of entertainment and self-enrichment. Photo courtesy of U.S. Department of Housing and Urban Development.

place is anticipated as part of the career pattern. These renters would seek spacious rentals in good locations, and luxury amenities, not so much to be enjoyed as to provide a sense of status.

Traditional Lifestyles and Dual-Income Families. It would be easy to assume that all families with both husband and wife working are representative of the careerism lifestyle. This may be the case, particularly if both have jobs in which advancement requires signs of dedication beyond eight-hours-a-day competence. Very often though, at least one of the partners, not necessarily the woman, has a job that does not interfere with nonwork time. Two-paycheck families can be just as oriented to familism as a one-paycheck family, and, in fact, some employed mothers will argue they can provide better for their children because they are employed. A college education for several children could easily be a motivation for a second paycheck. Some families, perhaps without children, see their dual-income affluence as a means to the good life associated with consumerism. In any case, more and more wives and mothers are employed, and there is a definite effect on the options for lifestyle open to these families. At the very least, this phenomenon challenges previous self-definitions of role emphasis and central life interest for both men and women.

CONTEMPORARY LIFESTYLE DIVERSITY AND HOUSING

In this section, three contemporary lifestyles are identified and discussed. Since they are currently popular, particularly with young people, they should be considered in conjunction with the traditional types already covered. Leisure, self-reliance, and ecology have emerged in recent years as themes of American life. The effect these themes have had on lifestyle, and in turn on housing, is the subject of this section.

Leisure

All of us are interested in leisure, and all of us find some form to fit into our lives. When leisure affects housing choice, it takes on a different importance. Leisure activities such as boating, fishing, skiing, flying, and maybe even jogging might be time-consuming enough to require low-maintenance housing. Conflicts affecting personal happiness and harmonious family life can arise from the need, on the one hand, to maintain the family home and derive the status benefits of home ownership,

Families with the advantage of two incomes have lifestyle options. For some, this type of urban high-rise housing in a central location close to both places of employment might be ideal. Photo courtesy of U.S. Department of Housing and Urban Development.

and the need, on the other hand, to enjoy oneself in the manner one prefers and can afford.

Leisure and Planned Communities. The importance of leisure as an integrated part of housing choice has become apparent to many planners and developers. Large rental complexes might be designed to include a range of leisure facilities such as swimming pools, saunas, and tennis courts. Country-club suburbs are not uncommon, and the appeal, besides the adjacent golf course, is a guaranteed social life. Some large-scale condominium developments are centered around golf courses, lakes for boating and fishing, as well as the standard swimming pools and clubhouses. Clubhouses, swim-

"*I wish we had a life style.*"

Drawing by Lorenz; ©
1973 The New Yorker
Magazine, Inc.

ming pools and other recreational facilities are an inherent part of large, high-quality mobile home parks. Many mobile home parks are located in recreational areas such as lakeside or beach communities. Many new towns have been planned with a recreational body of water in them and undeveloped open space intended for activities such as hiking, picnicking, or bird-watching. These large-scale leisure settings are planned into the community along with the standard recreational amenities already mentioned.

Second Homes. Many families have aspired to, and fewer have achieved, a second home located specifically for leisure purposes. Thousands of ski-resort condominiums, lakeside cabins, and beachfront cottages have been built in the past few decades, peaking in the 1960s when housing construction costs and automobile fuel costs were not yet unpredictably high. By the mid-1970s, the trend had subsided, but there are still thousands of such homes, and leisure lifestyles associated with them.

One trend that emerged in the 1970s was "time shared" ownership. Several families invested in the second home and agreed on which weekends and vacation periods each would have its exclusive use. Another method of keeping the purchase price within reach of some families is to buy a housing unit expecting to use it a small portion of the year, and renting it the rest of the time. Usually rental arrangements, maintenance, and ordinary cleaning are handled by a third party, not the owner, but the owner has some tax advantages of ownership (tax write-offs are relatively small) as well as the limited use of a home away from home.

Recreational Vehicles. Sales of recreational vehicles (campers, travel trailers, motor homes) have increased enormously in the past decade, in spite of threatened and real fuel cost increases. Apparently many families are choosing the **R V** as a substitute for the second home. The advantage is obvious—the family can spend its leisure time in different places depending on the season, amount of time available, and changing interests of its members.

The design of recreational vehicles indicates something about attitudes toward leisure and housing. Newer designs are literally homes in themselves. They are characterized by electrical appliances, including television sets, generous storage, sleeping for six to eight persons, carpeting throughout, comfortable upholstered furnishings, and so on. It seems we want to leave home without leaving home, and a surprising number of families can afford to do so. However, by 1980, high gas prices affected sales of the more fuel-inefficient R Vs.

Leisure and House as One. Finally, a leisure lifestyle can manifest itself by giving up a standard housing type altogether, and simply living in the leisure home. **House-**

This tennis court in Reston, Virginia, is typical of the types of leisure and recreational facilities planned into new towns and other large-scale developments. Many condominium rental complexes, and mobile home parks are also developed with easy access to leisure facilities in mind. Photo courtesy of U.S. Department of Housing and Urban Development.

boat living has been popular in some areas for years, but with rising costs of housing in the 1970s, more and more people were opting to give up their on-land home base and to turn their houseboat attraction into a form of permanent residence. Other types of boats are used as homes also. They include power cruisers, small sailboats, converted trawlers, former ferry boats, what have you. These "boat people" have been described as single men and women, young and middle-aged couples, and traditional nuclear families.[19]

Another leisure home that lends itself to residency is the travel trailer. Trailer parks are often nearly filled with travel trailers that more or less stay put. The occupants might be students, young couples, retirees, maybe a young family. In some cases, the economic advantages of low-cost housing, cheap rent (only a few dollars a night) and no taxes or maintenance, might be the primary motivation for living in this way. In many cases though, the ability to move on is very much part of the travel trailer phenomenon. The parks in the South, Southwest and West find that for the six months of the year, when northern climates are at their worst, their parks are full of out-of-state families.

Some persons buy old campers and buses and convert them into living quarters. Students usually know of a campus subculture of students living in vehicles of one sort or another, legally and illegally. There are some bus residents, however, who have spent a lot of time and care in creating a highly personal handcrafted place to live. It may be that the ability to travel in their home is less important to these people than self-expression, economy, and self-reliance.

Self-Reliance

Self-reliance can be the foundation for a quite different lifestyle. It is associated with

Sausalito, California is one of several places in which entire communities of houseboats have developed. Photo by author.

rural environments more than urban environments because it usually involves growing food supplies, including animals, so as to rely as little as possible on commercially produced food products. Old farmhouses on small farms are very like the farms of the nineteenth century, after which this lifestyle is modelled. The back-to-the-land

Turning older vehicles such as buses and trucks into places of residence has become a popular trend among college students. They are sometimes highly individual hand-crafted homes. Photo by author.

Plop! Waldon Drops Out

BY MIKE ROYKO

CHICAGO—One of the interesting social developments of our time has been the large number of people who have changed lifestyles and careers when they reach their middle years.

Not long ago, I met Waldon Pond, 46, and his wife, Murky, 42, who, with their two children, have thrown aside their former lifestyle and taken another.

Until recently, the Pond family lived high in the mountains of Utah. Their home was the wilderness log cabin in which Waldon was born. It was more than 50 miles from their nearest neighbor and 150 miles from the closest town.

Waldon had made a modest living digging rare roots out of the earth for shipment to natural health-food stores. This had been his career since graduating from Rutabaga Agricultural College, also in a remote section of Utah, where he met his wife.

In their wilderness home, his wife contributed to the family income by crafting treebark belts for shipment to natural clothing stores. She also grew her own vegetables, while Waldon trapped and fished and the children gathered edible berries and leaves.

For recreation the family would gather in the log cabin in the evening and read the classics aloud or, as a string quartet they played music by Bach, Haydn and Mozart as well as authentic folk songs handed down by their ancestors.

The children had few friends of their own age, but they enjoyed frolicking with their pet deer, squirrel, fox, raccoon, otter, mountain goat, elk and moose, which the family had tamed and which lived with them.

Then their lives abruptly changed.

"One day I was digging up a rare root," Waldon recalled. "In a tree above me, a beautiful bird began singing a sweet song. I lay down on the grass and looked at the puffy white clouds drifting across the blue sky, and I listened to the bird sing, as I often do.

"And I asked myself: 'Is this what I want to do with the rest of my life?'

"At that moment, a bird dropping landed in my eye. I took that to be a sign.

"That night I sat down with my wife and asked if she was content with our simple, natural life, away from the hurly-burly and close to nature. She said, frankly, she could take it or leave it. She was getting a little tired of having all those animals around the cabin, especially the tame moose.

"So we packed our few simple possessions and in a week we were living in Chicago. And this is where we have been for the last year."

Waldon, who now calls himself Wally, has become the sales manager of the used-car division of a large auto agency.

"I love it," he said. "I love the rat race. To me, seeing some unsuspecting soul walk into my lot, and pouncing on him and talking him into buying a clunker that might explode when it hits the first pothole, is infinitely more challenging than finding a silly, edible root."

Don't you miss the quiet simplicity of your cabin?

"Not a bit. I live in a large condo apartment and since I bought it, it has increased in value by $40,000. Hell, my doorknobs are worth more than my whole log cabin was. In fact, my wife now has a real-estate license and she's selling condos herself."

What about communing with nature? Don't you miss being close to creatures of the wild?

"Miss watching a lot of damn boring birds and squirrels and chipmunks from my front porch? Listen, all they ever did was dig holes or eat nuts or worms. What's so exciting about eating worms?

"I can sit on my condo balcony and see a lot more wildlife than I ever saw in the woods. Last night I saw an old lady get mugged by a street gang that sprayed 'Insane Idiots' on her coat with a paint can.

"And last week I watched two guys strip a car of everything but the ashtray in less than five minutes. The owner showed up while they were doing it and they stripped him of everything but his hairpiece. This is far more exciting than life in the wilderness."

Do you still spend evenings reading and sharing music with your children?

"As a matter of fact,

no. My son has moved in with a young woman. If they still like each other after three months, they're going to tell each other their names. And my daughter has joined a religious cult and is making a very good living. She poses as a paralyzed deaf mute and sells religious tracts in the Loop or at the airport. She gets 20% of the take, and just bought her own Mazda sports car."

But don't you miss hunting and fishing?

"I still do it, in a different way. You see, my wife is studying gourmet cooking at night, so I hit the discos and do a little hunting. And I'm buying my own 30-foot cabin cruiser, just as soon as the precinct captain can pay somebody off and get me a mooring. Then whatever I hunt down in the discos I can take with

me on my fishing trips. So I'm still a sportsman at heart."

But you're no longer a mountain man.

"No. I'm a high-rise man now. The closest I get to my old lifestyle is when I put on my Eddie Bauer boots and bush jacket on Saturdays and ride my high-rise elevator."

Do you think you'll ever change lifestyles again— maybe return to your wilderness cabin?

"It's too late. I just sold it to a middle-aged stockbroker from La Salle St. who quit his job to seek the simple life."

Do you think he'll like his new lifestyle?

"Maybe, especially if he can housebreak that damn moose."
© Chicago Sun Times, 1979. Article by Mike Royko. Reprinted with permission.

movement was dramatized by the growth of communes in the 1960s but it lingers as a lifestyle trend not only for experimental young people, but also for middle-aged urban folk searching for a simpler, healthier, less materialistic way to live.

Self-reliance can be expressed by building your own home. Many young people decide to construct their own homes mainly to save labor costs, but also to directly involve themselves in creating a personal living space. Some housing "kits" are designed to satisfy this lifestyle need. The purchasers follow the manufacturers directions for the house's construction, and can successfully build a home without previous experience. Some families, as well as singles, construct

houses that do not meet building codes.

Perhaps the most extreme form of self-reliance is teepee living. On the West Coast, hundreds, if not thousands, of people live in teepees, sometimes purchased but largely handmade. Since local housing controls do not allow this form of living, the residents generally seek out-of-the-way spots to place their tents. Some live in clusters, but nearly all are near a standard housing unit with normal provisions of running water and electricity.

Ecology and Lifestyle

Some of the ecological concerns of the 1960s and 1970s have become in all likelihood a permanent part of our culture. Bio-

This recycled older house with its solar panels symbolizes an ecology lifestyle in which persons apply their concern for the environment to their housing choice. Photo courtesy of U.S. Department of Housing and Urban Development.

degradable detergents, recycled paper, and litter laws are not going to disappear, but neither are smog, oil spills or polluted lakes and rivers. A lifestyle based on ecology goes much further than being a careful consumer and an aware citizen. It has its effects on daily life as well as on house design.

The recycled house is probably the most dramatic instance of ecology and lifestyle as they affect housing. Some whimsical architecture has resulted from reusing old wood, old windows, old anything to make a highly individualized living place.[20] Using abandoned or run-down buildings intended for other uses—old schools, churches, railway stations—for housing is recycling in another way. One could argue that rehabilitating an urban townhouse is equally conserving and therefore fitting of this lifestyle.

An ecology lifestyle is usually coupled with a concern for the consumption of energy. Besides the everyday measures of conserving fuel in the use of water, appliances,

and heating, the typical family in this lifestyle seeks ways to provide alternative energy sources. The most popular means at this time is solar energy.

Ecology and self-sufficiency overlap in the matter of waste disposal. Several publications have appeared which are essentially how-to-do-it manuals for using waste as a resource. In *Other Homes and Garbage*, the advantages, functions and technology of methane digesters and clivus multrums are explained. The former uses human wastes to produce gas for heating and cooking, as well as compost, and the latter produces reusable water from human waste.[21] Other subjects covered include generating your own electricity, providing your own water supply, and, of course, solar heating. *The Integral Urban House* describes "how to achieve a high quality urban way of life using a fraction of the resources we are accustomed to, at lower cost, with less waste, pollution and ugliness."[22]

An Ecological Village

2,000 PEOPLE

1200 ACRES

NO CARS

On 1200 acres of forest and meadow near Eugene, Oregon, a new community for 2,000 people is being planned and built by its future residents. An ecological village with shops, light industries, organic agriculture, experiential education, town meetings and community transit replacing the automobile.

Our first 100 households are a varied bunch, but we're all committed to ecological harmony, appropriate technology, personal growth and a neighborly community.

We're looking for fellow pioneers and supporters to join our adventure. Send for our introductory book on our long range goals, our progress to date, our participatory process for getting from here to there, and an invitation to take part in our extended community. We'll include information about our summer visitors programs and our involvement programs in several West Coast cities. Please enclose $2 for printing, postage and handling.

The Cerro Gordo Community

Dorena Lake, Box 569   Cottage Grove, Oregon 97424

Source: Mother Jones, *February/March, 1979, p. 65.*

SUMMARY

The traditional stages of the life cycle can be used to predict housing choices. Typically, the single person rents a small housing unit, and the young couple rents or buys a larger apartment, mobile home, condominium or small house. The formation of a nuclear family is strongly associated with the purchase of a single-family detached dwelling in a suburban neighborhood with its own school. When the children have left home, housing needs can be met with a smaller unit, whether owned or rented.

Singles adults often form one or several nontraditional stages in the life cycle. Single-parent families are a growing segment of the nation's housing consumers. Unrelated adults may form an alternative family type for which housing must be suited in a variety of ways. Housing for these alternative stages in the life cycle is drawn from the normal housing associated with traditional stages in the life cycle.

Lifestyle can be defined in terms of dominant role emphasis and central life interest, taking sociological variables into account. Three lifestyle prototypes can be related to housing very clearly. Familism is identified with the suburban environment of single-family, owned homes. The consumerism lifestyle is found in a fashionable setting for the good life. Careerism lifestyle can adapt to many types of high-status housing, either rented or owned, since housing and home life is secondary to work.

Leisure as a dominant lifestyle factor can affect housing in that it creates a market for second homes and recreational vehicles, but it also can be the motivation for unusual forms of housing such as boats. Self-reliance and ecology are parallel and often interrelated lifestyles which are manifested in rural farm housing, handmade houses, solar supplied space and hot water heating, and even converted vehicles and teepees.

Stage in the life cycle and lifestyle are two basics of housing choice important to consumers. The better the housing consumers recognize their own stage of the life cycle and lifestyle characteristics, the more satisfied they will be with their housing choices.

Notes

1. Morris, E. W., and M. Winter, *Housing, Family and Society* (New York: Wiley, 1978).
2. Michelson, W. H., *Man and His Urban Environment: A Sociological Approach* (Reading, Mass.: Addison-Wesley, 1976), p. 104.
3. Morris and Winter, *Housing, Family and Society*, p. 112.
4. Perin, C., *Everything in Its Place: Social Order and Land Use in America* (Princton, N.J.: Princeton University Press, 1977), p. 47.
5. Michelson, *Man and His Urban Environment*, pp. 99–101.
6. Strong, L. D., "Alternative Marital and Family Forms: Their Relative Attractiveness to College Students and Correlates of Willingness to Participate in Nontraditional Forms," *Journal of Marriage and the Family*, 1978, 40, pp. 493–503.
7. Profeta, S., "Singles Are Buying and Are an Expanding Market," *Builder*, June 1978, pp. 24–26.
8. Bernard, J., "Note on Changing Lifestyles, 1970–1974," *Journal of Marriage and the Family*, 1975, 37, pp. 582–93.
9. Profeta, "Singles Are Buying," p. 24.
10. Raimy, E., *Shared Houses, Shared Lives: The New Extended Families and How They Work* (Los Angeles: J. P. Tarcher, 1979), pp. 4–5; 11.
11. Ibid., pp. 16–17.
12. Public Broadcast System, KQED, "*Americans and the California dream*," Mar. 7, 1979.
13. Michelson, *Man and His Urban Environment*, p. 62.
14. Feldman, S. D., and G. W. Thielbar, eds., *Lifestyles: Diversity in American Society* (Boston: Little, Brown and Co., 1972), p. 2.
15. Ibid.

16. Michelson, *Man and His Urban Environment*, p. 62.

17. Fried, M., and P. Gleicker, "Some Sources of Residential Satisfaction in an Urban Slum," *Journal of the American Institute of Planners*, 1961, 27, pp. 305–315.

18. Howard, J., *Families* (New York: Simon and Schuster, 1978), pp. 98–112.

19. "Boat People, American-style," *Time,*

Mar. 5, 1979, pp. 82–83.

20. Boericke, A. and B. Shapiro, *Handmade Houses: A Guide to the Wood-butchers Art* (San Francisco: Scrimshaw Press, 1973).

21. Leckie, J. et al., *Other Homes and Garbage* (San Francisco: Sierra Club Books, 1975).

22. Farallones Institute, *The Integral Urban House: Self-reliant Living in the City* (San Franciso: Sierra Club Books, 1979).

Suggested Readings

Angell, W. J. "Housing alternatives." In C. S. Wedin and L. G. Nygren, eds. *Housing Perspectives* (2nd ed.). Minneapolis: Burgess, 1979.

Borden, R. J., Fisher, W. A., and Doyle, L. J. "Ecology and Changing Lifestyles: Environmental Concern as a Determinant of Household Items and Activities." *Housing Educators Journal*, 1977, 4, 29–34.

"The Condominium Home: A Lifestyle Decision." *Real Estate Today*, 1981, *14* (2) 12–17.

Gardner, H. "Dropping into Utopia." *Human Behavior*, 1978, 7 (3), 43–47.

Hinshaw, M. L., and Allott, K. J. "Environmental Preferences of Future Housing Consumers." In J. Pynoos, R. Schafer, and C. W. Hartman, eds. *Housing Urban America*. Chicago: Aldine, 1973.

Kelly, J. R. "Housing and Leisure in a Planned Community." *Housing Educators Journal*, 1977, *4* (1) 14–18.

"Lifestyles." *The Futurist*, February, 1979, entire issue.

Michelson, W. H. *Man and His Urban Environment: A Sociological Approach* (2nd ed.). Reading, Mass: Addison-Wesley, 1976, (chap. 3 "Lifestyle and Urban Environment," chap. 4 "Stage in the Life Cycle and Urban Environment").

Perin, C. *Everything in Its Place*. Princeton, N.J.: Princeton University Press, 1977, (chap. 2 "The Ladder of Life: From Renter to Owner").

Pollowy, A. M. "Children in High-rise Buildings." In D. J. Conway, ed. *Human Response to Tall Buildings*. Stoudsburg, Pa.: Dowden Hutchinson & Ross, 1977.

Raimy, E. *Shared Houses, Shared Lives: The New Extended Families and How They Work*. Los Angeles: J P. Tarcher, 1979.

Wekerle, G. R.; Peterson, R.; and Moreley, D. *New Space for Women*. Boulder, Colo.: Westview Press, 1980.

Influences on Housing Choice

5

Two concepts besides stage in the life cycle and lifestyle are important in our understanding of the many factors that make up housing decisions. They are social class and values. These two are closely connected with each other and with the two concepts discussed in the last chapter. The interrelationship of all of them is the subject of the last section in this chapter.

Nearly everyone has some kind of understanding of social class and housing. Nearly every community, however large or small, has its "nice" section and its poorer sec-

tions. We all subconsciously measure our own housing (and ourselves) in terms of the placement we think our house, or more exactly our neighborhood, has when compared to others in the community. A rough evaluation system results; we live in a poor, average, or good part of town.

Our sense of housing values is similarly simplistic. When asked what housing value is important to them, most students will respond that it is privacy. Given the usual student living circumstances, this is no surprise. But students usually cannot define a range of housing values for either themselves or their families without some familiarity with values used in housing research.

Both social class and values, then, are commonly known terms, but not commonly well-developed concepts. The complexity of social class and values as they re-

Jampackedness is a value expressed by some housing critics. Residents of this type of housing have favorable attitudes about higher density so long as they have nearby open space, good soundproofing, small parking areas, and pleasant views. Photo by author.

late to housing will become apparent in the following sections.

SOCIAL CLASS AND HOUSING

In American society, **social mobility** and equal opportunity are democratic ideals as well as, to some extent, social realities. We resist class differentiation. Most Americans think of themselves as middle-class no matter what their income level, educational achievement, or ethnic background. This is probably because middle-class norms dominate our culture, including our beliefs about housing. Nevertheless, social class is a useful concept in analyzing social problems, housing among them.

Low-income, middle-income, and occasionally high-income are terms used to describe groups of people, whether discussing their income tax, shopping habits, or housing. Income is, of course, one measure of class differences, but not the only one. Class is also determined by educational level achieved and occupation. Blue-collar workers are distinguished from white-collar workers by most sociologists. A professional person, such as a school teacher, may well make less money than a plumber, but the teacher would have a higher status in society, therefore be considered of a higher class.

Defining Social Class
The descriptions of the major classes of our society listed below are based on the work of three sociologists.[1] The very broad generalities used to distinguish one class from another should be seen as a basic framework. Many individuals may not fit into only one category.

1. *Lower class.* Employment is intermit-tent in poorly paying jobs. Educational achievement is low. Men are action-seeking, preferring an unpredictable life pattern to a stable one. The woman maintains the family, usually without steady income and without steady male support. The outside world is viewed as hostile.

2. *Working class.* Employment may be regular in blue-collar jobs. Educational achievement is average, stressing employable skills over intellectual goals. Family life is important for both men and women, but roles are separated—women have supportive relationships with other women in the extended family, men with other men in the family.

3. *Middle class.* Job satisfaction and job advancement are important aspects of work. Family life is focused on the nuclear family, and the outside world is viewed as supportive to their well-being. Education is used to achieve a satisfactory career, proper use of leisure time and participation in the community. For the *lower middle class*, white-collar employment, even when regular, yields a modest salary. Education through college is stressed for children. Religion, respectability and home ownership are especially important to this group. For the *upper middle class*, employment is at the managerial or professional level, and career goals are viewed as the basis for achieving a rewarding lifestyle for the nuclear family. Individual self-fulfillment within the family, and within work is stressed. Educational level is high and so is salary level.

4. *Upper class.* Great personal wealth is achieved either in the past or in the present. Education level is respectable and it leads to work of a respectable nature or community service. Class consciousness governs marriage choices and leisure activities. A graceful lifestyle sets it apart from other classes.

This large house in a desirable and expensive area typifies the housing choice of upper class families who desire a distinctive and graceful lifestyle. Photo by author.

Slum dwellers experience very real physical and psychological threats to their well-being. Photo courtesy of U.S. Department of Housing and Urban Development.

Social Class and Housing Differences

Does social class make a difference in the housing preference of the family? There is no simple yes or no answer. Obviously, a poor income, especially if it is unstable, will drastically limit the choices a family can make. There is evidence that **low-income families** strive for different kinds of housing satisfactions than do working-class or middle-class families. **Slum** dwellers live in environments with very real threats to their well-being. Some examples of non-human threats are rats, trash, cold, fires, poor plumbing, and general structural deterioration. Human threats accompany these in the form of violence, assault, rape, stealing, verbal abuse and fighting even within the family and immediate neighborhood. It is no wonder that the house, however poor in its space and facilities, is viewed as a haven from this outside environment.[2] If basic needs for air, light, warmth, and protection are met, then the family can attend to satisfying needs for comfort and convenience. Working-class families probably have the economic means to achieve housing that is basically safe and provides the higher level needs. Middle-class housing, because it has met the basic need for shelter and safety and the higher level needs of comfort and convenience, can also be expected to provide other kinds of satisfaction. The house can take on the personal trappings of expressive self-fulfillment as well as provide a setting for family recreation.

Do income, education and occupation alone determine housing quality? There are other factors involved. Morris and Winter have identified these factors as extrafamilial and intrafamilial constraints.[3] If the family happens to be black, Mexican-American, or Puerto Rican, they run into social barriers in trying to obtain the best housing available within their income level. They may be excluded outright from renting some housing units; they may be charged higher rents than if they were white; or they may simply be prevented from getting information about housing availability. Even though the Civil Rights Act of 1968 prohibits discriminatory practices of this sort, they, in fact, still exist. These barriers, along with the limitations the family already has with a low income, a poor education, and limited job skills, are called extrafamilial constraints to obtaining satisfactory housing.

There may be problems within the family as well. Typical intrafamilial constraints can result in the lack of functioning as a cohesive, decision-making unit. If there is no one in the family with authority or leadership, if the family communicates poorly about its goals, if the family is not in agreement about achieving its goals, then it cannot cope well with its problems with poor housing.

We can assume that lower-income families have housing that is inferior, generally, to middle-class and upper-class housing. Do they, then, have lower levels of housing satisfaction because they have poorer quality housing? Generally, no. It might be logical to assume that the worse the housing, the more intense housing dissatisfaction, and the greater probability that the family would try to do something about it, either by seeking different housing, or improving what they have. That is not the case. Lower income affects improving housing as severely as it does acquiring it. Constraints, particularly intrafamilial ones, are impediments to bettering the housing situation once the family is settled.

There are different patterns in home maintenance and improvement activities among classes. Home owners in the lower class will postpone improvements until they

Toward a Human Architecture

If social scientists are too often marching to theoretical rather than practical (architectural) drummers, architects are frequently at fault for asking the wrong questions. For one thing, some still want to be social reconstructionists and reject social-science findings that indicate that an architectural solution is irrelevant. Having once done a study of a low-income ethnic neighborhood, I am sometimes asked by architects how one designs buildings and neighborhoods that respond to the distinctive culture of low-income people or of an ethnic group; this is a good example of the wrong question. The fundamental, or at least most urgent, user patterns do not vary by class or ethnicity; that is, different income and ethnic groups do not use dwelling units all that differently. They all need living rooms, bedrooms, kitchens, etc,

and they all put these rooms to roughly the same use. True, low-income people have traditionally socialized informally and in the kitchen, while high-income people entertain more formally and in the living room, but such class differences are few, and in most cases would not affect design.

The main distinction between the rich and the poor is in their ability to pay for space, and the main problem of the poor is to get enough of it. Of course, poor people virtually never get new housing and they cannot hire architects, but when architects design projects for low-income people, they should worry less about designing for the distinctive characteristics of low-income social life, and more about how to design functional, comfortable and beautiful architecture in a space. In addition, they should use their professional expertise and status to

fight against low-income housing projects that try to cram their occupants into an unreasonably small amount of space. Together with researchers, they ought to determine the space requirements of low-income families so that they can develop minimal space standards for the poor. I suspect that these standards will require as much space as the standards for everyone else, thus casting doubt on the desirability of special (and especially small) housing units for the poor. Instead, housing will need to meet a universal threshold of space, with rent supplements for those too poor to afford the minimum. *Excerpted from: Gans, H. J., "Toward a Human Architecture: A Sociologist's View of the Profession." Reprinted from the Journal of Architectural Education, 1978, 31 (2), p. 29, courtesy of the Association of Collegiate Schools of Architecture.*

expect to move. In order to increase the selling price of their property they will fix it up. The next family benefits, for a price, rather than themselves. Middle-class families routinely maintain and occasionally improve their homes for their own satisfaction and to maintain the house's value. Upper-class families maintain their homes, or rather pay to have them maintained. If an improvement is sought, such as more space

or newer equipment, they are more likely to buy a new home rather than improve the existing one.[4]

There is no clear picture of class differences in expressed satisfaction. When asked if they are satisfied with their housing, the subjects of one study were very positive in their responses regardless of their present housing type and whether renters or owners.[5] It is not surprising that when asked what type of dwelling they preferred, nearly 85 percent said the single-family detached house. It may seem inconsistent that the same people who express great satisfaction can also state that they desire something different from what they have. This may be the result of lower expectations, as well as apathy in actually achieving their housing goals. Nevertheless, there is no reason to believe that a low-income family wants less space, wants to rent, or wants poorer neighborhoods than the middle-income family. Their housing experience shapes their housing expectations, and housing satisfaction can result. Just as a middle-class individual might desire a trip around the world, and be very satisfied with a week of camping, the lower-class individual may want a three-bedroom suburban home, and be satisfied with a subsidized townhouse apartment in a familiar neighborhood.

Homogeneity and Heterogeneity

When most of the residents of a small area—a housing project, a block, a neighborhood—have the same social class they are said to be homogeneous. Even if these people are not strictly alike in a socioeconomic sense, but view themselves as alike (perceived homogeneity), then they will probably have a higher degree of social interaction than if they did not perceive themselves as homogeneous. So-called "friendly" neigh-

Homogeneous communities of all class levels often band together regarding housing issues. This protest sign was photographed in Chinatown, San Francisco. Photo courtesy of U.S. Department of Housing and Urban Development.

_____ There Goes the Neighborhood _____

"There goes the neighborhood!"

borhoods are not so much the result of individual outgoing personalities as they are the result of homogeneity.

Heterogeneity is the opposite—a mixture of social classes within a given housing environment. Heterogeneity can also mean a mixture of ages or a mixture of ethnic groups. Some sociologists and professional planners in the past have favored heterogeneity over homogeneity for several reasons. One is that the individuals involved will have richer, more balanced lives, because they will live among people different from themselves. In a democratic society, this is desirable because people need a higher level of tolerance of social and cultural differences. Children have a broader education built into their daily experience with diverse people. Lastly, lower-class and working-class families can benefit by the exposure to middle-class daily life and attitudes.[6]

The ideals listed above may be controversial in themselves, but the more important question is, do they actually occur in heterogeneous neighborhoods? Intermingling of the sort expected by the planners does not. For instance, working-class wives, living in a neighborhood of mostly middle-class

The decision about housing space within units, siting, management, as well as overall appearance, of public housing (such as the Tiano Towers public housing project in New York City shown here) are usually made by persons from a different social class than those the project is designed to house. Photo courtesy of U.S. Department of Housing and Urban Development.

wives, did not join in their casual everyday social activities. Considering the differences outlined above between working-class and middle-class families regarding their relations with their families, attitudes about work, and goals for their children's education, it is no wonder that there was no common ground. By and large, families living in heterogeneous areas will seek out others like themselves whether or not they are close neighbors.

Gans, a sociologist who has studied this question intensely, surmises that homogeneity is desirable at the block level so that houses facing and next to each other, say a group of twelve, have a built-in basis for friendship-making. Since we are not so likely to cross the paths of our neighbors over a back fence, the next block could be comprised of a different social group. The neighborhood, as a whole could be heterogeneous, and the immediate residential environment homogeneous. Whether or not the ideals of heterogeneity are thus accomplished is very much open to question.

The housing consumer influences the patterns of homogeneity that dominate our society. There is a common fear that property values will not be maintained if families in a lower social class are allowed into a given area of higher status. Whether the invading group is upper-middle-class in a high-class neighborhood, or a lower-class group in a working-class neighborhood, does not matter; the fear is the same. The fear manifests itself in the housing choice in the first place, efforts to prevent housing being built for a different class of people, and, as a last resort, moving out.

Social Class and Housing Policy

To analyze how governmental housing policy has affected social classes in our society would take an entire book by itself. The details of housing policy are dealt with later in this book. But there is one major point to be made here. Generally in the past, the policy makers have been members of higher classes than the families for whom the policy has been made. Most federal housing assistance programs have been designed to aid members of the lower and lower-middle class. But the designers have largely been middle-class bureaucrats. Since the decisions about every detail of amounts and arrangements of housing space, siting, management, and costs of this housing have been made by persons without familiarity with the lives of the persons most directly affected, there were bound to be mistakes.

Urban renewal has been criticized in past years for not sufficiently attending to the needs of the lower class families whose housing environment is destroyed in the renewal process. Slum clearance satisfies a middle-and upper-class need to improve the physical condition of some cities. It is doubtful that any person residing in a slum thought it was a good idea to tear his or her house down. Even though slum clearance residents found other places to live, they were not necessarily better and often were worse. The cleared area was redeveloped according to middle-class criteria of what was better. Usually this has been expensive housing, hotels, civic centers, commercial buildings, anything that improved the appearance, function, and tax base of the city in middle-class terms. This was the pattern of urban renewal until the late 1960s. The program later required satisfactory relocation for the people in the area, and the provision of some new low-income family housing.

The beneficiaries of The Federal Housing Administration home insurance program have been largely first-time home buyers.

In the past many families achieved middle-class status through home ownership aided by the Federal Housing Administration home insurance program. Home ownership has been supported by federal housing policy to a greater extent than direct aid to lower-income families in all its forms. Photo by author.

Since home ownership has grown in the decades of the program's influence, two conclusions can be drawn. One is that many thousands of people in the working class and lower-middle class have indeed achieved the middle-class status of home ownership because of the program. Home ownership for all classes has been indirectly supported by federal housing policy (tax incentives) to a much greater extent than direct housing assistance in all forms. This "bias" in housing policy may reflect the class origins of most legislators.

HOUSING VALUES

Housing values are often confused with needs and preferences, therefore each is discussed. The section continues with a brief examination of sources of housing values, and is followed by a survey of some studies in housing values.

Defining Values, Needs and Preferences

We use the word value to mean a lot of things, and in connection with housing, common usage can be confusing. We have "valuable belongings" and they are in a house with a "fair market value" of so much (and going up). We "want" fireplaces and large master bedrooms. We "need" space, so big yards are necessary. We "prefer" single-family homes over condominiums. In other words, what we prefer, need, or want in housing is an expression of what we value in housing. Our values, then, can be expressed in many ways, and our verbal expression of values may not match our actual housing choices made in the real world of limitations.

Values. Values are the underlying criteria for our choices in housing and all aspects of life. Values are concepts we have about what is desirable, what ought to be. We Americans mostly share the concept that is desirable to have privacy, comfort, and safety in our houses. These are three examples of common housing values. Values can also be abstract goals. Personal dignity and equality are examples of these.

Needs. Needs should be distinguished from values in that they are derived from deprivation or disruption. The need for shelter from the elements is a real one, as is the need for heating in most climates.

Lack of indoor plumbing or electricity would create a disruptive living pattern that can be said to be unsatisfactory because basic needs have not been met. Psychological needs are explored in the next chapter.

Preferences. Preferences are expressions of values but an expressed preference may not directly relate to a single or obvious value. A 1978 survey of housing preferences of prospective home buyers, done by the home builder's magazine, *Housing*, identified specific housing choices.[7] Tudor exterior style, family room with a fireplace, one extra bedroom, good insulation, microwave oven equipped kitchens, and greenhouse windows were some of the preferences that were strongly expressed in some, but not all, areas surveyed. The preference for insulation may relate to a value of economy, and an extra bedroom probably expresses a value in convenience and hospitality, but it is more difficult to identify basic housing values underlying preferences for Tudor style and greenhouse windows.

Attitudes. One definition of attitude is that it is one's disposition, opinion or mental set. Attitudes obviously can apply to housing. Many housing consumers have the attitude that mobile home construction is inferior to standard on-site home construction. This attitude is an opinion but it may be related to housing values, such as safety and security. We express our attitudes more easily than we do our values. Since there is a possible connection between attitudes and values, research that focuses on attitudes can help in our understanding of housing values.

Sources of Housing Values

The sources of housing values are categorized here as traditional housing values and the implied values of housing literature.

Traditional Values. The Rokeach Value Survey includes thirty-six values in all, eighteen of which are instrumental values, those that are ideal modes of behavior.[8] Ambitious, broadminded, capable, cheerful, clean and courageous are among them. These are difficult to relate to housing because they have more to do with human relations than objects. Rokeach's eighteen terminal values can partially be related to housing. The following are examples:

1. *A comfortable life.* Our homes are the major area of control in which we can define a prosperous comfortable sense of well-being.
2. *A sense of accomplishment.* Home ownership is an accomplishment for most families; residence in a prestigious neighborhood gives a sense of accomplishment to older couples.
3. *Family security.* This is the primary function of housing.
4. *Self-respect and social recognition.* Although two separate values, the former generally having more importance than the latter, they compliment one another regarding housing. A well-maintained home in a satisfying residential setting can achieve both for its occupants.
5. *A world of beauty.* Creating a personally pleasing environment can be accomplished in the most humble housing circumstances.
6. *Pleasure and happiness.* Again, two different values can be accomplished with the choice of a residential setting that completely meets the needs of its occupants.

Other terminal values that relate less specifically to housing are: an exciting life, a world at peace, equality, freedom, inner harmony, mature love, national security, salvation, true friendship, and wisdom.

Implied Values of Housing Literature. As early as 1916, a building show that produced housing designs for the average man (approximate cost—$3,000) had as its purpose to meet the needs of anyone with sufficient interest in himself and his family and his city to want to own a home.[9] The value link between home ownership, good citizenship, and family orientation was not unique at the time. Home ownership was also encouraged for immigrant working men so that they would settle down and become responsible community members. A 1930s housing publication refers to the belief that well-housed, preferably home-owning, people are better citizens and more efficient workers.[10] Another 1930s value was expressed by the editors of *Fortune* who reported that half of American homes were said to not measure up to minimum standards of health and decency.[11] What is implied here is that we not only value decent and healthy housing, but that we believe American society can collectively do something to attain it for all its population. The 1930s gave birth to the government programs aimed in part at accomplishing that end. Another American value implied in this is that we can and should be able to solve our problems through ingenuity, cooperation, long-range planning, massive effort, and so on.

Perhaps the single most important value implied in housing literature is that of home-ownership. Dean argued in 1951 that home-ownership can be traced to two "ghosts"—one is the Prostestant ethic and the other is classical economics.[12] We believe in being rewarded for hard work, thrift, individual responsibility, and moral integrity. Rosow, writing in 1948, said that home ownership relates to other motives, but what he called motives have also been identified as values. Possessing property is

The American frontier heritage of plenty of room for everyone has led to the value of possession of space itself, often reduced as in this example, to the standard suburban lot. Photo by author.

related to individualism and independence. Financial goals of ownership relate to long-range economy and security. The family is benefitted by status, stability, and a secure setting for children's development.[13]

We also have a frontier heritage tied into housing values. Everybody wants elbow room, so the value of possessing space in itself is tied to the single-family detached dwelling. Bauer related the values of hard work, thrift, and honesty to being able to go out and find the site of one's dreams, and build on it the ideal American home.[14]

Housing values can also be derived from architectural criticism. Mumford, for instance, praised early development of the neighborhood concept, implying a valuing of social contact as part of the residential setting.[15] Scully criticized the 1940s trend of split-level **tract housing** as having the pretense of freedom with superficially varied facades, when in fact the housing was fundamentally "unfree" since it was set in a confining grid pattern.[16] The inhumaneness of highrise housing has been attacked by many architectural critics.

Another strong value theme in architectural criticism has been mediocrity of design. The editors of *Architectural Forum* spoke of the "dreariness" and "corrupted fantasy" of a major part of our building in 1957.[17] Architects and architectural critics have often seen popular taste as their fundamental enemy. But they also recognize that popular taste, and its manifestation in suburban sameness has been fostered by our democratic institutions.

Some critics have spoken strongly in favor of higher-density housing than popular preference would support. "Jampackedness" is the main value expressed in Whyte's work.[18] It is paralleled by Jacob's praise of the cul-

American Values and the Indian Fabric of Life

For the BIA agent the outdoors is frightening. His culture has won "the battle against nature," and has little direct contact with the outdoors. The fact that the Indians choose to sit outside seems inappropriate to him. The Indians, on the other hand, love the earth and take comfort in it; they are unable to understand the government's attitudes and feel victimized by them.

The Indians' bare feet also offend the BIA man, in whose culture "cleanliness is next to godliness." But the Indians remove their moccasins "to walk with bare feet upon the sacred earth," according to their beliefs. The soil is seen not as dirty, but as soothing and cleansing. For them cleanliness is more than skin deep, and this feeling conditions their perceptions and uses of space.

The government either does not care about or is unaware of the consequences of these ethnic differences. The result is that the Indians are dealt with not in terms of their own cultural heritage, but as deviant heirs of the policymakers' culture and values. They are consequently considered dirty, lazy, primitive and so forth, and are continually forced into situations which have no precedent in their own history and seem ridiculous and meaningless.

When traditional methods of perceiving and using space are tampered with by outsiders, the fabric of life unravels. The world view and system of roles, obligations and interactions upon which the society is based and which are transmitted from generation to generation, fall apart and society itself can degenerate into anomie and deviance. This is expressed by Black Elk, a member of the Oglala Sioux, when he talks about his house on the reservation:

"All our people are now settled down in square gray houses, scattered here and there across this hungry land, and around them the Wasichus [Americans] have drawn a line to keep them in. The nation's hoop is broken, and there is no center any longer for the flowering tree. It is a bad way to live, for there can be no power in a square.

"You have noticed that everything an Indian does is in a circle, and that is because the power of the world always works in a circle, and everything tries to be round. The sky is round, and I have heard that the earth is round like a ball, and so are all the stars. The wind, in its greatest power, whirls. Birds make their nests in circles, for theirs is the same religion as ours. The sun comes forth and goes down again in a circle. The moon does the same, and they are both round. Even the seasons form a great circle in their changing, and always come back again to where they were. The life of a man is a circle from childhood to childhood, and so it is in everything where power moves. Our teepees were round like the nests of birds, and these were always set in a circle, the nation's hoop, a nest of many nests, where the Great Spirit meant for us to hatch our children.

"But the Wasichus have put us in these square boxes. Our power is gone and we are dying, for the power is not in us anymore."

Excerpted from: Freeman, M., "Ethnic Differences in Perceiving and Using Space." AIA Journal, *1977, 66 (2), p. 47. Reproduced with the permission of the* AIA Journal, *copyright 1977: The American Instititute of Architects.*

tural diversity found in medium-density, inner-city living.[19] That cluster housing has become more acceptable to the house-buying public may represent a sharing of these values. One study found that there are definite factors related to the attitudes condominium residents have regarding their higher-density housing—nearby open space, small-scale development, good sound-proofing, pleasant views, varied designs, private outdoor space, and small parking areas. These preferences surely reflect the values of privacy, aesthetic appearance, and individuality.[20]

Studies in Housing Values

Measuring Values Related to Housing. A pioneer study of nine personal values that related to housing was done in 1955. It identified family centrism, equality, physical health, economy, freedom, aesthetics, prestige, mental health, and leisure.[21] In a follow-up study, statements were made reflecting these values, and the respondents, from both urban and rural areas, marked their level of agreement or disagreement with each statement.[22] Family centrism was expressed most strongly by wanting a house where family members can spend time together, and secondarily by wanting a house where relatives can get together. Children's needs being considered before others was the strongest expression for the value of equality. Physical health was strongly related to having fresh air in every room of the house. A location where neighboring houses would not lower resale value, selling a house at a profit, and selecting a house with low maintenance costs were, in that order, expressions of valuing economy in housing.

Freedom as a value had strong responses in four items: moving furniture around, doing as one pleases, not being interrupted

by family members, and not being interrupted by neighbors. A strong valuing of aesthetics was expressed through having a pleasant looking house, having a garden, and having a beautifully decorated interior. Prestige related to pride, social class consciousness, maintaining social contacts, and getting friends' admiration. Orderliness and calmness in a house were related to mental health. The value of leisure was related most strongly to having a house that is a primary setting for having fun, and having room for recreation.

Values as Behavioral Potentials. One study done in 1974 was aimed at helping students become more aware of their values as they relate to making consumer housing decisions.[23] Beyer's nine housing values were used. They also used his clustering of values into two groups as a basis for determining a value type. The person who ranked highest in any of the values of economy, family centrism, equality or physical health tended to be in a group classified by all of these. The other group of values discovered in Beyer's research was aesthetics, freedom, and mental health. But this study showed that people could not necessarily be typed with this cluster. Home economics students ranked aesthetics, family centrism and freedom most highly. But personal values changed order when they were applied to housing. The students' parents (also asked to rank personal values, and values as they relate to housing) stressed the value of importance of family, equality, and economy. This may indicate the effect the stage of the life cycle has on value orientation.

Values Among Multifamily Housing Residents. Apartment and condominium residents (100 of each) were the focus of another value study which attempted to find a relationship between values and satisfactions with present housing and plans for future housing.[24] Apartment residents ranked location, comfort and convenience, and privacy as their highest values, and condominium residents ranked comfort and convenience, location and friends and visitors as the highest. Economy was least important for both. The condominium residents perceived their housing as meeting their housing aspirations better than did the apartment residents. Both types of residents would give up eating out, children, purchasing goods, transportation, recreation, even utilities and telephone, in order to achieve a housing goal. When asked to identify the constraints preventing achievement of their housing goals, the respondents largely answered cost or lack of funds. Economy, then, did emerge as an important factor even if it was not recognized as an important value.

Value Change and Housing

Values do not change easily and neither do attitudes. We are, however, living at a time when rapid social change has dramatic effects on some aspects of society. Housing is one aspect for which this is the case. The rising number of mobile homes and condominiums is an example. If the residents of these types of housing have not changed their values, they have at least adapted their attitudes to accommodate the housing they have acquired. Even though it is difficult to measure attitude and value change, it is logical to suppose that changes are taking place in values, as our housing picture changes.

If one examines the typical values used in housing value research, questions are raised of how they can endure, given the housing circumstances in our society. What follows is a discussion of values in conflict. Even though it is highly speculative, it seems reasonable to assume that values not only are a strong influence in housing

decision-making, but that they cannot remain intact when the process of decision-making includes only a part of those values and necessarily disregards others.

Privacy—Economy. Privacy has traditionally been translated into private space, both indoors and outdoors. People express a "need" to have lots of room around them, and, when asked why, will give privacy as a reason. Economy, as a value, is becoming a primary concern, if not consciously recognized as a high priority value. Given the increasing cost of land, and the cost of house construction, can the need for pri-

---

This condominium satisfies the values of economy and convenience, but it compromises the satisfaction of privacy through spacious surroundings. However private these tiny outdoor spaces are, they represent a value conflict of privacy—economy. Photo by author.

vacy through space be satisfied? Probably not. Can privacy and economy be achieved simultaneously? Probably so.

The house-consuming public may believe privacy and economy to be in conflict. If a condominium, townhouse, or apartment is being considered by a family hoping for a single-family detached house, it will be assumed that the former would provide less privacy. If the condominium is less costly to purchase and maintain, then the trade-off might be in favor of the value of economy. Designers and builders can provide a great deal of visual and aural privacy in multifamily housing—for a price. If, indeed, our values do not change easily, then the housing producers may recognize the desirability of providing housing designs and construction that meet both value requirements.

Location—Health and Safety. One of the strongest motivations for moving to the suburbs has been to provide a physically and mentally healthy environment for childrearing, and to escape the unsafe (real and imagined) characteristics of the urban environment. The suburban location has typically had physical and social characteristics to support the nuclear family.

Set against the value satisfaction of most suburbs is the growing problem of transportation costs. If major employment centers are to remain in highly urbanized areas, then the desire (the value) for living in the suburbs may be in conflict with the desire of a location convenient to work. This may be an even more dramatic problem for working couples, particularly if they have children. Not only is commuting expense involved, but commuting time. For the tightly scheduled family, saving time for the family by cutting down travel to work is an obvious solution. Can a location near

one or two inner-city jobs be found that does not sacrifice the safety and health of outlying areas? Perhaps. It is more probable that the family would feel that they were sacrificing one value for another. Does that mean the sacrificed value would shrink in importance? Or does it mean the house-consuming public will seek innovative ways in which the value conflict can be resolved?

Aesthetics—Convenience. The conflict imagined in this discussion is more than just aesthetics set against convenience. It involves the pattern of values that results in a large comfortable house with each person well provided with space and storage and plenty of room for family activities and entertaining. It suggests a house designed and furnished to suit its occupants, hence the key word of aesthetics. The conflicting value of convenience is used to symbolize the pattern of values associated with the need for a living space that takes care of itself, is efficient to work and relax in, but probably has no excess room for guests, parties, and even family togetherness. Economy is part of this picture.

Do working women, single people, single-parent families necessarily value the latter? It can be assumed that busy, budget-conscious families are concerned about keeping utility and maintenance costs to a minimum, as well as keeping their housing responsibilities within manageable time limits. Is the aesthetic value, with its attendant picture here of space, comfort, hospitality, and family self-indulgence incompatible with the convenience and economy of an efficient easy-to-care-for housing unit? Maybe some middle ground can be found. No doubt some families make personal sacrifices in order to satisfy these conflicting values.

LIFE CYCLE, LIFESTYLE, SOCIAL CLASS, AND VALUES

The interconnectedness of these concepts has probably been apparent throughout Chapters 4 and 5. When the nuclear family is described as being suited to the suburban single-family home environment, one also associates a family-centered lifestyle, one assumes a middle-class status, and one could safely predict a value hierarchy of family centeredness, economy, comfort and convenience, health and safety, and so on. Even though this pattern may be predictable, it is also stereotypical. Stereotypes are easy to manufacture in describing a family's stage in the life cycle, lifestyle, social class and housing value system. It is the purpose of this section to point out alternative ways of linking these four concepts.

Family Diversity

To begin with, stage in the life cycle cuts across all social classes. Alternative forms of family were introduced in the last chapter because they account for more and more housing. These, too, cut across all segments of society. The single-parent family, for instance, is not an exclusive problem for urban black women, as might be supposed. Cohabitation is not an exclusive prerogative for college-aged or middle-class, experimental adults.

Even though it is easy to suppose that alternative forms of family relate to alternative forms of lifestyle, and no doubt oftentimes this is true, they should be considered separately. The supposedly typical suburban family might indeed be attempting to live a lifestyle of self-sufficiency. The inner-city apartment dweller, perhaps single, and upper middle class might well pursue a leisure lifestyle, on weekends at least. Not all owners of travel trailers and recreational vehicles are healthy retirees, a stereotypical association of stage in the life cycle and lifestyle.

Lifestyle links tightly with values. If consumerism is a dominant aspect of a family's life, one might believe aesthetics, comfort, or prestige to dominate the value picture of the same family. It is conceivable, however, that family centrism, convenience, and even economy could link strongly with a consumerism lifestyle. If the purchase decisions are made with family welfare and budget limitations in mind, the latter would be the case.

There have been value studies which have been aimed at finding out if different classes have different values, and if they are transmitted to children. But the argument here is, again, to allow for individual diversity rather than to oversimplify the asso-

The housing environment including the unit, neighborhood, and amenities can provide satisfaction regarding a family's stage in the life cycle, lifestyle, social class, and values. How well a family "fits" its housing environment depends on all these variables. Photo by author.

ciation of social class and values. Are only upper-middle-class families primarily interested in aesthetics? Certainly not. Are only working-class families primarily interested in economy?

Congruence

Michelson explored the concepts of stage in the life cycle, lifestyle, social class and values in his book *Man and His Urban Environment: A Sociological Approach.*[25] His theory of congruence is the result of his analysis. Congruence means that the cultural, social and personal variables of individuals and families "fit" with the variables of the physical environment. Put simply, the stage of the life cycle, lifestyle, social class, and values of a given family should fit with the environment in which it lives. The environment includes the housing unit, the neighborhood, related services, and amenities that make up residential satisfaction.

What takes place in the housing environment is not social class, values, stage in the life cycle, or lifestyle. It is behavior. Individuals and families use their housing environment to carry out the behaviors important to them. Behaviors are determined directly and indirectly by stage in the life cycle, lifestyle, social class and values. Lifestyle emerges in this analysis as having the widest behavioral choice, so the "fit" of the housing environment with lifestyle is the most important. The degree to which the physical aspect of housing design provides the opportunity to carry out desired behaviors is the degree of its success for its residents.

SUMMARY

Social class is a useful concept in looking at housing differences. Social class is based on educational achievement, type of employment and income level. Class differences in housing conditions are very real, and it is supposed that housing needs are met in a hierarchical manner, physical needs before comfort needs, and comfort needs before expressive needs.

Constraints related to jobs and income levels are accompanied by constraints within some families. Achievement of housing goals may be affected by these constraints. There are class differences in home maintenance and improvement activities. There is a tendency for lower-class families to be satisfied with smaller housing space of poorer quality than they would desire.

People generally associate with their own kind, an argument in favor of homogeneity, but the social goal of heterogeneity has not been ignored by professional planners. A serious issue regarding social class is the differences between those people making housing decisions, and the class of the residents for whom the housing is built.

Housing values can be distinguished from attitudes, needs, and preferences. American values affecting more or less the whole society have been identified and classified as terminal or instrumental. The implied values of housing literature are equally important in understanding the values in our culture. The values of home ownership, of individual private space, of mediocre design, and of higher density living were given special attention. Selected studies that focused especially on housing values were reviewed. Some housing values, such as economy, family centrism, comfort, aesthetics, and convenience weave a common thread throughout these studies, done over a period of about twenty-five years.

There may be a shift in values taking place, mainly because traditional values can easily be set against one another in making housing decisions. Contemporary housing trends would suggest this might be the case.

Stage in the life cycle, lifestyle, social class and values are linking concepts in understanding individual and family differences; housing needs and satisfactions are more comprehensively evaluated when the four concepts are interrelated. There is a diversity of possibilities in linking these four concepts together regarding housing decisions. The theory of congruence links them regarding behavior, and argues, sensibly, that the physical environment should fit the behavior patterns of individuals and families that derive from, directly or indirectly, all four concepts.

Notes

1. Gans, H. J., *The Urban Villagers* (Glencoe, N.Y.: Free Press of Glencoe, 1962), chap. 11; Michelson, W. H., *Man and His Urban Environment: A Sociological Approach* (Reading, Mass: Addison-Wesley, 1976), chap. 5; and Rodman, H., "Stratification: class culture," in *International Encyclopedia of the Social Sciences* (New York: Macmillan and Free Press), 1968, pp. 332–37.

2. Rainwater, L., "Fear and the House-as-Haven in the Lower Class," *Journal of the American Institute of Planners*, 1966, 32, pp. 23–31.

3. Morris, E. W., and M. Winter, *Housing, Family and Society* (New York: Wiley, 1978), pp. 273–74.

4. Ibid., p. 199.

5. Rent, G. S., and C. S. Rent, "Low-income Housing: Factors Related to Residential Satisfaction," *Environment and Behavior*, 1978, 10, pp. 459–88.

6. Gans, H. J., "The Balanced Community: Homogeneity or Heterogeneity in Residential Areas?" *The Journal of the American Institute of Planners*, 1961, 27 (3), pp. 176–84.

7. "Consumer Study: What Home Seekers Seek in Six Major Markets," *Housing*, Oct. 1978, pp. 51–76.

8. Rokeach, M., "Change and Stability in American Value Systems, 1968–1971," *Public Opinion Quarterly*, 1974, 38, pp. 222–38.

9. *The Average Man's Home* (Cleveland, Ohio: Complete Building Show Company, 1916).

10. Gries, L. M., and J. Ford, eds., *House Design, Construction and Equipment* (vol. 5) (Washington, D. C.: President's Conference on Home Building and Home Ownership, 1932), p. 192.

11. Editors of Fortune, *Housing America* (New York: Harcourt Brace and Co., 1932), p. 5.

12. Dean, J. P., "The Ghosts of Homeownership," *Journal of Social Issues*, 1951, 7, pp. 59–68.

13. Rosow, I., "Homeownership Motives," *American Sociological Review*, 1948, 13, pp. 751–56.

14. Bauer, C., *Modern Housing* (Boston: Houghton Mifflin, 1934), p. 53.

15. Mumford, L., *The Urban Prospect* (New York: Harcourt, Brace and World, 1956), pp. 56–59.

16. Scully, V., "American Houses: Thomas Jefferson to Frank Lloyd Wright," in E. Kaufmann, ed., *The Rise of American Architecture* (New York: Praeger, 1970), p. 184.

17. Editor of Architectural Forum, *Building*

    U.S.A (New York: McGraw Hill, 1957),
    p. 115.
18. Whyte, W., "The Tightened City," in
    C. L. Stater, ed. *The Cultural Landscape*
    (Belmont, Cal.: Duxbury Press, 1971),
    p. 263.
19. Jacobs, J., *The Death and Life of Great*
    American Cities (New York: Vintage
    Books, 1961).
20. Norcross, C., *Townhouses and*
    Condominium Residents' Likes and Dislikes
    (Washington, D.C.: Urban Land Institute
    (No. 67), 1973), p. 9.
21. Beyer, G. H., T. W. Mackesey, and J. E.
    Montgomery, *Houses Are for People*
    (Ithaca, N.Y.: Cornell University Housing
    Research Center, 1955).

22. Beyer, G. H., *Housing and Personal*
    Values (Memoir 364) (Ithaca, N.Y.:
    Cornell University Agricultural Experiment
    Station, 1959).
23. Stoeckeler, H. S., and M. Hasegawa, "A
    Technique for Identifying Values as
    Behavioral Potentials in Making Consumer
    Housing Decisions," *Home Economics*
    Research Journal, 1974, 2, 268–80.
24. Humphries, G. M., "Values,
    Satisfactions, Aspirations, and Goal
    Commitment among Multiunit Housing
    Residents," *Housing Educators Journal*
    (Proceedings 1976 Annual Conference),
    pp. 62–65.
25. Michelson, *Man and His Urban*
    Environment, pp. 228–32.

Suggested Readings

Blake, P. *God's Own Junkyard*. New York:
    Holt Rinehart and Winston, 1964.
Gans, H. J. "The Balanced Community:
    Homogeneity or Heterogeneity in Residential
    Areas?" *The Journal of the American*
    Institute of Planners, 1961, 27 (3) 176–84.
Michelson, W. H. *Man and His Urban*
    Environment: A Sociological Approach (2nd
    ed.). Reading, Mass.: Addison-Wesley,
    1976, (chap. 5 "Social Class and the Urban
    Environment"; chap. 6 "Values and the
    Urban Environment"; and chap. 10
    "Epilogue: Retrospect and Context").
"A Note on Housing Class." In R. Montgomery
    and D. R. Mandelker, eds., *Housing in*
    America: Problems and Perspectives (2nd ed.).
    Indianapolis: Bobbs-Merrill, 1979.
Nygren, L. G. "Planning for Ourselves." In
    C. S. Wedin and L. G. Nygren, eds.
    Housing Perspectives (2nd ed.). Minneapolis:
    Burgess, 1979.
Perin, C. *Everything in Its Place; Social Order*

    and Land Use in America. Princeton, N. J.:
    Princeton University Press, 1977, (chap. 6
    "Principles of Social Order").
Rainwater, L. "Fear and the House-as-Haven
    in the Lower Class." *Journal of the*
    American Institute of Planners, 1966, 32,
    23–31.
Scheflen, A. E. "Living Space in an Urban
    Ghetto." *Family Process*, 1971, *10*,
    429–50.
Williams, R. M., Jr. *American Society: A*
    Sociological Interpretation (3rd ed.). New
    York: Alfred A. Knopf, 1970. (chap. 5
    "Social Stratification in the United States";
    chap 11 "Values in American Society").
Zeisel, J. "Fundamental Values in Planning
    with the Nonpaying Client." In J. Lang, C.
    Burnette, W. Moleski, and D. Vachon,
    eds. *Designing for Human Behavior:*
    Architecture and the Behavioral Sciences.
    Stroudsburg, Pa.: Dowden, Hutchison &
    Ross, 1974.

The Psychology
of Housing

6

Whatever type, size, condition, and location of housing unit we have, it serves a primary function in our psychological well-being. We spend more time in our houses than in any other place, and we return to them, usually daily, to restore our bodies and minds. Houses are the places where we go to get away from the business of the world. They are the places where we can be most content, where we can be ourselves.

In order to explore the psychology of housing in some depth, several aspects of environmental psychology will be discussed in this chapter. Surprisingly recently, there

was a breakthrough in thinking by some psychologists: to understand human behavior fully, it must be studied in the environment in which it takes place. That is, the place itself is important in understanding what transpires between humans in it. Thus was born a theoretical perspective called **man-environment relations.** People act on their environments, and their environments in turn help determine behavior. The emphasis in this chapter is on the connection between people and houses.

HUMAN NEEDS
AND HOUSING

Need suggests something that cannot be done without, and human needs are those human requirements without which life

High-rise housing is often rejected by persons who feel that a single-family house on its own lot is the only way in which a house can be a symbol for self. Photo courtesy of U.S. Department of Housing and Urban Development.

would not be maintained. Physiological needs, such as air, food, water, and rest are easy to associate with this definition. Psychological needs are somewhat more difficult to grasp in this regard. If human needs include psychological needs or those requirements humans have for maintaining a contented and fulfilled life, then a broader and more interesting spectrum of human needs comes into focus.

Many psychologists have discussed human needs, among them Freud, Maslow, Murry, Horney, Adler, and Fromm. Not all of them have identified the same needs, nor do they agree on which ones are basic to human functioning. By combining their efforts, an extensive list of human needs results. Such a list was compiled by Peterson who was interested in exploring the implications regarding the designed environment.[1] She categorized human needs into six areas: semiphysiological, social, stabilizing, individual, self-expression, and enrichment. These are discussed in the subsections that follow.

Affiliation needs can be met in many ways in housing. These elderly women, each with a private apartment, can use the lobby to meet this human psychological need. Photo courtesy of U.S. Department of Housing and Urban Development.

Semiphysiological Needs

Two semiphysiological needs are identified—harm avoidance and sex. Safety was discussed as a value in the last chapter. Here we see safety as a basic human need which helps us avoid harm, avoid pain. Much of the body of law that protects us from inadequate building methods and materials is based on the need for safety. Electrical wiring is hidden in walls to avoid electrocution and fireplaces are built so that houses will not burn down with their use. The current interest in smoke alarms fits a traditional pattern of protecting ourselves from harm. Needless to say, our homes are not entirely safe. Slippery floors and sharp corners, for instance, cause common household accidents.

Home is the place most people associate with sexual intimacy. On the other hand, rarely is sex used as a design criterion along with food preparation, television viewing, or conversation. Even if master bedrooms are thought of by their occupants as primarily places for sex, they are not always designed in a direct and obvious way for audio and visual privacy, warm and soft intimacy, or even sensual comfort.

Social Needs

The association between affiliation, which embodies belongingness, relatedness, affection and approval, and housing is obvious. As the seat of family life, we are sustained in our closest relationships in the home. We also gather with friends in our homes. What may be less obvious is that affiliation happens in places other than areas specifically designed for it: for example, living rooms, family rooms, or recreation rooms. Kitchens are notorious for providing a place to air family problems, or to catch up on the day's activities of family members, and sometimes they become the center of a party gathering.

Massive housing often denies the human need for autonomy and identity. Residents might compensate for the lack of autonomy and identity on the exterior by the way they design their interior space. Photo courtesy of U.S. Department of Housing and Urban Development.

Nurturance and succorance are two human needs that are two sides of the same coin. We need to be needed, expressed usually by giving assistance, sympathy, support, or comfort to others, but we also need to be on the receiving end of these behaviors. Fixing food for someone else is an everyday activity related to nurturance, being served it is related to succorance. At times of illness, special behaviors come into play, and houses provide ways of allowing special privileges.

Stabilizing Needs

Security is the most familiar stabilizing need. It is the desire to be free from fear, anxiety, risk or danger. We usually satisfy this need by seeking housing in an area that offers us security when we leave the house. Some multifamily housing residents can satisfy their need for security through controlled access to their building and lock and alarm systems that prevent intrusion. The walls and security gates at many subdivisions, mobile home parks, and condominium developments provide this psychological satisfaction.

Individuals vary greatly in their need for order, but even the messiest among us needs some sense of things in their place, organization, neatness and precision. Some people with a high-level need for order are truly disturbed if a book is out of place or an ashtray moved a few inches from its designated spot.

Yet another stabilizing need is frame of orientation. This refers to a feeling of belonging to the world, a feeling of rootedness. We rely on the landmarks and familiarities of our neighborhood as well as the familiar arrangements of space and objects within our houses.

Individual Needs

There are three specific needs within this category: solitude, autonomy, and identity. The first is a need that is often overlooked. Even when children are provided private bedrooms and husbands their dens, offices, or workrooms, women are presumed to always be (and presumed to want to be) at the hub of family activity—in the kitchen or living room. Each of us, however busy, sociable, or responsible for comforts of others, needs to be alone.

Autonomy and identity are very close in definition. Children often satisfy their need for autonomy by having their own rooms "off limits." In them they can be themselves, do as they please, and avoid direction from domineering parents. But they also need to be recognized for their uniqueness. So their rooms are often cluttered with posters of their choice, and their doors with personally meaningful memorabilia. Both autonomy and identity are manifested in the desire for a "place of one's own" where one can do as one pleases. Thus the move from an apartment into an owned single-family dwelling is not entirely a matter of stage in the life cycle, lifestyle, values, or social class; it also fulfills psychological needs.

Self-expression Needs

Surely most of us select housing and then furnish it with the hope of bringing attention to ourselves, at least among our families and friends. This fulfills a need for exhibition. The need for dominance is similar—we need to influence or direct the behavior of others. The exercise of dominance usually takes place within the home, and the house space and its furnishings can reflect the dominant roles of certain family members. Most of us grow up with a room (den, master bedroom, the living room), or a piece of furniture (chair, desk, antique) that is off limits. Is it any wonder that parents get the biggest bedroom?

When we move into a bigger and better housing unit, we satisfy a need for achievement. When we gain admiration from friends and family for this achievement, we have our need for prestige fulfilled. On the other hand, we also have a need for deference, that is the admiration applied to another person or to someone else's house.

If there is a human need for aggression, and some psychologists say there is, then housing should provide a safe means for expressing it. Perhaps doors serve a basic human need, because they can be slammed. We also have a need for rejection, and the front door may be our main means of satisfying that need. We can control who is admitted and who is not by controlling passage through the house's entry.

Play and variety are also self-expressive human needs, and housing provides a major setting for both. Much of our leisure time is spent within the home, whether in actively pursuing a hobby in appropriately equipped space, or passively watching television. Of course game rooms, and back yards are meant to provide play space for children and adults. Variety is achieved through the kinds of spaces in and around the house, as well as the interior design—variety in color, texture, pattern, furniture, lighting, and so on. Some people need to change their interior environments often, through rearranging rooms, or by redoing them.

Four other self-expression needs have been identified. Since each is less familiar than those discussed above, they will be briefly identified with a single example regarding housing: (1) infavoidance, the avoidance of inferiority, probably prompts most of us to maintain the exterior appearance of our houses to meet the standards of our neighbors; (2) defendance, the defense against blame or humiliation, sometimes takes the form of an explanation of why the house is a mess; (3) counteraction, actively making up for failure or weakness, could translate into assertive nonconformity, such as pouring cement all over one's suburban front yard; and (4) abasement, the need to submit or surrender, might be illustrated by a family's satisfaction with housing conditions of lower quality than they could afford.

Enrichment Needs

One of the enrichment needs psychologists have identified is understanding. A need to speculate, formulate, and analyze; that is, a thirst for knowledge, could be satisfied with the decision-making process in selecting a house. Building one's own house would provide a special opportunity to investigate materials and techniques involved in housing, as well as the satisfaction that one knew exactly how one's house was put together, an area of ignorance and mystery to most of us.

Meaningfulness in life can mean goals or a sense of purpose. Surely the acquisition of a house, particularly the first home purchase, fulfills this need. A long residency in the same neighborhood could also provide a sense of endurance and establishment, aspects of the feeling that life has meaning.

Self-actualization can be viewed as a higher goal, one in which one transcends ordinary accomplishments, such as home ownership, to reach one's full potential in a creative way. An unusual hideaway for the painter or writer may come to mind as an example of the relationship of housing to self-actualization, but other individuals could achieve self-actualization in their housing in other ways.

Last, but not least, there is a human need for beauty, for aesthetically pleasing surroundings. It is curious that "aesthetic" in the abstract is an important value, but as a human need identified by psychologists it plays a very small role. Even so, it is probably safe to suppose everyone to some degree controls the appearance of his or her housing environment to suit personal ideas of what is beautiful.

HOUSING AND SELF-IDENTITY

Identity is one of the individual human needs. Self-identity is a more complex concept and one that has been given special attention by some leaders in environmental psychology. For most of us, "self" means what we are as unique human beings. We think of ourselves as inner beings, and each of us separates our own inner being, or soul if you will, from what is outside us, that is, the rest of the world. The importance of housing and neighborhoods in helping individuals define their unique selves is the substance of this section.

House as Symbol of Self

In a landmark paper, Cooper explored the concept of self as it relates to the house. Her ideas were based on Jungian psychology, in which symbols are linked to "timeless nodes of psychic energy."[2] We carry around unconscious ideas linking us to a primitive past. These archetypes manifest themselves into symbols which are the here and now reality of the unconscious past we all share. Cooper articulates the notion that houses are just such symbols, because they are the basic protection of the self of our inner beings.

Even though we want our personal identities to be unique, we do not want to be thought of as nonconformist. Our housing expresses this need accurately. A street of houses may look generally alike, but each has its stamp of self-identity. In American culture, where we place such a high premium on self-made men, and now self-made women, we resist the idea that housing is provided in a nonindividualistic way. Society's resistance to government housing and factory-made housing is a logical extension of this unconsious need to have a house symbolize oneself. Highrise buildings are rejected for family living primarily for the reason that the house as symbol is seen as a single-family, detached dwelling on the ground. There seems to be a "universal need for a house form in which the self and family can be seen as separate, unique, and protected."[3]

The housing types associated with alternative lifestyles are supportive of the house as symbol of self-concept. As people seek to find a new kind of life, they also seek to define their selves in new ways. Nonconformist forms of housing, such as vans, teepees, and houseboats, are supporting symbols in that psychic endeavor. Most of us are resistant to unusual housing forms for the very reason that we need a familiar, solid, even static way of viewing ourselves. The self is a fragile and vulnerable entity, so we need, in a profound psychic way, to surround the self with a symbol that is unchanging. To live in an unfamiliar form of housing is threatening because it threatens the self-concept.

Conflicts in Person-Environment Relations

Since sex roles are changing, the ways in which the home relates to self-identity is also undergoing change. Self-identity, self-image, and role identity all overlap. The transition of many women from homemakers, for whom a self-identity in the home is

easily proscribed, into self-developed persons outside the home has altered self-identities for themselves as well as for other members of their families.

If what is emerging from this role transition is a new meaning of the characteristics of housing, then it needs to be carefully examined. Saegert, a researcher in this area, believes the differences of men and women's views are related to their roles regarding work, children, household chores, and other uses of the home. She and a team of researchers identified four kinds of conflicts within the home.[4] (1) Person/structure conflicts occur when there is a misfit between what the residents expect and need from a home, and what its physical capacity can provide. (2) Role conflicts are those in which wife, husband, and parent roles cause dissatisfaction, but the personalities of the people involved are not the cause of dissatisfaction. (3) Interpersonal conflicts are those in which personalities are very much involved. (4) Intrapersonal conflict derives from a misfit between the characteristics of the self as is, and the characteristics of the self one would like to be. Conflicts within the home may be a mixture of these four types, but the fourth of these appears to be crucial in the context of housing and self-identity.

PRIVACY AND PERSONAL SPACE

The importance of privacy in housing is apparent to everyone. When we think of our own privacy we think of home, and probably the reverse is also true—thoughts of home

The need for play and variety can be met in individual housing or with facilities within a housing environment, such as this recreation center. Photo courtesy of Del E. Webb Development Co.

The human need for asthetically pleasing housing can be met in very individual ways. Photo by author.

are intermingled with thoughts of privacy. Privacy as an area of study in environmental psychology has given birth to a wide range of theoretical probings into the meanings of privacy, personality differences regarding privacy, and human needs regarding privacy. Clearly, this area of environmental design research has many implications for housing in the future.

The concept of personal space was also born and developed in environmental psychology. It relates to privacy and to territoriality, therefore both are discussed in this chapter section.

Privacy

Altman has defined privacy as "selective control of access to the self or to one's group."[5] The implication is that we have options, devices and mechanisms to prevent unwanted interaction. We can foster desired interaction. We can achieve privacy through solitude, and we can also achieve it through behavior (being reserved with some people or in some situations, for instance. Most of us seek a balance between times we are open and times we are closed.

Privacy functions in four basic ways. Personal autonomy is one of them, and as a basic human need identified earlier, it relates to self-identity, or being free to be oneself. Privacy is also associated with emotional release, that is letting down our hair, relaxing, and being off stage. Privacy allows us time for self-evaluation in which we can reflect on past experiences and plan future actions. Finally, privacy provides the opportunity to share confidences with the people of our choice. This means that we bring others into our private worlds. Intimacy then is a dimension of privacy.[6]

We control our privacy in several ways. The simplest way is through verbal communication. We tell people, "No we don't want to go to the movie; yes, come over

Controlled access to the front door is one major way in which we achieve privacy. This house has a double layer of control—the front gate as well as the front door. Photo by author.

and talk; come in; keep out." A more subtle form of controlling privacy is nonverbal behavior. We use our facial expressions, our arms, our whole bodies to give off signals that say, "Don't intrude."

In our homes, we control privacy in physical ways. The mere separation of one house from another by means of a space achieves privacy for most suburban residents. Within the house, walls separate spaces so that privacy is achieved for individual family members. The importance of doors to psychological well-being must be brought up again here in the context of privacy. In large families and in some student housing situations the bathroom may be the only place of total privacy, behind a closed and locked door, and not even this last resort is always honored.

Not much is known about the use of privacy within homes. We can guess that there

Personal Space

The concept of personal space is very simple. We each carry around with us a bubble of space which is private and personal. The bubble is not a static one, nor do its dimensions remain constant around the body. As we find ourselves in tight situations (for example, waiting in line for admission to a theater), the bubble shrinks. When we are seeking solitude, the bubble could be quite large. [8]

Personal space can also be thought of as successive layers, the most private layer being closest to the body, and the least private, further out. In decreasing order of intimacy they can be described in this way: (1) intimate distance is from the skin to about eighteen inches out, and only the closest of friends, family and lovers are allowed in

is a higher level of intimacy between adults than between adults and children, and the spatial divisions of the home support this kind of privacy by giving the adults a private bedroom and the children their own play space. Are siblings in the same bedroom more intimate than those who do not share bedrooms? Does intimacy occur along sex lines, women sharing secrets with other women and girls, and men sharing secrets with other men and boys. If this is true, how does the home support it?

All these privacy mechanisms help define limits and boundaries of the self. Individuality is developed by being able to, at times, incorporate others into our private worlds, at other times, to leave them out. Altman says, "If I can control what is me and not me; if I can define what is me and not me; if I can observe the limits and scope of my control, then I have taken major steps toward understanding and defining what I am."[7]

Territoriality—the staking out of what is ours—can take many forms. The elaborate fence as well as the row of potted plants serves the same purpose. Photos by author.

this zone of personal space; (2) personal distance is that which is comfortable for one-to-one conversation, about one and a half to four feet; (3) social distance is from four to twelve feet and it defines the area in which we comfortably converse in small groups (also a design criterion for furniture arrangements in living rooms); (4) the public zone is that which we use for our most formal and impersonal interactions, more than twelve feet.[9]

Despite the research that has taken place in the pursuit of defining personal space, almost nothing is known about its effects within a personal living environment. We can assume that some of the phenomena observed in public spaces apply also to interior spaces of private dwellings. The parents of a family may position themselves closer together in a living room than would their children, with boys maintaining the greatest distance between themselves and other boys. The filling up of chairs in a living room is probably no different than the filling up of chairs in a library or waiting room. We tend to space ourselves in equal distances around the room. We have probably all observed how the late-comers to parties squeeze between already seated persons, an acceptable and predictable behavior that would be thought odd and rude by the first to arrive.

Should personal space be considered in designing more psychologically satisfying homes? The behavior of people in a given space and the requirements of effective spatial design are much more complex considerations than the concept of personal space, but an awareness of personal space does draw attention to individual and situational differences of people and environments, and requires designers and builders to pay more attention to variety, flexibility and personalization.[10]

Territoriality

In public places, such as libraries or waiting rooms, we tend to claim a territory for ourselves and our belongings as an extension of personal space. Territories are also claimed inside houses. Kitchen cabinets are usually considered the mother's domain. A child's dresser drawers are a private territory not to be invaded by parents or siblings. Every family member may have certain seating or play places that are respected territories, the familiar "dad's chair" coming to mind.

One common way to lay claim to private space, and to insure the functioning of personal space, is to mark out territory for one's exclusive use. Pieces of property are territories for individuals just as towns, counties, states and nations are territories for governments. The edges of our personal territory are very important to us. We erect fences or plant hedges, not because we need to keep out wild animals or dangerous intruders, but because we want, in a deeply psychological way, to identify what is ours for the outside world to see.

Territoriality is a manifestation of self-identity and place identity. By building a fence, wall, or edge marker of any kind, we express our skills and personal preferences as an integral part of marking our territory. The process also helps identify the place which is synonymous with our identity. Becker has stated it well: "The occupant can develop a 'place' with which to identify and from which he or she can send messages about status, class, prestige, values, political ideology and taste with the knowledge that the conditions he or she places on behavior within the territory will be recognized and respected."[11]

Territoriality is more difficult to accommodate in multifamily housing than in single-family, owned housing. Apartment dwellers are usually restricted to making personal statements about themselves within

Suburban Turf: Second Stage Territoriality

Now let us move to suburbia to observe the process of staking out a new house lot on what was open farmland.

1. Legal and speculative claim-staking. The first surveyors arrive; measure out the metes and bounds; post zoning notices, clear paths through woods, put up stakes and other evidence to upset neighbors.

2. Developers set up outposts: a contractor's trailer-office, a sales office converted from a mobile home, stacks of sewer pipe, etc., as visible evidence of future construction.

3. First houses built and occupied.

4. Occupation. In countless colorful ways, new homeowners stake out claims, put down their own markers on the landscape: possessions laid out in front yard by moving crew; pickup truck, sports car, trail bike, garden tractor, and other symbolic possessions stationed strategically; temporary fences, sod, seed or ground cover, and hedges of yucca, barberry or other prickly vegetational defenses. . . ; outriders go out— sometimes a shed at the rear corner of property, a junkpile at another corner, incinerator elsewhere.

Such constellations of signals set up by the incoming family are immediately read by neighbors. One set conveys "Keep your distance"; another says plainly, "Come in." Spacious grounds in many suburbs indicate that the settlers want privacy. Especially in the newer brick and stone enclaves—exclusive residential subdivisions with gates and gatekeepers being built at the edges of many cities—many signals are preplanned. . . . In working-class suburbs the rituals are less evident and less formal. Painting one's own name on the R.F.D. mailbox or handcrafting the mailbox support from a welded chain or an old milk can is an easy opener of conversations with passersby. In denser neighborhoods, what happens on the stoop is everybody's business. One observes frequent neighboring, fewer fences between yards, more openings and paths through hedges— pathways kept hard by pets, kids, parents, postman, and paperboy.

Excerpted from: Clay, G., Close-up, How to Read the American City. (New York: Praeger, 1973) pp. 162–164.

their dwellings. Even in garden apartments, which might be designed with individual patios or small gardens, there may be restrictions as to the kinds of alterations that are acceptable to the management. Condominium developments are also restrictive in their management policies. Residents often may not build decks, patios, fences, extended roofs, nor may they paint the outside of their units, nor in some cases plant flowers and shrubs of their choice. Even though architectural unity and cohesive landscaping may be the result, these constraints on human territoriality should not be overlooked.

THE EFFECTS OF CROWDED HOUSING

Crowding and its effects on behavior have been a subject of great interest in environmental psychology. There has probably been more research in this area than in personal space and privacy. However, as we will see throughout this discussion, attempts at determining whether crowded housing causes poor mental health have resulted in more questions than answers.

Defining Crowding and Density

"Crowding" and "density" are used interchangeably in both popular and scientific literature, but they are quite different people/space phenomena, and the distinction is important to keep in mind when dealing with research findings. Density refers to a measure of the number of people in a given area of land. But the measure shifts depending on the perspective. Planners use the number of housing units per acre of land as a measure of density, and generally, that is also the definition of density used in this book. For instance, most suburban neighborhoods have six houses per acre. Fourteen houses per acre (a typical lowrise apartment development) would indicate a very high density by comparison. Obviously, one acre in the suburban environment might house a great many more people, say six to a house, than another acre, with two to a house, yet the density would be considered the same. Some studies have been based on the average density measure of census tracts without taking into account the fact that the tract may not be entirely residential. In another method of **areal density** measurement, the number of housing units per building are counted, again without regard to the number of people living in each unit.

High density housing in which a great number of housing units are built per acre of land is not synonymous with crowded housing in which a great number of people live in one unit. Photo courtesy of U.S. Department of Housing and Urban Development.

A measurement of crowding specifically identifies the number of people within a dwelling unit. A standard way of measuring crowding is by using a persons-per-room ratio. This ratio is calculated by dividing the number of persons in the household by the number of rooms in the housing unit (leaving out bathrooms). For example, a six-room house with a family of three as its occupants has a persons-per-room ratio of .5. Any unit measuring over 1.0 is considered crowded. over 1.5 severely overcrowded.

Minimum space standards have been established by public agencies such as the American Public Health Association (APHA) and the U.S. Department of Housing and Urban Development (HUD) as well as in building and housing codes. These standards often specify the minimum number of square feet in each room of the dwelling with differences depending on whether it is in single-family, multifamily, or public housing. Sometimes the amount is expressed as square feet per family; of course, the larger the family, the more space needed. The APHA declared in 1971 that the minimum amount of habitable space for a five-person family was 550 square feet, slightly more than a double-car garage. HUD, using a five-person family, agreed with this minimum standard for **subsidized housing,** but set higher minimum standards for multifamily housing (630 square feet) and one- or two-family housing (615 square feet). These discrepancies are disturbing; the implication is that lower-income families can or should be more crowded than middle-income families.[12]

Even though these measures for density and crowding appear to be concrete, there are problems with their use in research. The arrangements of space, that is, types of rooms, dimensions of the rooms, and rooms in relation to one another, are not taken into account, nor is the quality or character of surrounding space or access to it. The age and size of occupants are not taken into account. Residents on the top floor of a highrise building may feel more crowded than their neighbors on lower floors because they do not have easy access to the ground. On the other hand, their view out of windows may compensate, and they might be better off than midrise neighbors whose windows face an adjacent building.

In addition to all of these problems in defining density and crowding, there is difficulty in accounting for effects of light, sound, or temperature. Neighbor noise and street noise surely have an enclosing effect, and so might poor access to natural light and ventilation.

Although there are weaknesses in the measures of density and crowding, the experience of crowding is a serious matter indeed. One could feel restricted, for instance, by isolation in a housing unit surrounded by a threatening environment. An elderly person in a crime-ridden neighborhood might experience such restriction. One could also experience crowding because the living unit itself did not allow personal privacy or personal space. Stokols states the essential point about crowding in his definition: ". . .a state of crowding exists, and is perceived as such by an individual, when the individual's demand for space exceeds the available supply of such space."[13]

Density and Social Pathology

It has been assumed by most researchers that high density causes stress, and that stress will result in long-term psychological consequences.[14] These consequences manifest themselves as social pathologies such as "morbidity, mortality, fertility, ineffectual parenting and psychiatric disturbance."[15]

Living Space in an Urban Ghetto

The shape of your living space and mine probably looks something like this. One has a closet, bureau, and desk for his possessions. A husband and wife probably share one or two rooms they can call their own. One can exclude other household members from a den or bedroom. One also has a series of specialized rooms equipped with a variety of appliances and furniture where a variety of activities can be carried on. As an adult one has priority in using any of these and can exclude all people who are not members of the household from the apartment or at least from parts of it.

A child in such a middle class household has somewhat more constricted living space. The mother can probably come into the child's bedroom without permission and open the bureau drawers or closet. A child's use of the activity sites of the household may have low priority. Also areas outside the house or apartment are restricted by parental command, and a child cannot visit remote areas without parental permission and fiscal support until he is about fifteen years of age.

If you are a child in East Tremont your territory in the home and your home range will be even smaller. There is probably but one bureau drawer and a quarter of a closet for your use, because there may be three sisters sharing your room. There is no chair in your bedroom for it measures eight by ten feet and holds two beds, a crib, and two bureaus. If the whole family is home, there may not be one vacant chair in the household.

The most crowded household we have so far found in our studies of ghetto territoriality is a Yugoslavian family—two parents and five teen-aged sons, all of whom live in a one-bedroom apartment. In a case like this the living room and kitchen have beds in them. More often eight or nine people live in a two or three-bedroom apartment. As a consequence, the two parents may have a bedroom, the mother's sister and two girls may share another, and three boys have the third bedroom.

The average kitchen in East Tremont is nine by twelve. At least three feet of two walls are taken up by closets, cabinets, a sink and a stove. So, the remaining floor space is six by nine feet. But the apartment was probably built about 1920 when refrigerators were smaller, and now the family has purchased a large refrigerator-freezer. It will not fit in the original space, so the family now uses that space as a clothes and broom closet. The refrigerator itself is half way across the kitchen door and the remaining floor space is reduced to six by seven. A kitchen table and two or three chairs are located in this remaining area. One or two of the chairs is jammed against the wall so that only a child can sit in it, and two adults can hardly pass each other in the kitchen.

Therefore, some kind of adaptation has to be made. In East Tremont there are several common ones. In one kind the mother simply does not let anyone into her kitchen. At dinner time the plates of each member of the family are filled and taken to the living room. If father is home and has company, the children may not be allowed to use the living room either, for there is likely to be but one sofa and one chair. In another kind of adaptation, the kitchen table is dispensed with and an end table or a child's play table is used. In this case no adult can eat in the kitchen.

The living room is also short of space. There is room for a sofa (sometimes a sectional), one or two chairs and a television set. Maybe there is another bed and crib. The rest of the room may be cluttered with customary, but useless,

American junk. Maybe there is a Duncan Phyfe table with a vase on it or a huge hi-fi console.

In the Puerto Rican household when there is no company, things may not be too bad. All the family members seem comfortable huddling together on the sofa and chair. If crowded they put their arms around each other's shoulders and talk as they watch television. If there is company, the children play or sit on the floor. It is more difficult for many Black children. Parents and children do not huddle. Children are likely to be chased off the sofa if the parents sit there, and children are often sent out of the room if there is company.

In one Black family we studied intensively, four boys between six and twelve were kept out of both the kitchen and the living room. Every night they did their homework and reading and most of their playing sitting on the floor of the dimly lit hallway of the apartment. Sometimes, in addition, they got whipped if they blocked traffic.

Excerpted from:
Scheflen, A. E., "Living Space in an Urban Ghetto." Family Process, 1971, 10, 435–437.

Rates of juvenile delinquency and rates of reported crime have also been associated with areal density. There is no certainty, however, that the reported crimes accurately reflect the real crime rate or that those committing the crimes reside in the areas in which they take place. Mental illness has been related to density rates by the number of suicides or admissions to mental hospitals, and mortality has been measured by death rates.

Research in this area is inconclusive. While some research has found a correlation between high areal density and social pathology, other research has found just the opposite. Kirmeyer concludes, after reviewing much of this research, that "the more recent and methodologically sound sociological investigations suggest that high areal and in-dwelling (crowding) densities are not necessarily associated with morbidity, mortality, crime, or mental illness."[16] When income level, ethnicity, or familism are used to correlate these pathologies, the impact of density is relatively small. Another review of this research reached the following conclusion:

Density is disliked, makes most people uncomfortable and probably reduces . . .

local social interaction. It is *associated* with "pathology," but there is not much reason to believe that density (short of great extremes) *causes* pathology. The effects of density are highly dependent on individual, situational (social and architectural) and cultural factors.[17]

Perhaps the safest conclusion to make is that high density probably has a negative effect on the quality of life of the persons living in it, but that there is a vast range of individual experiences with the high-density residential environment that must be taken into account in order to reach sound general conclusions as to just what effect is.

Crowding and Stress

It is thought that overcrowded conditions can lead to increased social demand on the residents involved. Each person in a crowded situation is constantly aware of the other's presence and the inherent demands that such human contact brings. As a consequence of this, each person has less control over his or her social (familial) interactions. Most important of all, there is a lack of privacy. All of these interpersonal phenomena cause an increase in what one psychologist has labeled "psychological energy."[18] Each person must think and feel with regard to others at all times. Just coping on a day-to-day basis with such a living situation can cause frustration, physical weakness, and little time for long-range planning.

An overcrowded housing unit may have its most severe effects on children. Physical weakness can lead to a susceptibility to disease in children and adults. Parents can be more irritable than they might be in less crowded housing. Even though overcrowding may not cause juvenile delinquency in a provable way, it is sensible to suppose that the decision of teenagers to seek activity and social relations outside the home could be related to overcrowding. "In some cases parents may attempt to increase privacy and reduce crowding by encouraging children to spend more time outside the home, thus diminishing their supervision and control of children's activities."[19]

Intrusion is another stress-producing result of overcrowded housing. Unwanted social contact with other people, and restrictions regarding the use of space and the amount of noise can have distressing long-range effects. Coping behavior in these situations could result in psychological withdrawal.

One might conclude that crowding decreases socialization in the home, manifested as a reduction of intrafamilial socialization and decreased contact with friends, but the research on crowding and stress is inconclusive. Even though there is a relationship between overcrowded housing and signs of stress, the relationship is coincidental and not causal. Research in this field must also examine individual expectations, design, social situations, and cultural differences. Of all the research done in crowding and density in housing, one finding is dramatically clear. It is that "people prefer more to less space and will move, if possible, when household density becomes personally uncomfortable."[20]

HOME AS A PSYCHOLOGICAL CONCEPT

Is home a place, or the feeling we have about it? Do we have more than one home? Which is more important, the more recent, the longest lived in, the one in which we have been happiest? The psychological importance of "home" as a concept will be discussed in this section by examining the effects of residential change, that is, a change in homes.

The Concept of Home

Hayward, who has researched the concept of home, states that "'home' is a label applied voluntarily and selectively to one or more environments to which a person feels some attachment."[21] He categorizes nine meanings of home. Five are briefly identified here because they reflect some of the same psychological themes previously mentioned in this chapter.[22]

Home as Intimate Others. A sense of belonging or of togetherness, of caring, of warmth and security are embodied in this concept. Home is the place of our most intense emotional experiences. The importance of home as a center for the affection and security of family and friends is emphasized.

Home as Self-identity. Home is a symbol of how we see ourselves as well as how we wish to be seen by others. Our values are reflected in our home.

Home as a Place of Privacy and Refuge. Home is where we go to get away from the outside world. Home is freedom from pressures, a place to relax, a place of peace. Safety and security are also embodied in this concept.

Home as Continuity. Hometowns or permanent family homes embody this concept. Returning home after an absence is the essence of a feeling of continuity.

Home as Personalized Space. Being able to create a personally satisfying home is the meaning of home as personalized space. Control of the space, surfaces, and furnishings to reflect personal tastes is an important aspect of housing satisfaction.

Four other concepts of home were identified in Hayward's research. He found that people have strong feelings about their childhood home. Home is also the major base for daily activity. Home can also mean the center of a social network. Finally, the home is a physical structure. Housing literature often stresses this last concept without consideration of the other, psychologically more important, concepts of home.

We have emotional attachments to **neighborhoods** as well as the homes in which we live and the homes of our childhood. The importance of neighborhood is implied in Hayward's concepts of home as social network and home as a base for activity. Other psychologists have explored the attachment to neighborhood in different ways. One is the investigation of "home range." Studies have attempted to describe

Overcrowded housing units can lead to the stress related to constant human contact and lack of privacy. Overcrowded housing has more severe effects on children than adults. Photo courtesy of U.S. Department of Housing and Urban Development.

Home as a psychological concept includes home as self-identity and home as personalized space. This resident has surrounded herself with furnishings and personal belongings to create her psychological as well as physical home. Photo courtesy of U.S. Department of Housing and Urban Development.

the physical boundaries for these home areas, and how they differ among individuals. One study showed that the actual use of the space around the home becomes critical to each person's home area concept. Married couples were analyzed regarding their **home ranges.** When maps were drawn of individual home ranges, it was found wives had larger home areas than husbands. The husbands' home area "leaned" in the direction of their work, whereas the women's "leaned" in the direction of their shopping, and they shopped in more than one area. Women also had a sense of neighborhood that was bounded by main thoroughfares.[23]

Another area of research is **cognitive mapping.** Cognitive mapping is the mental process by which we form a picture in our minds of the areas we live in. Our individual sense of home range is probably one part of a mental picture of not only the neighborhood but the city in which we live. Cognitive mapping depends on direct experience with the area thus pictured.

A study was done comparing the image of Los Angeles in the minds of affluent residents in West Los Angeles, to the residents in a poorer section of the city. The image of the affluent was a thousand times bigger than was the image of the poor people. Given the fact that the affluent residents knew the city literally from one end to the other (about sixty miles) through personal experience, and the poor people knew only the few blocks in which they lived and worked, the dramatic difference in their cognitive maps is not surprising.

Effects of Residential Change

Probably the most critical factor in any consideration of the effects of residential change is whether or not the change was desired. Many millions of families move every year without detriment to their physical or mental health. Nevertheless, it is an oversimplification to say that everyone who moves voluntarily does not have any ill effects. Even a desired change can result in unfamiliar surroundings, a severance of old friendships, new social requirements, possibly higher rent and related experiences. Any of these can cause stress and its consequences to health.

A classic study done of relocated families compared 300 rehoused families with 300 nonrehoused families (control group) over a period of three years. The rehoused families appreciated their increased amounts of space, better heating and refrigeration, plumbing (hot and cold running water), screens, garbage disposal and absence of rodents.[24] Even though the rehoused group said they felt they were better off, there was no difference between the two groups in moodiness, nervousness, self-esteem or general morale. No differences were found in family relations. It should be noted that some of the rehoused residents returned to the slums from which they were moved (presumably because they were unhappy), and some of the control group found better housing on their own. These families were removed

from the study, therefore not giving an accurate picture of rehoused versus nonrehoused families.

Moves from cities to suburbs have also been studied. When working-class residents move to the suburbs they express satisfaction with more space, increased social life, and involvement with the community. But there seems to be no effect on mental health, family life, or marital happiness. Furthermore, working-class residents do not adopt the lifestyle of the middle class, contrary to the predictions of planners who favor neighborhood heterogeneity.[25]

Being forced to move is quite another matter. Many thousands of families have been forced to move due to highway construction or urban renewal. If slum residents have to seek their own housing, they not only leave familiar home ranges, but often pay more rent, usually without the benefit of better housing, and they sever familiar social networks. A common symptom in this circumstance is what has been labeled the "grief syndrome." "Grief is a psychosomatic syndrome that may include intestinal disorders, nausea, vomiting, and crying spells, for example, over an extended period of time.[26] When a person has a strong attachment not only to a house, but also to a neighborhood, the loss is felt as severely as the death of a relative or friend. The grief syndrome is more severe for those residents who like their previous neighborhood very much. Other factors include how well a person knew the previous neighborhood, and the number of friends there.[27] The West End of Boston provided the setting for a study of forced rehousing due to urban renewal. Two years after the move, 40 percent of the sample gave evidence of the grief syndrome.[28]

_____ SUMMARY_____

In addition to providing us with shelter, housing provides us with satisfaction of basic psychological needs. We have social, semiphysiological, stabilizing, individual, self-expression, and enrichment needs which can be identified and related to specific aspects of housing. The physical setting of housing provides the arena in which these psychological needs are met.

The particular home we have helps us define our inner being, and the housing unit in turn takes on personally identifying characteristics. Thus the house and self are mutually supporting. Because we see our houses as symbols of ourselves, acceptance of impersonal and all-alike housing is slow. On the other hand, people wishing to identify themselves as unconventional do so with untypical forms of housing. The changing roles of women and men have led to conflicts regarding self-identity and housing. Person/structure, role, interpersonal, and intrapersonal conflicts can all occur within the home in working-wife families. The place in which we live also helps us define who we are. Many factors come to bear on our place-identity, among them the feelings we have about a place, as well as our experiences there.

Privacy is one of the most important concepts in the psychology of housing. Home is where we let down our hair, are free to be ourselves, find solitude, control access to our innermost feelings, and so on. Privacy is also satisfied by spatial separation from neighbors, walls between rooms, and sound barriers.

Personal space can be visualized as a space bubble we carry around with us which protects us from intrusion by others. It has dimensioned layers from the most intimate zone to the most formal public zone.

The concept of personal space has been given much attention by environmental psychologists, but little is known about how it functions within family relationships in the home.

The strongest manifestation of territoriality in housing is the marking of private property. Within houses, territories are more subtle, with certain spaces off limits to other members of the family as well as guests. Multifamily housing in all its forms can also include provisions for territoriality.

Crowding and density, although frequently used interchangeably, refer to the in-house relationship of people to space (crowding) and the out-of-house relationship of housing units to land area (density). Space standards are a means of defining crowding, and have been used by the APHA and HUD. These standards are inadequate because they overlook other aspects of space that may be equally important.

The efforts to link density with social pathologies have resulted in inconclusive findings. For all the studies that have correlated high densities with morbidity, mortality, ineffectual parenting, and psychiatric disturbances, there are other studies that do not. The social problems associated with high density areas find their roots not in the density itself but in the socioeconomic characteristics of the people who often reside there. The studies that attempt to link crowding within the housing unit with social pathologies are also inconclusive, but signs of stress do exist in overcrowded housing.

"Home" can have many meanings. It has been defined as a place of intimate others, self-identity, privacy, continuity and personalized space. Home range is the area, including our houses, that we use as an extension of our homes. Our individual homes, and home ranges help form a cognitive map of, say a city, but our total experience in that city will help formulate the size and accuracy of the cognitive map.

Moving from one home to another can have psychological consequences. When the move is voluntary, there are few detrimental effects, but when the move is involuntary, the effects can be severe. The grief syndrome has been found to persist over a long period of time for people strongly (socially and emotionally) attached to a neighborhood.

Notes

1. Peterson, P., "The Id and the Image: Human Needs and Design Implications," unpublished paper (Eugene, Or.: University of Oregon, 1969).
2. Cooper, C., "The House as Symbol of the Self," in J. Lang et al., eds., *Designing for Human Behavior: Architecture and the Behavioral Sciences.* (Stroudsburg, Pa.: Dowden Hutchison & Ross, 1974); also in C. S. Wedin and L. G. Nygren, *Housing Perspectives* (Minneapolis, Minn.: Burgess, 1979).
3. Ibid., pp. 133–34.
4. Saegert, S., "Towards Better Person-Environment Relations: The Changing Relationship of Women and Men to the Environment," in P. Suedfeld et al., eds., *The Behavioral Basis of Design; Book 2: Session Summaries and Papers* (EDRA7) (Stroudsburg, Pa.: Dowden Hutchison & Ross, 1977).
5. Altman, I., "Privacy, a Conceptual Analysis," *Environment and Behavior*, 1976, 8, p. 8.
6. Westin, A., *Privacy and Freedom* (New York: Atheneum, 1970).
7. Altman, "Privacy," p. 26.
8. Sommer, R., *Personal Space: The Behavioral Basis of Design* (Englewood Cliffs, N J: Prentice-Hall, 1969).
9. Altman, "Privacy," p. 20.
10. Sommer, R., "Looking Back at Personal Space," in J. Lang et al., eds., *Designing for Human Behavior*, p. 207.
11. Becker, F. D., *Housing Messages* (Stroudsburg, Pa.: Dowden Hutchison & Ross, 1977), p. 52.
12. Morris, E. W. and M. Winter, *Housing Family and Society* (New York: Wiley, 1978), pp. 91–93.
13. Stokols, D., "A Social-Psychological Model of Human Crowding Phenomenon," in C. M. Loo, ed., *Crowding and Behavior* (New York: MSS Information Corp., 1974), p. 111.
14. Kirmeyer, S. L., "Urban Density and Pathology: A Review of Research," *Environment and Behavior*, 1978, 10, pp. 247–69.
15. Ibid., p. 251.
16. Ibid., p. 258.
17. Fischer, C. S., M. Baldassare, and R. J. Ofshe, "Crowding Studies and Urban Life: A Critical Review," *Journal of the American Institute of Planners*, 1975, 41, p. 411.
18. Altman, "Privacy," p. 24.
19. Kirmeyer, "Urban Density," p. 251.
20. Fischer, et al., "Crowding Studies," p. 408.
21. Hayward, D. G., "Home as an Environmental and Psychological Concept," *Landscape*, 1975, 20(1), p. 3.
22. Hayward, D. G., "Housing Research and the Concept of Home," *Housing Educators Journal*, 1977, 4 (3), p. 10.
23. Everitt, J., and M. Cadwallader, "The Home Area Concept in Urban Analysis: The Use of Cognitive Mapping and Computer Procedures," in W. J. Mitchell, ed., *Environmental Design Research and Practice: Proceedings of the EDRA/AR8 Conference* (Los Angeles: University of California, 1972).

24. Kasl, S. V., "Effects of housing on mental and physical health," *Man-Environment Systems*, 1974, *4*, pp. 207–226.
25. Ibid., p. 214.
26. Michelson, W. H., *Man and His Urban Environment: A Sociological Approach*

(Reading, Mass.: Addison-Wesley, 1976), p. 163.
27. Kasl, "Effects of Housing," p. 215.
28. Fried, M., "Grieving for a Lost Home," in L. J. Duhl, ed., *The Urban Condition* (New York: Basic Books, 1963).

Suggested Readings

Altman, I. "Privacy, a Conceptual Analysis." *Environment and Behavior*, 1976, *8*, 7–29.

Ashcroft, N., and Scheflen, A. E. *People Space*. Garden City, N.Y.: Anchor Press, 1976.

Becker, F. D. *Housing Messages*. Stroudsburg, Pa.: Dowden, Hutchison & Ross, 1977, (chap. 1, "Environmental Messages"; chap. 2, "Images of Home"; chap. 4, "Personalization").

Cooper, C. "The House as Symbol." In C. S. Wedin and L. G. Nygren, eds. *Housing Perspectives* (2nd ed.). Minneapolis: Burgess, 1979.

Evans, G. W., and Howard, R. B. "Personal Space." In D. S. Stokols, ed. *Readings in Environmental Psychology*. New York: MSS Information Corp., 1974.

Fischer, C. S.; Baldassare, M.; and Ofshe, R. J. "Crowding Studies and Urban Life: A Critical Review." *Journal of the American Institute of Planners*, 1975, *41*, 406–418.

Hall, E. T. "Meeting Man's Basic Spatial Needs in Artificial Environments." In J. Lang, D. Burnette, W. Moleski, and D. Vachon. *Designing for Human Behavior: Architecture and the Behavioral Sciences*. Stroudsburg, Pa.: Dowden, Hutchison & Ross, 1974.

Heimstra, N. W., and McFarling, L. H. *Environmental Psychology*. Monterey, Cal.: Brooks Cole, 1974, (chap. 2 "The Built Environment: Rooms and Housing").

Sadalla, E. K., and Stea, D., eds. "Psychology of Urban Life." *Environment and Behavior*, 1978, *10* (2) (entire issue).

Saegert, S. *House and Home in the Lives of Women*. New York: City University of New York Graduate Center, Center for Human Environments, 1975.

Sommer, R. *Personal Space: The Behavioral Basis of Design*. Englewood Cliffs, N.J.: Prentice-Hall, 1969.

"Toward a Social Psychology of Housing. *Housing Educators Journal*, 1977, *4* (3) (special issue).

Buying and Selling Your First Home

7

Home ownership dominates American housing. There are many more home owners than renters, but an even more significant fact is that nearly all housing consumers aspire to home ownership at some point in their lives. It is not only the American dream, it is also considered the basic ingredient of the American way of life.

Since house prices and interest rates have skyrocketed in a short period of time, many young families have been priced out of the market. Others are managing home

ownership at great personal costs. The family budget may be unreasonably distorted to allow for big monthly home ownership expenditures. When hobbies, entertainment, vacations, and leisure activities are sacrificed in order to achieve home ownership, the emotional effects are as difficult to withstand as the financial effects.

This chapter will examine, first, what is involved in making the decision to buy. The business of home buying, for most of us, depends on the borrowing of a large sum of money to be paid back over a long period of time. The many types of home mortgages, and their advantages and disadvantages, are the substance of the second chapter section. Qualifying for a home mortgage is discussed in the third section. That is followed by an explanation of the

---

There are a great many steps in homebuying from the first shopping trip to the closing: a contract of sale must be signed, a loan obtained, the house appraised, and closing costs estimated. Photo by author.

buying and selling process. The last section covers three unusual means of achieving home ownership.

MAKING THE DECISION TO BUY A HOUSE

The average price of a new or used house is so high that it may seem beside the point to discuss the care with which the decision to buy a house should be made. One may have all the right reasons to buy but be unable to do so from a strictly financial standpoint. This is the case more frequently now than in the recent past. Nevertheless, people should not feel they ought to buy a house simply because they can manage it financially, even though a social pressure may exist to do so. When the housing market is as volatile as it has been in recent years, there is a temptation to jump on the bandwagon of home ownership profits. That money can be made in buying and selling property should not, in itself, motivate home ownership for young families with no **real estate** experience.

What follows is a list of reasons for not buying a house. You are *not* ready to buy if one or more of these factors is present in your personal housing situation.

Job Permanency

You may not be ready to buy if your job future is uncertain either because your employment does not appear permanent, or because you are uncertain of your job satisfaction. Young people are expected to make several job shifts before they settle into a truly satisfactory position. When both the husband's and wife's careers are at stake, the job permanency factor is more difficult to assess realistically than when only one career is in question.

A job change often means a location

change. A quick move can put home sellers at a disadvantage in a fluctuating housing market. More importantly, the financial burden of home ownership can only be sustained with reliable income. Even a short period of unemployment could be disastrous to a family on a tight budget.

Space Needs

You may not be ready to buy if your space needs are met adequately with a one- or two-bedroom apartment. If a couple is not anticipating the birth of a child, there may be no logical reason to buy a three- or four-bedroom home. It is all too easy to overlook the disadvantages of excess space. Such space has to be heated, cleaned, furnished, and maintained. The costs in time and money for unneeded space may not be worth it.

The need for outdoor space is a factor too. A single-family house has private outdoor space which is useful to a young family with children but which could be burdensome to a couple without children. The ownership of a mobile home or condominium may be a suitable compromise for a couple needing limited indoor and outdoor space, since two-bedroom units are more commonly available in these housing types than in single-family, detached dwellings.

Stage in the Life Cycle

You may not be ready for home ownership if your stage in the life cycle is better suited by housing flexibility. When a stage of the life cycle is not viewed as permanent, such as for a single person between marriages, the decision to buy would seem inappropriate. Of course, there are stages in the life cycle for which home ownership is almost considered a must in our society—families with young or teenage children. Even such families may have good reasons, including those enumerated above, for not buying a

This large house should not be bought by a small family for whom there might be too much space to heat, maintain, and furnish. A young family's lifestyle might not be compatible with the costs in time and money that landscaping require. Photo by author.

house. Similarly, couples, singles, and elderly people may choose to buy, even though the renting option is more freely open to them.

Lifestyle

You may not be ready for home ownership if your lifestyle depends on a great deal of free time. Each person or couple should weigh very carefully the time and energy they are willing to give to house and yard maintenance. A new house may require landscaping. The installation and care of a yard, even a small one, can take many, if not most weekends. Most couples want to personalize interiors with painting, wallpapering, and other small home improvement projects. Major home improvements, often necessary in older, less expensive houses, could take months of free time. All of these time-consuming activities associated with home ownership could interfere with hobbies, entertainment, travel, education, and regular visits with family and friends.

Values

You may not be ready to buy if your housing values can be satisfied with rental housing. Little can be said in this area that is objective. Values are very individual, and emotions play an important role in determining value satisfaction. For instance, one person may feel that privacy can only be attained with space between living units, whereas another might feel very private in a well-constructed, attached-wall townhouse. Valuing leisure, economy, independence, freedom, and beauty could lead to housing of many types, owned or rented.

Home ownership requires an attitude of responsibility and the time and energy to fulfill that responsibility. Many individuals and couples are happier and have more balanced lives without fulfilling this American dream. Social pressures and the financial advantages of home ownership do not require all families to assume it is their best course of action. The decision to buy is a highly personal one, and it should be carefully thought through.

Psychological Needs

You may not be ready to buy a house if your psychological needs are satisfied with rental housing. For many people, psychological needs are more easily fulfilled with home ownership. For instance, identity, autonomy, security, and achievement are associated with the ownership of a single-family residence. But the many other psychological needs, as well as these, may be met with well-designed and well-constructed rental housing.

Home buying is a stressful experience for most people. The decision to buy (the decision to incur great indebtedness) is in itself an emotional one, and the associated decisions of location, price, and financing alternatives are often difficult. If the person or family has other stressful factors to deal with at the same time, such as job change, marital difficulties, or financial uncertainty, the home buying process may be very difficult to cope with. The responsibilities of ownership and the time required to carry them out add another kind of stress once the home buying transaction and move to the new home are completed.

Advantages of Renting

Most of the advantages of renting have been implied in the discussion above. Flexibility in housing choice is one of them. One can move in and move out without a time-consuming ordeal, and a change of location within the same housing market is easy to accomplish. A move from one housing market to another is also without complication.

Yard maintenance may be a part of a very few rental agreements, but by and large rentals are free of maintenance responsibilities, inside and out. When the heating or plumbing needs repair, the landlord is responsible. Keeping up the property value through regular painting and small repairs is the owner's responsibility, not the tenant's.

It is possible that rental housing includes amenities unavailable in single-family detached dwellings within a prospective buyer's price range. A swimming pool, game room, sauna, or tennis court are too expensive for most first-time buyers to include in their individual homes. These amenities are not uncommon in newer large apartment developments, where their cost is distributed among many residents.

Last, but not least, renting is generally less costly than home ownership. Even if people can afford the financial obligations of home ownership, they may choose to rent because it means more disposable income for other aspects of their lives. People

Some rental housing provides adequate space, privacy, and economy along with freedom from responsibilities and flexibility. Photo by author.

who enjoy sports, travel, eating out, theater, entertaining, quality clothes, and expensive cars may choose renting in order to maintain their lifestyle, tastes and preferences.

THE BASIC COMPONENT— A HOME MORTGAGE

Houses are bought for cash. It is difficult to imagine anyone walking into a house for sale and being in a financial position to write out a check for, say, $125,000, but it has happened more than once. For families in more ordinary circumstances, a home purchase can only be achieved with the help of a loan.

A loan made to a home buyer is called a mortgage because the real property (the house and land) is used as security for the debt. The lender holds a **lien** or claim against the real property being purchased. The buyer (mortgagor) agrees through a legal document called a mortgage note to repay the loan in a certain amount of monthly payments such as 360, or 30 years. Should the mortgagor **default,** that is neglect to make the regular monthly payments, the property reverts to the lender (the mortgagee). **Foreclosure** would be the legal process used in this case so that the lender could sell the property to recover the debt owed on the mortgage.

The amount of money that can be borrowed depends on many factors, but in general, the loan to value ratio is 80 percent of the value of the house. Some loans are for more, 90 to 95 percent. If the mortgagee agrees that the estimated value of the house, the **appraised value,** is the same as the selling price, then 80 percent of the sale price would be the amount of the loan. If the appraised value is less than the sale price, the loan to value ratio is smaller. The amount of the loan is critical because everything not borrowed must be paid by the purchaser in the form of a down payment.

There are three factors that affect the monthly payment of a mortgage. One is the amount of money paid in the down payment. If more than the typical 20 percent was paid down, then the amount of money borrowed on the mortgage would be less. Each monthly payment would be less, and the total amount of money paid back over the term of the mortgage would be less.

Time is the second factor. If the term of repayment is less than the typical 30 years, then less total interest is paid on the amount of money borrowed. The monthly payments in this case, however, would be higher. If a home buyer can afford extraordinarily high monthly payments, and is interested in paying as little as possible in the long run, obtaining a mortgage for 15, 20, or 25 years would be an advantage. On the other hand, more and more 40-year mortgages are being used in order to bring the monthly payment down. This allows someone with limited income to afford the

The monthly mortgage cost of every house regardless of its size and location is affected by three factors—the amount of down payment, the term of repayment, and the interest rate (APR). Photo courtesy of U.S. Department of Housing and Urban Development.

monthly mortgage payment. The long-range penalty for this financing arrangement is that the total cost of the house is higher than with a 30-year mortgage.

The **interest** rate, or **APR (annual percentage rate),** is the third factor. The lower the APR, the less each monthly payment will be, and the lower the total amount paid over the term of the mortgage. Housing consumers have very little control over interest rates because they are set in relation to national economic policies. If interest rates at the federal level are raised, the local lending institutions will also raise its home mortgage rates. If the national money supply is curtailed, the local lending institutions may have little money to lend, resulting also in raised interest rates.

In areas that have many competing lenders, it may be worthwhile to shop around for the best interest rate available, especially when it is not a tight money market, that is, money is not in short supply. The amount of down payment can affect interest rate—the larger the down payment, the lower the interest rate. The age of the house may have some bearing on both. Older houses usually require larger down payments; the interest rates may be slightly higher than those available for newer properties.

Table 7–1 (page 146) compares different interest rates and loan repayment periods keeping the amount of the mortgage the same. If a $90,000 house is being purchased, the standard 20 percent down payment would be $18,000. A 30 percent down payment ($27,000) would have the effect of lowering the monthly costs at each of the interest rates shown, and the total cost over the term of the loan would be comparatively smaller. A smaller down payment (10 percent or $9,000) would have the reverse effect—larger monthly payments and higher total costs. The decrease in monthly payment due to a longer term is greater between 20 and 30 years than it is between 30 and 40 years. This decrease in monthly payment also diminishes at higher interest rates.

The Conventional Amortized Mortgage

The **conventional mortgage** (also called a standard mortgage) is paid in even monthly payments determined by the down payment, interest rate, and the length of repayment period as seen in Table 7–1. A part of each month's payment goes toward paying the **principal** amount of the loan, and the rest goes toward paying interest. In a conventional **amortized** mortgage, these amounts toward paying interest change proportionally with each monthly payment even though the total amount of the payment does not. At the outset of paying back a mortgage, the amount that goes toward principal is extremely small and the amount toward interest huge. Very gradually, the

amount of principal paid becomes larger and the interest smaller. The interest is computed on the unpaid balance of the principal. This is significant in determining tax deductions and the amount of one's **equity** (the proportion of the house really owned), but it is not significant in determining how much monthly payment can be afforded.

Conventional mortgages have been the most commonly used method of home buying. They are arranged between the lender and the borrower without any intervening parties. Therefore, they are generally the least complicated to get. The lender, who is taking the risk, can determine relatively quickly the borrower's ability to pay back the loan. The lender also knows the local housing market and can competently determine the quality of investment a house in a particular neighborhood represents.

A conventional mortgage may be insured through private mortgage insurance. This insurance immediately pays off the mortgage debt in case of death or disability of the insured, thus protecting the remaining family members from undue financial hardship. Private mortgage insurance is required by most savings and loan institutions when the amount of the mortgage is more than 80 percent of the value of the house.

FHA and VA Mortgages

An FHA loan, as it is commonly called, is actually not a loan from FHA, the Federal Housing Administration. Rather the FHA guarantees the loan which is made by a local lender, who then carries little risk because the federal government insures repayment of the loan in case of default. The intention of this program, begun in the 1930s, was to assist families without large savings to buy homes. A 3 or 5 percent down payment is now typical. The APR for an FHA mortgage as well as the maximum

TABLE 7–1   Monthly Payments and Total Costs of a $72,000 Mortgage
(Principal and Interest)

A.P.R.	20 YEAR TERM		30 YEAR TERM		40 YEAR TERM	
	MO. PMT	TOTAL (PMT × 240)	MO. PMT	TOTAL (PMT × 360)	MO. PMT	TOTAL (PMT × 480)
9%	$ 648	$155,520	$ 579	$208,440	$ 555	$266,400
10-1/2	719	172,560	659	237,240	640	307,200
12	793	190,320	741	266,760	726	348,480
13-1/2	869	208,560	825	297,000	814	390,720
15	948	227,520	910	327,600	902	432,960
16-1/2	1,029	246,960	997	358,920	991	475,680
18	1,111	266,640	1,085	390,600	1,081	518,880

All figures rounded to nearest dollar.

loan amount available are determined at the federal level. Borrowers are also charged an extra half percent interest to cover the cost of FHA insurance.

Applying for a FHA insured mortgage is done through the local lender, but the loan must be approved by the FHA as well as the lender. This takes time. Furthermore, the house being purchased, whether new or old, must meet FHA standards. This requires an inspection, perhaps money and time for repairs to be made, and a second inspection for final approval. The advantage to the consumer is that high quality of construction is assured.

The FHA home-ownership program has declined in popularity. Its peak was in the early 1940s when nearly half of all privately owned housing units were financed with FHA mortgages. By 1978, fewer than 9 percent were financed through FHA.[1] The reasons are explained by Dasso, Ring and McFall:

The advantages of FHA borrowing are offset by red tape delays, and sometimes high foreclosure rates. Also, FHA loans are often difficult to obtain in periods of increasing interest rates because the administrative interest rate is way under the market interest rate. In fact, faster processing of loan applications by private mortgage insurance companies is a major reason why privately insured conventional loans have become more popular with lenders and borrowers in recent years. In addition, lack of regulation of interest rates with privately insured conventional mortgages has led to their wider use in times of increasing or high interest rates relative to FHA insured mortgages.[2]

A **VA mortgage** is one that is guaranteed by the Veterans Administration. VA mortgages have many of the characteristics of FHA mortgages. The lender carries little risk, and the loan must be approved at offices other than the lending institution. Interest rates are set by law, and the terms of the mortgage benefit young home buyers who might otherwise not qualify for a conventional loan. Both FHA and VA loans have upper lending limits. Only veterans and unremarried spouses of deceased veterans are eligible for VA mortgages, and they may use them only once. The VA loan does not require a minimum down payment, but the local lender may make this a condition of handling the loan.

Mortgage Alternatives

Rising interest rates, along with rising prices of houses, have resulted in many thousands of first-time buyers being turned down for conventional loans. A rise of half a percent in interest rate can mean a $20 or $30 a month difference in house payments. Although this amount may seem small, it can mean the difference between being able to handle a monthly house payment, and not being able to handle a monthly house payment, at least from the point of view of the person making the decision, the lender. In order to help moderate-income families qualify for home loans, new mortgage instruments are being used in some areas. There are advantages and disadvantages to each.

Variable Rate Mortgage (VRM). The advantage of a variable interest rate is that initially the buyer gets a mortgage with a slightly lower (half a percent usually) interest rate than a conventional mortgage would have. The disadvantage is that if federal money market interest rates go up, so will the interest rate on the VRM mortgage. Usually, a VRM is restricted so that the interest rate cannot go up any more than $1/4$ percent every 6 months, and no more than $2^1/2$ percent over the term of the mortgage. Clearly, the home buyer could have much higher house payments several years after buying the house. Although interest rates could go down, and the VRM with them, the history of interest rates indicates that they would more likely rise. The buyer gambles, or, to put it another way, the lender is transferring some of the risk of

Some new housing developments advertise the availability of FHA (Federal Housing Administration) and VA (Veterans Administration) financing. Photo by author.

fixed interest rates onto the borrower. In some VRMs, the term of the loan can be extended instead of, or in addition to, increased interest rates so that the monthly payment stays about the same.

Home buyers may find that a VRM is to their liking because they can keep the initial house payment lower at a time when their budget is the most strained with home ownership and related costs. Later, their income is likely to increase more than enough to include a larger house payment when and if the interest rate goes up. Considering the mobility of Americans, especially first-time buyers, most VRM borrowers would not stay in the house long enough to experience a maximum increase in interest rate.

Adjustable Rate Mortgage (ARM). In 1981, federally chartered savings and loan institutions were allowed to make a new type of loan called an adjustable rate mortgage (ARM). The interest rate on an ARM is based on an index chosen by the lender and the borrower, and it would rise or fall accordingly. There is no limit on the rate or frequency of fluctuation. The change in the interest rate can be handled by the borrower in three ways: (1) the monthly payments can change; (2) the term of the mortgage can be extended up to 40 years; and (3) the payments can remain the same but the amount of the outstanding principal increased (**negative amortization**). In the latter case, the owner's equity might be less than it would be with a fixed-rate mortgage when the house is sold. The ARM transfers all the risk of unpredictable changes (increases) in interest rates to the borrower.

Graduated Payment Mortgage (GPM). Home buyers looking for a very low initial house payment with the expectation that it will increase over time would be interested in the graduated payment mortgage. The early payments do not pay off even all the interest owed, and none of the principal. In effect, the amount of money borrowed increases (negative amortization). Over a 5- to 10-year time period, the monthly principal and interest payments increase at predictable and even amounts—from 2 to $7\frac{1}{2}$ percent per year. In other words, buyers can opt for a financially suitable plan ranging from very small increases over a long period of time, to higher increases over a shorter period of time depending on their prospective income levels and other living expenses. In either case, the payments eventually level off and stay constant for the remainder of the mortgage term. Thus an initial house payment could be as much as $100 a month lower than a level-payment mortgage, but end up being $30 to $40 a month higher.

Since the principal is paid back much more slowly in a GPM than in a conventional mortgage, the building of equity depends entirely on the increased value of the property in the first few years. Consumers cannot be assured of as rapid increases in property values as in the past few years. Therefore, home buyers assume some financial risk in a GPM mortgage unless they are sure of staying in the house until substantial principal is paid off or until it goes up in value.

Rollover Mortgages. This mortgaging idea is borrowed from Canada where it is a standard procedure. Rather than having the interest rate change automatically with money market conditions (VRM), or have the monthly payment increase in a predetermined pattern (GPM), the interest rate is reevaluated, and renegotiated every few years; 1 to 4 year rollover mortgages are not unheard of, but normally the time period is 5 years. A maximum amount of interest rate increase may be set. This type of mortgage would not have the same advantages as the VRM and the GPM for young home buyers on a tight budget because initial monthly payments would not be slightly lower than with conventional financing. On the other hand, the interest rate increases might not be as rapid, and the amount of principal, the term of the loan, as well as interest rate can be renegotiated. In effect, refinancing is possible without the usual costs.

Flexible Mortgage. Yet another type of loan designed to benefit first-time home buyers is the flexible mortgage. It allows the payment of interest only for the first part of the term, usually 5 years, after which the mortgage shifts to a conventional amortized loan repayment. For a 30-year mortgage, the first 5 years would have lower than conventional payments. Since no principal would be paid off in the first 5 years, equity would be limited as with GPM mortgage.

FLIP Mortgage. This alternative has been available since 1977. FLIP stands for the Flexible Loan Insurance Program. This type of mortgage is like the others in that the aim is to reduce monthly payments during the first few years of the repayment term. The down payment, or part of it, is put into an interest-earning savings account that is pledged to the lender. The lender can loan as much as 100 percent of the price of the house. The buyer has monthly payments supplemented with predetermined amounts for 5 years, because the lender depletes the savings account and its earned interest over that period of time. Payments level off for the buyer after 5 years, and the balance of the mortgage is amortized in a conventional way.[3]

Wrap-around Mortgage. A so-called "wrap-around mortgage" (All-Inclusive Trust Deed) is an innovative form of financing used at a time when interest rates are much higher than they have been in the past and the house being purchased has an existing mortgage at a relatively low interest rate. "A second lender simply makes a new, larger loan to the borrower at an interest rate between that on the [existing] first mortgage and that in the market."[4] The actual amount of money owed is the amount of the existing mortgage plus the amount of a new loan, but the lender continues to pay off the old first mortgage. The buyer benefits by having a lower interest rate than with a mortgage that would require the first mortgage to be paid off in full. In this way, both the second lender and the buyer benefit by the lower interest rate on the existing first mortgage.

Equity Sharing Mortgage. The concept of equity sharing between lender and buyer was applied to home buying in 1980. The lender becomes part owner of the property so that when the home is sold, both the lender and the buyer benefit from the increased value. Usually they split the appreciation in half. This type of mortgage is also termed "shared appreciation mortgage" or

Houses nowadays are more likely to be financed with mortgage alternatives (such as the variable rate mortgage, adjustable rate mortgage, or rollover mortgage) than they are with conventional mortgages. Photo courtesy of Scholz Homes, Inc. Toledo OH.

SAM. The following example using the Denver housing market explains how it works:

> On the purchase of a $60,000 home, the buyer would put $10,000 down. The lender would put up $50,000 to buy the house and let a 9% mortgage—well below market rate. Five years later the house would be worth $115,500, if home prices in Denver kept increasing 14 percent annually, as they have on average since 1973. So the value of the house would have grown by $55,500 in five years. This would be split equally by the lender and buyer when the house was again sold. Each would receive $27,750.[5]

The buyer has the advantage of an interest rate lower than that available with other types of mortgages, and the down payment is less than normally required. Both features would assist families in a slightly lower income bracket to qualify for this mortgage whereas they might not qualify for a conventional mortgage.

Another version of equity sharing helps the home buyer with the down payment, closing costs, taxes and insurance. The lender helps pay these items, but the buyer in turn is charged on "occupancy fee" to pay them back. This, in addition to the monthly payment for principal and interest, can make a sizable monthly house payment, typically over $1,000. This program was designed for prospective home buyers without sufficient cash for a down payment, but with high income levels. First-time buyers, divorced singles, and renters are part of the housing market for which it was designed.[6]

Junior Mortgages. Second mortgages are used in home buying, and they are explained in the section on the buying and selling process. Such mortgages are generally shorter term and have higher interest rates than first mortgages. The holder of the second mortgage has second rights to the property. If the borrower defaults, the first mortgage holder will collect the outstanding balance if the property is sold. If there is any money left over, the second mortgage holder will also be paid. Some properties carry third and fourth mortgages. All of the mortgages other than the first mortgage are called "junior mortgages."

When house prices inflate dramatically, as they have in recent years, home owners may find themselves with very high equities. They may choose to take out second mortgages on part of their equity in order to accommodate a personal financial need, for instance, sending a child to college. A second mortgage can be one means of borrowing a large sum of money for 5 to 10 years.

Reverse Annuity Mortgages (RAMs). RAMs are designed for the elderly who live in homes with high equities. A wide variety of RAMs are available. One version is a rising debt RAM in which the lender contracts to pay a monthly annuity to the homeowner. The recipient of the reverse annuity mortgage continues to own, live in, and maintain the home. The debt owed the lender increases over time, and it is payable when the house is sold, the owner dies, or at some specific date, whichever comes first.[7] The lender appraises the property and lends a percentage of the value (usually 80 percent). When all of the funds have been used, a new RAM may be arranged if there has been a further increase in the value of the property.

In another form of RAM, the full amount of the loan is used to purchase an insurance company annuity. The monthly payments of the annuity are used to pay back the loan as well as to provide supplemental income for the home owner. Still another type combines features of the two types described above.[8] Regardless of type of RAM, many elderly people are reluctant to diminish the amounts of their estates which they wish to pass on to their heirs.

Mortgage Provisions

Mortgages can be written with various provisions, some of which primarily benefit the lender, and some of which primarily benefit the borrower. The more available loan money, the more willing a lender is to negotiate these terms. Even at times when lenders are unwilling to yield to the housing consumer's wishes, it is best to be well informed of the implications of all the terms of the mortgage contract.

Escrow or Impound Accounts. Some lenders require, and some borrowers might prefer, putting part of the annual costs of property taxes and hazard insurance into an account to be used for paying them when due. This spreads out the cost to the home owner over 12 months, which is an advantage to families without regular savings programs. A controversial aspect of an impound account is that it may not earn interest. These accounts are more likely to be required of loans made in excess of the typical 80 percent of the value of the house.

Prepayment Penalty. Even though the borrower agrees to repay the amount of the mortgage over a period of time, it is possible that financial circumstances would allow paying off the loan many years sooner than expected. Most homes are resold within 8 years, so mortgages are more often repaid than carried for the full term. Most lenders allow prepayment but charge a penalty for it. This penalty may be spelled out exactly, such as the amount of interest in the last house payment made times six, in effect reducing the penalty as the mortgage progresses. The penalty may be dropped after a certain number of years, say 10, and may be waived if the new buyer finances the purchase with the same institution.

Open-Ended Mortgage. Although not common, this clause is an advantage to the consumer because it allows the retrieval of money paid toward principal of the mortgage. If a home owner wished to borrow some of the paid-off principal, the lender would grant the loan, and the borrower would then pay more per month for the remaining term of the original mortgage. This is done without prepayment penalty or the cost of refinancing. Such a mortgage may have a higher interest rate and the house must be of the same or higher value as when originally purchased.

Flexibility Clause. A clause that allows for a few skipped house payments, to be paid in due time, might be an advantage to some home owners. This would allow a period of unexpected unemployment or ill-

ness, to be weathered without risk of losing the property. Such a clause is rarely used by most lenders.

Assumption of Mortgage. Mortgages range all the way from prohibiting the home owner from turning over the mortgage to another person, as might happen when the house is sold, to specifically allowing it. In some mortgages, neither is the case, so assumption of the mortgage is negotiable with the lender at the time of sale. If interest rates have risen, the lender may require a higher interest rate even if the mortgage is assumed (prohibited in some states). More of this is explained in the section on the process of buying and selling.

Package Mortgage. When appliances, carpeting, installed draperies, and sometimes furnishings, are included in the mortgage, it is referred to as a package mortgage. Many builders provide built-in appliances and an allowance for non-built-in appliances, such as a refrigerators, washers and dryers. Paying for these large-cost items on a monthly basis for the term of the mortgage reduces their immediate cost to the family. On the other hand, paying 25 or 30 years of interest for items that would not last that long may not be sound financial management.

THE HOME BUYING AND SELLING PROCEDURE

The old rules of thumb about how much house one can afford are worth noting, even though they are being broken in today's housing market. A conservative gauge is that the mortgage amount should be no more than 2 to $2\frac{1}{2}$ times gross annual income. Thus a $15,000 annual income could comfortably cover the cost of a $37,500 conventional mortgage (of which there are not

A very large and expensive house requires a very high income to qualify for a mortgage that is 80 percent of its selling price. Photo by author.

many anymore), a $20,000 income, a $50,000 mortgage, and $30,000 income, a $75,000 mortgage (many two-income families might fall into this category). Conversely, the $125,000 house, no longer in the luxury range of home building, requires a $40,000 annual income for an 80 percent mortgage.

Another traditional guideline is that only 25 percent of a family's monthly income should go towards housing. By 1979, two out of every five home buyers exceeded this amount.[9] By adding in monthly utility costs, property taxes, and hazard insurance to the monthly repayment of principal and interest, average housing costs nationally ranged in 1979 from $400 to $600 a month, depending on location. Using the 25 percent of family income criterion, the following table shows the relationship of income to monthly house payments (including principal, interest, taxes and insurance) to the needed down payment (figured at 20 percent) and the house price. These figures are categorized according to 10 percent, 12 percent, 14 percent, and 16 percent interest rates.

One real estate expert advises an approach that includes the above items of principal and interest, taxes and insurance, but also includes the costs of maintenance and repairs (not a monthly expenditure but calculated on a monthly basis), and interest

lost. This last item refers to the amount of money that could have been earned had the down payment been invested differently. Using the price of the house, these costs added together amount to about 1.2 percent of that price. The formula applied to a $60,000 house would indicate a monthly housing expenditure of about $720, a $75,000 house about $900, a $90,000 house about $1080, and so on. This method of calculating how much monthly costs might run is perhaps a more realistic way of determining how much house can be afforded, given a family's income, other financial commitments, lifestyle, and all other factors that determine personal spending.[10]

Loan Criteria

Even if first-time buyers have convinced themselves they can afford to buy the house of their dreams, the lender is the person who makes the final decision. The savings and loan institutions, commercial banks, mutual savings banks, and other sources of mortgage money (insurance companies, and some credit unions) have their own guidelines, and they are not all the same. Generally, the following considerations are evaluated before a loan decision is made:

1. *Monthly income.* This is the starting point, but it includes more than the breadwinner's paycheck. The spouse's paycheck

10% APR

TABLE 7-2 How Much Home Can You Afford?

IF YOUR FAMILY INCOME IS...	YOU SHOULD BE ABLE TO HANDLE MONTHLY PAYMENTS OF...	AND, YOU'LL NEED A DOWN PAYMENT OF ABOUT...	TO AFFORD A HOME COSTING... (THOUSANDS OF $)	IF YOU CAN MAKE A BIGGER DOWN PAYMENT, YOU CAN AFFORD A HOME IN THE HIGHER RANGES BELOW. (THOUSANDS OF $)	
				INCREASE D.P. $10,000	INCREASE D.P. $20,000
$15,000	$ 310	$ 6,600	$ 32–35	$ 39–44	$ 47–52
20,000	420	8,800	42–46	50–55	57–63
25,000	520	11,000	53–58	60–67	68–75
30,000	625	13,200	63–70	71–79	78–87
35,000	730	15,400	73–81	81–90	88–97
40,000	830	17,600	84–92	92–101	99–109
45,000	940	19,800	94–104	102–113	110–121
50,000	1040	21,800	104–115	112–124	120–133

Note: Based on a 20% down payment and a 30-year 10% mortgage with 25% of your total family income for house payments (principal, interest, taxes and insurance).
Reprinted courtesy of the Chicago Title Insurance Company, copyright 1980.

TABLE 7-2 (continued)
12% APR

IF YOUR FAMILY INCOME IS...	YOU SHOULD BE ABLE TO HANDLE MONTHLY PAYMENTS OF...	AND YOU'LL NEED A DOWN PAYMENT OF ABOUT...	TO AFFORD A HOME COSTING... (THOUSANDS OF $)	IF YOU CAN MAKE A BIGGER DOWN PAYMENT, YOU CAN AFFORD A HOME IN THE HIGHER RANGES BELOW. (THOUSANDS OF $)	
				INCREASE D.P. $10,000	INCREASE D.P. $20,000
$15,000	$ 310	$ 5,800	$ 28–31	$ 36–39	$ 43–48
20,000	420	7,800	37–41	45–50	53–58
25,000	520	10,000	46–51	55–60	62–69
30,000	625	12,000	56–62	64–71	72–79
35,000	730	14,000	65–72	73–81	81–89
40,000	830	16,200	74–82	83–92	91–100
45,000	940	18,200	83–92	92–101	99–110
50,000	1040	20,000	92–102	101–112	109–120

Note: Based on 20% down payment and a 30-year 12% mortgage with 25% of your total family income for house payments (principal, interest, taxes and insurance).

TABLE 7–2 (continued)
14% APR

IF YOUR FAMILY INCOME IS. . .	YOU SHOULD BE ABLE TO HANDLE MONTHLY PAYMENTS OF. . .	AND YOU'LL NEED A DOWN PAYMENT OF ABOUT. . .	TO AFFORD A HOME COSTING. . . (THOUSANDS OF $)	IF YOU CAN MAKE A BIGGER DOWN PAYMENT, YOU CAN AFFORD A HOME IN THE HIGHER RANGES BELOW. (THOUSANDS OF $)	
				INCREASE D.P. $10,000	INCREASE D.P. $20,000
$15,000	$ 310	$ 5,400	$ 25–28	$ 33–37	$ 41–46
20,000	420	7,200	33–37	41–46	50–55
25,000	520	9,000	42–46	50–55	58–64
30,000	625	10,800	50–55	58–64	66–73
35,000	730	12,600	58–64	66–73	75–83
40,000	830	14,400	66–73	75–82	83–91
45,000	940	16,200	75–83	83–92	99–101
50,000	1040	18,200	83–92	91–101	100–110

Note: Based on a 20% down payment and 30-year 14% mortgage with 25% of your total family income for house payments (principal, interest, taxes and insurance).

TABLE 7-2 (continued)
16% APR

IF YOUR FAMILY INCOME IS...	YOU SHOULD BE ABLE TO HANDLE MONTHLY PAYMENTS OF...	AND YOU'LL NEED A DOWN PAYMENT OF ABOUT...	TO AFFORD A HOME COSTING... (THOUSANDS OF $)	IF YOU CAN MAKE A BIGGER DOWN PAYMENT, YOU CAN AFFORD A HOME IN THE HIGHER RANGES BELOW. (THOUSANDS OF $)	
				INCREASE D.P. $10,000	INCREASE D.P $20,000
$15,000	$ 310	$ 4,800	$ 23-25	$ 31-34	$ 39-43
20,000	420	6,400	30-33	38-42	46-51
25,000	520	8,000	38-42	46-51	54-60
30,000	625	9,400	45-50	53-59	61-68
35,000	730	11,000	53-58	61-67	69-76
40,000	830	12,600	60-66	68-75	76-84
45,000	940	14,200	68-75	76-84	84-92
50,000	1040	15,800	75-83	83-92	91-101

Note: Based on a 20% down payment and 30-year 16% mortgage with 25% of your total family income for house payments (principal, interest, taxes and insurance).

must by law be added in, even though only a few years ago this was not common practice. If a wife plans to quit work for pregnancy or other reasons, calculating the loan liability on her income would be a mistake. Couples have a right to have both incomes included, but they also have a responsibility to show that the double income is a true picture of their financial reliability. Alimony, child support, part-time employment, and all other steady sources of income must be considered by law.

2. *Employment.* How long the borrower has had the same job is as important from the point of view of the lender as the type of work involved. Whether or not the work is steady and whether or not it is likely to result in increased income are important factors. Established employment (two or more years) with a successful company in an expanding field is most desirable.

3. *Credit.* Above all, the lender needs to be convinced that the money borrowed will be paid back. The borrower's ability to repay a loan is best proven with past experience in doing so. Young first-time buyers need to have established good credit records to meet this requirement. A furniture, appliance, or car purchase (better yet, all three) over time will accomplish this goal, and housing consumers should build their credit ratings carefully over a period of several years. Multiple debts at the time of loan application can defeat their purpose. Some first-time buyers are required to have cosigners for their mortgage if their credit standing is doubtful to the lender.

4. *Debt and net worth.* The lender wants to know as completely as possible what the borrower's financial posture is. The loan application includes information on checking and savings accounts, securities, and possessions such as cars and furniture. Debts include monthly payments for car purchases, bank credit cards, store pur-

Older houses might be viewed as being a risky investment from a lender's point of view. This older house is being remodeled to increase its present and future value to both the lender and the homebuyer. Photo by author.

chases, installment buying of any sort, and personal loans. The net worth is arrived at by subtracting everything owed from everything owned. The lender looks for the borrower's capacity to handle housing costs, taking into account the regular monthly picture of what money is coming in and what money is going out. Most lenders set a limit of 35 percent of gross monthly income to be used for all installment debts lasting longer than seven months, including the house payment.

5. *Purchasing and related housing costs.* The borrower must have the down payment. Most lenders want to be assured that the borrower has saved at least that amount of money and also has that much personal investment in the property. Many first-time buyers have been given money gifts by their relatives to aid in their "saving" for a down payment. Another immediate out-of-pocket expense is closing or settlement costs. These are outlined in detail elsewhere in this chapter. The several hundred dollars they cost the buyer must be available.

The related housing costs of property

taxes, insurance, and utility costs are estimated by the lender in determining the borrower's ability to repay the loan. These, like installment debts, are figured into the applicant's monthly financial picture.

6. *The house*. Not the least worry for the lender is the age and condition of the house, and the quality and character of its neighborhood. Is it a good investment? The risk the lender takes involves assessing the house's long-range value, should it become the lender's property anytime during the long period of repayment. The lender protects the buyer from a poor investment by protecting the institution's best interests.

First-time home buyers would be wise to investigate financing alternatives with the lenders in their area. A knowledgeable and honest discussion of mortgaging alternatives, mortgage provisions, and borrowing capability paves the way for making a decision on which lender should be used for a loan application. The house shopper would not actually apply for the loan until a specific house choice was made, and a **contract of sale** was signed.

The Steps in Home Buying

A **contract of sale** is the legal document which binds the seller and the buyer to an agreed-upon price. It is also called an "agreement of sale," a "purchase agreement," and "contract of purchase." At the time of signing, the buyer pays so-called **"earnest money"** or **"binder,"** an amount adequate to demonstrate serious intent to buy. This deposit may not be refundable in case the buyer does not obtain financing, or if for any other reason the deal falls through, unless the contract so states. The earnest money becomes part of the down payment when the sale is completed.

The contract should include all provisions important to both buyer and seller. Verbal agreements should be put in writing about such critical matters as when the

closing will take place. This is typically thirty days from the date of signing the contract but either party may have good reason to need less or more time than that. Exactly what is included in the house should be identified—draperies, appliances, and other accessories to the house and land. Minor repairs can be required by the buyer along with insurance coverage until the date of closing. Termite inspection and needed treatment, if any, should also be covered in the contract. The buyer may wish to state contingencies which allow voiding of the contract without loss of earnest money. An example of such a contingency is failure to obtain financing.

The buyers fill out a loan application with the lender of their choice. The type of loan requested is indicated at this time. FHA and VA loans require more time to process than conventional loans (from three to six weeks or longer). When the loan application is submitted, the lender must make a good faith effort to accurately estimate what the closing costs will be so that the buyer is prepared to pay them at the time of closing. A credit check on the buyers is made and all information on the application verified.

The next step in the loan-approval process is an **appraisal** of the house. This is an important step, because if the appraisal by the lender is less than the selling price, the loan amount may be less than the buyer had counted on. For instance, an appraisal of $75,000 on a house to be bought for $80,000 could mean an 80 percent mortgage for $60,000 instead of $64,000. The buyer would have to have $4,000 more for a down payment than anticipated, $20,000 instead of $16,000. Lenders vary in their appraisal methods and in the conservatism of their point of view. Preliminary discussions with lenders could clarify a lender's standard approach to appraisal. Finally, a loan commitment is issued offering the terms of the loan.

The closing is the final step in the home buying procedure. This refers to the actual transfer of the property from one party to another. Rather large amounts of money change hands, papers are signed, and all legal aspects of the sale are completed. The buyer signs the mortgage note agreeing to repay the loan in a specified period of time at agreed upon interest. **Closing costs** are paid. The **deed** to the property is transferred from seller to buyer.

The Real Estate Settlement Procedures Act of 1974 (RESPA) affected real estate sales in all states, even though there are differences in what is included in closing cost and local practices. The good faith effort of the lender to estimate closing costs at the time the loan application is submitted is only one part of the RESPA requirements. Borrowers as well as sellers may also see the exact closing charges one business day ahead of actual closing. The lender is also required to provide a truth in lending disclosure wherein the annual percentage rate (APR) is accurately stated.

Consumers are protected under RESPA against the practice of kickbacks and referrals in which a specific person or business is referred for the consumer's use. The lender may not require the purchase of title insurance from any particular company. Buyers are not required to deposit excess amounts of money in an impound or escrow account. RESPA has specific guidelines as to what is a reasonable deposit regarding the date of house purchase, the due dates for payments of taxes and insurance, and predictable amounts of these bills. RESPA also specifies legal remedies for violations of its consumer protection provisions.

The Selling Process

First-time home buyers all too soon may become first-time home sellers. In today's mobile society, a change of residence is very common, and a couple or young family are more likely to make a move to a different area or to a larger house than an older group of home owners. Many of the steps taken in selling a home affect the home buyer, so this discussion of selling includes information valuable in the buying process as well.

Real Estate Agents. One of the first decisions a home owner will make after deciding to sell is whether or not to list the property with a professional **realtor. Real estate agents,** brokers, and salespersons have the advantage of knowing the local housing market, being responsible for the selling process, coming in contact with prospective buyers, and advertising the property properly. They can be fair, unemotional participants in the price negotiating process. But these services cost money, and in the light of very high priced houses, the standard 6 or 7 percent fee can represent thousands of dollars to the seller. The home owner may choose to sell the house without professional advice and service, and set the price a little lower, in effect sharing the saved fees with the buyer. When there is a sellers' market, that is there are few houses for sale and many prospective buyers in the area, selling without a realtor is more prevalent. Some areas have firms which charge low fees for minimal service to aid home owners in selling their homes themselves.

Listing with an agent can be done several ways. The way most commonly used is multiple listing. The agency with whom the house is listed shares the selling information with all other multiple listing agencies in the area so the seller has the advantage of the widest possible contact with prospective buyers. Another agency can sell the home and the **commission** is split with the listing agency. An exclusive listing refers to limiting the sale to one agency, or to one salesperson within an agency.

The Closing Process

A TYPICAL CLOSING is a meeting between the buyer(s), seller(s), representatives or agents for the lender (and title insurance company in some cases) and the real estate broker. THE PURPOSE OF THE MEETING IS TO TRANSFER TITLE (OWNERSHIP) OF THE PROPERTY FROM THE SELLER TO YOU, THE BUYER.

In some states the broker may represent both you and the seller; or the closing process may be handled by an "escrow agent."

- The lender's agent will ask for your paid Insurance Policy (or binder) on the house.
- The agent will list the *adjustments* (what you owe the seller: remainder of the down payment, pre-paid taxes, etc.; and what the seller owes you: unpaid taxes, pre-paid rents, etc.).
- You will sign the *mortgage* or *deed of trust* (the legal document giving the lender the right to take back your property if you fail to make your mortgage payments).
- You will also sign the *mortgage note* (the promise to repay the loan in regular monthly payments of a certain amount).
- You will then be "loaned" the money to pay the seller for the house.
- The *Title* (proof of ownership of the property) passes from the seller to you, usually in the form of a *Deed* (the document that transfers the title) signed by the seller.
- The lender's agent will collect the "closing costs" from you, and give you a *Loan Disclosure Statement* (a list of all the items you have paid for. Be sure to keep this).
- The deed and mortgage will then be *recorded* (put on file) in the town or county Registry of Deeds.
- Federal law requires your lender to provide you with a "good faith estimate" of your closing costs. Normally, you will receive this soon after your loan application has been submitted to the lender (RESPA).
- Since most closing costs cannot usually be paid for by a personal check, be sure you bring a CERTIFIED CHECK with you to the closing.

WHAT DO CLOSING COSTS INCLUDE? (Lawyer's fees, title insurance, mortgage application fees, appraisal fees, real estate taxes, and other costs *over* the purchase price of the property).

SOME TYPICAL ITEMS ARE:

- Legal Fees—what the lender charges for preparing and recording legal documents, searching the title, and other services performed to *protect the lender's interests*.
- Origination Fee— lender's charge to make the loan (usually 1% of the mortgage).
- Appraisal Fees— charge by the lender for an *inspection* of the property to determine its value. (FHA and VA appraisal fees are fixed by law.)
- Inspection Fees—cost of any other inspections required by local housing codes, government agencies, or individual lenders, such as termite or lead paint inspections (if you haven't already paid for them yourself).
- Mortgage Insurance— fee to the company or government agency which *insures the loan* in case you fail to make your payments.
- Credit Report—all lenders require a credit history of the buyer; this may be included in the application fee.
- Application Fee—the charge by the lender for *processing your loan application*.
- Survey Fees—the lender may require a registered survey or a map showing the

location of the house and the boundaries of the property.

Excerpted from: U.S.

Department of Housing and Urban Development, Homebuyer's Information Package: A Guidebook for Buying and Owning a

Home, (Washington, D.C.: U.S. Government Printing Office, 1979), pp. 62–63.

Purchase Negotiation. Whether sold by the owner or by a real estate agent, the house's price is negotiated, usually in a series of steps. The prospective buyer may make an offer much below the advertised price. The seller usually "counter offers" instead of agreeing to the first offer. Then the prospective buyer might counter offer the counter offer. So it goes until the price is agreed upon, usually somewhere between the two starting points. When a house sells for very nearly its asking price, it can be an indication of how tight the market is, or how desperately the buyers wanted it. If the house sells for far below the asking price, it may mean it was priced unrealistically high in the first place, or that the seller, in desperation, was willing to settle below the original price. The point is that although the house is a specific commodity in a limited housing market, the setting of price is an emotional process into which a great many factors enter on both sides.

Equity. The amount of equity the seller has in the house becomes one of the most important factors in determining how many options for method of purchase are open to a new home buyer. Equity is the actual amount of the house's cash value owned at any time, and in this case, at the time of resale. It can be determined by the market value, minus the outstanding principal on the mortgage. It also can be determined by adding the original down payment, the amount of principal paid off on the mortgage and the increased value of the home,

or **appreciation.** A house purchased for $80,000, with a $16,000 down payment (80 percent loan, $64,000) can be used as a simple example. By the time the house is sold, its value has appreciated to $80,000. Assuming $4,000 had by then been paid toward the principal borrowed, the equity could be figured two ways:

Value of the house	$100,000
Less unpaid loan	60,000
Equity	$40,000
Down payment	$16,000
Principal paid	4,000
Appreciation	20,000
Equity	$40,000

Mortgage Assumption. One option available to the buyer is to assume the existing mortgage. If this can be done with the original interest rate, probably lower than the interest rate charged on a new mortgage, there is a definite advantage to the buyer. There may also be substantial savings in closing costs. But the down payment to cover this arrangement would have to be the owner's equity. As can be seen in the example above, such a down payment can be very high indeed.

One way a buyer might be able to take advantage of assuming the original mortgage is to finance part of the down payment with a second mortgage. In order to be able to assume the mortgage, the buyer would have to have some amount of down payment. Even if it were only ten percent of the selling price, the rest could be borrowed on a short term basis, and at a high interest rate. The buyer would have very high house payments for the term of the second mortgage. After that, the house payments would drop to the amount of the original first mortgage, and by that time the costs would be very low when compared to then current housing costs, assuming inflation, whether rampant or normal, had driven house prices up.

The seller might be willing to carry (or "take back") a second mortgage. The seller in effect loans part of the equity to the new buyer, but earns high interest in the process. The second mortgage may be arranged with interest only paid for a specified time with the principal due at the end of the period. Other second mortgages are fully amortized during the term. The wrap-around mortgage described above has been used by some sellers. Many sellers want and need full equity in order to be able to purchase another, probably more expensive, house, and such sellers would find carrying a second mortgage undesirable. The buyer could find another party to carry the second mortgage, such as a realty firm or a private investor.

The buyer, of course, can obtain a new mortgage. The terms of the mortgage would be negotiated in the same way the original buyer had negotiated them. The lender may not be the same one, in which case, the seller would have to pay prepayment penalty, if required, at the closing.

Points. When a lender contracts for a mortgage at a fixed interest rate, the investment may not be the best one compared to higher earning alternatives. This is nearly always the case where interest rates are fixed by law, such as in FHA and VA mortgages. Because the money is lent at a rate lower than could be otherwise earned, points are

charged, which are a fee paid at the time of closing. Each point is one percent of the amount of the money borrowed, for example, $600 for each point on a $60,000 mortgage. If a few points are charged, the fee is not large, but if the money market is tight, many points may be charged (10 points in this case would be $6,000). Since FHA and VA programs are designed specifically to keep the intial costs down for home buyers, home buyers are not allowed by law to pay the points. The seller pays them.

Some sellers simply refuse to sell through these programs in order to avoid paying points. Other sellers set their prices higher than they might with conventional financing in order to pass on the costs of points to the buyer. In any case, points can be a critical issue in arriving at a house price and a financial arrangement with the seller. In recent years even conventional mortgages have required points (often called "loan fees"). The buyer generally pays for them when doing so is not prohibited by law.

Points are also referred to by lenders as discounted loans. In effect, less money is actually transferred in the closing than is written on the mortgage note, and the difference is made up with cash out of the buyer's or seller's pocket. Even though paying of points can vary from time to time and from lender to lender, the practice seems to be a permanent part of the home financing process. Housing consumers are well advised to understand the practice, but to shop for lowest possible points in a given time and place.

Other Costs. The real property taxes on a piece of property are paid for a year, often in two installments. Hazard insurance is another annual expense. If the seller has paid for these items prior to the date of clos-

The additional costs of property taxes and hazard insurance are part of the financial responsibilities of home ownership. When buying a home, these costs for the year are divided between the seller and the buyer. Photo courtesy of U.S. Department of Housing and Urban Development.

ing, there should be an adjustment made to reimburse the seller for the portion of the year to be used by the buyer. If the amounts owed the seller for the remaining time of taxes and insurance paid are not written into the closing costs, some other compensation for these costs to the seller should be made.

OTHER MEANS OF SINGLE-FAMILY HOME OWNERSHIP

There are several other ways in which housing consumers attain the goal of single-family home ownership. Three are discussed here. They are: purchase through land contract, leasing land and purchasing only the house, and purchase of undeveloped land for future house construction.

Installment Land Contract

A house may be sold to a buyer without a mortgage involved. The seller extends credit to the buyer, and the installment land contract, signed by both parties, sets up the schedule of payments, the length of time for repayment, interest rates, and so on. In effect, the homeowner becomes the lending institution. The buyer must maintain the property, pay its property taxes and insurance, and agree to pay for the house in full by agreed upon date, often only a few years later. At that time, the buyer may obtain a mortgage to pay for the house. The seller does not transfer title to the property until the term of the contract is up. Property is sold by land contract in some states more commonly than in others. A land contract sale may be necessary when mortgage money is tight. The seller may charge higher interest than a lending institution, but the buyer has the advantage of purchasing a house with a delayed promise to obtain a mortgage.

Leased-Land Home Purchase

A home buying device that is not new, but that has gained acceptance, is the leasing of land with the purchase of a home. It is commonly used in Hawaii, and it has also been used in Arizona and some parts of California. In development near Minneapolis-St. Paul, thousands of dollars (as much as $15,000) were saved on the purchase price of houses by leasing the land for 99 years.[11] In this case there was an option to buy at any time. Most long-term leases are of a type in which the tenants, in these cases the home buyers, pay all taxes, assessment, and other operating expenses associated with the property.

Land Purchase for Future Construction

Land purchase as a form of attaining an owned, single-family house is rarely used by first-time buyers: nevertheless, it appeals to some home buyers, particularly those who want to build a house of their own design. Traditionally, land was purchased and

The purchase of land for the purpose of building a uniquely designed home may be done with a packaged mortgage. The land is bought, and the house is constructed with one long-term mortgage. Photo by author.

A Self-Contractor's Aptitude Test

1. Do you or your spouse have enough free time to spend up to 2 hours a day at the building site?
2. Are you good at fixing things around the house?
3. Is your credit rating strong enough to persuade a skeptical banker to give you a mortgage?
4. Are you well organized and methodical?
5. Do you like to coordinate complicated projects involving many other people?
6. Are you persistent and willing to nag people to get things done even at the risk of annoying them?
7. Can you and your spouse compromise on disagreements without letting them escalate into major battles?
8. Would you look on a major construction project as an exciting challenge rather than a burdensome task?

If you have more than 2 "no" answers, you probably are not cut out to be a do-it-yourself contractor. If you answered "no" on more than 4 questions or are the kind of person, as one builder put it, "who needs a contractor to fix a sticky door," hire someone else to do the job.

Excerpted from "Being Your Own General Contractor" by Jerry Edgerton, Money Magazine, *Sept. 1976, by special permission. Copyright © 1976 Time Inc. All rights reserved.*

completely paid for before house construction began, and often lenders made land ownership a condition of loaning money for construction and for mortgaging the house itself. Today, it is more common for the lender to agree to a packaged mortgage in which the land is bought, the construction begun and the long-term mortgage arranged all at once.

Some young families are willing to delay home construction by either renting an apartment while they pay off the land purchase loan, or where zoning permits, by living in a mobile home on the land until the time they can build the house of their dreams. If an unusual home with unique features is desired (architect designed or not), this method of home ownership should be considered. Even a stock plan from a building contractor can be turned into a "custom designed" house reflecting the personal preferences of the home buyer.

SUMMARY

The decision to buy depends on a number of factors. Job permanence, space needs, stage of the life cycle, lifestyle, housing values and psychological needs can all contribute to a readiness for home ownership. The renting alternative has many advantages for families whose lifestyle, stage of the life cycle, and so on, require flexi-

bility, freedom from responsibility, recreational facilities, and, above all, lower cost.

The conventional home mortgage can be arranged with different lengths of time for repayment, different interest rates, different loan to value ratios and down payments. FHA and VA mortgages usually have interest rates, down payment, and terms of repayment advantageous to the moderate-income housing consumer. Since they are government-supported programs, additional paperwork and loan requirements are imposed on the borrower.

Variable and adjustable rate mortgages (VRM, ARM) are used by lenders so that higher (or lower) interest rates can be charged in the future reflecting changes in economic conditions. A graduated payment mortgage (GPM) allows for low initial payments with periodic increases to a level higher than normal. A rollover mortgage is one in which the interest rates are adjusted after a predetermined period of time, such as every five years. Flexible mortgages permit interest only payment for the early period of the loan, and then complete repayment on a fixed schedule. Both FLIP and "wrap-around" mortgages have had limited use in assisting first-time buyers. Reverse annuity mortgages (RAMs) benefit elderly people living in paid-for homes with high equities because they can be used to supplement retirement income.

Several mortgage provisions may be written into the agreement which benefit the borrower: allowing assumption of a mortgage, no repayment penalty, flexibility and open-ended clauses, and packaged mortgages. Impound or escrow accounts are an advantage to the lender in that money is paid monthly to pay annual costs of hazard insurance and real property taxes.

The lender determines whether or not a mortgage applicant qualifies. Income level, employment record, good credit rating, amount of debt and net worth are all carefully evaluated. Above all, the lender has to judge the soundness of the house as an investment and the reliability of the borrower in paying back many thousands of dollars over a long period of time.

Wise home buyers comparison shop among local mortgage lenders to determine the best available terms for their borrowing needs. The selection of a house is followed by appropriate legal steps to secure the purchase, obtain the loan, and close the sale during which property is transferred to the buyer. Closing costs include many items, and they can be a sizable portion of the total initial costs of home ownership. RESPA offers protection to consumers in the home purchasing transaction.

Listing a home for sale with a real estate agent can be done in several ways, with multiple listing reaching the widest possible market. The sale price is usually reached through a series of offers and counter offers. Buyers of existing homes may purchase in three major ways: (1) by assuming the existing loan, requiring a very large down payment; (2) supplementing the assumed mortgage with a second mortgage to help with part of the down payment; or (3) by refinancing with an entirely new loan. The seller needs to consider the possibility of paying points, required in FHA and VA loans, when setting an asking price. Other costs of selling include realtor's fees, repairs, and some closing costs.

Home ownership can also be achieved with an installment land contract, in which the seller finances the buyer without transferring title of the property. Purchase of a home on leased land can save money for the home buyer. Some families prefer to buy undeveloped land to be used for the construction of a house at a later time. This method may be desirable if a unique house design is the home buyer's goal.

Notes

1. U.S. Department of Housing and Urban Development, *1978 Statistical Yearbook* (Washington, D.C.: U.S. Government Printing Office, 1978), p. 65.

2. Dasso, J., A. A. Ring, and D. McFall, *Fundamentals of Real Estate* (Englewood Cliffs, N J: Prentice-Hall, 1977), p. 337.
3. "The New Mortgages: Betting on Inflation," *Housing*, 1979, *56* (2), pp. 61–62.
4. Dasso, et al., *Fundamentals of Real Estate*, p. 308.
5. "An Old Mortgage Learns a Few New Tricks," *Housing*, 1980, *58* (3), p. 11.
6. Ibid., p. 12.
7. McFarland, S. A., "Alternative Mortgage Instruments Offer Key to Expanded Lending Market," *Mortgage Banker*, 1978, 38 (12), p. 10.
8. Ibid.
9. "Can You Really Afford It?" in Better Homes and Gardens Building Ideas, *How to Buy and Sell Your Home* (Des Moines, Iowa: Special Interest Publication, Meredith Corporation, 1979), p. 98.
10. Hess, N. R., *The Home Buyer's Guide* (Englewood Cliffs, N.J.: Prentice-Hall, 1976), pp. 5–9.
11. "Minneapolis Buying on Leased Lots," *Housing*, 1979, *55* (2), p. 22.

Suggested Readings

Better Homes and Gardens Building Ideas. *How to Buy and Sell Your Home*. Des Moines, Iowa: Meredith Corporation, 1979.

Creative Financing. *Real Estate Today*, 1980, *13* (3) 24–31.

Dasso, J., Ring, A. A., and McFall, D. *Fundamentals of Real Estate*. Englewood Cliffs, N.J.: Prentice-Hall, 1977.

Davis, J. C., and Walker, C. *Buying Your House: A Complete Guide to Inspection & Evaluation*. New York: Berkeley Windover Books, 1978.

"A Guide to the Mortgage Maze." *Housing*, 1981, *59* (6) 70–74.

Harl, H. E. "Some Legal Aspects of House Buying." In C. S. Wedin and L. G. Nygren, eds. *Housing Perspectives* (2nd ed.). Minneapolis: Burgess, 1979.

Lee, S. L. *Buyer's Handbook for the Single-family Home*. New York: Van Nostrand Reinhold, 1979.

Meeks, C. B., and Bilderback, R. *Alternative Mortgage Instruments: Consumer Bane or Boon* (Conference Proceedings). Ithaca, N.Y.: Department of Consumer Economics and Housing, New York State College of Human Ecology, 1979.

Sumichrast, M., and Shafer, R. G. *The Complete Book of Home Buying*. Princeton, N.J.: Dow Jones Books, 1980.

Tuck, C., ed. *The Fannie Mae Guide to Buying, Financing & Selling Your Home*. Garden City, N.Y.: Dolphin Books, 1978.

U.S. Department of Housing and Urban Development. *Homebuyer's Information Package: A Guidebook for Buying and Owning a Home*. Washington, D.C.: U.S. Government Printing Office, 1979.

U.S. Department of Housing and Urban Development. *Settlement Costs* (revised ed.). Washington, D.C.: U.S. Government Printing Office, 1978.

U.S. Department of Labor. *Rent or Buy? Evaluating Alternatives in the Shelter Market*. Washington, D.C.: U.S. Government Printing Office, 1979.

Home Ownership in Other Forms

8

Home ownership has traditionally been associated with single-family, detached housing throughout American housing history. Home ownership, however, can be achieved in other forms, specifically condominiums, cooperatives and mobile homes. Such alternative types of ownership have in part replaced ownership of single-family, detached dwellings, and this trend may be the most important aspect of American housing in transition.

The scale of condominium building or mobile home sales are evidence of the trend. No doubt many owners bought such housing in the hope of some time in the future acquiring a single-family, detached house. Having experienced an alternative form, however, it may be that given the option to acquire their old dream, they choose to stay in the housing they have.

Each of the major alternative forms of home ownership has distinct financing and legal characteristics. These will be discussed separately in the first three chapter sections. "**Kit**" houses are also a trend worth noting. The purchase of a packaged house to be erected on the site by a contractor or the owners themselves, is an alternative form of ownership especially appealing to young people. Kit houses are discussed in the fourth section of this chapter. Then the related costs of home ownership in all its forms are considered. Finally, the financial advantages of home ownership will be discussed as a way of concluding both chapters 7 and 8.

The geodesic dome shown in one form of kit house. Photo courtesy of Cathedralite, Inc., Capitola, Ca.

Horizontal Property

To most people the idea of condominiums is relatively new—a product of American real estate ingenuity in the past two decades. If you're one who thinks so, you're off by nearly 4,000 years.

The earliest known record of the condominium has been traced to Babylonian documents dated to 2000 B.C., which show the sale of the first floor of a house with the owner retaining the title to the second floor. A papyrus in the Brooklyn Museum, dated 434 B.C., describes an apartment, its boundaries and specific instructions about the right of sale—and even title insurance.

As the Roman Empire grew, desirable land, especially near the Forum, become scarce and expensive. The squeeze led the Senate to pass a law that permitted Romans to own their own homes in multiunit buildings. Retired Roman generals were often given an apartment—a condominium—in the city as reward for their service to the Empire.

In western Europe's walled cities during the Middle Ages, condominiums were popular. Early in the 20th century, the condo concept spread to Spain, Italy, Belgium, the Netherlands and France, where statutes were enacted to permit them.

When the condominium reached Latin America, it was dubbed "horizontal property." Brazil adopted "horizontal property" legislation as early as 1928, and Chile followed with similar legislation in 1937. In Venezuela, condominiums are about the only type of house that one can buy.

There were a few condominiums in the U.S. in 1947, but there were no laws governing them. Puerto Rico enacted condo legislation in 1951 and then again in 1958. It took until the Sixties before the condominium gained a foothold in the U.S. In 1962 the Federal Housing Administration drew up a condominium statute based on the Puerto Rican laws that has since served as a model for states enacting their own laws. By 1967 all 50 states had enacted some form of condominium legislation.

It wasn't until the mid-Seventies that the condo impact was felt. In 1970 there were only 85,000 condo units in the entire U.S., according to census figures. By April of 1975, there were 1.25 million condo units. Today there are nearly 2 million.

Source: Tamarkin, B., "Condomania in Chicago," Reprinted by permission of Forbes Magazine from the Nov. 13, 1978 issue.

CONDOMINIUMS

Nearly everyone has seen a housing development advertised as a condominium, and because the type of structure seen becomes synonomous with that term, there is a popular assumption that a condominium refers to a type of housing rather than a type of ownership. A condominium is not necessarily a highrise building, nor a townhouse development including open space, nor a large-scale retirement community, even though the condominium method of ownership could be used with any of these housing types.

Condominium ownership is of two kinds: (1) ownership of the individual interior space in which the family lives, and (2) a share in the structure, facilities, and grounds associated with the individual housing unit (common elements). What is privately owned is the enclosed space, what is jointly owned is everything that surrounds it. The owner has an individual mortgage

The home owners association to which every condominium owner belongs manages and maintains all the shared grounds and facilities. The rules for use of the clubhouse and pool in this condominium are decided by the home owners as a group. Photo by author.

and a deed to the individual space. The owner also has a proportionate share of ownership of the common elements. The rights and privileges of that ownership are the same as with a single-family, detached dwelling on its own land—it may be leased, sold, bequeathed, and remodeled.

The shared ownership of buildings, facilities and grounds can be managed only if all participants are involved. Therefore, every condominium owner automatically belongs to the **home owners' association** for which the board of directors acts on behalf of the membership. The actual management of the condominium might be hired, but the board of directors decides whom to hire. The costs of maintenance are paid for by all owners. The monthly **home owners or maintenance fee,** covers the cost of landscaping, grounds maintenance, repairs, repainting, taxes and insurance on the common elements, and regular costs of water, sewage, and trash disposal.

The shared ownership and management aspects of condominiums have been an area

of disappointment for many buyers. In some cases, low management fees have been quoted at the time of purchase (intentionally or not) so that residents find their expected housing costs greatly increased a few months after moving in. Some condominiums have been sold and monthly fees charged, but with the management retained by the developer until the project was nearly sold out. In such cases the first buyers may wait a year or two before having any say about management policies. Even where the home owners function in a democratic fashion, the policies thus derived may not please every owner. Minor details such as scheduling of pool use or choice of entryway plants can become major sources of housing dissatisfaction. Prospective condominium home owners should be aware of all governing policies before investing.

Because the home owners share management decision making, there is also a tendency for the residents to be socially connected. Even though residents are not necessarily one big happy family (quite the contrary can be the case), there is less personal privacy and autonomy than might be achieved in other forms of ownership. Visual and aural privacy may or may not be well provided for in the structural design. This too should be checked out by prospective buyers as well as the general age level and lifestyle characteristics of other residents. A middle-aged childless couple might be miserable living among young families with children. Some condominiums restrict ownership to adults with no children under sixteen.

There are many advantages to condominiums. The most often cited one is price. Many housing consumers have bought condominiums in highly desirable areas where a single-family house purchase would have been prohibitive. Even though very expensive condominiums are common in some resort areas, and they are bought as second homes, the average price of condominium units within urban areas is below the average price of single-family housing.

The maintenance-free aspect of condominiums is attractive to many people for different reasons. Employed couples may not have time for or interest in yard maintenance, and as mentioned before, their priorities might favor hobbies, sports, recreation, and social contact over home care. Many condominium residents are previous single-family home owners. Having spent many years devoted to the care and feeding of a suburban plot of land, empty-nesters and retirees may prefer to turn over such chores to others and to pay for them gladly. Lifestyle, too, can determine a preference for built-in recreational facilities that might not be attainable on an individual basis.

The financing of condominiums is the same as single-family house financing. Owners obtain their own mortgage loans, but sometimes one lending institution may handle all the loans for a new project. Generally, 80 or 90 percent loans are available at the same interest rates as for house mortgages. The mortgage terms can be arranged with the same flexibility and care of a standard mortgage. The availability of FHA and VA financing for condominiums is one factor in their recent growth and popularity. Newer forms of financing—GPM, ARM, and so on—could also be applied to condominium purchases.

Besides the standard forms used in home buying, condominium purchases involve additional legal papers. One form is a **nonbinding reservation** which allows the buyer to hold a condominium even before construction is completed and allows the builder to verify the saleability of the project to the construction lender well before the project has begun. If the project falls through, the buyer can have the deposit re-

Each condominium owner independently buys and sells the individual unit along with the share in ownership of the common areas. Many different realtors may be involved in resales in one development. Photo by author.

funded, but this should be so stated in the form. The sales contract, much like a single-family house sales contract, may contain a statement that the buyer acknowledges receipt and acceptance of the organizational documents. These documents are important to the buyer and the sales contract should not be signed until they have been studied, with professional help if necessary, and accepted.

The legal instrument that converts the real property into condominium ownership has many names: the declaration of conditions, covenants and restrictions, the enabling declaration, the master deed, or the plan of condominium ownership.[1] This document extends the effective condominium laws, which can vary from state to state, to a particular project, and establishes the home owners association. It should describe the individual units as well

The Epidemic Has Spread Nationwide
Everybody's Buying, Selling, Building Condos

BY DIANE WHITE
The Boston Globe

Whiling away a few minutes in an incredibly *au courant* bar, I overheard the beginnings of what promised to be a fascinating conversation.

"How big is yours?" the woman asked.

"Enormous," the man said. "I'll show it to you sometime if you want."

"How about tonight?" said the woman.

To make a short story as short as possible, they were talking about his condominium.

I was more disappointed than surprised at the direction their conversation took, because lately it seems as if everybody is talking about condominiums. The calls of condo buyers fill the air:

"Mortgage rates are going down!"

"Has your building been converted yet?"

"Should I buy the adjoining unit and break through the wall?"

"Hardwood floors!"

"Working fireplace!"

"Water view!"

"Roof deck!"

When I first heard the word "condomania" I assumed it referred to certain developers who, seized by greed, are frantically converting any property they can grab—

wharves, warehouses, subway stations, outhouses, chicken coops—into condos.

Now I realize that condomania strikes those who buy even more severely than those who sell. Everybody wants to get in on the action. Condominiums have replaced drugs, divorce, roller skating, sex, vasectomies, weight lifting, joint custody, high fiber diets, baseball, even Cuisinarts as a conversational topic. (What's the point of having a Cuisinart if you don't have a condo to keep it in?)

Not having a condominium puts you at a certain social disadvantage. If you don't own a condo what can you talk about? Who'll want to talk to you?

Condomaniacs have an esprit de corps that makes the U.S. Marines seem like a bunch of anarchists by comparison. Within minutes strangers become blood brothers swapping lies about heating bills, discussing wiring defects, comparing square footage.

Condo owners don't talk rooms; they talk square feet.

I asked a friend how many rooms he has in his

condominium. "About 1,200 square feet," he said.

What does that mean? How big is that compared to a football field? A tennis court? A telephone booth? Only another condomaniac knows.

Even more than talking square feet, condo owners enjoy telling tall stories made even taller by hindsight:

It just went for $125,000 and I could have bought it three years ago for nothing. How was I to know people would pay that to live in an abattoir?"

If you confess to condomaniacs that you rent and have no intention of buying, they tend to treat you like a simpleton who hasn't got the brains to telephone a real estate agent. Or they try to convert you.

They will lecture you about the wisdom of property ownership, the benefits of equity, the romance of being part of the condo-owning class. They will try to convince you that you're passing up the chance of a lifetime by not buying into their building.

For only $20,000 down and mammoth monthly payments the rest of your life, you could own three little rooms and a walk-in closet that doubles as a guest room for a midget. That price also includes the opportunity to attend monthly co-owners' meetings where you can argue with the man who wants to replace the laundry room with a hot tub, lock horns with the faction that wants to build a paddle tennis court on the roof and in general get to know your other neighbors as you never would in an apartment building.

That's the sort of opportunity that makes renting look like a good deal.

Reprinted courtesy of the Boston Globe.

as all commonly held property, and should specify arrangements for hazard and liability insurance on this property. The percentage of common interest an owner has may affect the weight of that owner's vote in policy making. This percentage may also determine the amount of monthly maintenance and the portion of real estate taxes to be paid as part of the shared ownership responsibility.

The association bylaws set up the internal condominium government. This little democracy, as has been explained, can have critical importance in the ultimate housing satisfaction of the owner. How the home owners' business will be conducted, and how their monthly assessments will be decided and used should be spelled out in detail and should meet the prospective owner's approval. Critical questions to be answered by this document include: when does the builder release controls, what extra fees (if any) are charged for recreational facilities, and what are the restrictions on renting or selling individual units.[2] House rules are specified in another governing document. Such rules can determine restrictions on pets, ages of children, and some personal living habits such as how loud and how late a stereo may be played.[3]

The purchase of a condominium conversion development requires some special considerations. Condominium conversions are rental housing units converted to ownership units, either to the previous tenants or to others. Typically, the structure may have been renovated, so the quality of the original structure as well as the new additions and equipment would have to be evaluated by potential buyers. The walls, roofs, heating and cooling systems, plumbing, and appliances should be checked. Are they improved or restored? Are they "like new" or are they new? "Make sure the building and the unit conform to local government requirements. A refurbished heating system not in compliance could be costly and inconvenient to the new unit owners association."[4]

COOPERATIVES

Cooperative ownership is now a less favored form than condominium ownership, but during the 1950s and 1960s it was used a great deal in some cities, particularly New York. The common ownership is much the same but with very different legal implications.

The building or buildings and the land on which they stand are owned by a group of people (shareholders) who form a closed corporation. The residents own shares in the corporation which owns the real property, but the shares they own entitle them to occupy a specified space. The more desirable the living space, the more shares that resident would own in relation to others. A blanket mortgage and one deed is used for the entire development. The shareholders (the residents) elect a board of directors which is responsible for management, as in the case of a condominium. A maintenance fee is assessed to each resident.

One disadvantage of cooperatives, as compared to condominiums, is that a resident cannot sell to another person without the approval of the board of directors. Since title to an individual piece of property is not obtained, it cannot be transferred to anyone. The resident's shares may be sold to a buyer meeting the approval of the board of directors.

The main advantage of cooperative ownership is essentially the same as condominium ownership. An investment can be made that will likely increase in value, but the housing itself is without individual maintenance responsibilities, excepting routine care of the individual living space. The corporation, through its board of directors, determines selling prices for shares, and rent levels if rentals are allowed. The same forces that drive up housing costs of other types would affect the costs of cooperative housing. Some cooperatives in New York City are among the most expensive housing in the country.

The financing of a cooperative purchase is different from home financing. Mortgages are not available for the purchase of shares in a corporation, even if the sole purpose of the corporation is ownership of real estate. Individuals may arrange personal loans for the purchase of their shares. In some areas, a special "co-op mortgage" may be used for this purpose.[5] The corporation can mortgage the property as a whole, and individuals then pay their share of the monthly mortgage obligation. The shareholders are charged a portion of operating expenses, real property taxes, and insurance costs.

They may use their share of interest and property taxes as an income tax deduction.

There is a major disadvantage of cooperative ownership. It is the liability shareholders have regarding defaults by other shareholders. Dasso, Ring, and McFall explain:

> The major difference between condominium and cooperative ownership is the relative independence from the group. . . . In cooperative ownership the corporation or

Any type of housing may be either a condominium or a cooperative. In a cooperative, owners buy shares of stock in the corporation that owns the property. Photo courtesy of U.S. Department of Housing and Urban Development.

When purchasing a mobile home, both the home and the park in which it is or will be located should be evaluated. The appearance, facilities, and management of the park may affect housing satisfaction. Photo by author.

trust owns the property. A mortgage or tax lien against the property is therefore the obligation of the corporation or trust. This implies that the failure of one owner to pay taxes or meet debt service becomes a burden on the other shareholders in the cooperative. The shareholders must make up the deficiency to protect their own interests. This group liability also extends to mechanics' liens or operating expenses.[6]

MOBILE HOMES

As housing prices have risen dramatically, more and more people have bought mobile homes as an ownership alternative. Mobile home owners represent a wide spectrum of lifestyles and stages in the life cycle. Young couples, especially, are finding that a well-constructed mobile home in a well-equipped park can be a satisfying housing choice.

The purchase of a mobile home involves many considerations and may be more complex than the purchase of a single-family, detached house in the suburbs. There are three ways a mobile home can be purchased: (1) from a private mobile home owner; (2) from a real estate agent selling used mobile homes, and (3) from a dealer selling new mobile homes. Each of these ways of buying has different characteristics.

The mobile home owner is both owner and renter if the unit is in a mobile home park. The purchase of a mobile home from a previous owner is similar to the purchase of a conventional house. If the cost of moving it is to be avoided both the home and the park have to be evaluated. The park's management affects the happiness of the residents in it, so checking out the management policies is as important as checking out the construction of the home to be lived in.

Purchase of a used mobile home through a real estate agent is similar to buying directly from an owner, except that the agent may offer helpful services such as showing several homes to choose from or sharing insightful information about the park and its management. With or without an agent, the sale of a used mobile home should be handled by written contract.

A purchase from a dealer is more complicated. First of all, the decision has to be made whether to buy a new mobile home on the dealer's lot or to order one from a factory. In the latter case, special features and finishes can be chosen, and a "custom designed" interior can be selected from available materials, carpeting, draperies, appliances, and, if desired, furnishings. The selection of a mobile home must be accompanied by a selection of a place to put it. The park chosen may not have an available and desirable space. The purchaser has to coordinate the space reservation with the mobile home delivery.

The setting up of a mobile home is an important step in its purchase. If anything goes wrong, the dealer should stand in back of the product and the agreement to set it up. Dealers without solid reputations for good and prompt service and a supply of spare parts should be avoided. A great deal of comparison shopping should take place for dealers, for manufacturers, for models available from any single manufacturer, and for parks with available spaces. The appropriateness of design and construction for a particular locale should be checked, keeping in mind that the place of manufacture may be several hundred miles away and in quite a different climate than the eventual place of residence. Federal Construction and Safety Standards must be met by all manufacturers in all regions.

Manufacturers warrant their products, but only for a period of one year. Defects in set-up are a dealer problem, but there should be a written agreement regarding this. Installation may require a permit and

an inspection by either state or local enforcement agencies.

Some parks require that covered carports, skirting, porches, and storage sheds be installed along with the mobile homes. Such requirements are desirable in that the better quality parks function and look better because of them, but the cost of the additional items should be calculated into the mobile home purchase.

Mobile home financing is similar to automobile financing. Even though the term of repayment has increased in recent years, usually to 15 years, interest rates have also gone up and they are generally higher than interest rates on mortgage loans. The terms of financing often involve higher monthly payments than conventional single-family home mortgaging does. In addition, the space rent must be added to monthly housing costs.

An advertisement for the "cadillac of mobile home parks" included this financing information for a $52,748.03 home, with a 20-year loan.

> You pay $10,549.60 down. Your finance charge is $71,091.17. Monthly payments will be $472.04. That's on a 12½% simple interest loan. Interest may vary. . . . Our lot prices range from $190–$260 a month. We will also offer a 1-year lease with two 1-year options.[7]

This advertisement is clearly directed at the affluent older person: it boasts of the clubhouse, lawn bowling green, swimming pool, exercise room, billiard room, tennis court, and more.[8]

For several decades there has been a pattern of mobile home **depreciation** but that pattern has been reversed in recent years. It is not unheard of to sell a mobile home in good condition, located in a desirable park, for much more than its original purchase price. Trends in mobile home market values vary by region; the type of mobile home and the park's location and amenities are also factors affecting market values. If investment is one motivation for buying a mobile home, factors affecting resale appeal should be considered.

Mobile homes are taxed by some states as vehicles or personal property. Thus real property taxes may be avoided except as they are paid through the monthly rental charge on the parking space. A few states tax mobile homes by their value, just as site-built homes are taxed. Should a mobile home be placed on private property, the tax on the land plus the vehicle tax on the mobile home would be part of the housing costs to be estimated. Maintenance costs are relatively low. The typical metal exterior has the advantage of requiring very little care. The park space around the house, if minimal, also requires very little planting and yard care.

Mobile home residents can easily look out for each other. Having a neighbor keep an eye on the house during absence may have more psychological than financial benefits, but for people with valuable furnishings and possessions this feature of mobile home park living may have real rewards.

Some mobile home subdivisions have been developed in Las Vegas and in Florida, and others are planned in the Washington, D.C. and Chicago suburban areas.[9] A mobile home subdivision allows the standard purchase of land in a suburban community to be combined with the relatively low-cost purchase of a mobile home to put on it. In Sunbelt states where housing demand has risen rapidly, mobile home subdivisions are a quick way to achieve acceptable housing for a moderate-income group. Many communities will not allow such subdivisions at the present time, but if a few areas find them an acceptable alterna-

tive housing form, the trend toward mobile home subdivisions may grow.

KIT HOUSES

"Kit house" is a term used for houses bought and shipped to the owner in parts that are then put together at the site. Such houses are also called packaged houses. They differ from modular houses in that construction at the site is required and the kit may not be complete. Often plumbing fixtures, kitchen cabinetry, and fixed glass windows must be purchased separately at the site. Transportation to the site must also be added to the price.

There are a variety of kit houses on the market and each has its own characteristics. One northeastern firm specializes in barn houses. These can take on a contemporary look or a traditional look, but the construction idea is the same, a post and lintel framework. The package is a materials-only package.[10] Acorn, established in 1947, is another company in the Northeast. Complete houses are sold through their own dealer-builder organization, which offers fifty single-family house designs and other designs used in multifamily construction. A house may be purchased as an "erected shell," "rough finish," or "finished house," ranging in 1980 from $30,000 to over $140,000.[11] Acorn, as well as other kit-house producers, offer a solar heating system for both hot water and space heating with house designs especially suitable for them.

Geodesic domes are another type of kit house. The parts can be trucked in flat sections, and erection can be completed in a few days. Manufacturers claim that one person working alone can erect a dome. Dome sizes range from 20 to 45 feet in diameter, and the houses can be one, two or more floors in height. They can be outfitted

Geodesic dome kit houses may be erected easily by inexperienced persons in a few days. The finished home may have oddly shaped rooms as a result of the efficient structural design. Photo courtesy of Cathedralite, Inc., Capitola, CA.

with solar heating systems, and they are an economic use of materials since one-seventh as much material is used in a dome as is used in a conventional house enclosing a similar amount of floor space. The plans for domes are unlike those for conventional homes, because all rooms must fit into the overall shape. Oddly designed bedrooms, kitchens and living rooms are the result. These may be both challenging and appealing to some home buyers but awkward, if not seemingly unusable, to others.

Some kit-house companies do not extend credit for the purchase of their houses. Others require a monthly interest only payment and a balloon payment of the principal amount upon completion of the house

when conventional mortgage financing may be obtained. In both cases, loans must be obtained from local lenders for the purchase of the packaged materials, as well as for the land and the on-site construction costs. There may be resistance in some communities to lending money for the purchase of this type of housing if the local attitude is that site-built housing is superior.

Another difficulty could arise with meeting local building codes. The companies attempt to meet building code requirements, but local codes might be very specific about materials and techniques, disallowing innovative methods and materials which might perform equally well. The prospective kit-house buyer should investigate lend-

The Log Package

Generally, owners of log homes purchase a particular log package, rather than a total home containing all the components for a completed house. With the majority of log home kits, the following parts are offered: precut wall logs; precut second floor joists; precut rafters; precut gable ends; all windows, often including the door jambs; two prehung doors; gaskets; fiberboard splines; ten-inch spikes; windstop; caulking compound; and blueprints.

Homeowners must provide the finishing materials, as well as the roofing and flooring, although some companies offer flooring and roofing as options. The owner also must supply the electrical and plumbing systems, cabinets, foundation, fireplace, subflooring and labor to construct the home.

Generally, precut log homes are shipped Freight on Board (FOB) from the manufacturer's nearest plant. That means that you, the buyer, will need to pay transportation charges. Transportation charges are based on a trailer load, per mile rate. Most log homes require two such trailer loads. You should ask the manufacturer to supply you with estimated freight charges.

Although financing may not be as easy as for more conventional housing, you can usually obtain the same type of mortgage as you would for another type of home. If you have questions on financing, you may wish to talk with your personal banker as well as the dealer of log homes in your area. Many log homes also have been structurally approved by the Federal Housing Authority (FHA), which qualifies them for FHA-, VA- and HUD-backed financing. Check with the dealer to make sure the home you plan to buy does meet FHA standards.

In the manufacturing plant, precut logs are soaked in a wood preservative, which is both odorless and colorless, and which has proven itself in many applications. Most manufacturers recommend that the homeowner protect the house with repeated applications of the wood preservative on an annual or a biannual basis. To apply the preservative, an ordinary fruit tree sprayer can be used, after you have covered the shrubbery and windows. Interior applications are not needed. The length of time between applications of the wood preservative varies with the location of your home. Homes located in the South will require treatment more frequently than those in the North. Spraying the average house with the preservative will require about a day of your time and twenty gallons of preservative.

Treatment of your log home with a wood preservative will result in a beautiful home that will be able to withstand the weather. Some homeowners also finish exterior logs with linseed oil or polyurethane liquids, but this is not a common practice.

Reprinted with permission from: Tatum, B., The Alternative House: A Complete Guide to Building and Buying (Reed Books, 1978), pp. 128–130. Copyright 1978, Book Developers, Inc.

ing practices and local codes to see if the chosen house meets the requirements.

If a building contractor is involved with the construction, the choice of such a con-

tractor must be a careful one. Not all contractors are willing to attempt nor are they all experienced with kit-house construction, which nearly always differs in method from conventional practice. Some kit houses are designed to be put together by an amateur, and the kit not only includes directions, but might even include necessary tools. This is done to encourage the inexperienced to achieve a house of their dreams. Many kit-house owners have relied only on electrical and plumbing subcontractors, and have done all other work themselves. This is the least costly means of achieving a finished kit house.

THE RELATED COSTS OF HOME OWNERSHIP

The costs related to home ownership apply regardless of the type of home purchased. These costs do vary, however, depending on the location, size, condition of the house, and the personal preferences of its residents.

Maintenance Costs

A traditional equation for the annual costs of maintenance for single-family houses is that they equal one percent of the value of the house. It is difficult to imagine that a $90,000 house would require $900 of maintenance year after year. In fact, the actual cost might be much higher, but annual costs are not predictably steady. The most consistent home ownership cost in single-family suburban houses is yard care. Initial landscaping can cost many thousands of dollars, and subsequent expenditures on tools, equipment, plant materials, fertilizers, insecticides, and so on, may add up to a few hundred dollars each year. The landscaping choices can be made with low maintenance in mind, and some home owners choose not to landscape their entire plot of land.

Routine maintenance on houses includes painting and small repairs. When people undertake their own painting and wallpapering a great deal of money can be saved, even though the cost of materials and tools has steadily risen. Minor plumbing, carpentry, and electrical repairs can be accomplished by

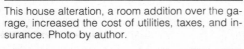

This house alteration, a room addition over the garage, increased the cost of utilities, taxes, and insurance. Photo by author.

Families living in identical housing units may have different utility costs. Habits and preferences as well as orientation, wind, and climate affect the costs of heating and cooling a home. Photo courtesy of U.S. Department of Housing and Urban Development.

most do-it-yourselfers, aided by many instructive publications. Major repairs such as replacing a water heater or a roof are undertaken by more ambitious home owners. If labor is contracted for a job, the cost can be very large, but maintenance on this scale does not occur very often. The purchase of an older house is likely to include such major repairs unless they have been done in the recent past.

Carpeting wears out, kitchen and bath flooring usually become out-of-date (even if still serviceable), and appliances are troublesome over time. The costs of replacing these major household items may be included in major remodeling. In any case, they are part of the long-range costs of owned housing.

Home owners are more likely than renters to undertake major housing alterations. The addition of a room, remodeling of a kitchen or bathroom or any change of internal arrangement of space will become a major investment on the part of the home owner. If equity in the property is sufficient, one way to finance major alterations is with a second mortgage. Home improvement loans of any type add monthly expenses to the existing mortgage costs. Housing alterations usually increase costs of utilities, property taxes and hazard insurance.

When housing production is at a low point, usually because mortgage money is unavailable and interest rates are high, then housing alterations are more numerous. Families may find they cannot easily acquire a larger or better house so they improve the one they have. If housing production is high, then the family may find a more suitable house within their price range and move rather than improve an existing structure.

Utilities

The most certain thing that can be said about utility costs at a time when the growth of nuclear energy is in doubt, and the supply and costs of home heating fuels are causing great public concern, is that utilities costs are high and rising. There are not clear and simple answers as to how we can provide ourselves with the cheap and readily available sources of fuel we have enjoyed in the past. Whether a home's reliance is on electricity, gas, oil, or a combination of these does not matter—all energy resources will cost more in the future. There are regional differences in the availability and cost of energy, and they certainly should be studied before a buying decision is made. Past records of heating and electrical use are a basis on which to calculate expected monthly costs at different times of the year. However, because lifestyle differences affect fuel consumption, costs of a previous owner may not match the new owner's costs.

Identical houses can have extremely different utility costs. The differences have to do with family habits and preferences (for instance, degree of comfort required for heating and air conditioning). Orientation of the house, local climatic conditions, particularly wind patterns, also greatly affect costs of heating and cooling. These along with the kinds and amounts of insulation, weatherstripping, caulking, and storm windows become critical in assessing expected utility costs.

The cost of services provided by the community is also increasing. Trash, water, and sewage charges have risen. Some areas have a history of water shortages, and the housing consumer would be wise to expect future shortages, or increased charges in times of shortages, or both.

Other utility costs include personal telephone bills and perhaps cable television. Some communities might undertake large expenditure improvements such as paving of streets or installation of sewers. These normally are paid for by property owners, who are assessed according to the total amount of land or the amount of street frontage they have within the improvement district. Such special assessments could become very burdensome to a family purchasing a house with the assumption that their monthly costs were fixed.

Home Insurance

Most lenders require that the property be insured with a home owners policy while the house is mortgaged. The house, garage and any other structures on the piece of owned land are covered in the policy, so is personal property such as household furnishings, clothing, typewriters, and so on, usually expressed in the policy as half the amount of the dwelling. Especially expensive items such as cameras and jewelry should be covered with separate policies to guarantee their full value coverage. A home owner's policy also pays for living expenses of the family in case of the need to live elsewhere, during a time of repair after a fire for instance.

Many home owners' policies include personal liability insurance as well. This insurance protects the home owner from suits regarding accidents and injury that occur on the property. Most people want to believe that a best friend having fallen and broken a leg on a slippery front walk would not sue for damages, but it can happen.

The cost of insurance varies by area. The location of fire fighting services can affect insurance rates. Of course, the more expensive the house, the more costly the insurance to cover its replacement costs. The higher the deductible amount, the portion to be paid by the owner before insurance applies, the lower the annual costs. Usually insurance premiums are renewed every year, and the cost is modest compared to automobile insurance. The following example is of a basic home owner's insurance policy in 1980.

There are basic perils which are covered in most insurance policies. They include fire or lightning, windstorm or hail, explosions, smoke, vandalism, theft, among other things. Some policies include many more hazards, and of course, these policies

Section - 1	Basic Coverages	Limit of Liability
A.	Dwelling	$54,000
B.	Appurtenant structures	5,400
C.	Unscheduled personal property	27,000
D.	Additional living expense	10,800
	Extended theft	Included
	Credit card & depositor's forgery	1,000
	Deductible - Section I $100	
Section - II		
E.	Personal liability (including	
	personal injury)	$100,000
	Each occurrence	
F.	Medical payments to others	
	Each person	500
	Each accident	25,000
	Each occurrence	500
G.	Damage to property of others	
	Basic Premium	$ 155

Condominium owners have individual home insurance, but the commonly owned areas are insured by the homeowners association. Photo by author.

are more costly. Comprehensive insurance covers nearly every possible peril, but there are always exceptions listed. Flood and earthquake insurance policies are available in some communities.

Insurance companies compute payments in two ways: the replacement cost of the building and the cash value of personal property. A critical factor in the computation is whether or not the insurance coverage is at least 80 percent of the cost of replacement at the time of the damage. If the insurance coverage is at least 80 percent, the full cost is paid without depreciation or deductions. If less than 80 percent is carried, only a proportion of the replacement cost is paid. "Thus if you have $40,000 of insurance but need $60,000 to come up with the 80 percent, the company will pay two-thirds of the loss. You would receive

only $4,000 for a $6,000 loss, $6,000 for a $9,000 loss, and so on."[12] The insurance company may prefer to pay what they call a "cash value" of the damaged part of the house which also is less than full replacement cost.

Most people are underinsured. The original policy is usually written at the time of purchase, but as the value of the house increases so do the costs of replacement. Many people, feeling secure with their home owners coverage, are caught with too little insurance to replace their houses without major outlays of money and/or borrowing at the time of rebuilding. Such was the case with the majority of home owners in a fire that destroyed about 200 houses in Santa Barbara, California in 1977. This dilemma can be avoided by updating the amount of replacement cost coverage to keep pace with true construction costs in the area. Some policies have a built-in increase, such as 10 percent a year, but the increased coverage in these policies should be checked against cost-per-square-foot construction estimates every year or two.

Condominium home owners have a slightly more complicated insurance situation than do single-family home owners. The liability insurance is usually covered by the condominium home owners association as a whole. The common buildings and facilities are also insured jointly. Each home owner, however, may have insurance coverage for personal property and for additions and alterations on individual units within the development. Cooperatives are similarly insured.

Mobile home owners should have basic hazard insurance. Because mobile homes are more susceptible to fire and wind damage than site-built homes, the insurance rates on mobile homes are generally higher. Basic home owners' insurance policies especially designed for mobile home owners are available and they provide the same kinds of coverage as single-family home owners' policies.

Insurance can be purchased against unusual catastrophes. Flood insurance is available, and the federal government pays part of the losses to home owners whose insurance coverage is insufficient to cover the total loss. This insurance is available only in areas that have made plans for flood control according to guidelines of the U.S. Department of Housing and Urban Development. Earthquake insurance is used in some areas with a high incidence of earthquakes such as California. Very few people, however, have earthquake insurance even in areas where it may be needed. In some areas, it is relatively inexpensive and may be a wise insurance investment.

Not all insurance is designed for home owners. Renters may have their personal property insured against all of the same perils that home owners are insured for, and they also may carry liability insurance. Some renters' policies include emergency living expenses as well.

Property Taxes

Property taxes, a traditional form of taxation in this country, differ from income taxes in that they tax wealth instead of income. This essential difference is important to remember when weighing the arguments for and against property tax increases. The so-called "property tax revolt" has been felt in nearly every part of the country. At the heart of the revolt is the following basic problem—the rapid increases in the value of real property result in more taxes on that wealth.

Property taxes are used to support local governmental operations such as schools, water districts, fire departments, libraries, parks and recreation facilities, and police protection. These services are also supported through other monies as well, but the amount of property tax is determined in part by the number of districts in which one's property lies. Some municipalities, because they include tax-paying industries, have a high tax base which results in lower taxes paid per home owner. Poorer communities might partially support local schools and services with half of the revenue of richer communities.

Two specific economic considerations are used to calculate the taxes due annually on any piece of property—**assessed value** and **tax rate**. The assessed value is not the same as the appraised value used by lenders or realtors. It is a percentage of the market value put upon the house and land by the governmental authority whose responsibility this is, such as the county assessor. One of the major factors that led to the passage of

PERILS AGAINST WHICH PROPERTIES ARE INSURED: HOMEOWNERS POLICY

BASIC HO-1	BROAD HO-2	SPECIAL HO-3	RENTER'S HO-4	COMPRE-HENSIVE HO-5	CONDO-MINIUM HO-6	OLDER HOME HO-8	PERILS
▨	▨	▦	█	▨	█	▨	1. Fire or lightning
▨	▨	▦	█	▨	█	▨	2. Loss of property removed from premises endangered by fire or other perils*
▨	▨	▦	█	▨	█	▨	3. Windstorm or hail
▨	▨	▦	█	▨	█	▨	4. Explosion
▨	▨	▦	█	▨	█	▨	5. Riot or civil commotion
▨	▨	▦	█	▨	█	▨	6. Aircraft
▨	▨	▦	█	▨	█	▨	7. Vehicles
▨	▨	▦	█	▨	█	▨	8. Smoke
▨	▨	▦	█	▨	█	▨	9. Vandalism and malicious mischief
▨	▨	▦	█	▨	█	▨	10. Theft
▨	▨	▦	█	▨	█	▨	11. Breakage of glass constituting a part of the building
	▨	▦	█	▨	█		12. Falling objects
	▨	▦	█	▨	█		13. Weight of ice, snow, sleet
	▨	▦	█	▨	█		14. Collapse of building(s) or any part thereof
	▨	▦	█	▨	█		15. Sudden and accidental tearing asunder, cracking, burning, or bulging of a steam or hot water heating system or of appliances for heating water
	▨	▦	█	▨	█		16. Accidental discharge, leakage or overflow of water or steam from within a plumbing, heating or air-conditioning system or domestic appliance
	▨	▦	█	▨	█		17. Freezing of plumbing, heating and air-conditioning systems and domestic appliances
	▨	▦	█	▨	█		18. Sudden and accidental injury from artificially generated currents to electrical appliances, devices, fixtures and wiring (TV and radio tubes not included)
		▦		█			All perils except flood, earthquake, war, nuclear accident and others specified in your policy. Check your policy for a complete listing of perils excluded.

▨ Dwelling and Personal Property

▦ Dwelling only

█ Personal Property only

*Included as a peril in traditional forms of the homeowners policy; as an additional coverage in the simplified (HO-76) policies.

Source: Insurance Information Institute, New York

California's Proposition 13, was that market values had jumped in what seemed to be outrageous leaps. Assessments are not usually done annually, and when they are done every three or five years, the increased market value they represent is not only shocking, but also the taxes often double or triple. Were assessments done annually, the true rise in property values would be reflected gradually over time, as in fact they occur.

Even where property market values have jumped dramatically, they very rarely are as high as the true selling price of the property would be. Generally, market values are conservative, but the slightest improvement to property will increase them. The addition of a room, improved landscaping, even wall-to-wall carpeting, can result in an increased assessment. Sometimes home owners feel they have been unfairly assessed because their house has not had the additions or improvements of neighboring houses, and neighborhoods are rated at about the same market value. If unfairness can be proved, through an assessment appeals process, the assessment and the consequent taxes may be lowered.

The tax rate that applies to all property is determined by the municipality in which the property exists. All of the taxing district's revenue needs are determined, and the tax rate set accordingly. Thus it can vary from year to year, and generally it will go up over time. Just as the cost of living has risen with inflation, so has the cost of running schools and public services. If the assessed values of properties to be taxed have kept pace with inflationary costs, there would be no need to raise the tax rate. Unfortunately for home owners, both assessed values and tax rates have gone up in most communities.

Home buyers should attempt to calculate their annual property taxes before purchasing a house. If they are more than a few hundred dollars, budgeting for them during the first year of ownership, when other related expenses are high, might be difficult. The taxes paid in the past are not always a true indication of taxes to be paid in the future, because the property's assessment may go up with the new market value based on the selling price. There may also be reason to suspect that the tax rate will increase as well. Either a cut-back or an expansion of public services and facilities will affect local tax rates. Knowing the area's political climate (proposed future developments) and economic climate (growth rate) may be important to making a housing decision, and these factors, of course, can change over time.

Improvement of any kind to a home will increase its market value on which property taxes are based. Remodeling this older house, resulted in a dramatic jump in property taxes whereas neighboring houses stayed at about the same assessment. Photo by author.

THE FINANCIAL ADVANTAGES OF ALL FORMS OF HOME OWNERSHIP

That home ownership brings a feeling of achievement, security, privacy, and prestige for most people has been established elsewhere in this text. The focus in this section is on the financial advantages of home ownership. There are many, but only the following are discussed: tax savings, investment, forced savings, inflated dollars, and credit.

Tax Savings

Having just read about property taxes, it may seem odd to the reader that there is an advantage to home ownership related to taxes. This advantage is in income taxes, both at the federal and state level and it is not only important; it can become a very strong motivation for home ownership.

The interest paid on a mortgage loan and

The buyers of these condominiums will have very high tax deductions for mortgage interest and property taxes in their first year of ownership. The substantial savings in income taxes is a strong motivation for many prospective homeowners. Photo by author.

the property taxes paid per year are tax deductions that may be itemized. There can be a sizable difference in amount of income taxes paid, especially in the first years of home ownership. There is so much of the mortgage payment going toward interest in the first monthly payments, that many thousands of dollars are normally accumulated as a tax deduction. The property taxes paid, whether low or high, add another substantial deduction.

A very simple example will explain how these deductions affect income taxes paid. If a couple earning together $30,000 a year purchase an $80,000 home with the standard 20 percent down payment, their first year's interest with a 14 percent, 30-year loan, would be roughly $8,950. Their property taxes could be as much as $1,500. These two figures amount to a $10,450 deduction their first year of ownership that they did not have the year before. All other considerations aside, their income taxes will be lower for two reasons—a smaller amount of money to be taxed, and a lower rate of taxation that applies to it. Using 1980 IRS tax tables, disregarding any other tax factors, and assuming a stable income, home ownership results in $2,610 less taxes. In most cases, the couple would have other deductions they would claim along with the ownership deductions, but it is the latter which puts them in a much lower tax category.

Many first-time buyers view this advantage as a monthly saving on their house payment. In the example above, the monthly payment of $758.33 would be "reduced" with tax savings by $217.50, calculated by dividing the tax savings by 12. This tax advantage gradually decreases over the term of the mortgage as the amount paid to interest decreases and the amount paid to principal increases. However, as property taxes increase over time, the deduction for them also increases.

Investment
House values do not always go up even though recent housing inflation would belie this. There are communities that experience a sudden loss of a major industry, and the large number of surplus houses then on the market can dramatically deflate house prices for several years. A community can get overbuilt with the same results. General demographic trends, discussed in chapter 2, can cause faster rates of price increases in some areas, such as the South and West, and slower rates of price increases in other areas, such as the Northeast. Depreciation can occur in some declining urban neighborhoods. In any case, inflation does not affect house price increases in a steady and predictable pattern.

Nevertheless, in most locations house values have gone up over the past several decades. That a home will likely be sold for many thousands of dollars more than its purchase price motivates many home buyers. This return on the initial investment, the down payment, can be greater than the return on any other form of investment. In the past few years, the difference between the investment in real estate and the investment in the stock market or savings and bonds has been dramatic for most people.

The pattern is by no means constant, and it will probably change in time.

It should be remembered that there are a great many costs related to home buying and to home ownership. In any estimation or calculation of return on investment in home ownership, the closing costs, real estate sales commission, improvements, repairs and maintenance costs, should be subtracted from the selling price for a true picture of "profit."

Forced Savings
The idea of forced savings is closely related to housing as an investment. The down payment and each monthly payment's portion repaying the principal is money that is "saved" unless the house is lower in value when sold than when purchased. When the house is sold, presumably at a profit, all that money is returned, just as it would be if put into a regular savings plan. The interest that would have been earned is compensated for by whatever investment return is realized at the time of sale.

Renters often feel they are throwing money away, because their monthly rent is not returned in any form. The forced savings aspect of home ownership may be especially important to young growing families with high living expenses, who find it difficult to save in any other more direct manner. The "savings" locked up in the equity of a house is very much different from a savings account. Funds may not be drawn out in case of emergencies. Sound financial planning would include liquid assets in addition to the money "saved" through home ownership.

Inflated Dollars
With the exception of some of the alternative mortgage loans in which house payments may be increased over time because of increased interest rates (ARM, rollover

mortgages), principal and interest payments are a fixed amount of money for the term of the loan. Since the value of the dollar has tended to decrease over time because of inflation, house payments actually have become cheaper. When this fact is combined with the tendency of young families to increase their incomes, home ownership can become in time a negligible monthly expense. This is only true if the owners stay on the same property.

The American housing tradition of "moving up" or "trading up" may cancel out this effect of inflation dollars. When a family sells a $60,000 house for a price of $100,000, they are in a position to use their equity for a much more expensive house. The house payments involved could easily triple due to both the higher mortgage and higher interest rates. The dollars may indeed be cheaper in buying power, but tripling the amount used for housing each month can cancel the benefit.

Credit

Even though it is necessary to have good credit in the first place in order to obtain a mortgage, one's credit rating improves once home ownership is achieved. Home owners are assumed to be more financially stable than renters, and as permanent members of the community they are more trusted in lending practices. Negotiating large bank loans for other purposes can be more easily done with home ownership status then with renter status.

It has already been mentioned that the equity in the home can be used for borrowing purposes. Second mortgages can be made for several thousand dollars using the equity in the home as collateral. Refinancing, for the purpose of gaining a large sum of money, is possible once the house has increased in value and much of the principal is paid off.

SUMMARY

The condominium method of ownership allows individual ownership of a housing unit along with shared ownership of grounds and facilities. The harmony or lack of harmony with which the home owners' association functions, and the degree to which it represents the majority's wishes can determine whether or not condominium living is a pleasant and satisfying experience. Condominiums have several housing advantages, among them lower price, lack of maintenance responsibilities, and recreational facilities. There are more complicated legal documents involved with a condominium purchase than with a single-family house purchase.

Cooperatives, like condominiums, are a form of ownership, not a housing type.

Owners buy shares of stock in the corporation that owns the land and housing buildings, and in return are allowed to live in the housing units. Financing of cooperatives differs from standard home mortgaging.

The rise of mobile homes as a substantial part of American housing is due mainly to the lower price of mobile homes. Whether or not a mobile home purchase is made from a previous owner, a real estate agent, or from a dealer, the major factor in mobile home satisfaction is the location and quality of the park in which the home exists or will be placed.

Mobile-home financing is similar to automobile financing. The park rental, as well as the required additions, are also part of the total financing picture. Mobile homes may or may not depreciate in value, and the taxation varies from state to state.

A trend toward kit houses is evident in some parts of the country. All construction materials are purchased and then erected at the site either by the home owners or by a contractor. Usually the house is finished with plumbing, cabinetry, and other interior equipment from local suppliers. The prices range from very modest to very expensive. Building codes may be a problem for the more experimental designs available in kit houses, even though their construction may be sound from a performance standpoint.

Maintenance costs are one part of the financial responsibilities associated with home ownership. Landscaping, painting, repairs, and equipment replacement can be very costly, and these expenses are not easy to budget for since they occur at irregular times. Major housing alterations are undertaken when space needs expand or living style changes.

Utility costs vary by region, climate, size and quality of the house, type of fuels used, and so on. Such costs can be extremely high, particularly at a time when there are fuel shortages. Personal living habits and preferences affect utility costs.

Hazard insurance is required by lenders, and prudent home owners, whether living in a single-family home, a condominium, or mobile home, should insure themselves against major perils for the full replacement value of their property. Insurance policies have different kinds of coverage, and some include personal liability insurance. Home owners may be insured against earthquakes and floods. Renters may also carry insurance.

Property taxes are paid by home owners because the wealth of the community supports local schools and services. The 1980s will probably witness dramatic changes in property taxing methods, if not property tax use. Prospective home owners should attempt to get accurate information regarding tax rates and proposed tax increases. Property taxes can be a major housing expense, and one that will go up over time.

The financial advantages of home ownership include five specific considerations: (1) the mortgage interest paid and property taxes paid annually can be deducted from taxable income thus reducing the amount of income taxes paid to the federal and state government; (2) since homes are nearly always sold for more money than paid for them, they are considered a sound investment; (3) since money spent in a down payment and toward repaying the principal is returned when the house is sold, the purchase of a house is a form of forced savings; (4) the amount of money paid on a home loan will in reality decrease over time as the purchasing power of the dollar shrinks through the effect of inflation; (5) homeownership leads to more borrowing power because financial trustworthiness is established, and the equity itself can be used for collateral.

Notes

1. "The Papers That Make You a Condominium Owner," *Changing Times*, June 1975, pp. 21–22.
2. Ibid., p. 22.
3. Ibid.
4. National Association of Home Builders, *Condominium Buyers Guide* (Washington, D.C.: Author, 1976), p. 23.

5. Gallet, J. H., "The Costs of Going Co-op: Can You Afford to Buy?" *New York*, Mar. 31, 1980, p. 49.
6. Dasso, J., A. A. Ring, and D. McFall, *Fundamentals of Real Estate* (Englewood Cliffs, N J: Prentice-Hall, 1977), p. 416.
7. Advertisement for the Groves, in Irvine, *Los Angeles Times*, July 1, 1979, p. VIII–32.
8. Ibid.
9. Hershberg, B. Z., "Money Problems Slow the Mobiles," *Housing*, 1979, *55* (3), p. 16.
10. *The American Barn . . . Offering a New Way of Life* (Deerfield, Mass.: American Barn Corporation, 1976).
11. Acorn Houses (Concord, Mass.: Acorn Structures, 1980).
12. "Got Eough Insurance on Your Home?" *Changing Times*, 1980, *34* (1), p. 47.

Suggested Readings

Brooks, P. and Brooks, L. *How to Buy a Condominium*. New York: Stein and Day, 1975.

Butcher, L. *The Condominium Book*. Princeton, NJ: Dow Jones Books, 1980.

Holder, S. L. and Coulter, K. J. "The Importance of Mobile Home Characteristics to the Buyer and the Seller." *Housing Educators Journal*, 1977, *4* (2), 21–29.

"Homeowners Insurance: Part 1 of a Two-part Report." *Consumer Reports*, 1980, *45* (8) 484–489.

Jones, M. O. "Behavioral Factors in the Housing Market: How People Afford the Unaffordable." *Housing and Society*. (Proceedings of the AAHE Annual Conference), 1979.

Lee, S. J. *Buyer's Handbook for Cooperatives and Condominiums*. New York: Van Nostrand Reinhold, 1978.

Morris, E. W. and Woods, M. E. *Housing Crisis and Response: The Place of Mobile Homes in American Life*. Ithaca, N.Y.: New York State College of Human Ecology at Cornell University, 1971.

Tatum, R. *The Alternative House: A Complete Guide to Building and Buying*. Los Angeles: Reid Books, 1978.

Turner, J. F. C. and Fichter, R. *Freedom to Build*. New York: Macmillan Co., 1972.

U.S. Department of Housing and Urban Development. *Questions About Condominiums; What to Ask before You Buy*. Washington, D.C.: U.S. Government Printing Office, 1974.

Watkins, A. M. *The Complete Guide to Factory-made Houses*. New York: E. P. Dutton, 1980.

Housing Law and You

9

There is no such thing as living in a situation free from the effects of housing law. As a home owner, you are a property owner only insofar as the law specifies, and within a particular legal type of ownership. As a **tenant,** or as the landlord renting to tenants, you are in a legal relationship that has a heritage dating back many centuries.

Students should be aware that this chapter serves only as a brief introduction to the enormous body of law that affects their housing choices over a lifetime. Nevertheless, housing law is not a subject to be left to lawyers and housing experts. Housing law is subject to change at all levels of government. Insofar as housing law becomes part of your own experience with housing, and your housing satisfaction, you should become aware of the housing issues that are

involved in the lawmaking and law changing process.

The legal aspects of home ownership such as forms of ownership and their implications are detailed in this chapter to complete the student's understanding of the ownership role. With our recent interest in consumer protection, home ownership warranty plans have developed, and these will also be discussed in the first section.

Two types of codes affect housing quality. They are building codes and housing codes. Even though very few people are familiar with the details of their local codes,

Building codes control new construction and any future additions. They vary greatly between communities. Photo by author.

The Law is on Your Side

In recent years, several federal laws have been passed designed to help and protect the home buyer. (State laws vary. Check them carefully.)

The Equal Credit Opportunity Act. The law prohibits lenders from discriminating against applicants for credit because of race, color, religion, national origin, sex, marital status, and age (provided, of course, the applicant is old enough to enter into a legal contract). In addition, the Act forbids lenders from not considering applicants because part or all of their steady income comes from a public assistance program, alimony, or child support, or because they may in the past have sought to protect their rights under the Consumer Credit Protection Act. Consult a regional Federal Reserve Bank for more information.

The Fair Credit Reporting Act. Many lenders employ agencies to run credit checks on loan applicants. The law allows you to inspect a summary of the report (not the original credit check, however). If parts of it are wrong, you can require that corrections be made. To find out more about the Act, check a regional office of the Federal Trade Commission.

The Consumer Credit Protection Act. Often called Truth-in-Lending, the law requires a lender to disclose the *effective* interest rate on a mortgage loan (though not when you apply). The rate is usually higher than the one in the contract because it includes a varied list of charges, including financing fees and insurance premiums. The statement should also detail charges you may be assessed if the loan is paid off before it is due.

Though the law does not *require* the lender to disclose this information when you apply for a loan, ask for it at that time. The numbers are crucial, and you should know what they are as early in the search as possible.

The Real Estate Settlement Procedures Act. The law requires the lender to give a good-faith estimate of *all* closing costs within three days of the loan application (along with a booklet on the subject). Upon your request and one business day before closing, the lender must provide a list of the exact closing costs fixed at that time. By this point, most of them *will* be set exactly; the time to shop for settlement services (or negotiate their payment with the seller) is much earlier in the process— before you sign an offer to buy.

Reprinted from: Better Homes and Gardens How to Buy and Sell Your Home *(Des Moines, Iowa: Special Interest Publications, Meredith Corporation, 1979), p. 108. © Copyright Meredith Corporation, 1979. All rights reserved.*

the construction, materials, and techniques used in their own housing and its condition over time, are determined by these codes. Building codes and housing codes are the subject of the second section of this chapter.

Most college students first become aware of housing law when they feel they have been treated unfairly in a renting situation. The legal aspects of tenant-landlord law are all too often discovered when it is too late to remedy a problem. It is far better for tenants and landlords to understand the rights and responsibilities of both parties in advance of a rental or lease agreement. These will be discussed in the third section of the chapter.

Even though there are many fair housing laws protecting minorities and women against housing discrimination, the practice of it persists in subtle ways. The recent legislation against discrimination and its effectiveness will constitute the last section of this chapter.

LEGAL ASPECTS OF OWNERSHIP

The transfer of property in the buying and selling of homes is essentially a legal process. In fact all of the home buying processes discussed in the last two chapters are governed by housing law. For instance, state **usury laws** set upper limits on interest rates that may be charged on mortgages. These limits, and the laws that govern them, are one aspect of housing law being questioned at the present time, and a few states have changed their laws, raising the ceilings on interest rates to reflect the economic realities of the times.

In spite of a trend to single-person home ownership, first home purchases are usually made by couples, married or not. Various types of joint ownership should be understood in order to make the most appropriate choice.

Joint Ownership

There are both advantages and disadvantages to joint ownership. There are several kinds, and each determines how the property would be transferred to the other party in case of death.

Joint Tenancy. Joint tenancy with the **rights of survivorship** is the most common type of joint ownership. Each person in the agreement owns an equal share, and more than a couple could be involved. When one party dies, the other party or parties inherit that person's share, regardless of wills, court decisions, or other inheritance matters. In this arrangement, one person could sell his or her share without the approval of the other, but some states restrict this possibility to jointly owned property other than the family home. Costs of probate can be avoided if all property is in the form of joint tenancy, but a will for each party should also be written to insure intended inheritance decisions. Estate taxes are not avoided by joint tenancy.

Tenancy by the Entirety. This form of joint ownership applies only to married couples, but it is not recognized in many states. It does not allow the selling of property without the approval of the other person. In some states, this type of ownership is restricted to real estate. In states where tenancy of the entirety exists, couples must have both names on the title to the property.

Tenancy in Common. In tenancy in common, two or more people own individual shares in the property, but each controls his or her own share. It would be possible for the husband to will his share to heirs other than his wife, even if she is the other party in the tenancy in common ownership. In other words, it is like the joint tenancy form, but without the right of survivorship. Business partners might choose this form of ownership so that their respective families would inherit each share.

Community Property. Arizona, California, Idaho, Louisiana, Nevada, New Mexico, Texas, and Washington are community property states. This means that ownership laws presume that all property of the marriage is owned equally by each party. In these states, even where there is no will, the surviving spouse inherits half of everything owned after the date of marriage. A will can exist that turns over all of the estate to the surviving spouse. Divorce law in these states is also based on the assumption that each of the partners should take half of the assets of the marriage, even though it is difficult to divide a house in half without a sale and a disruptive move for a family with children.

Property Rights

Home ownership actually involves the ownership of rights to a specific piece of land, not ownership of the land itself. Very often, the rights to the land are shared with other parties. For instance, the home owner may have rights to the surface of the land purchased, but the oil and mineral rights underneath the surface may be owned by someone else who may also have the right to use the surface land to obtain them. Air rights above the property are important also. Highrise apartments and condominiums in dense urban areas may be affected by their rights to the space above them. When full rights to the land to the earth's core and into infinite space are owned, the form of ownership is "**fee simple.**" The owners have complete rights to do as they please with the land, within the limits set by local codes, zoning, and other ordinances to restrict land use for the public's benefit.

Deeds

The piece of paper that declares ownership comes in different forms, and each has different implications for the home buyer. A **general warranty deed** transfers all the rights to the property the seller had to the new owner or buyer. This is the most complete set of assurances the seller can give the buyer. The seller guarantees that there are no other claims or defects on the title. If there are, the seller is responsible. This deed, although desirable, may have little value if at some later time, defects or encumbrances (other legal claims) become apparent, because the seller may not then be available to back up the warranty.

A **special warranty deed**, when trans-ferred to the buyer, warrants that there is no transfer of claims upon the rights of the seller. This type of deed does not carry as much weight in a legal dispute as a general warranty deed because the liability of the seller is limited compared to a general warranty deed. A third type of deed is called a **quitclaim deed.** It merely transfers the rights the seller has, or claims to have, to the buyer, but there is no guarantee that the seller has any rights to the property at all.

A **deed of trust,** or trust deed, conveys the title to the property to a third party. It is held by that party until the objectives set forth in the agreement are accomplished. Such deeds are used in many states instead of mortgages to secure property. The lender is the trustee of the deed of trust until the loan is fully repaid. Then the deed of trust is conveyed to the owner. A deed of trust does not transfer rights of ownership to the trustee (lender) unless the borrower fails to live up to the trust agreement (make the loan payments). Then the lender has the power to sell the property and use the proceeds to pay off the debt obligation. States usually use either the mortgage or trust deed form of home loan.

Lawyers are often involved in searching the title to the property at the time of sale so that any difficulties in the future can be avoided. If the title is clear, that is there were no problems in any of the previous transfers of that piece of land, the buyer can obtain a certificate of title that states this. If there are "**clouds on the title,**" meaning that in the past the transfer of title had not been free and clear, then the certificate of title would state them.

Title Insurance. Title insurance is the best protection against defects in the title. Title insurance may be obtained from a lawyer in some states and from commercial title insurance companies in others. It is protection against financial loss due to flaws or defects in the title not known at the time of purchase. The policy protects the new home owner by guaranteeing the owner's interest in the property. The premium is paid only once, and either owners or lenders buy title insurance. Should a dispute arise over rights of ownership, the insurance company would defend the title for the policy holder. Should the owner purchase a title insurance policy, the fee for it is part of the closing costs.

Liens. If a home owner does not pay taxes or other charges related to the property, a court may decide that such costs must be paid at the time when the house is sold out of the proceeds of the sale. Such a charge is called a lien. When the money to be paid is the result of work done on the property, the labor used in remodeling for instance, these fees are called a mechanic's lien. Materials and tax liens are also commonly used. If a judgment has been made in favor of the claimant retroactive to the time of the original payment due, there could be sizable charges against the property at the time of sale.

The mortgage or deed of trust is, in fact, a lien on the property. It is taken as a matter of course that the previous lender in the transaction will be paid fully for his or her rights of ownership, that is the unpaid balance due on the mortgage.

Easements. The right to use the real property of another person is called an easement. A specific purpose for this use of property should be designated. Typical easements are for utility and telephone lines. A road used by service companies could also be an easement. One type of easement (easement appurtenant) involves the rights of one property owner to use part

of the property nearby and usually adjacent to another property owner. A driveway access to a piece of property across another piece of property is one example of this. Sometimes driveways, walls, patios, or walkways from a neighboring property encroach in part on the adjacent property through careless siting. When a new owner purchases the piece of property encroached upon, he or she must act to have the encroachment removed. If no action is taken at the time of purchase, an easement will arise that allows the driveway, wall, patio, or walkway to stay where it is.[1]

Deed Restrictions. A deed restriction is a requirement to do or not to do something on the property. The requirement to build a house of specific minimum size or not to keep farm animals are both restrictions. These kinds of restrictions are typically entered into the public record at the time of conveyance of title, so they are called deed restrictions. Generally, they are restrictions to keep the uses of property consistent with the neighborhood.

There are two major types of deed restrictions. A **restrictive covenant** is a written promise to use or not to use the property in a certain way. The promise transfers with the title. Should one property owner in a subdivision not keep the promise, the other subdivision owners or the developer can enforce the restrictive covenant through an injunction. A **restrictive condition,** on the other hand, is written so that if a certain use is made, or not made, then the title reverts to the grantor or heirs of the grantor. Courts prefer to interpret a restriction as a covenant because the enforcement is less harsh.[2] Deed restrictions of both types may be terminated through lapsed time, ownership mergers, mutual agreement of all parties, material change in the neighborhood, and abandonment.[3]

Dispute Settlement Procedure

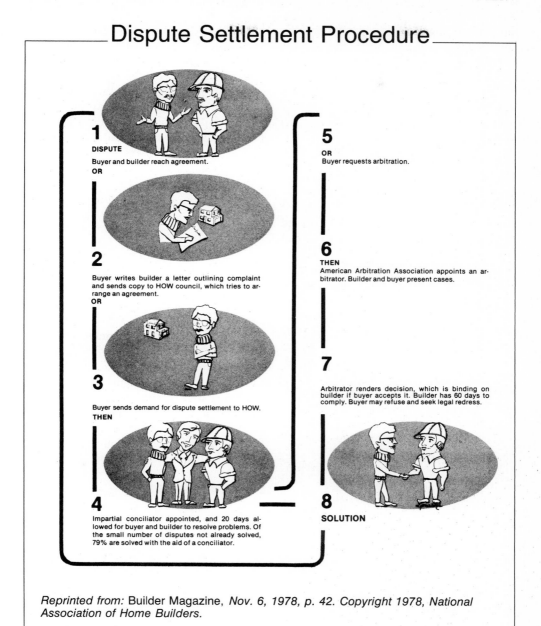

1

DISPUTE

Buyer and builder reach agreement.

OR

2

Buyer writes builder a letter outlining complaint and sends copy to HOW council, which tries to arrange an agreement.

OR

3

Buyer sends demand for dispute settlement to HOW.

THEN

4

Impartial conciliator appointed, and 20 days allowed for buyer and builder to resolve problems. Of the small number of disputes not already solved, 79% are solved with the aid of a conciliator.

5

OR

Buyer requests arbitration.

6

THEN

American Arbitration Association appoints an arbitrator. Builder and buyer present cases.

7

Arbitrator renders decision, which is binding on builder if buyer accepts it. Builder has 60 days to comply. Buyer may refuse and seek legal redress.

8

SOLUTION

Reprinted from: Builder Magazine, *Nov. 6, 1978, p. 42. Copyright 1978, National Association of Home Builders.*

Warranties on Houses

The Federal Housing Administration has warrantied houses against faulty workmanship and materials since 1954. The FHA plan, however, is effective for only one year, and available only on new houses financed with FHA loans. The FHA plan includes forcing the builder to make the repairs or fix the damage caused by faulty construction, or having the repairs made with the bill going to the builder. Considering the limited number of homes covered under the FHA warranty plan, and the limited time the warranty is in effect, other plans may be in the consumer's best interest.

HOW. HOW stands for the **Home Owners Warranty** plan initiated by the National Association of Homebuilders in 1974. In the first four years of the program, 10,000 builders and 375,000 homes were enrolled in forty-four states, and 2,000 disputes were settled out of court through the processes established by the program.[4] Many thousands of new homes are added to the program every year (188,000 in 1978). In the first year, workmanship and materials are warranted, and in the second year, defects in wiring, plumbing, electrical, and heating systems are warranted at no direct cost to the buyer. Major structural defects are warranted for ten years. The HOW is transferable if the house is sold during the ten year period. Single-family homes and condominiums of all housing types may be covered.

One of the strengths of the HOW program is the complaint handling procedure which can involve conciliation and arbitration. In recognition of the program's standards, both FHA and VA have waived some of their inspections and requirements for HOW houses. Some lenders acknowledge that HOW builders have met high standards for technical competence, and financial capacity.[5] Preferential interest rates may be granted to buyers of HOW homes.

NAR. The National Association of Realtors has a Home Protection Program for resold houses. The coverage is much the same as HOW's—operating defects such as heating, plumbing, electrical, heating and air conditioning systems, and soundness of walls, floors, ceilings. The coverage is limited to only those items approved after an independent inspection. There is a $100 deductible per element per occurrence limitation, and, in fact, the policy is more an insurance policy than a warranty.[6] The National Association of Realtors does not get directly involved with the program. Rather it sets up the program specification, and it has a ten member board that monitors the individual companies that participate.

CODES

Housing and building codes have been instituted in most communities in order to regulate the quality of housing. These codes are generally concerned with building and maintaining safe and durable housing. They set minimum standards of quality so that poor housing cannot be built in the first place, or poor housing allowed to be inhabited. Ideally, they regulate the overall quality of the housing stock in a given area, but it will become apparent in the sections that follow that the ideal and the reality of codes are quite different matters.

Building Codes

Most of us as housing consumers are ignorant about housing construction. It is a complete mystery to us where the wiring is in the walls, how the heat circulates throughout the interior space, even what holds the roof up. We are not uncomfortable with our ignorance, because we trust that our houses are built safely and soundly. In many parts of the country, we can attribute this faith in sound construction to building codes.

Building codes are designed to control new construction of all kinds. Regarding housing, they control the initial building of the house and any future additions or remodeling. Building code enforcement depends on permits and inspections as methods of regulation. In communities where building codes exist, they are more equitably enforced than housing codes. Violations of building codes may be punishable by fines and jail terms, however some do-it-yourself home alterations escape building official inspections without penalty. Home owners who bypass the irksome business of building permits, and their associated fees, risk stringent penalties. Buildings or additions that do not meet code requirements may have to be torn down or reworked to conform to building code standards.

Building Code Development. Traditionally, local communities develop and administer building codes. Even though building codes existed as early as 1925, it was not until the 1950s that they grew in popularity because of public concern about rapid and sometimes haphazard housing growth in many areas of the country, particularly suburban fringes around major metropolitan areas. The number of municipalities that had building codes grew from 20 percent to over 60 percent in that one decade.[7]

One of the major problems of building codes grew out of this rapid but local enactment. Building codes are not identical from one place to another. In the 1950s and 1960s, when building innovations were being promoted nationally, some local codes would not allow the use of roof trusses, prefabricated construction, or romex wiring. One town's code could specify use of copper water pipe, and the next town's specify galvanized steel pipe. Because of such differences, model building codes were suggested.

Professional groups and national committees conferred on the building code issue during the sixties. Even though a single code for the whole nation has been suggested by a few professionals, this has not gained widespread acceptance. Even though there have been twenty years of clamoring for uniformity of building codes, there still is a marked difference in building codes by state and by region. Generally, these codes are adaptations of the model building codes developed by building officials' professional organizations (Basic Building Code, Uniform Building Code, Southern Standard Building Code, and the National Building Code.)

Only eighteen states have adopted mandatory codes (1978). A few states have recommended codes, and two states have model codes which must be used if a code is adopted within a community. Generally, the states with codes are more populated than states without them. Illinois has not yet adopted a state code, but California has numerous building restrictions administered by different agencies. Very few states require licensing of building officials.[8]

The Building Code Procedure. Since many housing consumers will be involved with one or more building codes during their future housing experience, some knowledge of the procedure is advisable. When home building or remodeling are contracted, the contractor will attend to most of the procedural details. Do-it-yourselfers carry through the procedure themselves. Plans are submitted with the application and the fee, but it may take some time for approval to be granted. Some construction requires an electrical and plumbing permit as well. Complete information about the piece of property and the project must be provided such as the lot, block, tract and street address (or the assessor's parcel number), the occupancy, and the house's valuation. Plans should include set-

Major home improvements, and some minor improvements require a building permit. The homeowner is responsible for the application process, payment of fees, and provision of accurate and complete information. Photo by author.

backs, topographic features, easements, electricity and plumbing details, and so on. Fees charged may be very modest in some areas ($20) to very high in others.

Exceptions to building codes can be granted, if the need for the variance is logical and the interpretation of the code is flexible. The home owner may need to justify the code variance at a hearing, but complete information and sound reasoning can affect a favorable decision.

Some home improvement projects are not of much concern to the building official. Refinishing, cabinetry, and paneling that does not affect the structure itself may be exempt. Building codes differ greatly in what is included in their regulations and what specifically is not. Communities may place a dollar value limit on the work being done as a means of allowing minor projects to be done without permit.

Specification Versus Performance Standards. Building codes traditionally specified the exact materials and method to be used in housing construction. In doing so, they inhibited the development and use of new materials and building technology. A performance standard, on the other hand, describes what the materials and techniques must do, such as not burn up, support a certain weight, withstand a certain pressure. If a building code is written so that what the construction must achieve is made clear, then presumably any material and technique that accomplishes the goal is possible. This would allow building innovation and flexibility. **Specification building codes** are often accused of increasing the costs of construction because cheaper and equally effective materials are disallowed. **Performance building codes** could, therefore, reduce housing construction costs. The resistance to performance building codes is based on the foreseeable difficulty in testing new materials and techniques at the local level. If testing were done at the state or federal level, then some of the burden of local code enforcement could be alleviated.

In spite of apparent advantages to performance codes and uniform codes, little headway has been made toward their adoption. In spite of the shortcomings of existing codes, building officials and professional builders nevertheless work satisfactorily within them.

Housing Codes

The first housing codes were born out of public concern for the unsafe and unhealthy housing conditions that were dramatically obvious in New York City's tenements in the nineteenth century. Chapter 1 details how these tenements and the early legislation that regulated them were developed in that city. But it was not until 1949 that national concern was expressed for unsafe and unsanitary housing conditions. The Housing Act of 1954 provided the leg-

The condition, use, occupancy, and maintenance of all housing in a community is addressed in housing codes. Photo courtesy of U.S. Department of Housing and Urban Development.

islative weapon for enacting housing codes in all communities, even though some still have not done so, especially in rural areas where substandard housing may account for a higher percentage of the housing stock than in urban areas.

The first housing codes were intended to prevent unsafe and unsanitary conditions by establishing minimum standards for basic equipment, ventilation, and sanitation. They have evolved to include broader aspects of housing having to do with defining overall quality of life. For instance, the condition, use, occupancy and maintenance of residences may be expressed in terms of the welfare of their occupants. Codes vary greatly in the extent of their coverage and the specified elements of safe and sanitary housing. The lack of uniformity between codes is one of the recognized problems of housing codes.

Inspections. Whether or not a housing unit meets the minimum standards set forth in the community's housing code is determined by an on-site inspection. Some communities, which can afford sufficient personnel, might have systematic inspections occurring at regular intervals or at each time the housing unit is vacant. Licensing of housing units is one method of making sure housing units maintain housing code standards. It is much more typical that inspections occur only after a tenant has complained about specific housing code violations. Small communities may have only one inspector who cannot possibly check the conditions of all housing units. Furthermore, owner-occupied housing is, for all practical purposes, exempt from code compliance because (1) owners will not report bad conditions themselves, and (2) a concern for the rights of private property results in noninterference. In these times of limited tax revenues to support community services, the problem of too few inspectors will not soon be solved.

Effectiveness. Since housing codes are generally applied to rental properties, a large part of housing in most communities is overlooked. Further, not all rental property is subject to compliance with the housing code. Many tenants are either unaware of the housing code with which their rented unit should comply, or they are afraid of eviction or rent increases should they inform the building inspector of housing code problems. At the heart of this dilemma is a fundamental issue about housing codes: should housing codes eliminate all poor housing in a community? In reality, low-income people often cannot afford anything but poor housing. To state it differently, housing that is brought up to code may necessarily carry higher rents, thus effectively eliminating it as a housing option for low-income families.

In some communities, differential en-

Active code enforcement may result in abandoned housing. The owners may choose to abandon it instead of improving it and having their property taxes increased. Photo courtesy of U.S. Department of Housing and Urban Development.

forcement of housing codes has been the way around this dilemma. Housing codes are applied to middle-income or lower-middle-income neighborhoods, whereas low-income neighborhoods are more or less left to deteriorate further. Where then is the meaning of community standards for minimum quality housing? In effect, minimum quality is different depending on the income level of the residents being housed. Few thinking citizens would openly advocate unsafe and unsanitary housing for some members of our society. On the other hand, few citizens are openly advocating appropriate funding through taxes for more equitable enforcement of housing codes throughout their communities.

The problem would not be solved solely by numerous well-trained inspectors. An active code enforcement program could result in an increase in abandoned housing, because owners may choose to abandon the property rather than repair it. Landlords have also chosen to violate enforcement figuring that the fines thus levied are less than the costs of required repairs. Abandoned housing has the same effect as rent increases due to code enforcement. The displaced tenants seek housing elsewhere thus raising rents paid for available housing. In any case, strict housing code enforcement does not often result in improved housing conditions for low-income families.

There have been efforts in some areas to improve the situation of housing code effectiveness. By providing low-interest loans to owners to improve their house, some deteriorating housing may be restored. The back-to-the-city movement has been spurred by the urban homesteading programs in some cities in which abandoned housing is available to residents at minimal cost. In return, they bring the housing up to code within a limited period of time. Considering it is most often middle-class

families moving into these bargain houses, these programs do not usually benefit low-income families. Property taxes could also be restructured so that improved housing was rewarded rather than punished.

All in all, no large-scaled solution to the housing code dilemma has been found. As Meeks, Oudekerk, and Sherman state, "One of the discouraging realities of code enforcement is the recurrent nature of the problem. . . . housing code enforcement must be continuous and sustained in order to keep older housing from losing ground to the forces of deterioration and decay."[9] The web of political, economic, and legal factors woven around housing code enforcement is complex indeed.

RENTING

With a slowing down of production of rental housing, and the increasing number of previous rentals being converted to condominiums, fewer and fewer rental units are available for housing consumer choices. Because of limited rental availability, it is now critical that rental decisions be made cautiously and wisely. Understanding the rights and responsibilities of both the landlord and the tenant is important in entering into this legal relationship.

Tenant-Landlord Law

Even though tenants nowadays rent space rather than land from the landlord, the laws that govern the tenant-landlord relationship date from medieval times. The agrarian tradition is persistent to this day in some states in those laws which do not prevent the renting of substandard units, which relieve the landlord of maintenance and repairs responsibilities and which permit landlord access to the tenants' private quarters, among other things.[10] A few states, however, have tenant-landlord laws that are realistically concerned with the problems of tenants. The overall view expressed here by Mowery seems an accurate description of an essentially unfair situation:

> The two parties are not in an equitable bargaining position. Political power rests with the landlord. Economic power rests with the landlord. He controls the supply, and all of this is set against the historical background, . . . which establishes the framework of expectations on which common law decisions are usually based. Needless to say, legal decisions have tended to favor the property owner. Even if, [and where], . . . laws to protect the rental housing consumer are adopted, the tenant is still likely not to know what his rights are.[11]

Considering the costs involved in filing suit against a landlord and the fear of retaliatory actions, many tenants do not seek justice in unfair renting situations.

Rental Agreements. There are three kinds of rental agreements. One is simply an oral agreement to pay the rent at regular intervals for the use of the space. Nothing is written down, and no signatures are required. As the most informal type of rental agreement, it is the easiest one to get out of, but the tenant should give notice one rent period prior to leaving (one week, two weeks, one month, whichever is the rent payment period). Whatever rules, conditions, and waivers might be contained in a written agreement are thus avoided, but rents can be raised and rules changed because they are not agreed to in writing.

Oral agreements are legal and enforceable, but both parties are at a disadvantage (tenants more than landlords) as time goes by and memory fades. A judge would have to weigh the tenant's word against the landlord's. If verbal promises are made at the

outset, such as repairs to be made or deposits to be returned, it is best to have them confirmed in writing, with the date and landlord's signature on the written promise.

The written rental agreement does have all matters affecting the tenant-landlord relationship in writing, but it is a less formal agreement than a lease. It often permits month-to-month occupancy, and it permits rent increases. The move-out stipulation is the same as in an oral agreement. A written rental agreement may have legal terminology which protects the interest of the landlord.

A **lease** is a form of contract between the tenant and the landlord. In addition to the stipulations of a written rental agreement, which often looks like a lease because preprinted forms are used, the length of the rental period is specified. During that time, (six months, nine months, one year), the rent cannot be raised, nor can the tenant be **evicted** unless the tenant breaks the terms of the lease. Leases normally specify the property, the names of tenant and landlord, the rent due date, the amount of rent, the responsibilities for maintenance, and the landlord's rules and regulations. Tenants should understand that they cannot easily get out of a lease agreement; they are obligated to rent the housing unit for the period specified whether or not their housing needs change.

Preprinted forms used in both written rental agreements and leases generally favor the landlord. As three lawyers advise:

> These forms need not look like a death certificate, nor read like an act of Congress, but such is often the case. Some of the worst ones include paragraphs by which you sign away your privacy, accept shorter than normal notice periods for rent increases and termination, accept responsibility for fixing things that should be handled by your landlord and generally

A leased apartment involves a legal obligation to pay a specified amount of rent for a specified period of time. Tenants should understand the exact terms of their lease contracts. Photo by author.

elevate the landlord into the position of a minor dictator.[12]

Provisions. Some of the provisions that may be included in a lease agreement which place the tenant at a disadvantage are listed below. The tenant may strike out or rewrite these clauses to achieve a lease that is fair to both parties.

1. A provision against assignment or sublease without the landlord's consent might prevent you from finding another tenant to take your place. The tenant can change this to read that the landlord cannot reject any tenant unless there is a justifiable reason for doing so, such as a bad credit rating.

2. A provision that the landlord is not responsible for damage means that negligence which may result in accidents is not the landlord's fault.

3. A provision setting a notice period of less than thirty days should be changed so the tenant has at least this much advance notice of rent increases or other changes.

4. A provision of "right of re-entry" means the landlord can force the tenant out if rent is not paid. Most states protect tenants with legal eviction proceedings, so this provision is invalid.

5. A provision of late charges might be a problem for tenants who occasionally have valid reasons for being a few days late with the rent.

6. A provision which says that the agreement is the entire agreement means that any verbal promises made which were not written down are not valid.

7. Waivers to right of appeal or right to jury trial might be written in but they are illegal in some states, therefore may not be valid. These kinds of provisions are included to intimidate the tenant rather than to be used in legal proceedings.

It is obvious that leases and written rental agreements must be read carefully and understood thoroughly before they are signed. Help should be sought with the legal language of leases. Many tenants' groups, legal aid offices, and other housing agencies can provide such help or give directions to where it can be found. Tenants' rights handbooks are available in some states and on some campuses.

Landlords do have specific rights in tenant-landlord law. They can decide who can live in the housing units, so long as there is no discrimination because of race, creed, color, national origin, ancestry, and sex. There are legal exceptions, and illegal but persistent practices of such discrimination are discussed in the next chapter section. The landlord can sell the property or convert it to condominium ownership. Periods of leases, amounts of rent and deposits, and terms of the agreement can all be rightfully determined by the landlord.

Tenants have responsibilities that include keeping the unit as safe and clean as possible, disposing of garbage and rubbish in a safe and sanitary method, using facilities and appliances in a reasonable manner, and generally conducting themselves in a manner that is not disturbing to neighbors. Tenants may not "destroy, deface, damage, impair, or remove any part of the premises or knowingly permit any other person to do so."[13] A rowdy party guest who throws an open beer can across a living room is the tenant's responsibility.

Deposits. Several kinds of deposits are commonly used. Tenants tend to think of them as interchangeable because they all amount to the same thing—money. Deposits must be paid in addition to the first month's rent before moving in. Each has its specific purposes and characteristics.

1. **Security deposits** are used against unpaid rent, or damage done to the housing unit, or costs of cleaning when the tenant leaves. The security deposit may be as high as one month's rent, but all

The fees charged and the restrictions that are applied in rental apartments insure the landlord that the property will be well maintained over time. Photo by author.

or part of it should be refunded if all conditions are met; that is, no rent is unpaid, no damage is done, and the unit is left clean. The security deposit allows the landlord compensation for these costs instead of finding the negligent tenant and suing for them. Whatever amount is due the tenant should be paid within the time period stated in the lease or specified in state law.

2. **Cleaning deposits** are held specifically for cleaning after the tenant leaves. If the unit is left as clean as possible, with normal wear and tear taken into account, the cleaning deposit should be returned. This deposit should not be more than it costs to have the premises cleaned, which with inflation has increased. The cleaning deposit is generally lower than a normal security deposit. If a "cleaning fee" is charged instead, the landlord may have no intention of returning it no matter how clean the place is left.

3. **Damage deposits,** like cleaning deposits, are meant for one purpose. If the renter has not caused damage, the deposit should be refunded.

4. The last month's rent is often required in addition to the initial rent and deposits. This amounts to a large cash outlay before moving in, but the tenant has the advantage of having paid for the last month of the period of the lease in advance. This may be very attractive feature when it comes time to move, and the next landlord is requiring first and last month's rent, plus deposits, or when home ownership with all its attendant costs, is the next step.

5. Other fees might include the cost of a credit check and a holding deposit. The latter is used to hold the unit and is also called a "bond deposit." If prospective renters change their minds, the landlord probably keeps the deposit to pay for the loss of other prospective renters during the period the unit was held. This holding fee can be applied to the first month's rent.

Rental Restrictions. Most landlords have very specific rules and restrictions for the use not only of the housing units but also of the grounds and facilities. The welfare of all tenants is the primary goal, and the prevention of abuse to the property and other tenants is another goal. These may change over time, but the tenant has a right to be informed of them at the beginning of occupancy and afterwards if any changes occur. Whether or not the landlord accepts children or animals is his prerogative. Painting, papering, picture hanging, special furnishings (such as waterbeds), may not be allowed. Parties, use of television sets and musical equipment are usually limited to certain times of the day. Parking spaces for tenants and guests may be very specific. Pool rules, laundry room rules, and so on, are not uncommon. Some outdoor activities and gardening may be allowed. Even though these details affecting livability can be oppresive to renters, the landlord has the right to set them. It is the tenant's responsibility to make a housing choice that wisely considers them.

Uniform Residential Landlord Tenant Act (URLTA). There is a need in many places to eliminate those aspects of tenant-landlord law that do not recognize the full rights of tenants in a fair rental arrangement which is in keeping with contemporary times. The problems of tenants have been particularly noticeable in urban areas. The Uniform Residential Landlord Tenant Act was designed in 1972 (modified in 1974) to provide a model for all states so that the tenant-landlord law could be made uniform, modern, and simplified. The obligations of both tenants and landlords were spelled out clearly, and remedies for both

What to Ask the Landlord before Renting

Q: What is the proper proportion of your income for rent?

A: An old rule of thumb is that your total monthly shelter costs should not exceed one week's pay. That rule can be bent and should be, depending on the level of your income, extent of your obligations, and other safeguards. But it's a basic beginning.

Q: What type of shelter is best?

A: An apartment offers the most service and requires the least responsibility. The heating, yardwork and repairs are taken care of by building management.

An attached house, townhouse or duplex generally will give you a small yard, the care of which will be your responsibility. Your utilities also could be your responsibilities.

A detached house will provide you with more living space, a larger yard, frequently a carport, garage or parking space, and generally more privacy. In addition to your rent, you are responsible for the usual expenses of running a home, including utilities, trash collection and lawn maintenance.

Q: What are the best ways to find rental housing?

A: Start with your friends and acquaintances. Ask if they know of places coming up for rent. This could be a great source.

Check newspaper classified ads and brokers in the area. So-called "apartment finders" may be of help, but be wary of being charged merely for lists taken from daily papers also avaliable to you.

Ask apartment managers or superintendents of buildings in which you are interested if apartments are coming on the market.

Q: What should you ask the landlord if you find a place?

A: When you put down the application fee, ask if this commits you to take the dwelling if you are accepted. If you reject the unit, will any charges be deducted from your application payment? What happens to the fee of the prospective landlord fails to provide you with a satisfactory dwelling? How long will it take after the application for the landlord to advise you of an acceptance?

When you tour the dwelling, make a list of all damages and needed repairs. Ask the landlord if he will repair them before you sign a rental agreement. Have the landlord make a list of damages. Keep a copy of that list. Get a completion date for repair of damages.

If the landlord refuses to repair the damages, ask him to sign an acknowledgement that you have pointed them out to him. Have the landlord attach a copy of the reported damages to your lease.

If you still plan to rent despite the damages, keep a copy of the report for your records to protect you against claims when you move out. Find out what repairs are your responsibility as a tenant; have this spelled out in your rental agreement.

Get in writing the address and phone number where the owner or landlord can be contacted, so you can locate either one.

Be sure you understand all the terms in the rental agreement before you sign. Ask questions about the "legalese." Don't rely on any oral promises. Get everything in writing.

If the landlord has set up rules and regulations to preserve his property or to safeguard tenants, learn what they are before you enter into a rental agreement.

Be clear on all deposits required: a cleaning deposit which allows the landlord to clean, or paint after you move; a damage deposit which must be returned when you leave the premises unless you caused excess physical damage; and a security deposit, sometimes used interchangeably with a damage deposit. Read your lease with care to find out if there are any specified. The terms and conditions of rental agreements as well as prohibitions were designated. Some states have adopted URLTA and others are considering adoption. A few states have tenant-landlord laws that are more progressive than URLTA in dealing with tenant-landlord relations in modern urban areas.

Rent Control

Whether or not a community should control the amount of rent a landlord can charge is not a new controversy, but in these inflationary times, rent controls are being adopted by communities that never before considered them. When housing shortages occur, the demand for available vacant rental units drives up their market value. A case in point is the demand for housing in Alaska during the Alaskan pipeline construction which drove rents up 200 percent to 300 percent.[14] Such housing emergencies occur in different times and places, for different reasons, and to less dramatic degrees. Nevertheless, the past decade has witnessed a slowdown of rental housing production, an increase of rental housing condominium conversions, and a growing trend toward abandonment, all of which contribute to shortages. The results are rapid rent increases in many metropolitan areas. These areas in turn have enacted rent control as a means of consumer protection. By 1978, about one-eighth of the nation's rental units were subject to some form of rent regulation. Besides Alaska, cities

and towns in the Northeast, the District of Columbia, and California have enacted rent control programs.

The arguments in favor of rent control are based on a concern for low and moderate-income families and the elderly. The financial circumstances of these groups do not allow for enormous and rapid rent increases. An influx of population combined with a low vacancy rate does not increase the costs to the landlord of owning and maintaining rental housing, so why should he unduly profit from economic forces beyond the business of renting housing?

The point of view of landlords, real estate experts, and some housing economists is exactly the opposite. They argue that the long-range effects of rent control worsen the housing options for low-income families. Because landlords operating under rent control cannot, they argue, maintain their property properly, they eventually abandon it, adding to the problem of high demand and low housing availability. Rental housing investors are discouraged from producing housing in areas where their profits are unrealistically limited. Rent control has led to condominium conversions in some areas. That has led to another form of government control—the prevention of further condominium conversion. This controversial action is also meant to protect the present rental occupant but may, in the long run, worsen the rental housing situation.

The mechanisms of rent control can be suited to the particular housing situation in

Many cities and towns in the Northeast, as well as in Alaska and California, have rent control. While rent control is a temporary benefit to the consumer, it may worsen the long range availability of rental housing. Photo courtesy of U.S. Department of Housing and Urban Development.

the area of jurisdiction. Where a genuine emergency exists, stringent control may be necessary to prevent rent gouging. In this case, across-the-board controls are set with additional control over rent increases. Presumably, the emergency passes, but in the case of New York City, the housing emergency of the World War II era has persisted to this day. A less stringent form of rent control allows automatic rent increases because of increases in operating cost. The most limited form of rent control would allow the landlord to argue for rent setting and rent increases before a fair rent board or commission. In all cases, allowance for costs of housing code compliance should be considered necessary for proper maintenance of the housing stock.[15]

Adults-Only Rentals

A problem of significance to families with children seeking rental housing in many American cities is the common practice of some landlords of renting to adults only. For example, it was found that 70 percent of the apartment buildings in Los Angeles did not allow children in 1979.[16] The practice has been considered by many to be discriminating to children.

Since federal law prohibits housing discrimination based upon sex, race, color, religion, ancestry, and national origin, it seems odd that children as a class may be discriminated against. There have been efforts in some states to outlaw the practice, and some communities have adopted such legislation. Nevertheless, a California court case in 1979 established the right of landlords to rent to adults only on the grounds that children are noiser, more boisterous and cause higher maintenance costs than adults whose right to quiet enjoyment of their property must also be allowed.[17]

The issue of adults-only rental housing will continue to be the focus of local, state and possibly federal legislation, as well as court cases. As rental housing becomes more scarce, the greater the likelihood that landlords will prohibit children. At the same time, the more difficult it is for families to find suitable rentals, the greater the likelihood that there will be public action to prohibit this type of discrimination.

FAIR HOUSING

The Secretary of the U.S. Department of Housing and Urban Development said in 1977 that "public law and a continuing democratic tradition guarantee equality and make discrimination illegal. Far removed from this ideal, however, are the realities

Rentals for adults only have been viewed as discriminatory to children. This controversial issue is currently the focus of some court cases and local legislation. Photo by author.

of racially impacted neighborhoods, substandard ghetto housing, and untold instances of person-to-person discrimination in the sale, rental and financing of housing."[18] Although discrimination in housing is not limited to women and blacks, they comprise the two groups used to illustrate the problems in fair housing.

Women and Housing

The demographic characteristics outlined in chapter 2 include the trend toward delayed marriage. Consequently both men and women seek housing as singles in greater numbers than in the past. Of the one-fifth of all American households headed by a single person, the majority (62 percent) is maintained by women.[19] Divorced women and never-marrieds account for a large proportion of these households.

In 1978, there were eight million families maintained by women not living with a husband, an increase of 44 percent since the 1970 census. The number of black

women in this category increased 65 percent during that period.[20] Clearly, children are increasingly living with one-parent families, eleven times as many with their mothers as with their fathers. Nearly half of all children born today will spend "a meaningful portion of their lives before age eighteen in single-parent families."[21]

The above data dramatize the growing trend of single women as housing consumers. Obviously a great and growing number of women will seek housing for themselves and for their families in coming years. What then are the problems they face in finding satisfactory housing?

Renting. Whether unmarried, widowed, separated or divorced, women make up a large share of rental housing consumers. They seek, usually, medium-priced units in safe neighborhoods, convenient to jobs, transportation and shopping. Those with children are as concerned as suburban nuclear families with the quality of nearby schools. But in five urban areas studied regarding women and housing—Atlanta, St. Louis, San Antonio, San Francisco, and New York—such units were found to be (1) in increasingly short supply, and (2) subject to landlord bias.[22] The first of these factors affects all prospective renters by driving rents up. The effects of the limited number of units available at reasonable rents are especially severe on women. Women tend to be less economically well-off than their male counterparts. Furthermore, they tend to need larger units if they have children. To put it simply, women heads of households have housing needs that can be met only by larger and more expensive units available in the rental market, but they, on the average, have less money to pay for such adequate housing.

The sexism of landlords is a much more

Women with children often have a difficult time finding suitable rental housing. While discrimination based on sex is illegal, some landlords use subtle strategies to avoid renting to women with or without children. Photo courtesy of U.S. Department of Housing and Urban Development.

Home Ownership. Real estate brokers have a principal role to play in directing prospective buyers to houses on the market, steering buyers to lenders, and setting up secondary loan possibilities. The report published by HUD on discrimination in housing for women found brokers to exercise sexism in these ways: (1) brokers cling to prejudicial attitudes about women; (2) experienced brokers rarely sold houses to women or women heads of households; (3) brokers steer women to and away from certain available housing; (4) brokers employ discriminatory credit criteria in qualifying women buyers.[26]

Credit discrimination is another large area affecting accessibility to owned housing for women. Besides being refused home loans, women have been asked for additional requirements such as the payment of all outstanding loans, copies and verification of divorce papers, and so on. Male cosigners have been required by some lenders. Delaying tactics alone can discourage many women mortgage seekers. It must be pointed out that lenders are persisting in a long-established preference for male-headed nuclear families, and this preference has been given governmental sanction in the past.

In addition to dealing with all the discriminatory attitudes preventing single women access to mortgage money, divorced women have an additional burden of being considered unstable. Financial circumstances often complicate the picture. The attitudes towards divorced women who wish to rent housing also apply to women who wish to own housing.

Regarding still other forms of housing discrimination, the report states:

> Barriers to access, however important, emerge as but one dimension in the mosaic of sex discrimination in housing in

personal form of discrimination that that of the housing market described above. Women who have found suitable housing they can afford are often turned down in very obvious ways. Landlords may state openly that they prefer men, or that apartments are reserved for men.[23] It is assumed that men can and will keep up the property better than women. Male cosigners for leases are sometimes required.[24]

Separated or divorced women are considered unacceptable by many landlords. By renting "to married couples only" single women tenants are avoided. The prejudice that operates here is that single women are believed to have low moral standards. Landlords sometimes openly state that they fear single women will bring men into the house and give it a bad name.[25] Women are also assumed to have unstable incomes. A subtle technique is to take the woman's application and put her on a waiting list for an apartment, the vacancy for which somehow never materializes.

this country. Indisputably, shelter is more than a roof with supporting walls. With the physical structure, there must be related services and facilities for even modest enjoyment to be possible. . . . It's not enough to acquire a home if you can't get insurance, or anyone to assist with its maintenance without unconscionable gouging.[27]

Blacks and Housing

Racial discrimination in housing has a very firmly ingrained history in our institutions and in our practices. Because for centuries blacks have been allocated only certain areas in which to live, the patterns of racial segregation are only slightly blurred after recent decades of civil rights activities. The current controversy about school bussing in this country would not exist if non-segregated housing provided equal access to quality education.

Even though anti-discrimination laws exist (they are the subject of the next subsection), discrimination against blacks persists. Practices that are rooted in our racially separate past result in a racially separate present. Such practices include blockbusting, racial steering, denial of access to listings, differential pricing, selective advertising, redlining, and exclusionary zoning.[28] The last of these will be dealt with in the next chapter.

Most racially discriminating practices apply to the home-buying process. In blockbusting, a single home on a block is sold to a black family. The real estate agents inform the neighbors of this, seeking to list their houses, capitalizing on fears that the neighborhood will lose its value as it became more integrated. The panic selling often results in an all black block of owned homes. This practice is now illegal and has been professionally chastised by professional real estate organizations, but it still occurs.

Racial steering accompanies blockbusting: prospective black buyers are led to neighborhoods that are partly or mostly black already and are steered away from all white neighborhoods.

Redlining. Whether or not lending institutions use red pencils to mark areas on maps considered high risk, the practice of withholding loan money to certain deteriorating neighborhoods is termed "redlining." Insurance companies often follow suit, as has the FHA in years past. The result of redlining is discrimination against low-income families, and because blacks tend to live in low-income and deteriorating urban neighborhoods, the discrimination affects them as a group most directly. After an area has been so earmarked, it often declines more rapidly than if financial support had been available. It is ironic that some federal housing programs have been designed specifically to prevent further deterioration of some basically livable areas while at the same time, other forces are hastening the decay.

The practice of redlining became a public issue in the 1970s. The Home Mortgage Disclosure Act of 1975 was passed to prevent the practice. Banks that are part of the Federal Reserve Banking system are now required to disclose where they make loans, what type of loans they grant, and what loans they purchase. This provides the residents of a community the opportunity to obtain information on the lending practices in their neighborhoods.[29]

In some areas, local residents who have been denied home improvement loans even though they have put savings in local institutions, have protested loudly enough so that lenders have enacted programs distributing the risk area loans among several institutions. Most lending institutions will deny that redlining persists today, and they

will furnish information on property locations being financed as well as define the
needs for loans in their areas.

Black ghettos. This country's housing
has been, among other things, a history of
large migrations of poor people into urban
areas. The first chapter dealt with this phenomenon as it shaped forms of housing in
New York, Boston, St. Louis, and elsewhere. The largest migration into urban
areas in this century was the black movement from the rural South to the industrial
Northeast. Blacks tended to move into existing slum areas because the rents were low
and other blacks were already there. This
impacting of an area created a black ghetto
which was then reinforced by the real estate, banking and political components of
the city. One analyst describes the process
this way: "If there is a disproportionate
number of blacks with limited rent-paying
ability seeking housing accommodations, a
new ghetto cluster is sometimes formed in
an alternate low-income area."[30] Since
whites often do not want to share social
space with blacks, many cities have become
concentrated clusters of several black ghettos. As more blacks move in, more whites
flee.

Setting aside, for the movement, the
immensity of the social problems created for
the black population in the cities, and for
the nation as a whole, there are four specific housing problems for blacks in ghettos.
One is the availability of housing. As a low-
rent area fills to capacity, fewer units are
available for the continuing influx of people. The doubling and tripling within units
adds a further housing hardship on older
and incoming residents. A second problem
is one of cost. As the demand increases for
the very poorest of housing, the cost of rent
goes up. The quality of the shelter available
in urban ghettos is the very lowest in the

country, matched only by some substandard rural dwellings, and crowding only
worsens the quality of the structures. And
lastly, the provision of social services to
these neighborhoods is very inadequate.
Simple expectations in middle-class white
neighborhoods of trash removal, sewage
disposal, available heat and water become
major problems of everyday life in a ghetto.
The problems of maintaining such housing
to housing code levels have already been
discussed. In short, ghetto housing is
largely substandard and it will likely remain so.

Fair Housing Law
One may well ask why there are no laws
designed to prevent the kinds of discrimi-
nation that have been described. There are.
HUD has established the Office of the As-
sistant Secretary for Fair Housing and
Equal Opportunity to administer eight laws.
These are:

1. Title VIII of the Civil Rights Act of
   1968 relates to fair housing. It commits
   the government to equal opportunity in
   housing for all citizens regardless of
   race, sex, color, or national origin.
2. Title VI of the Civil Rights Act of 1964
   prohibits discrimination in programs or
   activities receiving federal financial assistance.
3. Section 3 of the Housing and Urban
   Development Act of 1968 as amended
   pertains to training and employment opportunities for low-income residents in
   HUD assisted projects.

The problems of black ghettos in many major
American cities are enormous. The crowding,
cost, and poor quality of available housing are
among many related social problems. Photo courtesy of U.S. Department of Housing and Urban
Development.

4. Section 109 of the Housing and Community Development Act of 1974 prohibits discrimination in programs it set up.
5. Four Executive Orders, numbers 11063, 11246, 11478, and 11625, refer to non-discrimination in assisted housing, hiring of construction contractors, employment within HUD, and business enterprises.[31]

Even though the impression may be that these laws and executive orders cover all the bases, the gains made by minority groups of all kinds have been small. Yes, many more women are being granted home loans than were ten years ago. Many more blacks live in middle-class neighborhoods. But the goal set in 1968 of eliminating ghettos through fair housing legislation has not been met.

The problem is one of enforcement. HUD has little power even though it is central in the process of receiving, investigating and conciliating complaints. Many people discriminated against are unaware of the practices to which they are subject. If they are aware they do not know whom to blame, where to complain, or even if it is worth their trouble. The processes are slow, often personally and financially expensive, and finally, conciliation is voluntary.

If a dramatic turnaround in centuries-old practices of discrimination was expected with the enactment of a few legislative acts, the entrenchment in our culture of these practices was overlooked. A stroke of a pen does not stop the way people think and behave. Nevertheless, the problem of fair housing is still one of urgency "for many Americans whose path to wider job markets, better schools, and safer neighborhoods—in short, to a more secure place in our society—is blocked by discriminatory housing barriers."[32]

_____ SUMMARY _____

Homes may be owned by a couple in several different ways. Joint ownership, joint tenancy, tenancy by entirety, or tenancy in common each has its advantages and disadvantages. The eight states that have community property laws automatically determine the form of ownership a home-buying couple will have.

The rights to property are often divided among several owners. Deeds vary in their legal implications. A general warranty deed is superior to a special warranty deed or a quitclaim deed. A title search and title insurance protect the home owner against claims of rights to ownership from other parties. A lien on property is a legal means of getting paid money rightfully due. Both easements and deed restrictions are legal infringements on property rights.

Home warranties have come into use in the past few years. The HOW program protects new houses for ten years. The NAR warranty covers used houses for one or two years. Building codes govern the quality of housing construction at the outset as well as construction during remodeling. Were building codes more uniform from community to community, and were they based on performance rather than specification standards, housing costs might be reduced through innovative building technology. The dilemma of housing code enforcement involves the inequitable lack of application of codes to owner-occupied housing, and the detrimental results of strict enforcement in low-income neighborhoods.

The traditions of tenant-landlord law have favored the landlord. As more and more tenants, individually and in groups, challenge unfair interpretations of the law, the balance has shifted. Verbal rental agreements are less satisfactory than written agreements or leases. The provisions in a lease should cover basic matters in the tenant-landlord contractural relationship, but leases often also include items that intimidate the tenant or that favor the landlord. The rights and responsibilities of both landlords and tenants have been clearly defined by URLTA.

Adults-only rentals which limit the availability of rental housing to families with children will continue to be a public issue. Rent control, another current issue, affects not only the amount of rent to be paid at a given time, but the overall quality of available rental housing in many urban areas where it is used. As inflation and the rental

unit shortage increase, the public pressure for rent control will also increase. The public issues involved should be considered by all housing consumers.

After more than ten years of fair housing law, many minority groups still experience overt and subtle forms of housing discrimination. Each of the two groups used to illustrate these problems, women and blacks, deals with specific practices. Women are prevented from renting and owning housing of their choice through both institutional and personal biases. Blacks are victimized by practices such as blockbusting, steering and redlining. The enormous problems created for low-income black renters in urban ghettos are related to the social problems these ghettos create for cities and the nation as a whole.

Notes

1. Lee, S. J., *Buyer's Handbook for the Single-Family Home* (New York: Van Nostrand Reinhold Co., 1979), p. 79.
2. Dasso, J., A. A. Ring, and D. McFall, *Fundamentals of Real Estate* (Englewood Cliffs, N.J.: Prentice-Hall, 1977), p. 114.
3. Ibid., pp. 114–15.
4. "HOW Protects 375,000 Homes," *Builder*, 1978, *1* (27), p. 39.
5. Ibid.
6. Nelson, D. R., "Why Builders Should Know HOW," *Real Estate Review*, 1978, *8* (1), p. 52.
7. Ryan, J. E., "State Building Codes— Their Evolution and Application," *The Building Official and Code Administrator*, 1978, *12* (5), p. 12.
8. Ryan, J. E., "State Building Codes— Their Evolution and Application," *The Building Official and Code Administrator*, 1978, *12* (10), p. 15.
9. Meeks, C. B., E. H. Oudekerk, and B. Sherman, "Housing Code Dilemmas,"

Real Estate Law Journal, 1978, *6* p. 313.
10. Angell, W. J., "A Forgotten Consumer (the Renter)," *Proceedings of the American Association of Housing Educators*, 1973, *8*, p. 73.
11. Mowery, E. B., "The Problem— Landlord-Tenant Relations." *Proceedings of the American Association of Housing Educators*, 1973, *8*, p. 76.
12. Moskovitz, M., R. Warner, and C. E. Sherman, *California Tenants' Handbook* 3rd ed. (Berkeley, Cal.: Nolo Press, 1975), p. 27.
13. U.S. Department of Housing and Urban Development, *Wise Rental Practice* (Washington, D.C.: Author, 1977), p. 23.
14. Lett, M. R., *Rent Control: Concepts, Realities, and Mechanisms* (New Brunswick, N J: Center of Urban Policy Research, Rutgers).
15. Ibid., p. 203.
16. Forster, M., "Campaign against 'Adults-

Only' Housing Growing in California,"
Los Angeles Times, Oct. 14, 1979, pp.
I–1; 28.
17. "Court Upholds Landlord's Right to
Exclude Children from Apartments,"
Housing, 1979, 56 (7), p. 16.
18. Harris, P. R., "Fair Housing—From the
Ideal to the Reality," *HUD Challenge*,
1977, 8 (4), p. 2.
19. "Single-person Households Increasing,
Says Report," *AHEA Action*, 1979,
6 (1), p. 2.
20. Ibid.
21. Ibid.
22. National Council of Negro Women,
*Women and Housing: A Report on Sex
Discrimination in Five American Cities*
(Washington, D.C.: U.S. Department
of Housing and Urban Development,
1975), p. 32.
23. Ibid., p. 35.
24. Ibid., p. 36.

25. Ibid., pp. 40–41.
26. Ibid., pp. 52–53.
27. Ibid., pp. 73–74.
28. Chandler, R. W., "Foundation and Fair
Housing," *HUD Challenge*, 1978, 9
(4), p. 10.
29. Kollias, K., *Disclosure and Neighborhood
Reinvestment: A Citizen's Guide*
(Washington, D.C.: National Center for
Urban Affairs, 1976), p. 1.
30. Rose, H. M., "Social Processes in the
City: Race and Urban Residential Choice,"
in D. R. Mandelker and R. Montgomery,
eds., *Housing in America: Problems and
Perspectives* (Indianapolis, Ind.: Bobbs-
Merrill, 1973), p. 369.
31. "The Office of Fair Housing and Equal
Opportunity: An Overview," *HUD
Challenge*, 1978, 9 (4), p. 4.
32. Chandler, "Foundation and Fair
Housing," p. 10.

Suggested Readings

Angell, W. J. "A Forgotten Consumer (The
Renter)." *Proceedings of the American
Association of Housing Educators*. 1973, 8,
72–96.
Case, D. "Segregation in Housing: Its Costs to
Life Chances and Some Solutions." In
C. S. Wedin and L. G. Nygren, eds.
Housing Perspectives (2nd ed.). Minneapolis:
Burgess, 1979.
Consumers Union of the United States. "How
to Read a Lease." In C. S. Wedin and
L. G. Nygren, eds. *Housing Perspectives*
(2nd ed.). Minneapolis: Burgess, 1979.
Conway, W. G. "Fair Housing: Not Here You
Won't." *Saturday Review*, February 18,
1978, pp. 23–24.
Fowler, G. "The Bitter Fruit of Rent Control."
Nations' Business, 1978, 66 (8) 63–66.
Harl, N. E. "Some Legal Aspects of House
Buying." In C. S. Wedin and L. G.
Nygren, eds. *Housing Perspectives* (2nd ed.).
Minneapolis: Burgess, 1979.

HUD Challenge, 1978, 9 (4), entire issue on
fair housing.
Meeks, C. B.; Oudekerk, E. H. and
Sherman, B. "Housing Code Dilemmas."
Real Estate Law Journal, 1978, 6,
297–319.
Milgram, M. *Good Housing*. New York:
W. W. Norton, 1977, (chap. 1 "United
States Housing Patterns and the Law").
National Council of Negro Women, Inc.
*Women & Housing: A Report on Sex
Discrimination in Five American Cities*.
Washington, D.C.: U.S. Department of
Housing and Urban Development, 1975.
U.S. Department of Housing and Urban
Development. *Wise Rental Practices*.
Washington, D.C.: Author, 1977.
Wedin, C. S. "Codes and Controls," and
"Home Warranties." In C. S. Wedin and
L. G. Nygren, eds. *Housing Perspectives*
(2nd ed.). Minneapolis: Burgess, 1979.

Planning Concepts and Housing Trends

10

New England towns, described in the first chapter, were planned communities in the strictest sense. Every aspect of family and community life was planned for with an appropriate allocation of land. Railroad towns, too, were planned communities. But there are many more examples of town nonplanning than planning in American housing development during the last two centuries. Villages grow into towns, into modest-sized cities, into metropolises, into enormous urban regions. The unplanned-for growth occurs in spite of the human lack of vision to plan for it.

The mid-twentieth century gave birth to formalized concern for the inevitable patterns of growth. A handful of professional planners in 1907 has grown to more than 10,000. Professional planning became widespread even in small, but growing, communities. City planning as a profession, and as a public ideal, is described well by Abrams:

> City planning is a profession, an art, a science, a governmental function, and a social and political movement. . . . City planning not only concerns urban communities and their relationship to the regions of which they are a part, but seeks or should seek to improve the conditions of urban and suburban life and well-being through sensibly arranging the residential, commercial, and industrial parts of areas;

This high-rise is in Roosevelt Island, a new-town-in-town in the East River adjacent to Manhattan in New York City. There are no cars in this community of 20,000 people. Photo courtesy of U.S. Department of Housing and Urban Development.

developing each section to standards of space consonant with health and safety; providing good housing at costs within the means of the inhabitants; supplying adequate recreational, educational, and other communal facilities; providing an efficient system of circulation and adequate utilities and public services; identifying the financial resources to fulfill these objectives; creating environments people can live and grow in decently, without unreasonable restraints on the lives they choose to lead.[1]

Professional planners then, are ideally suited to arrange the physical, social, economic, and political environments in such a way as to provide us with optimum conditions for the quality of life we might choose. Despite the fact that there is no known example of such an achievement in the United States, either because of or in spite of professional planning, the ideal is outlined so that the mechanisms planners use can be seen in their own philosophical context.

This chapter will begin with basics, that is, a consideration of the relationship of land and people. Land is a resource, just as water, air, oil, and minerals are resources. The way people use this limited resource is at the crux of planning issues and practice.

Next, the practice of planning is described by explaining the implementation and use of general plans for several levels of government. Zoning has been the traditional means of sorting out one kind of land use from another. Typical zoning within a community is covered. The second section ends with a discussion of the newer development of coastal zones.

Cluster housing is the subject of the third section. This trend toward using innovative means of allocating land between shared and private uses is looked at carefully because it sets a pattern for housing developments of the future. **Planned unit developments (PUDs)** are a type of special zoning that allows cluster housing innovations.

There are some "new towns" in this country, and even though governmental support for them is on the wane, they are a kind of planning that should not be ignored. A good living and working environment is planned more thoroughly and on a larger scale in a new town than in any other planning scheme, thus giving the housing consumer a valuable opportunity to examine basic questions: what is a good housing environment, and how best can it be achieved?

New towns have led to the development of **new-towns-in-town.** The seeming double talk refers to the adaptation of new-town planning scope and characteristics to problems of older urban areas. These are covered in the last section of this chapter.

LAND AND PEOPLE

Historically, this country has taken land for granted. At one time there was an abundance of it; in fact, plenty for everyone. Even as growth pressures within some northeastern cities resulted in high-density housing forms, the belief that land could be attained in large amounts was never threatened. If one had money to purchase a sizable plot of land for private living purposes, then that achievement was not only allowed, it was respected and admired. Large estates are still revered; they can become successful public attractions because of our reverence.

This American value of land—really a value of the-more-land-the-better—is paralleled by another strong value. It is the value of land as a commercial asset. "Land parcels have been allocated to different uses according to their private rate of return."[2]

Thus, land is thought to be fairly allocated when it is put to its highest and best use. But highest and best use has not been determined by what is best for the society at large. Instead, private developers have decided what needs to be developed where and when. These apparently public decisions have traditionally been privately made. Private developers do not make decisions unless the expected profit warrants them. At the heart, then, of the question of where housing is to be built is the question of where money can be made.

This traditional way of valuing and using land is now challenged by other values. The primary one that has become central to many social changes in the last decade is the value of preserving the natural environment. It has been the environmentalists who have raised the question of what kind of future are we creating if we spoil our water, pollute the air, and build foolishly on flood plains, fertile valleys, sand dunes, and so on. The environmentalists are joined by suburbanites who do not want to pay for additional housing services necessitated by increased development. (Roads, water and sewer lines, and schools are paid for by their property taxes.) To emphasize the complexity of the transition from old to new ways of valuing land, Solomon writes:

> Our land use controls, administrative processes, and laws are lagging behind new imperatives. Historical divisions between private and public spheres need to be bridged. What is clear is that the present deadlock over America's land use system will not be broken until we reach a new accommodation between collective and private interests, present and future generations, and racial and income classes.[3]

Communities no longer assume that unlimited growth is desirable. They now realize that natural resources are limited resources. How can communities preserve forests and wetlands, conserve water and land resources, protect coastal areas and other ecologically important regions, and at the same time provide housing, jobs, shopping, recreation and sufficient electricity for a growing population? There are no easy answers to this question. Solomon makes five specific recommendations which taken together mean no less than a major commitment to public planning and institutional change. They also mean a more active role in planning for local and state governments, and a change in legal doctrine. Solomon readily admits that there is much resistance to changing the status quo on the part of people who have most to gain from the present system. "But if we truly desire to make our land system more responsive to our new imperatives, as well as to our traditional values, we must change the ways in which we think about these problems and work for their solution."[4]

Accompanying the large issue of environmental protection and ecologically careful land use is another large issue, perhaps larger. It deals with how we sort out people by the ways we use land, especially the ways we use land for housing. Perin calls our planning, zoning, and development practices the "unstated rules governing what is widely regarded as correct social categories and relationships. . . ."[5] The land users, that is, the people who live in each category of land use, have their social relationships defined for them by the land use pattern in which they live: renters in inner-city zones of high density as opposed to home owners in suburban low-density zones of spacious single-family detached dwellings, for example. Traditional social categories such as income, race, occupation, educational level are accompanied in these housing categories by life cycle, renting and home ownership, citizenship, so-

Traditional methods of using land for housing has categorized people into social groups with renters nearly always in higher densities than suburban homeowners. Photo courtesy of U.S. Department of Housing and Urban Development.

cial homogeneity, and so on. In the major metropolitan areas, where most of the population lives, the social categorization of our land use system has resulted in a "white noose around the blacks and poor of central cities."[6] Our political and economic systems have resulted in conditions that do not measure up to the ideals of a great industrial democracy that we believe ourselves to be.

The "cultural artifacts" of our land use system are many, and they each affect the lives of everyone: (1) the chaotic patterns and the waste of energy and land in metropolitan development; (2) the procedural confusion, costly delays, and sometime bribery of zoning; (3) the monotony of speculators' subdivisions and the injustice of suburban exclusion (exclusionary zoning); (4) the ugliness and physical dangers of strip development along highways.[7] Why do we have land use regulations and taxing policies which result in these public problems? Because, Perin thinks, we have not asked

the right questions that might bring about a new way of thinking about the underlying issues. Her call to find new ways of thinking about the relationship of land and people echoes Solomon's conclusions about how to achieve a land use system based on new values.

PLANNING PRACTICES

In contrast to the very difficult questions raised in the analysis above, the questions normally dealt with in everyday planning practices are much less broad and challenging, even if their answers are not always simple. They tend to dwell simply on whether or not a particular development should take place on a given area of land.

The guidelines for these decisions at the local level are comprehensive plans, zoning ordinances, and subdivision regulations. In addition to discussing these basic tools of

The "Highest and Best" Use

By the late 1920s, largely through zoning, the one-family home was established as the "highest and best" use in the city planning schema of things. But the battle was not over. Just this year [1974] the U.S. Supreme Court had an important zoning case concerning the one-family zone. It arose in the village of Belle Terre, a Long Island town with only a few hundred residents, but a town near the State University of New York at Stony Brook. College students were renting houses in Belle Terre to the consternation of those townsfolk who wanted to keep Belle Terre as a place for families. So the town modified its zoning ordinance by defining the one-family zone as a zone in which no more than two persons not related by blood or marriage could live. This eliminated from the town all groups of college students living together since there were no apartments in Belle Terre. The ordinance had the effect of denying to Mr. Boraas, a homeowner in Belle Terre, the right to continue renting his house to college students as he had been. The "highest and best" use of his house, as far as Boraas was concerned, was the market price and students outbid everyone else. But that was not the determinant of the highest use in the political sense. The U.S. Supreme Court speaking through Justice Douglas, upheld the town ordinance, citing the fact that the people of Belle Terre could legislate the sort of environment they wanted. The noise, traffic, and general commotion of a neighborhood populated with groups of college students was not what they wanted. And Justice Douglas agreed that homeowners could utilize the powers of local government even in a very small town to secure the milieu that pleased them. Why, we might ask, did Justice Douglas, who is both an ardent environmentalist and an arch civil libertarian, perceive this case as one involving environmental protection and not as a civil liberties case? It could equally as well have been analyzed as a case in which people with one life-style (two children, three dogs, two cars, and a camper) were trying to ban people with differing life-styles ("hippies" or just plain college students wanting to keep house together outside the bounds of the traditional family unit). This case suggests some of the disputes now emerging over what shall be the "highest and best" use of land in the remaining years of this country.

Excerpted from: Lefcoe, G., "The 'Highest and Best' Use of Land: The Long Way Home." In E. Lenz and A. LeBel, eds. Land and the Pursuit of Happiness, (Los Angeles: Western Humanities Center, UCLA Extension, 1975), p. 28.

planning, this section will also address the issues of **exclusionary zoning** and **inclusionary zoning**. The implementation and problems of coastal zones are covered as well.

Comprehensive Plans

Planning processes are initiated at the local level. First, a community may recognize the need for a general **comprehensive plan** for future growth. Its governing body then appoints a planning commission made up of lay persons, not professional planners, to recommend to its governing body, such as a city council or county board of supervisors, planning decisions for the entire community. Planning commissions often have the assistance of professional planning staffs, but the power of decision making

Comprehensive planning is the realistic projection of future needs for housing, employment, shopping, educational, and recreational needs of a growing community. Photo courtesy of Del E. Webb Development Company.

rests with the commission which in turn must answer to the elected governing body. Public opinion weaves its way into this process by two means—through the election process of the governing body, and through direct comment at planning commission meetings and at higher levels of review.

When a community adopts a comprehensive plan, it sets out clear goals for itself regarding growth and development. The plan usually aims at a future date, perhaps twenty years hence, and attempts to project growth of population, industry, commerce, and other demographic and economic factors that will predictably affect the area. The present land use forms the basis for future land use. Allocations of land for future industrial sites and commercial areas are set in place with regard to housing, transportation, water and sewer resources, and so on. Future locations of schools, hospitals, churches, shopping centers are indicated. Existing agricultural and open space land uses may be earmarked for development, but some may be preserved in their present form. Housing areas of older low-density, single-family housing may be planned for higher-density multifamily housing in the future.

The comprehensiveness of a plan is its strength. It should attempt to project realistically the needs of the future, plan for reasonable development to accommodate those needs, and balance all aspects of a community. The housing, employment, shopping, educational, and recreational needs of the residents of the community all have to be thought through.

The public reviews all aspects of a comprehensive plan before it is adopted. Public hearings take place, often in different neighborhoods and over a long period of time, to insure a careful review by all interested citizens. Once the plan is approved, legislation is often adopted to facilitate its use. Zoning ordinances, subdivision controls, and capital improvement programs are typical government actions taken to implement a general plan.

Zoning and Subdivisions

The zoning ordinance allows a municipality to regulate what is to be built where. It

Zoning designates overall categories of land use. Residential land use is further subdivided into low-density, medium-density, and high-density housing. Rezoning can change the character of a neighborhood. Photo courtesy of U.S. Department of Housing and Urban Development.

specifies very exactly to what uses each plot of land can be put. Such uses are categorized broadly as residential, commercial, industrial, recreational, and agricultural. The broad categories usually have subcategories. For instance, residential areas are divided into single-family housing (designated in many areas by a R-1 zone), low-density multiple housing (designated by R-2 and R-3), medium-density housing (R-4, R-5), higher-density housing (R-6 and so on). Other codes may be used, but a land use map designates all land use by the locally adopted symbols. Each subcategory would specify exact density, setback from the street, types of structures, floor area to lot size ratios, maximum building height, and other matters determining the particular kind of housing permitted in each zoning area. The setting of density maximums for each residential category insures an even pattern of housing types within a given area. This sameness of housing, all single-family, or all townhouse, or all highrise, is precisely the housing segregation that Perin questions.

Zoning ordinances implement a general plan by allowing only those developments that comply with the long-range scheme. If a developer requests a building permit for housing that complies with the zoning controls on the selected land, there is no problem in the review process. It is when the developer wishes to develop housing (or whatever) of another zoning category that problems occur. Rezoning for the site is often requested for a nonconforming use. Whether or not the request is granted, the larger issues dealt with in the comprehensive plan come into question. If, for instance, the developer wants to build an R-4 type of development, medium-density midrise rental apartments, in an R-1 zone, the requested rezoning has implications for existing residents, the schools, demands on

transportation, and water and sewer systems, among other things. The entire balance thought through when the comprehensive plan was adopted may be challenged. This is not to say plans should be inflexible, nor that rezoning requests should be automatically granted. Needs change over time. In reality, the development process is largely one of rezoning. The public hearings that follow these requests are the public's opportunity to enter into the ongoing planning process.

The municipality's regulations for the development of raw land are called subdivision regulations. They prescribe in detail street and lot sizes and layout, sidewalks, utility provisions, and if required, street planting, street lighting, and open space. Most planning allows for coordination between subdivisions so that streets connect, adequate schools and parks are available, and the overall character of a community is consistent. Very often the growth of a town reflects different community attitudes about appropriate subdivision over a period of several decades.

The process of approval for subdivision plans is like the process of rezoning. The public planning agency, with or without the help of professionally trained staff, makes the decision by approving or not approving a developer's plan. Subdivision plans are often reworked to meet planning agency requirements.

Exclusionary Zoning Inclusionary Zoning

The purpose of fair housing law—the attempt to prevent discrimination in housing with regards to race, sex, or national origin was discussed in the previous chapter. Another kind of housing discrimination, however, is perfectly legal and is commonly practiced. It is exclusionary zoning. By requiring that lot sizes be large (one or two

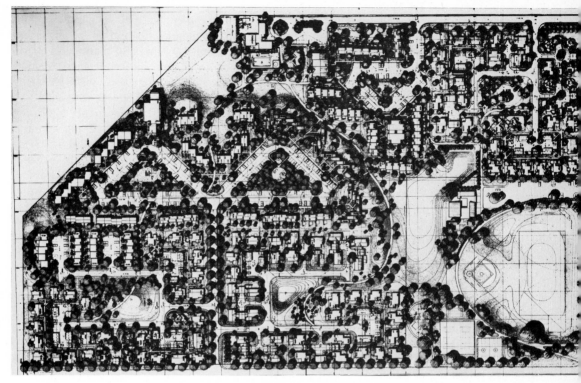

Subdivision plans are approved by a public planning agency. They may have to be redesigned several times to meet local requirements for development. Photo courtesy of U.S. Department of Housing and Urban Development.

acres), or that the houses built on home sites be a minimum size (1800 square feet, for instance), for all practical purposes, all but affluent middle-class families are excluded. Thus, the moderate and low-income families seeking refuge from city life must look elsewhere.

Restrictions on the development of mobile home parks and the building of low and moderate-income multifamily housing, directly affect low-income groups. Even though the discrimination is on the basis of income, it is, in effect, sexist and racial discrimination. Even though singles and young couples are affected, lower and moderate-income families tend to be nonwhite. Single-parent families are more often

than not headed by women. The elderly, who are frequently elderly women, are affected too.

More is at stake than the exclusion from desirable housing. It is also exclusion from the employment opportunities that are more likely to be available in the outlying suburban community, and from the good schools, shopping, and recreation that might provide a healthy and satisfying life.

Restrictions on growth, such as the no-growth controls discussed in chapter 3, can have the same effect. By limiting the number of housing units to be built within a given year, a community may prevent accommodation of the housing demand made on it by all income groups.

Many cases regarding exclusionary zoning, including the no-growth issue, have been tested in the courts. So far, there is no overall trend in the settlement of these cases. Racial prejudice as such has to be proved if that is the basis for bringing suit. Courts in some states have held that zoning ordinances cannot be used to keep people out or hold taxes down. Courts in other states have held that the zoning ordinance at the local level cannot be challenged for the same reasons. Some states, such as New York, insist that in the long run all income groups are accommodated. Zoning is considered a regional problem in some states, but not in others. What is the result of all of the legal battles over exclusionary zoning? Hutchins believes that "even if the price of housing goes down, the most likely residence of the poor will still be the central city. They will not be permitted to live in many other places."[8]

There has been a trend in a few places to reverse the effects of exclusionary zoning. In fact it is called inclusionary zoning. Because housing has become very high priced in many areas, partly through exclusionary ongoing practices and partly through housing economics in general, no housing developer can profitably provide low- or moderate-income housing. In order to provide incentives to developers to build lower-cost housing to meet the needs of low- and moderate-income families, some communities have specified provisions in their zoning laws.

Typically, 25 percent of the housing to be built in a development of a specified size must be "affordable" to families that are within the 80 percent to 120 percent range of the community's **median income.** Ownership and rental units that are below market rates (BMR units) may be included in this guideline. The reward for the developer can take the form of a **density bonus,** that

is the development may be allowed to have a higher density (for example, 25 percent more units on the site) than if developed normally. Other incentives may include: the exemption from fees; land for parks; community provided streets, sidewalks, and sewers; or the use of grant money to acquire land for the development. Some communities have set up a special board which selects the families for these units, oversees resale so that undue profits are not earned, checks that buyers are appropriately within the income limitations, and so on.

One of the complications regarding inclusionary zoning is the practice of allowing **"in lieu fees"** to be paid by developers who do not wish to participate. The question then is how to use the fees to improve the housing situation for families meant to benefit. Another problem, and the more controversial one, is the question of who really pays for the lower-cost housing? Doesn't the developer pass the loss of profits from the 25 percent of "affordable" units on to the cost of the 75 percent that are sold or rented at market rate? Or does the developer absorb the loss? If a community absorbs the loss, by in effect picking up some of the development costs for the developer, then the existing residents are supporting such housing with tax money. Is it appropriate for this form of subsidization to occur at the community level? From a societal standpoint, however, can we "afford" to have communities without all income levels represented?

Coastal Zones

The U.S. coastline, including the shores of the Great Lakes, contains the nation's seven largest cities, 53 percent of the population, and 90 percent of the population growth. Roughly half of all manufacturing jobs in the U.S. are located in coastal areas, and development pressures there

This Boston waterfront housing is a successful attempt to renew existing deteriorating development and make it an attractive part of the urban environment. Photo courtesy of U.S. Department of Housing and Urban Development.

are likely to accelerate with the pursuit of oil and gas beneath the ocean floor.[9]

The central role that the American coastline has in future housing development cannot, then, be overemphasized. The insensitivity with which the coastline has been developed in the past has come into question. Dunes, beaches and barrier islands offer natural defense against severe storms. To develop such areas carelessly is to destroy this natural resource. The problem of coastal development focuses on the same competing national goals present in all planning and development. We want to protect the environment, but we also want convenient housing, energy self-sufficiency, and recreational opportunities.

In 1972, the Coastal Zone Management Act provided legislation for coastal zone protection. Its amendments in 1976 provided a more balanced allowance of development. Thirty-five states can participate by enacting coastal zone plans, but less than half have done so. States implement coastal policies in two ways. One is to create a new enforcement authority, which about two-thirds of the coastal states have done. The other method is to work through existing agencies (Massachusetts is an example).

Urban waterfronts pose special problems. Often they are overdeveloped and deteriorating. To renew them so that they are not only accessible to the public but an attractive part of the urban environment is a monumental task. At least further bad development can be opposed, as it was in Jersey City where citizens prevented the siting of a deep-water terminal along the dock front.[10]

California has enacted one of the boldest and largest-scaled coastal plans. Although the plan was adopted in 1972, it is still considered a controversial issue. Because of the power of the state commission and its six regional coastal commissions to decide what can and cannot be developed within the coastal strip (three miles seaward and 1,000 yards landward), other planning control mechanisms are overshadowed. The specific purposes of the coastal plan are: (1) to improve the marine environment; (2) to protect the few remaining wetlands; (3) to provide for development of ports and marinas in such a way as to minimize environmental damage; (4) to retain natural habitat areas; (5) to protect coast-dependent agriculture; (6) to protect the scenic beauty of the coast; (7) to encourage orderly, balanced development; (8) to require the evaluation of both inland and coastal sites for future energy installations; (9) to improve the efficiency of existing roads with public transit; (10) to improve public access to the coast; and (11) to increase coastal recreation.[11]

All requests for development must be approved by the coastal commissions as well as other local planning jurisdictions. Building permits may be allowed by traditional planning agencies, but then denied by the regional coastal commission. An appeal can be made at the state level. Public opinion is welcomed, and, in fact, ordinary planning questions such as development consistency and traffic congestion tend to outweigh environmental concerns in the coastal commissions' deliberations. One significant issue is the requirement that low- and moderate-income housing be provided within the coastal area. This requirement has annoyed developers of high-income housing, a logical, profitable, and traditional development use of ocean-view land.

The California coastal commissions approve the majority of applications before them. Projects are refused if they are not in strict compliance with the coastal plan, and all projects are reviewed regarding their siting, sewage disposal, parking provisions,

public access, and the size, bulk and appearance of buildings.[12] Even though developers consider some commission decisions to be arbitrary and unreasonable, they have learned to tailor their proposals to meet commission requirements. That, after all, is proof that the coastal plan has some real effect.

State Land Use Planning

The implementation of planning through zoning, subdivision regulations, and capital improvements is usually carried out through local jursidictions. It has been recognized by planners and other governmental officials that neighboring jursidictions may need to coordinate their planning for the benefit of all. Planning problems usually pertain to the geography, economics and social areas of which the single jurisdiction is a small part. Planning solutions dealing with transportation in all forms, industrial development, parks and open space, and major civic and educational facilities affect whole regions rather than one particular community. The need for regional planning became especially clear in highly urbanized areas. For instance, the Regional Plan of New York and its Environs was developed as an unofficial guide to 1400 planning jurisdictions in three states.[13]

Some states have initiated state-level land use planning in an effort to provide a solution to the problems of local jurisdictions functioning independently. Hawaii was the first to adopt a state-level plan in 1961. All fifty states presently have some legislation affecting land use on a statewide basis, but there is diversity among states as to the purpose of state-level legislation. Although goals vary greatly, most states want to improve the public policy decision-making process through state coordination and to preserve the environment, natural resources, and other special sites.[14] Some states have land inventory systems. However, "despite growing recognition that some planning can be more effectively done at higher than local levels, the zoning authority is still predominately at the local level."[15] Even so, in some states, the local zoning decisions must be consistent with master plans. In only eleven states can it be said that the primary thrust of planning activities is at the state level.[16]

CLUSTER HOUSING

Cluster housing can be defined as a grouping of housing units on land to allow for communal open space and for economies of development.[17] A tract of land is developed as a whole rather than divided into many single small plots of land, each with its house placed in the center. In cluster housing, the houses are built on only part of the land in the development tract, and there is variation in the lot size and in the orientation on each lot.

The cluster housing idea borrows on a centuries-old tradition of home building. Mediterranean towns, so often admired by students of architecture and planning, are charming because of their tightly knit irregular patterns of housing and open space. The irregularity of house placement and the open common of New England towns are an American example of historical use of cluster housing. Row houses, used first in England, and then in American cities such as Philadelphia, Baltimore, and Washington, D.C., have been used as prototypes for row housing in cluster developments.

The overall density of a cluster project is an important consideration. A development may have a very high density in one part balanced by no density in another part. Since much of the land is left undeveloped, natural drainage, scenery, and attractive

Cluster housing borrows a centuries-old idea of tightly knit row housing. This example also has the borrowed idea of using roof space as an extension of the usable enclosed space. Photo by author.

topography can be used to advantage in the overall plan. Soil erosion can be avoided, and orientation to natural features, such as a view or a lake, can be enhanced. The lengths of streets and of utility lines can be economically shorter than in typical single-family subdivisions.

A comparison of single-family lot subdivision and cluster housing development on the same amount of land illustrates the advantages of cluster housing. If a six-acre parcel of land is subdivided, twelve lots could be developed with 20,000 square feet in each. A very low density of two dwelling units per acre could be created. If, instead, each lot is reduced by half, with only 10,000 square feet in each, the total amount of land in the six-acre plot could be alloted so that three acres are left in open space. The overall density remains the same in both examples. Further clustering would result in even more space left open for communal use, and lower costs of development for streets, water and sewer lines, and so on. Even in the case of only 5,000 square feet per lot (a 50 by 100 foot lot still allows private outdoor space), only 1.5 acres would be developed with housing, and 4.5 acres left open. The two houses per acre density is still maintained.[18]

PUDs

Some communities have developed special zoning and subdivision regulations to allow cluster housing called planned unit developments (PUDs). In these communities, an application for cluster housing would be treated under the zoning regulations for a PUD rather than for a conventional subdivision. Some PUD developments are large enough to include development of nonresidential facilities such as shopping and employment centers. Others are very small and are often called mini-PUDs.

Other communities do not have a special zoning classification for planned unit developments. Cluster housing is viewed as a form of single-family housing. Although conventional subdivision zoning is used, it is applied flexibly to cluster housing, allowing reduced private lots with compensating open space. A public hearing may be required although a conventional subdivision would not require it. Some communities regard cluster housing as a conventional subdivision with "special exemption" status. Developers may prefer getting approval for cluster housing through these less specific methods than through PUD zoning.

Other housing terms have come into popular use with the advent of cluster housing. "Townhouses" has traditionally meant houses in town. In older American cities, the type of house built in town has been row houses, so these two terms have become synonymous. "Garden homes" or "patio houses" are two more terms used in cluster housing advertisements. A cluster housing development may or may not be a PUD; it may or may not have townhouses, and to add another layer of definition, it may or may not be a condominium.

One other term needs explanation. It is "zero lot line." One means of achieving individual housing units on less privately owned land than in a typical subdivision is to place one or more of the house's outside walls on the property line. This is zero-lot-line planning, and it usually requires a special zoning ordinance to allow it, such as that available in planned unit developments. A zero-lot-line development house may be detached from adjacent houses, unlike row or townhouses. Each house has one side yard only, and the wall of the next house, presumably without windows, is also the boundary of the side yard.

Open Space

The open space created in cluster housing development can be handled in two ways. One is to dedicate it to the municipality. This is similar to the dedication of land for a park or school within a conventional subdivision. The municipality gets the land free in this case, but maintenance responsibilities are then assumed by it rather than by the home owners most likely to benefit.

The other method of handling open space is to form a home owners' association for the expressed purpose of maintaining and conserving common areas. The condominium form of ownership includes this kind of communal responsibility, as well as communal ownership. Condominium cluster housing includes its open-space maintenance along with its parking areas, swimming pool, and other facilities maintenance in the monthly fee.

In cluster housing and in other types of subdivisions which are not owned as con-

The open space in cluster housing developments including Planned Unit Developments (PUDs) can be handled in two ways—it can be dedicated to a municipality or it can be maintained by a home-owners association. Photo by author.

dominiums, the only communal responsibility may be maintaining the open space. Membership in the home owners' association may be automatic with the purchase of the home. The common land can be owned by a separate corporation, initially controlled by the developer, but later controlled by the home owners. A board of directors adopts a budget, assesses fees, selects management, purchases insurance, and establishes rules for the conduct of the association.[19] In these matters, the association's function is identical to that of a condominium homeowners' association.

Planning for open space within a community can have advantages for all. Small amounts of open space left within separate housing developments are not as beneficial as connected open space. If a community identifies especially desirable open spaces such as public parks, school sites, highway buffer zones and natural recreation areas, they can then be designed into an overall network of which cluster housing open space can become a part. Ideally, such

open spaces could be joined by walkways and bikeways threading throughout the whole.[20]

NEW TOWNS

As early as the 1920s, the traditional use of land for housing was questioned by far-sighted planners. Radburn, New Jersey, was designed to include cluster housing, open space, and separation of automobile and pedestrian traffic. The ideas were borrowed from England where new town planning was firmly established, but they were revolutionary in this country. By 1935, the federal government endorsed the pattern set by Radburn by sponsoring the building of three new towns (eight were originally planned). They were called greenbelt towns after their English prototypes, and are located in Maryland, Ohio, and Wisconsin.

Widespread adoption was made of the cul-de-sac, the superblock, and of curvilinear streets. But the new town concept as such did not catch on in this country. However, many successful new towns had been developed in western Europe with the help of strong government direction and support. Then, in the 1960s, with a spurt of population growth, housing industry activity, and a search for large-scale developments to meet housing demand, a renewed interest in new towns was born. As an alternative to additional suburban growth, new towns offered a fresh approach to planning for a complete working and housing environment.

Characteristics

Largeness of scale is the main characteristic of new towns. Very large amounts of land are developed with expected large numbers of eventual residents in mind. Lemkau describes new towns this way:

Recreation, usually involving a body of water, is nearly always planned into new towns, as in this Westlake, California, example. Photo by author.

The new cities obtain land in large parcels of tens or thousands of acres which allows planners to design the city with an eye to the terrain, to plan separate but coordinated communities within the area, to arrange for full service, to insure open land, to group schools and other service functions, to control traffic patterns, and to arrange for different communities to have some individual functions and characteristics.[21]

Ideally, new towns are planned at the outset for an optimum population. Streets and sewer lines are mapped out for their eventual capacity, thus avoiding the normally disruptive and very costly processes of ex-

pansion. Networks of open space can be mapped out and preserved as housing is built. Logical and convenient locations of shopping can be integrated into housing patterns.

New towns generally incorporate planning concepts that are intended to create an ideal living environment. They are worth detailing because they may be desirable in all planning, especially of large-scale.

1. *Neighborhood concept.* The neighborhood is thought by planners to be very important in the social function of housing environment. If a small area is identifiable to all residents within it, a home territory is automatically created (see chapter 6). Harmonious relations between neighbors might thus be stimulated. Neighborhoods have been created in most suburban developments with elementary schools as their central focus, but in new towns, such neighborhoods would be made physically separate by open space between them.

2. *Recreation.* The use of open space integrated into each neighborhood, and between each neighborhood, allows for the easy development of play areas, walkways, bike paths, and so on. Water is almost always a recreational asset in new towns. Small ponds, lakes, creeks, or bay access become focal points for housing orientation as well as sources of activities for children and adults.

3. *Vehicular and pedestrian traffic.* New towns are designed to be safe. Nearly always path systems are laid out so children can walk to school without crossing major streets. Underpasses or overpasses are employed to avoid surface street crossings. Where these pathways weave through open space adjacent to housing neighborhoods, they also become a resource for leisure activity.

Separating vehicular traffic from pedestrian traffic is one characteristic of new towns. This ensures the safety of children walking to school. Photo courtesy of U.S. Department of Housing and Urban Development.

4. *Self-sufficiency.* In addition to residential and recreational components in new towns, there are industrial and commercial components. Ideally, new towns provide work for their residents, thus avoiding dependence on large metropolitan areas, and the highway access to them, for employment. Services are provided at appropriate locations. Small village shopping areas might have a bank and a medical facility, but major offices, legal services, hospitals and medical specialists are centrally located for the convenience of new town residents.

5. *Size.* Since a new town starts on wholly undeveloped land, the eventual size is open to free choice. What then is the right size of a town for pleasant living with adequate service, shopping, and recreation built into its planning? New town planners projected their future populations in 1970 as 18,000 to 150,000. Larger new towns are usually broken up into smaller units of development sometimes called villages. The village size of 10,000 to 15,000 population is ideal for several reasons. Lemkau, a participant in the new town planning process, describes these considerations of size as having to do with "the size of junior and senior high schools, the economics of shopping centers, the number of people a physician could serve, estimates of the size of churches and the frequency of membership in various denominations, the number of people served by branch libraries, the sociology of towns versus cities, and the like."[22]

Federally Supported New Towns

The Housing and Urban Development Act of 1965 created mortgage insurance for private developers for the purchase of raw land on which to build new communities. There were few participants in this early program. The Housing and Urban Development Act of 1968 went a step further in order to stimulate new town development; $50 million became the mortgage insurance upper limit. Even though Congress allocated money for the program, the federal machinery to put it in motion was exercised very cautiously.

Finally, new legislation in 1970, Title VII of the Housing and Urban Development Act, provided a full-scaled federal effort to finance new towns. A Community Development Corporation was created

Jonathan, Minnesota

Physical Development Scheme:

Elementary schools. 5 villages of approximately 7,000. Basic living module.

Convenience services, shopping facilities, post office. Medical clinic with offices for doctors, advisors, out-patient facilities, and emergency care facilities. Offices. One or more primary schools.

Single multi-storied structure built over a rail line and a major highway. Learning center. General hospital, with specialist offices, inpatient facilities and staff for general coordination of medical services. Major retail and office facilities. Entertainment facilities. Apartment structures.

Land Use:

Excluding a 1,500-acre industrial tract, 45 percent residential; 18 percent open space; industrial 10 percent; lakes 8 percent; commercial 6 percent.

Reprinted from: Mields, H., Jr., Federally Assisted New Communities (Washington, D.C.: The Urban Land Institute, 1973), pp. 112–13. By permission.

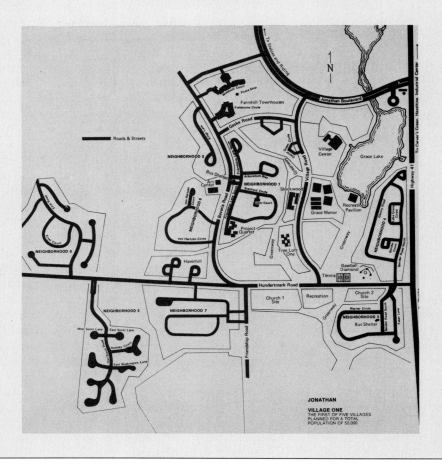

within the Department of Housing and Urban Development (HUD) "to assure that the new towns program would have special identification, would be highly visible, and that it would focus on the clear mandate in the Bill from Congress to actively and positively encourage large-scale rational development."[23] The criteria Title VII established for federally sponsored new towns complements the characteristics of new towns identified above. A new community must: (1) include most of the basic activities normally associated with a town, (2) combine these in a well-planned whole; (3) contribute to the social and economic welfare of the area; (4) provide employment; (5) provide an alternative to disorderly growth; and (6) increase housing choice, be open to all regardless of race and include housing for low-income groups.[24]

By 1973, HUD had processed applications for fifteen new towns from nine states. They are summarized in Table 10–1.

Four types of new towns are identified in Table 10–1. The **free-standing new community** was defined by the federal government in its 1970 legislation as one being self-sufficient and being some distance away from existing urban areas. Only one of the new towns listed is of this type—the type most closely meeting the utopian ideal of new town planning. A **satellite new town** may be economically balanced within its own range, but admittedly depends on the economy of an adjacent metropolitan area. Satellite new towns are planned as a suburban substitute for conventional urban sprawl. The table clearly shows that this kind of growth was needed in the 1970s. **Growth center new towns** are planned around smaller communities with growth potential in rural areas. The two new towns classified as combination satellite and growth center new towns are far enough away from metropolitan areas to eventually

become independent of them. New-towns-in-town, the subject of the next section, are planned for vacant land or land needing redevelopment within existing cities.

The mid-1970s housing industry slump affected the continued growth of new towns. As private funding became less available, federal spending also shrank. Many of the new towns, begun in hope and optimism, virtually never got off the drawing boards. Some, however, were begun and may again experience future growth as housing financing and demand combine to provide them a promising financial climate.

Successful New Towns

Park Forest, Illinois was begun in the 1940s, and it was the first private wholly new community in the United States. Its planner and developer adopted ideas used in the greenbelt new towns of the 1930s. A regional shopping center was planned as the hub of the new community, but most of its residents depended on Chicago for employment. During the 1950s, 3,000 rental housing units were built in Park Forest to ease the housing pressures of the Chicago metropolitan area, an accomplishment not matched by other communities. Park Forest South, developed in the 1970s, is an adjacent new town with an expected population of 110,000.

One man purchased 6,750 acres to develop a new town in Virginia. It is Reston, and some planners consider it to be one of the most successful new towns in this country. Its goals, set out in 1962, were:

(1) the widest choice of opportunities for full use of leisure time; (2) an environment flexible enough for people to remain in a single neighborhood throughout their lives; (3) priority in planning for the importance and dignity of the individual; (4) the chance for people to live and work in

TABLE 10–1 Summary of New Communities Guaranteed by HUD
(Dollars in Thousands)

COMMUNITY	TYPE	GUARANTEE COMMITMENT AMOUNT DATE	GUARANTEE ISSUES		POPULATION (PROJECTED)	DWELLING UNITS (PROJECTED)	LOCATION
			AMOUNT DATE	INTEREST RATE			
Jonathan, Minnesota	Satellite/Growth Center	$21,000 2/70	$ 8,000 10/70 $13,000 6/72	8.50% 7.20%	50,000 in 20 years	16,500 in 20 years	20 mi. S.W. of Minneapolis
St. Charles Communities, Maryland	Satellite	$24,000 6/70	$18,000 12/70	7.75%	75,000 in 20 years	25,000 in 20 years	25 mi. S.W. of Wash., D.C.
Park Forest South, Illinois	Satellite	$30,000 6/70	$30,000 3/71	7.00%	110,000 in 15 years	35,000 in 15 years	30 mi. S. of Chicago
Flower Mound, Texas	Satellite	$18,000 12/70	$14,000 10/71	7.60%	64,000 in 20 years	18,000 in 20 years	20 mi. S.W. of Dallas
Maumelle, Arkansas	Satellite	$ 7,500 12/70	$ 4,500 6/72	7.62%	45,000 in 20 years	14,000 in 20 years	12 mi. N.W. of Little Rock
Cedar-Riverside, Minnesota	New-Town-In-Town	$24,000 6/71	$24,000 12/71	7.20%	30,000 in 20 years	12,500 in 20 years	downtown Minneapolis
Riverton, New York	Satellite	$12,000	$12,000 5/72	7.125%	25,600 in 16 years	8,000 in 16 years	10 mi. S. of Rochester
San Antonio Ranch, Texas	Satellite	$18,000 2/72	— —	—	88,000 in 30 years	28,000 in 30 years	20 mi. N.W. of San Antonio
The Woodlands, Texas	Satellite	$50,000 4/72	$50,000 9/72	7.10%	150,000 in 20 years	49,160 in 20 years	30 mi. N.W. of Houston

TABLE 10-1   continued

Gananda, New York	Satellite	$22,000 4/72	$22,000 12/72	7.15%	50,000 in 20 years	17,200 in 20 years	12 mi. E. of Rochester
Soul City, North Carolina	Free Standing	$14,000 6/72	—	—	44,000 in 30 years	12,906 in 30 years	45 mi. N. of Raleigh-Durham
Harbison, South Carolina	Satellite	$13,000 10/72	—	—	23,000 in 20 years	6,750 in 20 years	8 mi. N.W. of Columbia
Lysander, New York	Satellite				18,300 in 8 years	5,000 in 8 years	12 mi. N.W. of Syracuse
Welfare Island, New York	New-Town-In-Town	12/72	—	—	18,000 in 7 years	5,000 in 7 years	in New York City
Shenandoah, Georgia	Satellite/ Growth Center	$40,000 2/73	—	—	70,000 in 20 years	23,000 in 20 years	35 mi. S.W. of Atlanta

Source: Mields, H., Jr., Federally Assisted New Communities: New Dimensions in Urban Development (Washington, D.C.: Urban Land Institute, 1973), p. 27.

One example of a successful new town is Reston, Virginia, a town that is a satellite to Washington, D.C. Photo courtesy of U.S. Department of Housing and Urban Development.

the same community; (5) the availability to residents of commercial, cultural, and recreation facilities from the outset of development; (6) preservation and encouragement of beauty; and finally, (7) financial success of the development.[25]

Original planning and development proceeded smoothly, and by 1965, a commercial center had been leased, 500 people had moved in; half of them were locally employed. By 1973, 22,000 persons lived in Reston, but the great majority of them worked in the Washington, D.C. metropolitan area. Reston has not been without financial setbacks, but it is generally ad-

mired for having achieved nearly ideal new town planning.

Columbia, Maryland is between Washington, D.C. and Baltimore. Its planning process was unique in that experts in housing, education, family life, recreation, sociology, transportation, and communications were all involved. The 10,000 to 15,000 ideal population for a village, referred to above, resulted in housing clustered in neighborhoods (each of 800 to 1200 families) and three to four neighborhoods making up a village. Twenty different private developers had built 8,000 single family detached houses, townhouses, and apartments by 1973. The projected population is over 100,000, to be reached in the 1980s.

Columbia set out to provide an ideal social environment as well as an ideal physical environment. It was planned to be conducive "to generating a broad range of friendships and community relationships, a sense of responsibility leading to an active involvement in community affairs, and a 'racial openness' which would not have developed in suburbs or conventional urban communities."[26] Although a 1973 survey of Columbia residents indicated that they did indeed have more interracial friendships than before living there, the open housing goal has not been achieved very successfully in Columbia or any other new town.

That this new town did not achieve a 10 percent low-income housing mix cannot be blamed solely on its planning processes and financial management. In fact, Columbia has a higher percentage of black residents than surrounding suburbs. The problems of providing adequately for low-and moderate-income families in new towns are the same as in all living environments; they are problems of the housing industry, of American values applied to land use, of social segregation, of an inflationary economy, and, as will be discussed at length in the next few

This model is of one neighborhood planned for Cedar-Riverside, a new-town-in-town planned in 1970 for downtown Minneapolis. It would have housed 6,000 of the total 30,000 expected population. Only a small part of Cedar-Riverside has been completed. Photo courtesy of U.S. Department of Housing and Urban Development.

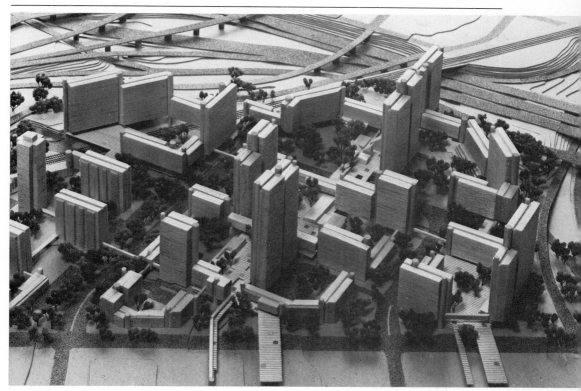

Fort Lincoln: A New-Town-in-Town

The conception of Fort Lincoln, as the town was to be called, was exhilarating. It started with a suggestion by sociologist Harvey Perloff that if new towns out in the country are a good idea, why not build "new towns—in town" on large vacant sites in the city? This was followed by an open letter to President Johnson in *The Washington Post,* suggesting that the site of the departing National Training School for Boys at the northeast gateway to Washington, D.C., was ideal for a national demonstration of the concept. (The Training School, a euphemism for a federal prison for juvenile delinquents, was moving to West Virginia.)

It took the White House almost two years to ponder the suggestion, but then President Johnson wanted action in a hurry.

HUD, on a day's notice, summoned Moshe Safdie, Paul Rudolph, and other leading architects to Washington to produce innovative and economical building designs. The city's local building code bureaucrats rejected them all.

Citizens living near the Fort Lincoln site tied the entire project into knots for months, quarreling about citizen participation in the planning of a town that was not to have any citizens for years to come.

The local urban renewal agency, known as the Redevelopment Land Agency, hurriedly built some housing for the elderly and a school on the site, only to satisfy White House demands for quick action. The housing is terrible and the school stood empty for years because the elderly don't have school children.

After these and many other grotesque shenanigans, Mayor Walter Washington commissioned a team, headed by Edward J. Logue, to produce a plan. Logue later headed the New York state Urban Development Corporation.

It was a dandy plan. Unlike most city plans, it resembled neither a Mondrian painting, nor a still life of potato sacks in diverse colors, denoting the kind of zoning proposed. Neither did it show a country club community. It showed a compact, urban place.

The plan focused on the workings of the proposed town, the human interaction, the life to be led there. It was to be a multiclass community going first class. It was to offer livability.

Foremost among the special features of Logue's Fort Lincoln plan were exceptionally good schools and a monorail to replace automobiles.

The superior schools, administered by a separate educational institution free of Washington's stifling school board bureaucracy, were to induce upper-and middle-income families to live alongside low-income families.

The monorail was to free space usually devoted to wide motor roads and parking, thus achieving high density amid greenery and clean air. The Logue plan called for housing for 4,500 families plus shopping, recreation, schools, a college, some industry, and much lively bustle on 335 acres.

What toppled the plan was precisely that which made it so convincing. It was designed, as a good community must be designed, as one intricate structure in which each part is dependent on the others, like a house of cards.

Take away the special schools, and hopes for attracting affluent families will vanish. Take away the monorail, and there will have to be expensive motor roads and parking lots, and far less lucrative space for people. And so it went. A bureaucracy, flabbergasted by the boldness of the plan, poked at card after card until the whole structure collapsed.

Excerpted from: Von Eckardt, W., Back to the Drawing Board! Planning Livable Cities (Washington, D.C.: New Republic Books, 1978), pp. 145–147.

chapters, of faulty governmental support programs.

Adopting New Towns to Urban Problems

Vacant land in American cities has increased with the process of housing abandonment. Combining these land resources with land made available through urban renewal (usually requiring the relocation of existing residents), sizable sites have been identified for major planning schemes. Rather than approaching the design and planning for these sites in traditional ways, the new town concept of planning has been applied to them. Thus was born the new-town-in-town. Title VII of the Housing and Urban Development Act of 1970 included funding for this type of new town.

The sites may be small, such as 25 acres, and the population requirements (perhaps 10,000) smaller than for outlying new towns, but high considering the size of the site. If social and economic balance as well as physical attractiveness are the main purposes of new town planning, it seems that to achieve these purposes is all the more difficult in the inner-city context. Nevertheless, two new-towns-in-town (really new-towns-in-cities) have proceeded in their development.

Cedar-Riverside is on the bank of the Mississippi River twelve blocks from downtown Minneapolis. An urban renewal plan was translated into a proposal for the first federally designated new-town-in-town after the 1970 legislation. Plans were made for a 340-acre site normally considered undesir-able, but 100 acres of this was designated for private development. A ten-stage plan provided for 12,500 dwellings of different sizes and architectural styles. The planners expected that by 1990 with a population of 30,000, "this new-town-in-town [would] stand as a self-contained city, with a prime commercial complex in an elongated center, convenience shopping distributed over a wide area and cultural and educational amenities to assure a well-balanced and stimulating urban environment.[27]

The high hope for Cedar-Riverside's success were dashed in 1973 when the development had reached its second stage. A group filed a suit claiming that a new Environmental Impact Statement (EIS) was required for this stage. Thus began a court battle which involved the management of Cedar-Riverside and HUD.[28] By 1976 housing for all income levels had been built, but the future of Cedar-Riverside as a prototypical urban new-town-in-town was in doubt. The need for an EIS dramatized some weaknesses in this kind of large-scale and multiple-agency planning.

Roosevelt Island, in New York City, was formerly known as Welfare Island. It is located in the East River, and is linked to Manhattan by monorail. Its unique planning feature is that 20,000 people will be housed in an automobile-free environment. The plan is sponsored by a subsidiary of the New York State Urban Development Corporation (UDC). As in Cedar-Riverside, most of the housing is high-rise. Since this housing type dominates the midtown Manhattan location to which it physically and economically relates, this is not a disadvantage. The high-rise structures in Cedar-Riverside have been criticized as being inappropriate.

However few and limited in scope the new-towns-in-towns are, they do provide an alternative to what a British critic describes as "the enormous number of communities which will spring up, planned or unplanned, over the next decades and which will be within existing towns surrounding large cities."[29] Since the holes, as it were, in urban development will be filled in one way or another, it is better that they be planned to provide a superior livable environment, and at the same time achieve economies in services and resources. Typical sporadic subdivisions do not often achieve these goals.

SUMMARY

The early tradition of town planning in America was reborn in this century with the advent of large-scale building to house a growing population. Professional planning attempts to incorporate all considerations for an environment supportive of a high quality of life.

At the root of all planning are the values we attribute to land. We have assumed traditionally that land was plentiful and commercial return determined its best use. Presently, alternative values have come into focus—specifically a concern for environmentally sensitive land use and a concern for social implications of land use segregation. Critics have called for new ways of thinking about the relationship of land and people.

Comprehensive plans are the formal recognition of a community's goals regarding growth. All aspects of planning are taken into account so that the growth can be balanced and logically accommodated by existing resources. Zoning ordinances accompany comprehensive plans by designating specific building types within each land use category. Subdivision regulations provide specific guidelines for developers to build housing.

A social issue related to planning is the practice of exclusionary zoning. Because low-income level also indicates a dominance of minority groups, especially blacks and women, they are indirectly affected by exclusionary zoning. Although many court cases have challenged this practice, there is no conclusive trend towards abolishing it. On the other hand, some communities have adopted inclusionary zoning to insure available housing for low- and moderate-income families.

Since much of the housing in the United States is in coastal metropolitan areas, the new emphasis on controlling the kind of development in coastal zones will affect future housing. California's coastal plan has been given special attention because it has had effective force since adoption.

The main advantages of cluster housing are that open space is preserved for the common use of all residents, and development can be done less expensively, thus cutting costs on individual houses. The planning tool most often used to build cluster housing is PUD, but some areas allow it within the planning framework of conventional zoning.

The largeness of scale of new town planning allows a comprehensive approach to residential, commercial, industrial, and other components. The major characteristics of new town planning are the neighborhood concept, recreation through open space, separation of vehicular and pedestrian traffic, and economic and social self-sufficiency. The federal sponsorship of new towns in the 1970s resulted in many new towns being planned and a few to be fully developed in the 1980s.

The most successful new towns have been privately developed. Park Forest, Reston and Columbia each exhibit application of new town principals. The new-town-in-town concept has been put into practice in several places, most notably in New York (Roosevelt Island) and in Minneapolis (Cedar-Riverside). These ambitious projects point the way for futher urban and suburban infill development.

Notes

1. Abrams, C., *The Language of Cities* (New York: Viking Press, 1971), p. 48.
2. Solomon, A. P.,"Five Land-use Reforms Suggested to Resolve Problems of Urban Growth," *Journal of Housing*, 1977, *34* (6), p. 276.
3. Ibid., p. 277.
4. Ibid., p. 281.
5. Perin, C., *Everything in Its Place: Social Order and Land Use in America* (Princeton, N.J.: Princeton University Press, 1977), p. 3.
6. Ibid., p. 4.
7. Ibid., p. 163.
8. Hutchins, R. M., "Environment and Civil Rights," *The Center Magazine*, 1975, *8* (6), p. 6.
9. Silverman, J. A., "The American Coastline: New Frontier of Planning," *AIA Journal*, 1978, *67* (9), p. 47.
10. Ibid., p. 49.
11. "The California Coastal Plan. . .How and Where to See for Yourself, in Two Counties," *Sunset*, May 1976, p. 105.
12. Healy, R. G., "California's Powerful Coastal Planning Apparatus," *AIA Journal*, 1978, *67* (9), p. 52.
13. Abrams, *The Language of Cities*, p. 262.
14. Mann, R. A., and M. Miles, "State Land Use Planning: The Current Status and Demographic Rationale," *APA Journal*, 1979, *45* (1), p. 51.
15. Ibid., p. 52.
16. Ibid., p. 54.
17. "Cluster: An Old Formula Solves New Problems," *Builder*, 1978, *1* (15), p. 24.
18. Ibid., p. 27.
19. "How to Form a Homeowners Association," *Builder*, 1978, *1* (15), p. 35.
20. The Citizens Advisory Committee on Environmental Quality, *Community Action for Environmental Quality* (Washington, D.C.: U.S. Government Printing Office, 1970), p. 15.
21. Lemkau, P. V., "Housing and Health," in C. S. Wedin and L. G. Nygren, *Housing Perspectives*, 2nd ed. (Minneapolis, Minn.: Burgess, 1979), pp. 151–152.
22. Lemkau, P. V., "Human factors in the new town," in C. S. Wedin and L. G. Nygren, *Housing Perspectives: Individuals and Families* (Minneapolis, Minn.: Burgess, 1976), p. 134.
23. Mields, H., Jr., *Federally Assisted New Communities: New Dimensions in Urban Development* (Washington, D.C.: Urban Land Institute, 1973), p. 26.
24. Turner, A., "New Communities in the United States: 1968–1973," *Town Planning Review*, 1974, *45* (3), pp. 264–65.
25. Mields, *Federally Assisted New Communities, p.* 16.
26. Milgram, M., *Good Neighborhood: The*

Challenge of Open Housing (New York: W. W. Norton, 1977), p. 184.
27. Ibid., p. 197.
28. Engelen, R. E., "A Case Study: Cedar-

Riverside," *Practicing Planner*, 1976, 6 (2), p. 36.
29. Turner, "New Communities," p. 271.

Suggested Readings

Babcock, R. F. *The Zoning Game : Municipal Principal Practices and Policies*. Madison, Wisc.: University of Wisconsin Press, 1969, (chap. VII "The Purpose of Zoning;" chap. VIII "The Principles of Zoning").

Barlowe, R. "Land for housing." In C. S. Wedin and L. G. Nygren, eds. *Housing Perspectives* (2nd ed.). Minneapolis: Burgess, 1979.

Gallogly, F. D. "Housing Decisions in Selecting a Residence in a Planned Townhouse Development." *Home Economics Research Journal*, 1974, 2 (4) 251–61.

Greer, G. G. "Sensible Growth in Housing: Four Winners Show the Way." *Better Homes and Gardens*, 1980, 58 (8) 19–26.

Hutchins, R. M. "Environment and Civil Rights." *The Center Magazine*, 1975, 8 (6) 2–5.

"A Marathon Victory over Snob Zoning." *Housing*, 1978, 53 (5) 79–83.

Mayer, M. *The Builders: Houses, People, Neighborhoods, Governments, Money*. New York: W. W. Norton, 1978, (chap. 3, "Situs"; chap. 4 "New Communities").

Milgram, M. *Good Neighborhood: The Challenge of Open Housing*. New York: W. W. Norton, 1977, (chap. 5, "The Future: Housing for Reality").

Perin, C. *Everything in Its Place: Social Order and Land Use in America*. Princton, N.J.: Princeton University Press, 1977, (chap. 4 "Many Wagons, Many Stars: The Uses of Land, Zoning, and Houses").

Solomon, A. P. "Five Land-Use Reforms Suggested to Resolve Problems of Urban Growth." *Journal of Housing*, 1977, 34 (6) 276–81.

Turner, A. "New Communities in the United States: 1968–1973." *Town Planning Review*, 1974, part 1, 45 (3) 259–73, part II 45 (4) 415–30.

Von Eckardt, W. "A Fresh Scene in the Clean Dream." *Saturday Review*, 1971, 54 (20) 21–23.

Zehner, R. B., and Morans, R. W. "Residential Density, Planning Objectives and Life in Planned Communities." *Journal of the American Institute of Planners*, 1973, 39 (5) 337–45.

Federal Housing Programs Before 1974

11

This chapter, along with the next one, attempts to cover the major efforts that have been made to solve housing problems at the national level. The first large-scale programs for housing assistance to low-income families were begun in the 1930s. Each era since then has given birth to new programs and a reevaluation of older ones. Some programs have endured for decades in spite of the criticisms, underfunding, and public lack of support. Other programs have been short lived. Regardless of success, or lack of it, the goals and approaches are worth studying because they are part of the long

search for national solutions to housing problems. Previously tried approaches may be restructured into viable programs in the future.

Although the chronology is not precise, the programs that dominated federal efforts in the earlier period, from 1934 to 1974, are emphasized in this chapter, and programs which dominated in the last decade are the focus of the next. The Housing and Community Development Acts of 1974 and 1977 have been the major instruments for shaping current housing solutions.

New York City had experienced housing problems before the turn of the century. With a heritage of public awareness followed by reform legislation, New York paved the way for a growing concern for housing conditions throughout the nation. Private enterprise had traditionally assumed

Urban renewal came to be called "the federal bulldozer" in the 1960s because it tore down more housing than it replaced. Photo courtesy of U.S. Department of Housing and Urban Development.

responsibility for all housing production. When it appeared that housing for the poor was not improving, many concerned citizens, including professionals in social work, economics, and government, campaigned for a public role in providing housing for the poor. In the era of the New Deal in the early 1930s, the first major housing act creating federal policy for housing the poor was passed. It was the United States Housing Act of 1937 (also known as the Wagner-Steagall Act). Thus was born **public housing,** the first of the federal programs discussed in this chapter.

Urban renewal is the second major federal program covered here. Although its impact was not felt until the 1950s, it too was a program intended to improve the housing in poor urban neighborhoods, among other things. The programs that grew out of urban renewal are the subjects of the third section. A program meant to stimulate home ownership for low- to moderate-income families is the subject of the fourth chapter section. Programs designed specifically to stimulate housing production are the subject of the fifth. Finally, miscellaneous programs are mentioned to demonstrate the breadth of HUD involvements with diverse housing problems.

PUBLIC HOUSING

The key to understanding how public housing works is the local public housing agency. The **LHA** (identified as PHA in HUD literature), is sometimes appointed by an established governmental body (city or county level). The LHA decides what the local housing need is, where housing should be built, who will live in it, how to manage it when completed, and all other matters regarding housing for low-income families in the community. The federal

government is in the background, and as may be supposed, very much in control, because all decisions regarding these issues must meet HUD standards. The selection of the site, the design of housing units, the amount of parking and play space, the durability of materials, to name a few technical components in the design of public housing, are approved by HUD officials.

HUD also provides the financing through loans during planning and construction. Thereafter, bonds issued by the local PHA are paid off by federal long-term contributions contracts. The local agency is thus "guaranteed" financial support for the financing of the housing. Rent is paid by the selected tenants, but it cannot be more than 25 percent of their income. Therefore, supplements of additional rent are also part of the federal funding for this program.

There are several ways in which the local PHA can provide housing for low-income families. The following procedures are outlined by HUD:

> Under the **"Turnkey" program,** the PHA invites private developers to submit proposals, selects the best proposal, and agrees to purchase the project on completion. Under conventional-bid construction, the PHA acts as its own developer, acquiring the site(s), preparing its own architectural plans, and advertising for competitive bids for construction. The PHA may also acquire existing housing with or without rehabilitation, from the private market under the acquisition program.[1]

The History of Public Housing

The first major step taken by the government to get involved with housing policy was the formation of the Federal Housing Administration (FHA) in 1934. Other New

Deal legislation, specifically the Public Works Administration attempted to improve slum conditions. But it was the 1937 housing act that created the United States Housing Authority which was the overseeing agency for the local public housing agencies and their efforts to solve local housing problems of low-income families.

Public programs during the Depression were as much concerned with creating jobs as with bettering living conditions for the poor. The high unemployment of the 1930s led to many families living in worse than standard housing conditions. Public housing was seen at the time as a two-part solution to the problem—workers would have jobs and a "decent, safe and sanitary" place to live.[2]

The first housing units built with this federal sponsorship were of low density and usually one to three stories high. Some developments had meeting rooms, playgrounds, and spacious sites. By 1941, no more than one percent of the 300 projects then completed were in ten-story buildings.[3]

The character of public housing changed by the mid-1950s. The working-class, upwardly mobile families housed during the earlier period were replaced by the permanently poor. Many were blacks who had migrated from the South into northern urban cities. Some were on welfare, and the cultural deprivations of these new urban poor led to problems within public housing. As the influx changed the nature of public housing, public resistance to its location, and indeed its very existence, built up. McFarland describes the process:

> As a result, it was difficult for local housing authorities to find sites on which to build. Where sites could be found, the land was expensive. Expensive land made high-rise construction an economic neces-

Much early public housing was built in low-rise and medium-rise structures. These children are working on a community garden in the grounds of public housing in Chicago. Photo courtesy of U.S. Department of Housing and Urban Development.

> sity. Too many public housing projects became concentrations of culturally deprived families packed into large, tall structures—an environment ill-suited for normal family life (what mother can supervise her children from the twelfth floor?) and very conducive to the disruptive behavior encouraged by the anonymity and monotony in which the deprived families lived.[4]

The then famous, and now infamous, project of Pruitt-Igoe in St. Louis was built in 1955. The concentration of poverty-level black families, a majority of which were headed by women, into sixteen highrise apartment towers is now easily viewed as a mistake. At the time it was hailed for its massive solution (2,764 units in all) to St. Louis' housing problems. The project that won design awards when it was built was then partly torn down, and finally abandoned, at no small cost in federal money.

Major Legislative Enactments and Executive Orders

1. Federal Home Loan Bank Act, 1932 (Federal Home Loan Bank Board)
2. Home Owners' Loan Act of 1933
3. National Housing Act, 1934 (Federal Housing Administration)
4. United States Housing Act of 1937 (Public Housing)
5. Lanham Act–War Housing, 1940
6. Establishment of the National Housing Agency, 1942
7. Veterans' Emergency Housing Act of 1946
8. Establishment of Housing and Home Finance Agency (by Executive Order), 1947
9. Housing Act of 1948 (Research)
10. Housing Act of 1949 (Slum Clearance and Urban Redevelopment)
11. Housing Act of 1954 (Research; Urban Planning, extension of slum clearance to include rehabilitation; first use of term *urban renewal;* additional public housing)
12. Housing Act of 1959 (Housing for Elderly)
13. Housing Act of 1961 (FHA below-market-rate housing, planning for urban mass transportation, open space land)
14. Housing Act of 1964 (Direct 3 percent loans for rehabilitation)
15. Housing and Urban Development Act of 1965 (Rent supplements; advanced acquisition of land)
16. Department of Housing and Urban Development Act, 1965
17. Demonstration Cities and Metropolitan Development Act of 1966 (Model Cities Program)
18. Civil Rights Act of 1968
19. Housing and Urban Development Act of 1968 (National Housing Goals, Sections 235 and 236, subsidized loans for ownership and rental of housing)
20. Moratorium on Housing Subsidy and Community Funds, Executive Decision, 1973
21. Housing and Community Development Act of 1974 (block grants for community development, Section 8 Program for subsidizing rents on new and existing housing)
22. The Housing and Community Development Act of 1977 (modification of block grant apportionment formula, special multiyear Urban Development Action Grants for neighborhood revitalization in severely distressed cities and counties)

Reprinted from: Federal Government and Urban Problems: HUD Successes, Failures, and the Fate of our Cities, *by M. C. McFarland. Copyright © 1978 by Westview Press, Boulder, Colorado. By permission.*

By the 1960s, many LHAs had shifted their emphasis to housing for the elderly. Elderly tenants did not create management problems nor did they have public disfavor to impede the process of building public housing for them.

The scattered site approach for public housing was adopted in many communities. When public housing is placed on several small sites in different neighborhoods with no cluster exceeding twenty units, the impact of hundreds or thousands of low-in-

High-rise public housing has been more satisfactory for elderly than it has been for families with children. This project in Philadelphia, built in 1960, houses both. Photo courtesy of U.S. Department of Housing and Urban Development.

come families on schools and community services is not dramatic. The families thus served benefit by smaller-scale housing environments placed in stable neighborhoods.

Another program of public housing came into favor during the 1960s. New, existing, or rehabilitated housing units were leased by the local housing authority to qualified low-income tenants. Section 23, as this rental housing program was called, had the advantage of providing housing throughout a community, often mixed in

This public housing is an example of the scattered site approach which began in the 1970s. No more than 20 units are in any one location so that the housing and the families assimilate easily into the existing neighborhood. Photo courtesy of the City of San Luis Obispo Housing Authority.

unnoticeably with both rental and owner-occupied housing. This program has been phased out. A rental assistance program currently in use is discussed in the next chapter.

The Present Status of Public Housing

Construction of new public housing units was stopped after 1973 when a freeze in funding occurred due to poor national economic conditions. When funding became available again, local housing authorities who attempted to develop new housing units following HUD guidelines and regulations were faced with new problems. Site availability is a major problem because few sites within housing authority jurisdiction meet HUD's stringent, although understandable, requirements (for example, cannot be near a railroad or freeway). Developers, who might have participated in the Turnkey method of public housing construction prior to 1973, are reluctant to involve themselves with the complicated review process required by HUD in addition to the impeding local review processes (discussed in chapter 3). LHAs who develop their own housing then experience the lengthy process of local and HUD approval, assuming they have been fortunate enough to gain some portion of limited housing construction money available in the past few years.

There are many public housing projects in disrepair, and the original poor designs have not inspired caring attitudes on the part of either the residents or the surrounding community. Futhermore, the high incidence of blacks and Spanish-Americans in some urban public housing has given federal government sanction to high levels of segregation. When HUD is faced with budget restraints due to a lack of public interest in all its housing programs, public housing is least likely to get funding adequate to maintain, manage, or rehabilitate existing units, let alone create additional units.

If providing a decent, safe and sanitary housing unit for every low-income family, as well as creating employment for a lagging housing industry, was the original and continuing purpose of public housing, it has failed. At best, it has accounted for about 4 percent of annual housing production, and in more than forty years, fewer than 1.25 million units have been built.

Proponents of public housing can boast of some success. Many more public housing units are in small- and medium-sized towns and cities than in large metropolitan areas. Waiting lists for existing public housing units are common, and it is not extreme that a family will wait for three or more years before getting into a desired unit. Since many families fall into the very low income category (50 percent or less of

This low-rise public housing has been designed to suit the needs of families. Adequate and safe play space is incorporated into the grounds for the use of small children. Photo courtesy of U.S. Department of Housing and Urban Development.

_____ The Failure of Public Housing _____

The history of public housing in the United States is most discouraging for anyone seriously concerned with the willingness and capacity of the democracies to deal with fundamental human problems. Clearly, the institutions responsible for the decisions that guided the development and operation of public housing failed miserably. Worse, they seem incapable of pursuing identifiable goals persistently or improving their performance with experience. They have not learned. And behind the failure of particular institutions lies the grim specter of a society utterly unwilling to accept the social and economic burdens required for even a modest effort to redress the more grievous inequities in the established order. Here, perhaps more than anywhere else, is where public housing's failure was decided. Until genuine changes are made in society's fundamental priorities, efforts to alleviate the suffering of the unfortunate will continue to fail, or at best succeed imperfectly and be expensively disguised as solutions to other problems that society *is* willing to tackle—with the additional risk that such accomplishments will be taken as surrogate for the humane considerations that ought to guide collective action in these spheres. Of those changes, there is no sign whatsoever.

Reprinted from: A Decent Home and Environment: Housing Urban America, *by D. Phares, Ed. Copyright 1977, Ballinger Publishing Company.*

the median income in the area), or the low income category (80 percent or less of the median income of the area), and pay more than 25 percent of their income for housing, public housing is relatively attractive. Thousands of families have been served, and the housing they live in is better than they otherwise could afford. The "bad name" public housing has gained because of its urban disasters is compensated for with small scattered-site developments in hundreds of smaller communities and by public housing for the elderly.

URBAN RENEWAL

The substandard housing conditions that were common to many areas of American cities were the best recognized of this nation's housing problems during the early twentieth century. The reform legislation of the 1930s attempted to deal with **"slum clearance"** at the national level. But it was not until 1949 that legislation was enacted to directly affect the slums in American cities.

The Purpose of Urban Renewal

The urban renewal program was designed to provide "federal financial assistance to eliminate blight in defined urban areas."[5] The concept of **blight** is fundamental to urban renewal. Abrams defines blight this way:

A metaphor from the plant world used to describe that concentration of forces which puts a building or a neighborhood on its way to becoming a slum. A blighted area is one that has deteriorated or has been arrested in its development by phys-

ical, economic, or social forces. . . . Statutes generally require that an area be blighted before it is eligible for urban renewal, but what constitutes blight is open to interpretation.[6]

Blight, as any disease, is best dealt with by getting rid of it. The most obvious way to get rid of deteriorated housing is to tear it down. Slum clearance, then, most often meant the stripping away of all existing structures in many urban neighborhoods. The land, cleared of its reminders of a previous commercial, industrial, and most often, residential use, could be used for whatever the city's governing officials wished.

The slum clearance program had the improvement of the city's tax base as one of its aims. The movement to the suburbs by many thousands of American families had caused a decrease in tax revenues from reliably middle-class home owners. This exodus had been followed by the movement of commerce and industry to the suburbs with their wealthier tax contributions. Urban renewal was an opportunity to bring both the residents and their supporting businesses back to the city. Public buildings such as sports arenas, theater complexes, and art museums were favored in urban renewal projects. The improvement of slum housing was a minor, and often forgotten, objective.

Federal grants were made to cities for two-thirds of the costs of slum clearance. In smaller cities, this portion could be three-fourths. Project planning and preparing for reuse were also federally funded. Real estate entrepreneurs were thus helped with government funds as they made their plans for large-scale, city-center construction.

The elimination of blight through slum clearance was a major motivation for early urban renewal projects. Photo courtesy of U.S. Department of Housing and Urban Development.

Criticisms of Urban Renewal

McFarland states the problems of urban renewal succinctly:

> By the early 1960s, the growing urban renewal program began to stagger under a barrage of criticism. It was charged with destroying neighborhoods, callously evicting poor families, and destroying countless small business firms. Beyond that, federal expenditures on urban renewal were said to be wasted.[7]

Public concern became focused on the plight of the slum dweller. The human aspects of urban renewal vied for attention with the commercial aspects. By 1968, 423,000 units were torn down and replaced by 125,000 units. Less than half of these were built for middle- and low-income families.[8] New federal approaches included a search for decent housing for those persons displaced by the "federal bulldozer," and some slum neighborhoods were scheduled for rehabilitation instead of clearance.

Urban Renewal in the 1960s

The idea of rehabilitating deteriorating structures, especially housing, in blighted urban areas had been part of the public debate on urban renewal in the 1950s. The part rehabilitation had to play in urban renewal was officially recognized in 1954 when FHA was encouraged to lend money for rehabilitation of one- or two-family housing unit structures (up to $20,000) that were within defined urban renewal project areas. Apartment buildings were also approved for larger loan amounts.

By 1961, the role of rehabilitation in urban renewal became more important. At that time it became possible for urban renewal agencies to purchase run-down houses, rehabilitate them and then sell them. But the 1964 Housing Act was the real turning point for rehabilitation. The objective then was to bring housing stock up to code. Generous HUD funding was made available for local efforts at what was called "concentrated code enforcement." The goals of this approach were described this way:

> Where building standards do not exist, they are to be established, and where they do exist, they are to be enforced. It must be remembered that in many instances the problem is not lack of regulations, but rather, lack of proper enforcement. This aspect of the program brings into play the local governmental role in inspection and enforcement, and makes these standards the responsibility of the local community.[9]

The 1964 Housing Act created direct funding for rehabilitation. Through **Section 312**, long-term loans became available at very low interest (3 percent). Both home owners and nonresidential owners were eligible. Rehabilitation had gained such favor that Congress required 10 percent of all urban renewal funds be devoted to grants and loans for low-income home owners.[10] The Housing Act of just one year later allowed the funding of small grants for rehabilitation in urban renewal and code enforcement areas. These Section 115 grants were intended for low-income families unable to qualify for loans.

Neighborhood development became another aspect of urban renewal in the late

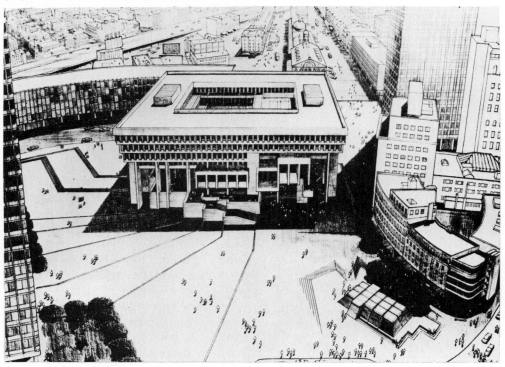

Urban renewal in Boston resulted in a new government center. The sketch is of the project as it was proposed. Photo courtesy of U.S. Department of Housing and Urban Development.

1960s. The Neighborhood Development Program was initiated in the Housing Act of 1968. Perhaps because of the urban riots of the 1960s, there was a recognized need for faster more flexible solutions to housing problems than those the urban renewal programs had produced. This program, therefore, encouraged the renewal of individual neighborhoods that needed urgent action. Funding was on an annual basis.

Model Cities Program. The Model Cities Program approach to the urban problems of the 1960s was bold and imaginative compared to the piece-by-piece legislation that had shaped other urban renewal programs. It was an ambitious and comprehensive attack on the social, economic, and physical problems of certain neighborhoods within urban areas. By concentrating many federal resources into a limited area, it was assumed that dramatic improvements for residents would quickly become evident. The funding aimed to provide job opportunities, educational facilities, disease control, reduction of crime and delinquency, recreational and cultural opportunities, social services, an improved physical environment, and last but not least, more and better housing. A key strategy of the program was local initiative and coordination. The neighborhood residents themselves were to set goals and coordinate efforts to achieve them.

Several significant problems became evident in the Model Cities Program's short and uneven history. One was that a HUD Secretary cannot easily orchestrate numerous programs within HUD, let alone deal sympathetically with the diverse needs of many different urban neighborhoods and neighborhood groups. The people within the target neighborhoods were themselves a problem in that they could not plan and execute long-range programs to achieve

The new government center shown on page 256 is now under construction.

agreed-upon goals. Also, too little money was allocated to accomplish too much in too many cities. Although the program held great promise for eight years, it was terminated in 1973.

One housing critic has summed up the whole experience of urban renewal and its turbulent history in these remarks:

The history of urban renewal reveals a pattern of changing emphasis. When the program began, new houses were to be built only if old ones were torn down; now, old houses are to be torn down only if new ones are to be built. Slum clearance was virtually the entire purpose of the program in 1949; today, it is close to the last thing mentioned by program advocates. . . . Each new direction in the program has been taken after severe criticism in earlier approaches. Each in turn generated new opposition, in many cases for the same reasons. To a substantial extent urban renewal has appeared to be a program in search of a purpose, or at least a search of means to achieve a vaguely stated purpose.[11]

On balance, conventional urban renewal has destroyed more housing units than it has created. Since the displaced families usually moved into surrounding neighborhoods, the housing for former slum dwellers was not improved, and often it was more costly. On the other hand, some cities have created large new downtown centers on sites of urban renewal— New York's Lincoln Center, St. Louis' Gateway Project, Denver's Mile High Project, and San Francisco's Embarcadero Development among them.

One positive accomplishment of urban renewal has been the racial integration in housing in the cities. Where housing was built to replace torn-down slums, it was both black and white middle-income and upper-income families who moved into it.

HOMEOWNERSHIP AS A HOUSING SOLUTION

When public housing lost favor during the 1960s because it appeared not to improve the housing environment of low-income families, there was national interest in allowing families to become home owners instead of renters. It was believed that home ownership could provide the incentive to adopt middle-class habits regarding steady work, educational achievement for children, and above all, responsibility for housing maintenance and repair.

Section 235 Program

Section 235 was part of the National Housing Act of 1934, but it was used infrequently until it was amended in 1968 legislation. The program was designed to insure mortgages to lenders (just like any other FHA insured mortgage), and also to make payments to the lender in order to reduce the amount of interest paid by the home owner. Originally, interest rates could be as low as 1 percent. Down payments were also kept at a minimum to facilitate home ownership for low- and moderate-income families. Applicants had to demonstrate a reliable income source, however, in order to qualify. In fact, the program was aimed at families above the income qualifications for public housing, but unable to buy homes in the private sector.

By 1971, Section 235 accounted for about 6 percent of all housing starts. These 125,000 new homes were supplemented with the purchase of 15,000 existing homes in what appeared to be a successful response to the program.

The construction of new homes brought about one of the major problems with Section 235. In many cities, HUD-controlled inspections, designed to prevent substandard construction materials and methods, were not carefully done. Scandals arose over payoffs to FHA inspectors who allowed faulty construction. As one housing analyst put it, "This was nothing less than a racket. . . ."[12] When the new home owners moved in, they found themselves burdened with cracked slabs, leaky roofs, nonfunctioning heating and plumbing systems, and so on. With the costs of repairs added to their new found expense of monthly mortgage, utilities, taxes, and maintenance costs, many families simply could not handle the financial dilemma in which they found themselves. Thousands of fore-closures occurred in many major cities. The responsibility of home ownership was difficult for the qualified families even without the added costs of poorly constructed housing.

Only two years after the program's peak year of 1971, Section 235 was suspended, along with a freeze of funding affecting other housing programs. When it was reactivated in 1975, new rules were written so that more moderate-income families would be served.

Home Ownership and Urban Renewal

People displaced by urban renewal became the focus of a program activated in 1954. Mortgage insurance was provided by the federal government so that low- and mod-erate-income families could purchase, construct, or rehabilitate housing of no more than four units. Anyone could apply, but displaced households were favored. This program has had far less publicity than others, and some measure of success. By 1977, it had produced over 800,000 units valued over $11 billion. By comparison, by 1977 Section 235 housing amounted to slightly over half that amount and had cost about 80 percent of that amount of money.[13]

Home ownership for the near poor may still have validity as an idea. Since home ownership is so strongly pursued by most American families to satisfy their housing norms, income level notwithstanding, federal government revenues might better be allocated in this direction rather than into rent supplement programs. As Morris and

Townhouses such as these could be built for cooperative ownership by moderate- and low-income families should federal assistance be directed toward owned rather than rented housing. Photo courtesy of U.S. Department of Housing and Urban Development.

Winter argue, ownership can take other forms:

> Would it be so difficult to explore cooperative ownership for low-income families? Of course not. Are townhouses out of the question for publicly sponsored housing? Of course not. Had there not been scandals in its administration, would not the 235 homeownership program for moderate income families have been successful? We think so.[14]

PROGRAMS TO STIMULATE HOUSING PRODUCTION

Housing production as a primary means of achieving quality housing for low- and moderate-income families became a dominant idea in housing legislation in the late 1960s. The Housing and Urban Development Act of 1968 provided a dramatic difference in federal legislation. For the first time in history, a housing goal was set in which 26 million housing units were to be built within a ten year period. Of these, 6 million units were to be replacements for substandard housing unfit for rehabilitation.

The Section 235 home ownership program, discussed above, was also part of this legislation. It stimulated housing production by providing builders with incentives to construct single-family homes for the low- and moderate-income target population. This was accomplished through the subsidizing of interest rates.

Multifamily Housing

Interest subsidy formed the backbone for another program meant to stimulate construction of multifamily housing to be used for the rental market. Again, the target population was of an income level above

The design needs of the handicapped are considered in Section 202 housing, a program aimed at constructing housing for elderly and handicapped persons. Photo courtesy of U.S. Department of Housing and Urban Development.

public housing qualifications, but below that which can afford typical market rents. **Section 236,** as this program is called, originally allowed the owner of multifamily housing to pay off mortgages with interest as low as 1 percent. This in turn allowed for lower rents to be charged to tenants. Some of the tenants, however, needed additional subsidies to pay the necessary rent when 25 percent of their income amounted to less than the fair market rent for the units.

Section 236 effectiveness in improving housing production has been uneven. In ten years of activity, only about 450,000 units have been produced. The program has been criticized for being inadequately managed and economically inefficient as a

This Section 202 housing for the elderly and handicapped was sponsored by the Baptist church, one of many non-profit organizations which have sponsored the construction of such housing. Photo by author.

means of housing production. One interesting issue here is the transfer of conventional housing production into government encouraged production. If no more total units are produced, and if they are produced at higher per-unit cost, what has been gained? Whether or not Section 236 was marginally successful, it was suspended in 1973.

New construction of a special type is encouraged through a program designed to benefit the elderly and handicapped. It is **Section 202** housing, and it differs from other programs in that loans are made directly to the sponsoring groups of the housing developments rather than indirectly

through subsidized interest paid to the lender. The sponsors have to be nonprofit organizations, and the tenants have to be sixty-two years or older or handicapped. The legislation setting up this program originated in 1959, but it was modified in subsequent housing acts. Now, at least 20 percent of the units must be rented to people with low income, whereas the other 80 percent of renters may be of moderate income. Construction of this special housing has been minimal over the long run. In average years, the program has produced only a few thousand units, however, the trend since 1977 has been to increase the number. An estimated 35,000 units were built in 1979, a figure more than ten times the number in 1977.[15]

The Federal Role in Housing Technology

Compared to other industrial methods, the home building process is archaic. With the majority of builders producing fewer than twenty-five houses a year, few builders have made advances in time-saving techniques or experimental use of less expensive materials.

Even though the Housing Acts of 1948 and 1959 had provided some funding for research and development in the building of houses, total research activity was "grossly inadequate," at least it produced no new money-saving technology.[16] By the late 1960s, this problem was recognized by the federal government.

The Office of Urban Technology and Research was established in 1967; 1968 and 1969 produced legislation that "further demonstrated that more significance was being placed on the role of research and technology as essential components of a systematic approach to achieving housing goals."[17] But it was not until a major program called "Operation Breakthrough" was begun that the federal government was involved in a significant way.

This program was devised to produce better housing in large volume, and to use better technology, materials, construction techniques, management and marketing. A second purpose of the program was to assure the housing industry that there were available markets (buyers) to absorb the increased volume of housing. It was believed that Operation Breakthrough would solve the problem of rising housing costs.

Proposals for funding were of two types. Those that described complete structural systems to achieve the desired increase in volume were one type, and those that described components of such systems were another. One of the major stumbling blocks to innovation in housing technology was building codes. The federal government in 1969 gave the HUD Secretary the power to override local building codes and zoning restrictions where they interfered with HUD sponsored housing technology innovations. The way was cleared for Operation Breakthrough to proceed.

Funding for Operation Breakthrough was planned for the selection of only 20 projects, but the proposals submitted numbered 600, the majority of them for components rather than whole building systems. When 22 of these systems were selected for demonstration on nine selected sites, major American companies were represented, such as ALCOA, General Electric, Republic Steel, and National Homes.

The 2,500 homes produced by Operation Breakthrough have been judged as attractive and livable, but the economies of scale necessary for cost reduction were not achieved. Transportation costs from factories to the selected sites proved to be a costly factor. The systems that were employed in the construction had been in existence before this program, but they were put together in fresh ways. In any case, Operation Breakthrough did not industrialize the housing industry.

SUPPLEMENTARY FEDERAL PROGRAMS

The emphasis in this chapter has been on the major programs that have had the greatest impact on current thinking regarding the federal government's role in low-income family housing assistance. In addition to the programs of public housing, urban renewal, home ownership for the near-poor,

This Operation Breakthrough site in Kalamazoo, Michigan, illustrates the type of modular units that were developed in an effort to reduce the cost of housing construction. Photo courtesy of U.S. Department of Housing and Urban Development.

and programs intended to increase production, there have been numerous other programs that relate to these major ones.

Three programs relate to public housing. The **Public Housing Modernization Program** finances capital improvements. Funds can be designated for correction of physical deficiencies, upgrading of living conditions, or for achieving operation efficiency and economy. During recent years (1974–1976), public housing projects that have encountered severe operational problems

Indian housing, such as this in Michigan, is produced in much the same way as public housing, but only Indian housing authorities are qualified for federal funding under this program. Photo courtesy of U.S. Department of Housing and Urban Development.

(Target Projects) have been the focus of the **Public Housing Operative Subsidies Program.** Operating deficits are currently offset by applying a formula based on what it costs to run a well-managed public housing project.

Providing community services for public housing tenants is the purpose of another program. HUD furnishes the technical assistance to the management of public housing, but the employment opportunities, social services, and recreational programs for tenants are arranged through state, regional, or local levels of government.

Both condominiums and cooperative housing have been aided by HUD programs. Condominium ownership was encouraged through federal mortgage insurance, just as the FHA aided single-family home ownership. It was updated legislation in 1961 that included condominiums. Federally insured loans are also available for mobile homes, but the mortgage limits may not be realistic in today's housing costs— $16,000 and fifteen years for a single-width mobile home and $24,000 for twenty-three years for a double-width.[18] Interest is held to a 12 percent rate.

Indian housing has been the focus of another HUD program. It produces housing for Indians in much the same way that any housing authority produces housing for its community, but only Indian Housing Authorities can apply for this particular program. Also, "mutual help" housing for Indians allows people to earn equity in a home by "contributing the site, indigenous building materials, labor and/or cash to its construction."[19]

SUMMARY

The earlier federal programs were designed primarily to aid poor families who had problems in achieving decent, safe and sanitary housing. Another motivation has been an interest in stimulating the housing industry and creating jobs. Public housing has a forty-year history of attempting to reach these two goals, and a mixed record regarding its success.

While much well-designed public housing exists on scattered sites in smaller communities, the remaining urban concentrations of highrise public housing dominate the public image of its failure. Less well-known is the noncontroversial success of public housing designed for the elderly and the rental units managed by public housing throughout the community (Section 23).

The history of urban renewal is second only to public housing in stirring up public controversy regarding the federal involvement with bettering the housing (and the lives) of poor people. Slum clearance was begun in the belief that ridding central cities of blighted areas would stimulate inner city growth for the benefit of the city, if not for individual residents living in these areas. Cities' tax bases were improved with the construction of downtown convention centers, hotels, art museums, theaters, and housing for middle- and upper-income residents. The slum residents were not housed in the new structures, and their housing conditions might have become worse.

Urban renewal in the 1960s attempted to offset the damaging effects of earlier policies. Rehabilitation and neighborhood development were emphasized instead of the tear-down-and-start-over approach. The Model Cities Program in the late 1960s concentrated federal funding for a wide range of neighborhood-level improvements.

The home ownership programs, too, met with early enthusiasm for their approach, then rapid public disfavor, and eventual inactivity. Many new homes built under the Section 235 program were constructed of cheap materials and short-cut methods. HUD inspection scandals and abandoned housing were the results. It is possible that this program could be revived with tighter regulations and alternative forms of ownership available.

Housing production was the major purpose of several programs initiated in the 1960s. Multifamily housing was stimulated by Section 236, and housing for the elderly and handicapped by Section 202. Both programs have been modestly successful.

By contrast, Operation Breakthrough was originated with much fanfare and with high hopes of industrializing, and therefore reducing the costs of housing production. Federal funding was used to support twenty-two projects demonstrating complete structural systems and parts of systems. It failed to industrialize the housing industry or even to demonstrate cost-cutting techniques.

Finally, numerous other programs supplement the major ones. Public housing is helped by programs to modernize facilities, to upgrade physical facilities, to support operational deficits, and to provide coordinated community services. Condominiums, cooperatives and mobile homes have all been included for federal mortgage insurance.

Notes

1. U.S. Department of Housing and Urban Development, *Programs of HUD* (Washington, D. C.: Author, 1978), p. 36.
2. Birch, E. L., "Women-made America: The Case of Early Public Housing Policy," *AIP Journal*, 1978, 44(2), p. 132.
3. Ibid., p. 141.
4. McFarland, M. C., *Federal Government and Urban Problems: HUD: Successes, Failures, and the Fate of Our Cities* (Boulder, Colo.: Westview Press, 1978), p. 131.
5. U.S. Department of Housing and Urban Development, *Programs*, p. 12.
6. Abrams, C., *The Language of Cities* (New York: Viking Press, 1971), p. 24.
7. McFarland, *Federal Government and Urban Problems*, p. 77.
8. Weicher, J. C., "Urban Renewal: National Program for Local Problems," in I. H. Welfeld et al., eds., *Perspectives on Housing and Urban Renewal* (New York: Praeger, 1974), p. 190.
9. Beyer, G. H., *Housing and Society* (New York: Macmillan Co., 1965), p. 470.
10. Weicher, "Urban Renewal," p. 193.
11. Ibid., p. 267.
12. McFarland, *Federal Government and Urban Problems*, p. 142.
13. U.S. Department of Housing and Urban Development, *Programs*, pp. 17–18.
14. Morris, E. W., and M. Winter, *Housing, Family, and Society* (New York: Wiley, 1978), p. 329.
15. U.S. Department of Housing and Urban Development, *The Tenth Annual Report on the National Housing Goal* (Washington, D.C.: Author, 1979), p. 21.
16. Rice, R. R., "Housing in the 1960s," in G. S. Fish, ed., *The Story of Housing* (New York: Macmillan Co., 1979), p. 358.
17. Ibid.
18. U.S. Department of Housing and Urban Development, *Programs*, p. 23.
19. U.S. Department of Housing and Urban Development, *Programs*, p. 50.

Suggested Readings

Cole, A. M."Federal Housing Program." In G. S. Fish, ed. *The Story of Housing*. New York: Macmillan Co., 1979.

Dolbeare, C. N. "How to Develop Creative Public Housing Communities for Low-Income People through Conventional and Leased Programs." In A. Greendale and S. F. Knock, Jr., eds. *Housing Costs and Housing Needs*. New York: Praeger, 1976.

Fish, G. S. "Housing Policy during the Great Depression." In G. S. Fish, ed. *The Story of Housing*. New York: Macmillan Co., 1979.

Holleb, D. B. "A Decent Home and Suitable Living Environment." *American Academy Political and Social Sciences Annals*, 1978, 435, 102–116.

McFarland, M. C. *Federal Government and Urban Problems, HUD: Successes, Failures, and the Fate of Our Cities*. Boulder, Colo.: Westview Press, 1978, (chap. 8 "Housing the Poor and Near-Poor").

Meehan, E. J. "The Rise and Fall of Public Housing: Condemnation without Trial." In D. Phares, ed. *A Decent Home and Environment: Housing Urban America*. Cambridge, Mass.: Ballinger, 1977.

Rice, R. R. "Housing in the 1960s." In G. S. Fish, ed. *The Story of Housing*. New York: Macmillan Co., 1979.

U.S. Department of Housing and Urban Development. *Occasional Papers in Housing and Community Affairs*, Vol. 2. Washington, D.C.: U.S. Government Printing Office, 1978.

U.S. Department of Housing and Urban Development. *Programs of HUD*. Washington, D. C.: Author, 1978.

Welfeld, I. H.; Muth, R. F.; Wehner, H. G. Jr.; and Weicher, J. C. *Perspectives on Housing and Urban Renewal*. New York: Praeger, 1974.

Government Solutions to Current Housing Problems

12

A major shift in emphasis in the federal government's role in housing took place in the early 1970s. Whereas from 1930 to 1968 many specific programs aimed at solving first one housing problem, then another, the 1970s witnessed a different governmental approach. Rather than directly controlling and centralizing many specific programs, the policy shifted towards a greater degree of local control and decision making.

The Housing Acts of 1974 and 1977 are the primary legislative vehicles for the updated and refocused housing policy. Both acts contain elements from the previous four decades of federal housing assistance. While redirection and new emphasis characterize these acts, their complexity is a reminder of the many directions previously taken in federal policy. A 1978 statement made by the Congressional Budget Office perhaps best illustrates the complexity of housing policy in the 1970s.

Among the objectives of federal housing policy are: reducing the incidence of substandard housing and overcrowding, and alleviating excessive housing costs; increasing residential construction and reducing cyclical instability in the home building industry; expanding access to mortgage credit and encouraging homeownership; encouraging residential integration and deconcentration of lower-income households; providing housing for individuals with special needs due to age or disability; and promoting community development, and neighborhood preservation and revitalization. Progress towards those objectives has been uneven. Improvements in one area have sometimes been at the expense of gains in other areas, creating shifting policy concerns.[1]

The 1970s approach to urban problems, especially urban housing, is the subject of the first section of this chapter. The **Community Development Block Grant Program** is aimed at solving interwoven urban problems. Rehabilitation and **urban homesteading** have also helped shape urban policy. The current form of rental assistance, **Section 8,** is examined in the second section and rural housing is the focus of the third section. While urban problems have often gotten more public and official attention, rural housing conditions have been improved through the programs of the **Farmers Home Administration.**

States have played an important role along with federal endeavors to remedy housing problems. The goals and effectiveness of state housing finance agencies are discussed in the fourth section. The last section returns to the federal role in housing and deals with the government's influence on the private sector of the housing market. This influence involves both federal taxation policies and mortgage market controls.

URBAN HOUSING

Since neither public housing nor urban renewal had abated the problems of inner city poverty-level populations, it was recognized that urban decay was a problem far more complex than any one-dimensional pro-

gram could solve. Slum clearance and commercial rebuilding did not change the social environment of the people who were slum residents and who were often ignored in urban renewal efforts.

> The realization that direct subsidies to households might be the proper role of the federal government was gaining momentum in academic circles as well as in political circles. By 1974, the nation began to explore the viability of block grants modeled after revenue sharing and direct subsidies to low-income households. In effect, the 1974 Housing Act was to be the turning point in the nation's thinking about housing.[2]

This section on urban housing deals first with the block grant program as it was defined in the 1974 Housing Act. Housing rehabilitation is the subject of the second subsection. Many popular magazines have focused on the success stories of urban homesteading, the subject of the third subsection.

Community Development Block Grants

Prior to 1974, grants had been given to communities for a variety of purposes. These so-called "categorical grants" were applied for by communities recognizing their own needs, but each need was funded by a separate program of HUD. The categorical grant programs were:

1. Model Cities
2. Neighborhood Development
3. Neighborhood Facilities
4. Open Space, Urban Beautification and Historic Preservation
5. Public Facility Loans
6. Urban Renewal
7. Water and Sewer Facilities

The most important programs with respect to the assistance given to low-and moderate-income families—Urban Renewal, Neighborhood Development, and Model Cities—were discussed in the last chapter.

Title I of the 1974 Housing Act authorized Community Development Block Grants (CDBG) to replace these categorical grants. This program was then amended by Title I of the 1977 Housing and Community Development Act. HUD describes the program with the brief phrase, "Federal aid to promote sound community development."[3] Creative and flexible solutions to local problems were encouraged. The way it works is a little more specific. Cities and qualified urban counties are guaranteed an amount of money called an "**entitlement**" which is based on local need. Smaller communities may receive "**discretionary**" **funds.** Factors used to determine need are population, poverty, overcrowded housing, age of housing, and rate of growth. The

Rehabilitation loans have been available to low-income owners of housing in need of major repairs. Photo courtesy of U.S. Department of Housing and Urban Development.

priorities for use of the entitlement money are determined at the local level, but the law provides general guidelines. Adequate housing and an improved living environment are primary among them, while economic opportunities for low-income residents are also given funding potential.

One of the requirements of the communities applying for CDBG funding is a **Housing Assistance Plan.** Local officials in the communities are required to survey their low- and moderate-income housing needs, and more importantly, to establish a program for meeting these needs. The resulting Housing Assistance Plan (HAP) is included in the application for funds.

As expected, CDBG funding has been used for a variety of purposes. In many communities, unfinished urban renewal projects have continued development with these funds. Where categorical funding had been used before, CDBG funds have been applied. Public works and facilities have been a major portion of their use. Rehabilitation activity has accounted for a steady portion of this funding (about 13 percent).[4]

Rehabilitation

Rehabilitation of rundown but salvageable homes in decaying urban neighborhoods was discussed in the last chapter in connection with urban renewal in the 1960s. Because so little housing for low-income families had been provided by the new construction of urban renewal, and because the urban renewal process was so disruptive to low-income urban neighborhoods, rehabilitation became a 1954 legislative reform.

Another HUD program has been aimed at providing loan money solely for property owners in federally assisted areas aided by Community Development Block Grants. These so-called "Section 312" loans, after Section 312 of the Housing Act of 1964, as

Federal Rehabilitation Programs

FHA Title I Nonsubsidized Home Improvement Loans— insured loans made by financial institutions to homeowners for home improvements. Maximum amount for a one-family home loan is $15,000 and the minimum term is 15 years. Current interest rate is 12 percent (HUD).

Community Development Block Grant Program—CDBG funds disbursed by localities in direct rehabilitation loans or as subsidies, deposits, or guarantees in leveraging programs with financial institutions. In 1977, approximately 13.5 percent of CDBG funds was budgeted for CD loans and grants (HUD).

Section 312 Rehabilitation Loans— federal loans for the rehabilitation of single- and multi-family residential properties and business properties. Loans currently bear an interest rate of 3 percent for terms not exceeding 20 years or three-fourths of the remaining life of the structure after rehabilitation, whichever is less (HUD).

Urban Homesteading Program—transfer of unoccupied one- to four-family HUD-owned properties without payment to units of general local government. Local governments, in turn, transfer such

properties at nominal costs to eligible families as well as provide public services and amenities designed to correct neighborhood decline and encourage private investment (HUD).

Section 8 Substantial Rehabilitation—long-term (30 to 40 years) housing assistance payments contracts are entered into by the federal government with owners of multi-family housing for structures to undergo substantial rehabilitation and be made available to eligible lower-income families (HUD).

Neighborhood Strategy Areas—allocations of Section 8 substantial rehabilitation funds for use by selected cities in neighborhood strategy areas to reverse deterioration. Under this targeted strategy, other programs including CDBG funds, urban development action grants, public housing modernization, and special mortgage insurance procedures will also be focussed on these designated areas (HUD).

Section 8 Moderate Rehabilitation—short-term (up to five years) leases of existing housing for lower-income families are combined with financing from Section 312, CDBG monies, state and local grants, or private financing to undertake capital improvements ranging from $1500 to $5000.

Allowable rents under Section 8 are adjusted to reflect the cost of upgrading (HUD).

Section 202 Loans for Elderly and Handicapped—a portion of Section 202 loans are combined with Section 8 substantial rehabilitation (HUD).

Public Housing Substantial Rehabilitation—a proportion of new long-term (40-year) contracts for public housing is allocated for substantial rehabilitation (HUD).

Public Housing Modernization—a set-aside of annual contribution funds is provided to modernize and upgrade older, existing housing projects (HUD).

Section 502 Rural Housing Programs—the Farmers Home Administration provides loans to low- and moderate-income families for rehabilitation and repairs of buildings located in rural areas. Interest rates vary but there are interest supplement payment provisions that can bring the effective interest rate down to 1 percent for low-income families. Loans to moderate-income families are made at an amount not less than a rate determined by the Secretary of the Treasury, taking into consideration the current average

market yield on outstanding obligations of the United States with comparable maturity (Department of Agriculture).
  FHA Mortgage Insurance Programs—

insures lenders against loss on mortgage loans for housing rehabilitated under its basic mortgage insurance programs (HUD).

Reprinted from: Journal of

Housing 36 (2) *1979; an official publication of the National Association of Housing and Redevelopment Officials, 2600 Virginia Avenue, N.W., Washington, D.C.*

amended, have upper limits. The owner of each dwelling may not be lent more than $27,000, while nonresidential properties may get more. Preference is given to low-income and moderate-income applicants.[5]

Both owner-occupants and investors may get Section 312 rehabilitation loans; about 80 percent of them, however, go to owner-occupants. In the ten-year period prior to 1977, 70 percent of the loans had gone to people with incomes under $12,000. A substantial proportion, however, went to people with incomes over $16,000 (12 percent), indicating that not only low-income families were served. Black households have been provided with 45 percent of the loans.[6]

Although the program has been relatively small throughout its history, it did survive the 1973 moratorium. More than 80,000 units had been rehabilitated by 1978.[7] Funding in recent years (1977 to 1979) had been increased from previous levels. Section 312 loans are used in conjunction with urban homesteading, discussed in the next subsection.

Rehabilitation has become part of other ongoing programs as well. Modernization of public housing, a program referred to in the last chapter, is, in effect, a rehabilitation program. The major rent supplement program now in use (Section 8) also has rehabilitation funding related to it.

Urban Homesteading

Homesteading is a term that dates back to the Homestead Act of 1862. That legislation was created to encourage the settlement and development of the western regions of what became the United States. Homesteading came to mean the farming of a 160-acre tract of land. Urban homesteading has become the twentieth century counterpart, only this time, it is for the purpose of redeveloping inner-city neighborhoods through the restoration and occupation of abandoned housing.

"Each year, property owners throughout the United States are simply walking away from about 70,000 units of housing."[8] Thus, abandonment has become a major urban phenomenon. Many of the buildings have become deteriorated to the point that owners can neither rehabilitate them at a reasonable cost nor rent them at adequate levels to warrant their restoration. In addition, the owner may perceive that the housing unit itself does not qualify for further maintenance and repair. Paul states,

> It may be too large, too expensive to heat, poorly planned, too costly to maintain, too small. It may be inadequately wired, need a new roof, a new heating system, offer no place to park. And, it may be seen as an unfashionable house in an unfashionable neighborhood. As many of these problems accrue, the possibility of remedying any problem is no longer considered to be worth the effort.[9]

Maintenance is ignored over a period of time, thus hastening the deterioration already taking place. When one or two owners abandon houses in a poor neighborhood, others lose value, and further

Housing abandonment has become a major problem in many American cities. Landlords simply give up property when maintenance and taxes become more burdensome than potential rents allow. Abandonment leads to further decay and vandalism. Photo courtesy of U.S. Department of Housing and Urban Development.

abandonment takes place. Some cities have blocks and blocks of abandoned housing. For the remaining residents in or near such areas, normal residential security and convenience is impossible.

Urban homesteading was a program designed to reverse this process. Wilmington, Delaware was the first city to attempt urban homesteading, and it intended low-income families to move into and fix up the abandoned housing. Instead, middle-income families were attracted to the opportunity to repair an inner-city house in exchange for the advantages of urban location. Abandoned houses are often purchased for one dollar. They may require virtual rebuilding, however, and the money and skills required for the job can be enormous.

HUD's urban homesteading program was part of the 1974 Housing Act (Section 810). In the program, HUD transfers houses it owns to local governments in communities with HUD approved Home-

steading Plans. These plans assure the availability of rehabilitation financing, technical assistance to prospective homesteaders, and municipal services in the homesteading neighborhoods. Section 312 and Community Development Block Grant funds are used in cooperation with urban homesteading funds.

After the small token sum is paid to the city for the property, the homesteader must make repairs to meet minimum health and safety standards. Then the homesteader must reside in the property for three years, and within eighteen months of occupying it, he or she must bring it up to local code standards. Finally, when all of the requirements have been met, the property is deeded to the homesteader, and it goes back on the city's tax rolls. The HUD homesteading program began with twenty-three cities, and it has grown to include at least forty cities. The funding has also in-

Urban homesteading allows the purchase of a piece of property for as little as one dollar providing the owners meet the requirements of residency (occupy it for three years) and of rehabilitation (bring it up to code within 18 months). Photo courtesy of U.S. Department of Housing and Urban Development.

An entire area may be subject to urban homesteading. This street of houses is the successful result of the program's application in Baltimore. Photo courtesy of U.S. Department of Housing and Urban Development.

creased—from $5 million in 1976 to triple that amount three years later.[10]

Where urban homesteading has been successful, abandonment of housing decreases, but does not disappear. In Baltimore, abandonment decreased from a rate of about 5,000 houses to half that—2,500 houses—in three years.[11] About that same number of houses was being homesteaded. In one of the homesteaded areas in Baltimore, forty-two houses were restored and the city participated by redoing streets and sidewalks. That success was followed by three other projects, each larger than the first.

RENTAL ASSISTANCE: SECTION 8

The Section 23 leased housing program was mentioned in the last chapter in connection with public housing. In this program, exist-ing housing units were leased from private owners for the use of low-income tenants selected by Local Housing Authorities. Landlords were paid the fair market rent for the leased units through rent supplements provided by HUD.

Another important rental assistance program was the Experimental Program in Housing Allowances. It was based on the belief that low-income families might do better in providing themselves with suitable housing than HUD had done, especially in light of public housing mistakes. Families were provided with cash instead of a housing unit with all of its implied cumbersome production problems and its lasting stigma. In theory, low-income families could find housing in the local market, thus stimulating that market to produce housing to meet their needs.

Twelve cities were selected for this experimental program in order to test how households used the allowance, how housing markets responded, and how well the program was administered. The ten-year experiment began in 1972 and served 20,000 households. Results of the program were mixed. In brief, they proved to dispel some myths about housing allowances as a better alternative in aiding low-income families.

It was the 1974 legislation that activated Section 8 of the U.S. Housing Act of 1937, calling it the Lower-Income Rental Assistance Program. Its intent is simply to subsidize the rent of low-income families "to help them afford decent housing in the private market."[12] Keeping in mind that eligible recipients need not pay more than 25 percent of their income on rent, and that the participating landlords must receive a "**fair market rent**" for the housing unit, HUD makes up the difference. HUD, however, determines what is fair market rent and has standards that must be met for the housing units to be rented. The rental assistance applies to existing housing, new construction, or rehabilitated units.

Local public housing agencies administer the program, and most LHAs who participate also have public housing programs. Other less experienced agencies may also participate in Section 8. Tenants apply for Section 8 with the LHA, and if their income is less than 80 percent of the area's median income, or if they are elderly or handicapped, they receive a certificate that enables them to search for an appropriate housing unit for 60 days. HUD requires that 30 percent of certificates must be given to very low income families—families with income levels below 50 percent of the area's median income. The number of certificates to be given is limited in any one LHA. Some give them out on a first-come-first-served basis, others on a priority basis such as unsafe housing, or very low income.

The major responsibility of the partici-

Housing of all types throughout a community may be rented under the Section 8 program. The certified tenant contracts with a landlord for a unit that meets HUD standards. A rent supplement is provided by HUD through the local Housing Authority. Photo by author.

pant, having received certification, is to find a unit that will pass HUD inspection and whose landlord will participate in the program. Single-family detached units, mobile homes, and multifamily apartments may qualify. When the participant is successful, a contract is made with the landlord for the share of the rent to be paid by the participant. Many of the participants who receive certification never find a suitable housing unit. Some do not search for them, but others do so unsuccessfully.

Section 8 Evaluation

A study of the program showed that a disproportionately large number of elderly women and female-headed households with children, compared to the eligible population, participated successfully. People with very low incomes are well served by the program (82 percent of recipients are in this category). Successful participants are to be found in all locations—central cities, suburbs, small towns and rural areas. About half of the participants stay in their present units, but they experience a rent increase, with the size of the increase related to the preprogram rent level (rents over $150 were increased by only five percent). It appears that those who want to move, do so, some to different neighborhoods (one-third). Movers reduced overcrowding by finding units with more bedrooms, but also by reducing household size with the move.[13]

The families who want to participate, but who are not successful in finding appropriate housing with a cooperative landlord have different characteristics from the successful participants to the program. They tend to be large families headed by females. They also tend to have very low incomes. Elderly persons experience a higher level of success that nonelderly, due mainly to their small household size, often one person. The larger the family, the less likely it is to find housing. Minorities have difficulty finding housing in this program, but the study did not indicate overt discrimination. The HUD study explains that households with incomes that allow only a modest benefit from the program may decide that it is not worth the added inconvenience of meeting the program's requirements to bother with becoming a program recipient. Even those paying more than the fair market rent may not wish to move to qualify for the program if the gain is low.

Section 8 Rehabilitation and Construction

Section 8 has been one of several means of rehabilitation for poor quality existing housing stock. Both nonprofit and for-profit developers may participate by submitting proposals for substantial rehabilitation to the Local Housing Authority of the State Housing Finance Agency, which handles some Section 8 funds. Once rehabilitated, the units are rented to eligible participants in the program.

Neighborhood revitalization is another purpose of Section 8 funding. Some of the rehabilitation funding is set aside especially for Neighborhood Strategy Areas (NSA). Proposals for eligible neighborhoods are made by local governments. The communities who participate in this program have Community Development Block Grant funding, along with local resources, to supplement the Section 8 funds.

Another aspect of Section 8 funding surpasses that of Section 8 rehabilitation, both for NSAs and non-NSAs. It is housing construction. New construction proposals are handled the same way rehabilitation proposals are handled, through LHAs or through state agencies. In recent years, the funding for new construction has increased whereas the funding for rehabilitation has remained about the same. In 1979, an es-

New construction is also possible with Section 8 funding. The project illustrated is for elderly tenants. Photo courtesy of U.S. Department of Housing and Urban Development.

timated 150,000 units were started under this program compared to about 20,000 rehabilitation units, and about 270,000 units received rental assistance.[14]

RURAL HOUSING

The emphasis so far has been on urban housing problems. Urban ills are intensified by their visibility and concentration. Nevertheless, rural America can match urban America in serious housing problems. This section examines the federal efforts to solve those problems.

Tabulating exactly how many rural houses are **substandard** is difficult. The definition of substandard may mean dilapidated or lacking complete plumbing, or it may mean something broader including such characteristics as overcrowding or leaky roofs. A conservative estimate is that half of all of the nation's bad housing is in small towns and rural areas. Put another way, more than 14 percent of all nonmet-

We Do Not Need an Urban Policy

It is wrong to say the nation has an urban problem. We have a settlement problem. We do not need an urban policy.

Development works like this: We build cities. We then construct in undeveloped areas—suburbs, small towns, woodlands, farm areas—without restraint. These areas become new cities with everything the old cities offered: jobs, stores, symphonies, colleges, cemeteries.

Periodically, between wars, following riots, when unemployment rises, pressures build to aid cities. Laws are passed. All miss the point. The problem is not the cities. The problem is what we call the suburbs.

Developers blackmail us. As open areas are developed, the developers play township against township, county against county, state against state to gain tax concessions for housing developments, shopping centers, factories. Asked to return to cities, they blackmail us again, saying they need government incentives—in criminal cases this is called a bribe—to develop in cities. Government plays the role of conspirator. Incentives are authorized. The people who destroyed us are supposed to save us.

Because we do not attack the problem—private money and new development—we spend billions of dollars in public money on urban programs. Many American cities are federal cities, as much tied to the federal government as Washington, D.C., or an infantry base, or an Asian government we support

against communism.

If we wish to assist cities, we must fashion a national development policy that preserves open land and forces development into cities.

We must pass a stringent federal land law that protects open land almost wherever it is found. We need federal laws to preserve family farms and small towns. We must expand wilderness preserves. We must establish parks and plan cities and metropolitan areas around them, not let cities and metropolitan areas straggle across the countryside, and save a pocket of trees here, a fifth-growth forest there.

Excerpted from: Serrin, W. Nation's Cities, 1978, 16 (6), p. 2. Reprinted by permission.

ropolitan housing is inadequate.[15] Compared to urban housing, "the non-metro household is substantially more likely to have a leaky roof, a leaky basement, or holes in the floor of the house. This is probably partly to be explained by the fact that there is 20% (sic) chance that they will be living in a pre-1940 house."[16]

HUD Programs in Rural Areas

Several of the programs initiated by HUD are applicable to rural housing problems as well as urban housing problems. Some programs have been specifically designed to be

shared by both metropolitan and nonmetropolitan areas. However, it should be recognized that regional offices of HUD are all in metropolitan areas, and that a dependence on local institutions limits the effectiveness of its programs in some areas. Half of the nation's counties, inhabited by one-fifth of the population, have no public housing agencies.[17] Even so, a few programs have been successful in rural areas.

Section 8 Rental Assistance. The **Lower Income Housing Assistance Program** (Section 8) legislation intended 25 percent of the funding to be directed into nonmetropolitan areas. The method of certification for low-income families, and their subsequent search for suitable housing and a cooperative landlord, is the same for rural as for urban residents. It may be that rural housing more easily meets HUD's requirements for rent levels than does urban housing, even though there is an effort to adjust rent levels according to local housing economics.

Community Development Block Grants. Although Title I block grants were designed primarily to solve the interrelated problems apparent in urban ghettos, they can be applied to rural towns as well. Rehabilitation of dilapidated housing is one of the several purposes to which block grants are applied. As cited earlier in this chapter, discretionary funds are used for smaller communities, and 1,800 such communities had received this funding in the 1978 through 1980 period.[18]

Public Housing. Certainly HUD's oldest active program cannot be forgotten as a viable means of assisting rural households in seeking better housing. As indicated in the last chapter, most of the more successful and enduring public housing projects have been constructed in smaller towns. But not all rural areas have public housing—new or old.

Farmers Home Administration (FmHA)

The federal agency whose major purpose is helping with housing problems of low-income families in rural areas is the Farmers Home Administration of the Department of Agriculture. The Housing Act of 1949 authorized the Farmers Home Administration to lend money for home ownership and home repairs as well as for farm operation and community facilities. Since then, much legislation has added further housing involvement for this federal agency.

The distinction between FmHA programs and HUD programs is that the FmHA programs must be limited to rural areas. Although rural areas were originally defined as places with less than 10,000 population, they now have a broader definition. The Housing and Community Development Act of 1974 included in their definition of rural areas "any open country, or any place, town, village or city with a population in excess of 10,000 but not more than 20,000 if they are not within a standard metropolitan statistical area and have a serious lack of mortgage credit as determined by the Secretary of Agriculture and the Secretary of Housing and Urban Development."[19]

Self-Help Housing Program. One of the most successful programs sponsored by the FmHA is self-help housing. It was begun by a nonprofit private corporation in California. Its success there led to the adoption of a national rural housing program in many other states. The program's main purpose is to provide newly constructed homes for ownership by low- to moderate-income families in rural areas. The families build the homes themselves thus saving the high costs of labor. The families are selected and

The foundation of one of several houses is constructed by residents who will become home owners through the FmHA Self-Help Program. Photo courtesy of People's Self-Help Housing Corp., San Luis Obispo.

Home improvements and repairs in rural housing are funded under a program administered by the Farmers Home Administration. The installation of a ramp for wheelchair access would qualify for this type of funding. Photo courtesy of U.S. Department of Housing and Urban Development.

trained by program directors and their technical assistants. It has been found that six to twelve families work well together. All able members of the family make a contract commitment for hours of labor on the project that includes their own and other's homes.

FmHA funds the program in two ways. Section 523 allows grant money (up to $200,000) for developing, administering and coordinating the technical assistance for a self-help housing program. Public bodies and nonprofit corporations can apply for these grants. Section 502 is a home ownership program used in conjunction with self-help housing to finance materials and land purchase. Mortgage credit is provided in this program. In addition, most self-help families also qualify for interest credits that further reduce their mortgage payments.

Rural Home Ownership. Section 502 has a broader range of purposes than im-

plied in its application to the self-help program. Section 502 loans can be used:

to construct, improve, weatherize or relocate a dwelling; to buy a building site; to buy a house and lot; to provide a water supply and sewage disposal facilities; to modernize a home by adding bathrooms, central heating, modern kitchens, including a range, refrigerator, clothes washer, clothes dryer; to provide foundation plantings, seeding or sodding of lawns; to buy and improve homes for farm laborers; to refinance debts under certain conditions; to pay legal expenses.[20]

Loans are made at below-market rates, and they may be repaid in thirty-three years. Interest rates to low-income families may be reduced further. All families qualifying for 502 loans must fall below income ceilings set by each state.

Other FmHA Programs. Another program is aimed specifically at home repairs. Minor repairs and improvements, such as roof repairs, water supply, plumbing, structural supports, can be funded by small loans of $2,500 under the Section 504 program. Home owners who may not qualify for 502, could qualify in this program. The elderly are benefitted in this program through the provision of grants to supplement loans.

Rental housing is a rural as well as an urban need. Section 515 provides loans to construct, purchase, improve, alter, or repair rental housing. Facilities for dining and recreation can be included along with housing units. Nonprofit corporations are the primary users of this program but individuals, consumer cooperatives, public bodies and some profit-making corporations may also qualify for 515 loans. HUD's Section 8 program may be used for rent subsidies for tenants in FmHA 515 rental housing.

Farm labor housing is another area of concern to the Farmers Home Administration. Sections 514 and 516 are programs aimed at construction and repair of farm labor housing used year-round. Again, nonprofit organizations and public bodies are the primary beneficiaries of this program, but loans may also be made to farm owners.

Another program is directed at the purchase and development of housing sites. The loans made in the program can be used for access roads, streets, utility lines, water and sewer systems, engineering and legal fees, and closing costs. Owners of self-help housing may apply for these loans as well as the other ones mentioned above. The sites developed in this program, when not used for self-help housing, may be "sold to families, nonprofit organizations, public agencies and cooperatives eligible for assistance under any law which provides financial assistance for housing low- and moderate-income families."[21]

Overall, the FmHA programs do not result in as much housing production as do HUD programs. Looking at new construction and rehabilitation combined, in 1979 for example, HUD provided about three times as much new housing starts as did FmHA (298,950 to 107,970). Looking just at new construction starts, the proportion of HUD units to FmHA units was far greater. Of the approximately 94,000 construction starts credited to FmHA in 1979, more than a third of them were for multifamily housing. In the same year, only a few hundred multifamily units were rehabilitated with FmHA funds, whereas HUD rehabilitated an estimated 25,000 multifamily housing units. In the one- to four-family home category, FmHA did much better. It assisted with about 13,000 homes compared to HUD's 2,250.[22] Clearly, new construction accounts for more housing production than rehabilitation by both of these federal agencies.

STATE PROGRAMS FOR HOUSING ASSISTANCE

New York in 1960 was the first state to form a housing finance agency. The federal Housing and Urban Development Act of 1968 mandated the formation of additional state agenices, because the Section 235 ownership program and the Section 236 rental programs outlined in this legislation were funded through state agencies. When HUD funding ceased during the 1973 moratorium, state agencies had to establish their own programs with less dependence on federal funding. By 1975, three-fourths of all states had housing finance agencies (HFAs).[23]

One of the major functions of HFAs is to make construction and permanent loans for the building of low- and moderate-income multifamily housing. The financial vehicle for these loans is the issuing of tax-exempt bonds, and the money thus raised is loaned directly to the housing developer or sponsor. In theory, the financial arrangement provides loans at reduced cost to the developer, and the developer in turn passes on the savings in reduced rents. Research has shown, however, that rents are often not low enough to benefit even moderate-income families.[24]

HFAs may also provide interest-free loans to public housing and other nonprofit groups for the development of housing. These so-called "seed money loans" help pay for the early development costs of land options, attorneys, architects, and so on. Seed money is repaid to the state agencies when permanent financing is found for the project.

Some state agencies have the power to

This housing development on Roosevelt Island in New York City was one of many projects undertaken by the Urban Development Corporation (UDC) of the State of New York. This particular state agency was very active in many kinds of developments, but it found itself in financial trouble in 1975. Photo courtesy of U.S. Department of Housing and Urban Development.

develop housing directly rather than funding private developers. New York has had the largest such program through its Urban Development Corporation (UDC). It can acquire land, select builders, provide financing, and provide technical assistance for the development of residential, commercial, civic and industrial projects. UDC found itself in serious financial trouble in 1975, so its development capacity was re-

duced by the New York State Legislature. Fourteen other states, however, have empowered their state housing finance agencies with development capabilities.

Even though the construction of housing has been the main purpose of HFAs, other housing needs have also been recognized. Some states have participated in experimental housing programs. For instance, West Virginia and Minnesota were selected by HUD to provide "basic homes" (homes designed to reduce costs for low-income families) in rural areas. Another example is the "add-a-bathroom" program in which a bathroom unit can be attached to an existing house at relatively low cost. This was done in South Carolina. West Virginia experimented with a program aimed at using home repair loans for the elderly. Two states, Massachusetts and Michigan, have been involved with rehabilitation programs.[25]

The efforts of several states have been directed to help special groups. The following list illustrates the variety of purposes and diverse target groups:

1. The Illinois Housing Development Authority has a special program to encourage housing for the elderly.
2. The HFAs in New York and Maine have been involved in projects on Indian reservations.
3. The Missouri Housing Development Commission builds housing designed for blind occupants.
4. California and Wisconsin provide mortgage financing especially for veterans.
5. Michigan operates a program for marginally mentally retarded adults.[26]

Even though this list is impressive in its variety and in its implied concern for low-income groups with special housing-related problems, by and large HFA activity has benefitted persons without low income or special problems. One study of housing produced by state agencies showed that 90 percent of it was for the moderate- to middle-income groups, and 80 percent of it was in suburbs.[27]

THE FEDERAL ROLE AND THE PRIVATE SECTOR

All of the programs discussed so far are aimed at providing public support for housing low- and moderate-income families. The impression has been made, no doubt, that the federal role has been dominated by a concern for these less affluent families in American society. This is not the case. A major and prominent role that the federal government plays is in its support of home ownership and its influence on the financing mechanism on which the private housing market depends. These indirect aids stimulate and regulate the housing industry by creating demand for housing on the one hand and aiding production on the other hand.

Taxation Policies

The advantages to home owners regarding the tax deductible items related to home ownership were discussed in chapter 8. Here they are viewed as one important aspect of federal housing policy. By allowing annual mortgage interest payments and property tax payments to be deducted from taxable income, the federal government is boosting home ownership through an **indirect subsidy**. This amounted to $7.6 billion in 1977, far more than the $2.9 billion spent in direct federal funding of housing assistance programs during the same year.[28]

Another tax advantage involves the capital gains resulting from selling a home. If money is invested in stocks or bonds, the

The owners of this home are indirectly subsidized by the federal taxation policies. By allowing deductions for interest and property taxes and deferring of capital gains when the house is sold, federal policy favors homeowners. Photo by author.

increased value of these investments is taxed upon their sale, even if the money so earned is reinvested in a similar way. This is not so with the sale and purchase of homes. If a family sells its home and reinvests the profits made from the sale into another home for themselves of equal or higher value, they owe the Internal Revenue Service nothing—at that time. The new home purchase or home construction must be completed within eighteen months, before or after the sale in most cases. The tax owed on this form of capital gains is deferred until such time as the home-selling profits are not reinvested in a primary residence. This usually does not occur until a family is retired.

When people over fifty-five sell their homes and do not reinvest the profits in primary residences, they may take advantage of a tax law that allows them to be exempt for one time only from capital gains amounting to $100,000. If the profits were more than that, capital gains taxes would have to be paid on the excess amount. But in addition to this one-time tax bonus, elderly people over sixty-five may deduct up to $35,000 of the capital gains value when calculating their taxes owed on a sale of property. If the profits earned from the sale exceed this amount, the rest is taxed at the rate of income level appropriate to retirement instead of rates appropriate during preretirement employment.

The federal government could choose to tax the equity one has in one's home, but it does not. If this income were earned on another form of investment, taxes would be paid. Interest and dividends are taxed, but increased value in real property is not. Again, the federal government is in effect supporting American home ownership through this tax advantage, probably because home ownership is valued for reasons other than investment potential.

The Mortgage Market

For the most part, home ownership is only possible when mortgage money is available to housing consumers. Unfortunately, the availability of mortgage money fluctuates. The major lending institutions cannot provide a steady supply of mortgage funds largely because people do not make savings in steady amounts at regular intervals.

Savings and loan associations have been the major supplier of home mortgages. The interest rates they pay for savings deposits must be competitive with other forms in investment. In recent years, U.S. Treasury Bills, corporate bonds, and various money market instruments have paid higher earnings than have savings deposits. Some consumers have preferred these other investments, causing withdrawals from savings accounts to finance them. This process is called "**disintermediation.**" When disinter-

mediation occurs, savings and loans must curtail lending which of course hurts the housing market.

Commercial banks also make real estate loans including, in some states, second mortgages and construction loans. But commercial banks are also the major source of loans for other consumer financing such as credit cards, car loans, and personal loans. Real estate loans have to compete for available funds with these other borrower needs. Banks prefer the shorter terms and higher interest earned on other competing forms of financing.

Mutual savings banks are a primary source of mortgage money in some states. They have affected by disintermediation as well. Life insurance companies have traditionally supplied funding for real estate investments, but usually not directly to home buyers. They often purchase mortgages from banks thus supplying additional funds for lending by them. Life insurance companies also finance large commercial construction such as shopping centers.

Interest Rates. Interest rates fluctuate according to the amount of loan money available and according to the number of people seeking loans at a given time. If mortgage money is plentiful, and if few people need it, interest rates will fall. If mortgage money is "tight" (that is, scarce), and demand is high, interest rates will rise. Generally, a growing economy will be accompanied by rising interest rates, and an economic downturn will be accompanied by falling interest rates.

Interest rates for home mortgages are affected by the interest rates banks have to pay for money they borrow from the **Federal Reserve System.** The Federal Reserve System functions as central bank of the United States. The "Fed," as it is called, has a great deal of influence not only on its member banks but on the economy as a whole.

Housing construction depends on the availability of money at interest rates within the means of both the builders and prospective buyers. Interest rates at the local level are determined at the federal level. Photo courtesy of U.S. Department of Housing and Urban Development.

Member banks borrow money from the Fed and the rate paid for these loans, the discount rate, is controlled by the Fed. The Fed can curtail consumer credit by raising the discount interest rate. A lowering of the discount rate encourages bank borrowing and consequent consumer borrowing. Whether the local bank has money enough to lend to a prospective home buyer and what interest rate will be charged is, in effect, largely decided in Washington, D.C.

Some states have usury laws which limit the amount of interest that can be paid on borrowed money. When these laws were written, 10 percent or 12 percent seemed to be as much as anyone should ever have to pay through legal borrowing channels. When tight money and inflationary economics drive interest rates up to 16 percent or 18 percent, money simply is not available for loan in usury law states. Lending institutions will direct their money out of the state in order to earn maximum interest on their investment. The savers who have deposited funds with those banks will have their money earning high interest, but they, in turn, cannot borrow from their own banks.

The Federal Role in the Mortgage Market. Federally chartered savings and loan associations are regulated by the **Federal Home Loan Bank Board (FHLBB)**. It operates in much the same way the Fed operates for commercial banks. The FHLBB lends money to its member savings and loans and thus controls both the supply and interest rates available at the local level. It also regulates the amount of reserve funds the savings and loans must keep on hand, and it can determine what proportion of loans must go to home mortgages.

A secondary mortgage market was created during the Depression by the federal government in the form of the **Federal National Mortgage Association (FNMA)**. This institution has gained the nickname of Fannie Mae. It is a government agency whose purpose is to buy and sell FHA mortgages. Local bankers lend money to FHA-qualified buyers, but they then sell these mortgages to FNMA. Thus the local banker has more money to lend. FNMA also buys mortgages in one area of the country and sells them in another area in order to even out the supply of mortgage money nationwide. This behind-the-scenes mortgage activity does not affect the home buyer. In most cases, the payments continue to be made to the original lending institution. Even though HUD influences FNMA policies, FNMA is a semi-private corporation at this time. It has added VA mortgages and conventional mortgages to its buying and selling activities.

Another agency was created when FNMA became a semi-private corporation. The **Government National Mortgage Association (GNMA** or Ginnie Mae) is a completely government-controlled (HUD) corporation. Its main purpose is buying and selling loans for the construction of low- and moderate-income families. Since GNMA is often involved in reduced interest rate housing programs, it purchases mortgages from private institutions at regular rates but sells them at the subsidized rate set by the program. Federal funding makes up the difference.

Still another federal agency, nicknamed Freddie Mac, is involved with the secondary mortgage market. The **Federal Home Loan Mortgage Corporation (FHLMC)** deals entirely with conventional mortgages. It buys mortgages from commercial banks and savings and loans and puts them together in large enough packages so that they can be sold to pension funds, insurance companies, and other large-scale financial institutions.

Recurring Housing Policy Issues

Each year, the Congress faces a number of recurring issues concerning the funding, design, and operation of federal housing programs. The still unmet housing policy objectives, the sheer complexity of current housing programs, and uncertainty as to their effectiveness give rise to these issues and contribute to their recurring nature.

- What level of funding should be provided for housing assistance programs and how should they be financed?
- What should be the mix of new construction, rehabilitation, and existing housing assistance?
- What kind of housing assistance should be provided to lower-income homeowners, and should direct assistance be extended to higher-income families?
- What mix of programs is most effective in encouraging housing production and providing countercyclical aid to the home building industry?
- How should housing assistance programs be used to encourage community development?

Excerpted from: Congressional Budget Office, Federal Housing Policy: Current Programs and Recurring Issues (Washington, D.C.: U.S. Government Printing Office, 1978), p. 61.

SUMMARY

The 1970s were a time when a shift in emphasis took place in government programs. More local control was encouraged with the federal legislation initiated in the housing acts of 1974 and 1977.

The Community Development Block Grant Program was deemed an all-purpose program to be used for whatever purpose local officials deem necessary to promote sound community development. Housing improvements, often in the form of neighborhood improvements, have high priority.

Urban housing has also been greatly affected by the many forms of rehabilitation programs. Rehabilitation was begun at the federal level through the Urban Renewal Program and has continued with loans available through Section 312 program. Even though rehabilitation efforts have succeeded in some areas, many difficulties in achieving success have been identified.

The Urban Homesteading Program parallels rehabilitation but generally it is middle-class families seeking an urban location who are the beneficiaries. Urban homesteading has attempted to reverse the process of housing decay and abandonment prevalent in many cities.

The dominant program created in 1974 was the Lower Assistance Rental Assistance Program (Section 8). Qualifying families find their own suitable housing and HUD subsidizes the fair market rent for units meeting their standards whose landlords are willing to cooperate with the program. Section 8 funding has also been used for new construction and rehabilitation.

Rural housing problems were not without attention in the 1970s. Some of HUD's programs have had a little impact on solving these problems, but the most effective programs especially for rural areas have been designed by the Farmers Home Administration. Self-help housing is an ongoing successful program in which families group together to build their own houses. Rural home ownership is supported by FmHA through their Section 502 program. Other programs are aimed at home repairs, rental housing assistance, farm labor housing, and development of housing sites.

State Housing Finance Agencies (HFAs) have had a major role financing construction of multifamily housing for low- and moderate-income families. A few states have sponsored rehabilitation, insurance programs, large-scale construction, rural housing, and housing for the elderly and handicapped.

The federal role in the private sector of the housing market has been much more prominent than its role in publicly supported housing assistance. The home ownership incentives built into federal taxation have been effective in stimulating home buying and, indirectly, new house construction. These incentives are in the form of income tax deductions and deferred or reduced capital gains taxes.

Federal agencies regulate lending institutions, and influence the fluctuations in interest rates. Usury laws in some states have deterred lending. The Federal Home Loan Bank Board (FHLBB), along with the Fed, control consumer interest rates and the amount of available mortgage money. The federal government has also created a secondary mortgage market through three agencies: FNMA (Fannie Mae) which buys and sells FHA mortgages; GNMA (Ginnie Mae) which buys and sells loans primarily for construction of low- and moderate-income housing; and FHLMC (Freddie Mac) which buys and sells conventional mortgages.

Notes

1. Congressional Budget Office, *Federal Housing Policy: Current Programs and Recurring Issues* (Washington, D.C. U.S. Government Printing Office, 1978), p. ix.
2. Sullivan, D., "Housing in the 1970s," in G. S. Fish, ed., *The Story of Housing* (New York: Macmillan Co., 1979), p. 391.
3. U.S. Department of Housing and Urban Development, *Programs of HUD* (Washington, D.C.: Author, 1978), p. 2.
4. Witte, W., "Community Development's Third Year: A Report on Trends and Findings of NAHRO's CD Monitoring Project," *Journal of Housing*, 1978, 35(2), pp. 69–70.
5. U.S. Department of Housing and Urban Development, *Programs*, p. 5.
6. Struyk, R. J. and B. J. Soldo, *Improving the Elderly's Housing: A Key to Preserving the Nation's Housing Stock and Neighborhoods* (Cambridge, Mass.: Ballinger, 1980), p. 209.
7. U.S. Department of Housing and Urban Development, *The Tenth Annual Report on the National Housing Goal* (Washington, D.C.: Author, 1979), p. 54.
8. Paul, P. D., "Abandoned Housing: An Urban Issue," *Practicing Planner*, 1978, 8(3), p. 24.
9. Ibid.
10. U.S. Department of Housing and Urban Development, *Programs*, p. 69.
11. Paul, "Abandoned Housing," p. 25.
12. U.S. Department of Housing and Urban Development, *Programs*, p. 33.
13. U.S. Department of Housing and Urban Development, *Lower Income Housing Assistance Program (Section 8): Nationwide Evaluation of the Existing Housing*

Program (Washington, D.C.: U.S. Government Printing Office, 1978), pp. xvi–xvii.

14. U.S. Department of Housing and Urban Development. *The Tenth Annual Report*, pp. 22–23; and U.S. Department of Housing and Urban Development, *Housing and Urban Development Trends* (Washington, D.C.: Author, 1979), p. 40.

15. Rural America, *Low-income Housing Programs for Rural America* (Washington, D.C.: Author, 1978), p. 1.

16. Ibid.

17. Ibid., p. 2.

18. U.S. Department of Housing and Urban Development. *Programs*, p. 3.

19. "Farmers Home Administration: Rural Housing, in *Housing and Development*

Reporter (Washington, D.C.: Bureau of National Affairs, 1979), p. 40:0011.

20. Rural America, *Low Income Housing Programs*, p. 3.

21. Ibid., p. 8.

22. U.S. Department of Housing and Urban Development. *The Tenth Annual Report*, pp. 22–23.

23. "State Housing Finance Agencies," in *Housing and Development Reporter* (Washington, D.C.: Bureau of National Affairs, 1979), p. 50:0011.

24. Ibid., p 50:0011–50:0012.

25. Ibid., p. 50:0016.

26. Ibid., p. 50:0017.

27. Ibid., p. 50:0011.

28. U.S. Department of Housing and Urban Development, *The Tenth Annual Report*, pp. 2; 20.

Suggested Readings

Congressional Budget Office. *Federal Housing Policy: Current Programs and Recurring Issues*. Washington, D.C.: U.S. Government Printing Office, 1978.

Montgomery, R. and Mandelker, D. R., eds. *Housing in America: Problems and Perspectives* (2nd ed.). Indianapolis: Bobbs-Merrill, 1979, (chap. 8 "Housing Subsidies"; chap. 9 "Neighborhood Revitalization").

————. "The 10-Year Housing Goals Show a Shortfall in Number of Units and a Need for Links to Fiscal Policy." *Journal of Housing*, 1978, 35, 342–46.

Rural America. *Low-Income Housing Programs for Rural America*. Washington, D.C.: Author, 1978.

Schwartz, A. L. "The Mortgage Market: A Basic Primer." *Real Estate Today*, 1979, 12(8), 3–7.

Sternleib, G. and Listoken, D. "Neighborhood Preservation." In A. Greendale and S. F. Knock, Jr., eds. *Housing Costs and Housing Needs*. New York: Praeger, 1976.

Sullivan, D. "Housing in the 1970s." In G. S. Fish, ed. *The Story of Housing*. New York: Macmillan Co., 1979.

U.S. Department of Housing and Urban Affairs. *Lower Income Housing Assistance Program (Section 8): Nationwide Evaluation of the Existing Housing Program*. Washington, D.C.: U.S. Government Printing Office, 1978.

————. *Programs of HUD*. Washington, D.C.: Author, 1978.

————. *Residents' Satisfaction in HUD-assisted Housing: Design and Management Factors*. Washington, D.C.: U.S. Government Printing Office, 1979.

Housing for the Elderly

13

If we think of housing for the elderly at all, we tend to think of a special kind of housing for a special group of people. We do not think of this housing as having much to do with us. And yet, the problems of housing older persons affect all of our lives—first through the observation of our grandparents, then through the housing experiences of our parents, and finally through the housing decisions we make for ourselves.

Just as the term "the young" misrepresents the wide range of people under thirty-five, so "the elderly" misrepresents the wide range of people over fifty-five. A sixty-five-year-old couple, not yet retired, living in a suburban single-family house, does not have much in common with a seventy-five-year-old couple living in a high-rise urban apartment, nor do they with their invalid ninety-five-year-old parents in a **nursing home.** It is absurd to lump rural and urban residents, the active and inactive, well and unwell, male and female, poor and well off, of all ethnic and socioeconomic backgrounds, into a single term to embody the characteristics of forty years of their lives.

This chapter begins with the concepts of challenge and support, opposite ideas which provide the framework for evaluating a variety of housing types with respect to their suitability for the elderly, ranging all the way from healthy active and independent people, requiring the stimulation of a challenging environment, to those im-

Sun City, Arizona has appealed to thousands of retired persons because of its well-planned recreational facilities throughout the community. Photo courtesy of Del E. Webb Development Company.

The "Average" Older Person

In spite of the fact that she is pure fiction, the average person is likely to be in reasonably good health. She can move about her neighborhood in or near an urban area without great difficulty, though longer trips are infrequent, unless it is to visit close relatives. In many areas, the only transportation possible is someone else's car. She is likely to live in the same household with one or more family members, though an elderly man is even more likely to have someone share his home. Like average people everywhere, her biggest problem is money. The house is paid for, but expenses appear to rise in advance of periodic Social Security adjustments. Both man and wife fill a substantial amount of the day doing everyday duties around the house. They may watch television about three hours a day. The wish to see more of other people is frequently voiced, though casual contacts with neighboring tradesmen can be satisfying. If older people are fortunately situated, they may richen their lives visiting in a park, attending a senior center, or continuing with earlier-life hobbies. Still, there are too many hours of inactivity. Though by most standards their spirits remain good, depression is a threat, and they may be anxious over the possibility of a catastrophic illness or loss of physical or financial independence. The average older person as an individual is thus pretty much like anyone else, but with somewhat less biological vigor. He must expend more than the usual amount of energy coping with social and environmental situations where he is selectively at risk: low income, poor transportation, and a shrinking social world.

Source: Lawton, M. P., Planning and Managing Housing for the Elderly (New York: Wiley, 1975), pp. 46–47. Reprinted by permission.

paired, often older people requiring a large number of social services in a protective housing environment. The second section examines the places in which the elderly actually live. These fall into the categories of single-family homes, retirement communities, mobile housing, and congregate housing.

The section on the housing-related problems of the well elderly is divided into two areas—personal impairments and social deprivations. These have been accounted for in detail in the designing of housing for the elderly. The location, design features and services of planned housing for the elderly are the topics of the fourth chapter section. Nursing homes deserve special attention, and are, along with their alternatives, the subject of the fifth section. The last section briefly examines the effects of federal housing programs intended partially or primarily to improve the housing situation of older persons.

CHALLENGE AND SUPPORT

Challenge and support are opposite ideas. An environment that provides opportunities for physical and social activity and is therefore stimulating and interesting is challenging. One that provides the kinds of services that make life easier is supportive. Most of us enjoy cultural and environmental diversity but at the same time require supportive municipal services and labor-saving devices. As people grow older, however, a different kind of balance of the two may be needed.

For elderly people to find the housing that offers the level of challenge and the level of support they need, they must realistically assess personal needs. This is not easily nor often done. It is important that a range of choices is available. This accommodates individual differences and allows for finding the housing environment most suitable for individual needs.

Lawton has conceptualized four types of housing environments using challenge and support as factors:[1]

1. *High competence—high challenge.* Everyone knows or has heard of people in their eighties or nineties who maintain a high level of creative activity. There are well-known authors and musicians who fit into this category. Even ordinary persons who participate in their families, churches, communities, giving of their time and energy to others, easily win the admiration of younger, less active relatives and friends. For these highly competent people, housing should offer a maximum opportunity for personal challenge. Their housing choice, whether single-family home, condominium, apartment, or mobile home, should allow a high level of independence.

2. *Low competence—high support.* The nursing home provides the highest level of support for people whose impairments require a great deal of assistance. Both mental and physical impairments can result in low competence where nearly all activities have to be supervised. Contrary to popular belief, very few highly competent elderly people are stuck away in nursing homes before they need be. Families also provide support for elderly people with low competence. As many such people live with supporting families as live in nursing homes. Semi-independent housing can be maintained by some if social services, homemaker services, or out-patient clinics can provide the needed assistance.

These patio apartment homes in Sun City, Arizona provide for high competence and high challenge living for elderly persons. They can maintain independent and active lives. Photo courtesy of Del E. Webb Development Company.

3. *High competence—high support.* The highly competent older person does not need a highly supportive environment. Although this is obvious, some elderly people find themselves in this mismatched situation. A major life disruption that motivates a change of residence can also lead to a housing choice that is in the long run inappropriate. For instance, the death of a spouse might cause a person to think there is a need for total dependence on services provided, rather than a need for maintaining independence and learning new skills. Even though some elderly, because of impaired health and depression, want to "give up" they might be better served through rehabilitation than by a move to a totally dependent housing environment.

4. *Low competence—high challenge.* The opposite mismatch is where a person has more to cope with than he or she is capable of. This is a common problem for the elderly who have all their lives been independent, self-reliant, and hard working. Even though it is desirable to maintain a strong self-image, it may be detrimental to a person's feeling of self-worth to be constantly reminded of fail-

ures by being in a situation where basic needs cannot be accommodated or typical behavior is no longer adequate. Some old people consciously or unconsciously choose an environment that is too challenging for them on the assumption that others will take care of them. The practice of screening applicants for housing is an attempt to avoid mismatching of this sort.

WHERE DO THE ELDERLY LIVE?

As might be expected, the housing that meets the needs of many different elderly people is of all types and in all locations. The main point is that no one type of housing satisfies the needs of all older individuals. Younger elderly in the fifty-five to seventy-five age range, are more likely to require housing that allows them a high degree of independence. But as the aging process continues, less and less independence may be possible. As a person's health and social well-being are impaired, there may be a need to find a more supportive housing environment. Of course, not everyone moves into an old age home at age seventy-five. Many younger elderly may need supportive services much sooner than others their age. Similarly, many very old people maintain self-sufficient independent housing until death.

Single-Family Homeowners

Several types of housing satisfy the needs of the independent elderly. Primary among them is the single-family owned home. Even though condominiums and mobile homes have played a major role in meeting the housing needs of active, well elderly people, many more live in their own homes in a community they know. Very few retirees pull up stakes and move, as is commonly believed to be typical.

Elderly who have their homes paid for (the majority of elderly homeowners) often have a difficult time with maintenance costs and property taxes. Many, however, enjoy the luxury of a recreational vehicle. Photo by author.

Single-family homes for the elderly tend to be smaller and older than average. Many housing units have deficiences such as incomplete plumbing or a dilapidated condition. Undertaking repairs is very difficult for many old people. The lower their income, the less likely that needed repairs will be attended to. The poor elderly make very few home improvements. Paradoxically, the elderly pay more for repairs on the average than nonelderly, probably because they cannot do part of the work themselves.[2]

The burden of property taxes has risen dramatically for many elderly home owners. When the place of residence is in an area of high housing demand, such as many growing metropolitan areas, land values may double or triple in value in the space of a few years. Since the property tax is ultimately based on the market value of real property, the taxes due on an owned home can seem to increase at an unfair rate. Inflation in the late 1970s only worsened the problem.

One form of relief for elderly home owners is the so-called **"circuit breaker."** When there is an "overload" of tax liability in relation to income, the circuit breaker "shuts off the property tax system."[3] The overload may be determined as a percentage of income or it may be determined as a percentage of property tax on a sliding scale, with tax rebates being much smaller for higher-income people than for lower-income people.

The use of circuit breakers as an aid to elderly home owners has increased in the last decade. Fifteen states in 1979 had circuit breakers benefiting elderly home owners and renters, and five had benefits for elderly homeowners only. Seven more states and the district of Columbia have circuit breakers benefiting all ages.[4]

Another form of tax relief is the homestead exemption. This tax credit is set up for elderly home owners in fourteen states, and fifteen states give elderly more liberal credits than nonelderly. Some states have both homestead and circuit breaker programs.[5] It has been argued that a better method of tax relief, and one that is fairer to other taxpayers, is tax deferral. Taxes are deferred until a person's house is sold, whether while still living or not, at which time all the unpaid taxes are due. This amount could sizably reduce the wealth then available to that person or to the heirs of the property. Tax deferral programs are available to the elderly in only a few states.

Retirement Communities

One type of housing is specifically designed to meet the needs of the active elderly. It is the retirement community. Leisure Worlds in California, Maryland, and New Jersey are one example. A single housing development includes detached houses, duplexes, townhouse condominiums, and high-rise apartments. All are expensive, but the attraction is the availability of leisure facilities. One Leisure World has four heated pools, a twenty-seven-hole golf course, horseback riding, not to mention crafts workrooms and clubhouses in which activities are scheduled day and night. A retirement community of this sort creates its own lifestyle, but it is cut off from ordinary community activities and from work opportunities.

The largest retirement community—Sun City, Arizona—has been defined as a new town by some planners. Its thousands of residents have all moved from some other place, usually another state. The same leisure activities of golf, swimming, parties and hobbies are integrated into the entire community, made up mostly of single-family detached homes.

Some mobile home parks are designed with the same housing aims in mind, but the scale is smaller. A single pool and clubhouse might serve the need for leisure. Condominium developments have been built around golf courses to take advantage on that source of leisure. Minimum age limits, such as fifty-two or fifty-five, insure the residents of perceived homogeneity, a prerequisite for friendship formation in an unfamiliar housing situation.

Mobile Housing

Another form of independent housing is mobile housing. Many retirees create a lifestyle around a recreational vehicle or a travel trailer. The recreational jaunts may be many and short, for a few days at a time, while some retired singles and couples simply leave their permanent residences for a large portion of the year. Campgrounds intended for short-stay recreational vehicles may find that available spaces are taken up by transients who, in fact, stay weeks at a time. In states with desirable climates, a six-month stay in one or more campgrounds is not uncommon. The advantages of condominium and mobile home living with respect to the freedom to travel has been stressed in a previous chapter.

Congregate Housing

Congregate housing is defined as a housing complex in which residents share buildings and services. Even if the only shared facility is a common dining facility for use at one meal a day, it is congregate housing. This type of housing can be highly supportive, and without much challenge.

Congregate housing is typically located in urban areas and it is often built in multistory buildings with as many as 300 to 400 units, which may each be no more than 400 feet square. Common spaces consist of a dining room, lounges (often on each floor), a game room, hobby and crafts rooms, and libraries. Single rooms within each congregate housing project may have kitchenettes. Many have one-bedroom units with private baths, and common baths between two units are also common.[6]

One- and two-story housing developments, called "low-rise," are more often located in suburban and rural areas than in urban areas. Where land is plentiful, the grounds, recreational facilities, and additional services can be part of the overall planning scheme for the project.

Gerontologists categorize housing for the elderly in terms of "age segregation." When people live in congregate housing with all residents over a certain age limit, the housing is age segregated. Many prefer this arrangement, however, studies in housing satisfaction have tended to overemphasize the desirability of age-segregated housing for all elderly people. Many of the elderly in public housing have contact with families and children of all ages and are happy with this age heterogeneity.

One form of housing for the elderly not popular in this country is "**proximate residences.**" These are individual detached housing units specifically designed for elderly people but near family residences. A whole neighborhood of proximate residences could provide the advantages of

This shared dining facility is typical of congregate housing for the elderly. Meals might be served one, two, or three times a day. Photo courtesy of U.S. Department of Housing and Urban Development.

both age-segregated and non-age-segregated housing. There have been small-scale efforts to place prefabricated housing units (granny houses) in existing backyards to fulfill this purpose.

One form of congregate housing that evolves in many downtown areas is the "**single room occupancy**" or **SRO hotel.** Individuals may reside in these hotels on an indefinite basis, often paying minimal rents. Typically, the elderly person, man or woman, has lived in single rooms for many years. The picture of unknown thousands of older people, poor and probably in ill health, living in a seemingly independent, even isolated manner is not a happy one. The positive aspects of this form of housing is that the residents do have potential social contacts available to them, their housing expenses are low, and their location may provide a high level of challenge.

A highly experimental form of congregate housing is home sharing. In one such program, Share-A-Home in Florida, eight to twenty people are housed in a variety of housing units, from mansions to modest houses in quiet neighborhoods. The idea is

Adaptive Strategies of Elderly Tenants in a Slum Hotel

In a population such as this, people often have difficulty budgeting their meager monies in order to meet such a basic expense as rent. Even when money is well budgeted, emergencies do occur, robberies are common, misplaced funds are not unknown. However, the most common source of disagreement over the issue of rent results from differing expectations. The manager expects his tenants to pay on time, and his understanding of "on time" means "in advance." Those who receive social security normally pay by the month, those on state aid, biweekly. The tenants, on the other hand, want to pay by the week: they see it as less expensive, less money going out at one time. Also, they define "on time" as payment *after* the service is rendered, that is, they want to be a week *behind* in their rent, they insist upon this. Constant battles are waged over this issue of the time that the rent is due; indeed, there are some elderly tenants who go through shouting matches with the manager twice a month and have been doing so for years.

Nonpayment of rent has reliable consequences. The transient who fails to pay is contacted by the manager. Either he pays up or he is evicted, and the hotel keeps the luggage until payment is made. In the case of an elderly permanent resident, the manager has his room "plugged." A small metal device is inserted into the lock of the door so that the key cannot be used to unlock the door, and the tenant loses access to his room. The tenants bitterly resent plugging; no other action or policy on the part of hotel personnel so outrages them. Tenants whose rooms are plugged—and there are a number to whom this happens with predictable regularity—become righteous martyrs and receive considerable verbal support and sympathy from the other tenants. That they may be several days or even weeks behind in their rent is deemed insufficient cause to treat them so poorly.

Some tenants anticipate being plugged and have stratagems to forestall it. The most often used ploy is the "con." Similar to the use of conning in manufacturing a personal history, the conning of the manager consists of an act and a convincing story designed to justify the fact that one is behind with the rent. The act may include other hotel employees if the tenant presents his "case" to them and requests that they "mention it" to the manager. The content of the con ranges from denial of being in arrears ("I'm sure that I already paid"), to indignation ("I always pay on time!"), to threats (accompanied by shouts and profanity), to sincere promises to pay, to the myriad versions of how the money has been lost or stolen, and "Could I just have a little more time?" On occasion, tenants will turn on the picture of helplessness and pitiful old age to add a convincing dimension to their battery of excuses. The list of excuses is endless, and ranges from claims of having been robbed, to the plea that an anticipated check has not arrived.

When the con fails and excuses can no longer forestall reprisals—in short, when plugging is imminent—the tenant may resort to a more extreme tactic. He may lock himself inside his room and refuse to come out or to answer his telephone. If his key is in the lock on the inside, the door cannot be plugged. This strategy is relatively effective, in that it can delay things for a few days at least. The manager waits it out, periodically sending up porters and desk clerks to knock on the door and issue threats. Eventually, the tenant has to come out, by which time he is usually willing to settle the dispute. Even in the unusual case where the rent still is not paid, the tenant can manage to avoid losing a place to sleep. One elderly woman who was six weeks behind in her rent was plugged, and for the next two weeks she slept in a chair in the television room.

Plugging denies one of the most crucial assumptions held by the individuals in this society—the privacy and sacrosanct character of their rooms. It is an affront to their insistence that these rooms are their homes and sanctuaries. For any permanent tenant, plugging cannot be justified; strategies employed to avoid it may

range from the furtive to the unrealistic, but all are understandable from their point of view.

Excerpt from: Stephens, J. Loners, Losers and Lovers: Elderly Tenants in a Slum Hotel (Seattle, Wash: University of Washington Press, 1976). Reprinted by permission.

based on the formation of a "family" of unrelated elderly people who care for and support each other. The main advantage is that each individual is freed from the burden of housekeeping and cooking. Expenses are divided, and a resident manager and staff provide needed services such as shopping, laundry, and transportation.[7]

HOUSING PROBLEMS OF THE WELL ELDERLY

Well elderly are those people who can and do maintain independent living arrangements. Only 5 percent of the nation's elderly are housed in institutions such as nursing homes, and another 8 percent are not well enough to leave their homes. The housing solutions for these persons are discussed in the last section of this chapter. The great majority of elderly may not enjoy perfect health and vigor but nonetheless carry out their daily social and personal affairs without assistance.

Even though there are few disabilities that are intrinsic to the aging process, changes do occur that affect the activities and well-being of older individuals. These impairments can be categorized as "per-

sonal" and "social." Not all young-old are without them, nor are all old-old impaired by them. Nevertheless, as chronological age increases, so does the likelihood of their occurrence.

Any one of these personal impairments or social deprivations can have limiting effects regarding other factors. For instance, an inability to walk up and down stairs can affect nutrition, socialization, access to medical resources, even personal care. Low income, of course, is related to inadequate housing, poor nutrition, and the likelihood of living in a crime-ridden neighborhood with poor transportation. When more than one or two of these impairments occur, the overall limiting effects can be very severe.

Personal Impairments

Since supportive services to alleviate the problems caused by personal impairments are part of a desirable housing environment for the elderly, they are listed below:

1. Physical illness—the acute and chronic illnesses of old age.
2. Mobility—arthritic pain, fatigability, paralysis, cardiac problems, lessened energy.

3. Self-care—deficits in ability to groom, control of bladder and bowel, food preparation, dressing, and other behaviors.
4. Speed-slowing down of the ability to move one's muscles, to respond to signals from the environment, and to make decisions regarding how one should behave.
5. Mental status—impairments in memory, ability to learn new behaviors, or to think abstractly.
6. Psychological adjustment—anxiety, depression, excessive dependence, antisocial behavior, alcoholism, suicidal thoughts.

When one of these occurs suddenly, and many do, they are considered a major life disruption. Whereas the onset of some physical disabilities is gradual, others are shockingly disruptive. A heart attack, an accident, a prolonged serious illness are typical physical major life disruptions.

Social Deprivations

Less easily recognized are the results of sudden social changes. Retirement alone can be disruptive. Death of a spouse is, of course, cause for a major life change, but the impact of a change in day to day activities is less well understood. An altered bus route, the closing of a market, the move (or death) of a close friend, and other more subtle disruptions in a stable pattern of life can have the effect of a major life disruption. Lawton's list of social deprivations identifies twelve specific problems.[8]

1. Low income.
2. Inadequate housing.
3. Poor nutrition.
4. Crime-ridden neighborhoods.
5. Lack of public transportation.
6. Enforced retirement.

7. Lack of continued educational opportunities.
8. The steady move of recreational resources to suburbs and resort areas.
9. Centralization of medical resources and their consequently increased distance from the older person.
10. The concurrent growth of the small family, smaller dwelling units, and decline in three-generation living.
11. Loss of friends through death, lowered mobility, and migration.
12. The youth culture and anti-elderly stereotyping.

Major life disruptions are a primary motivation for a change of residence. It may take more than one major life disruption to bring about a move, but the death of a relative or close friend has an especially strong impact on the desire to move. One study contradicts this, showing that physical or mental disability has more to do with the consideration of a move than death of a spouse or retirement. The same study concluded that the large majority of moves are to smaller housing units, closer to friends and relatives and to pleasanter climates. The death of a spouse often tends to motivate a move to the home of a child.[9]

PLANNED HOUSING FOR THE ELDERLY

When housing is planned and developed especially for the elderly, it can be ideally suited to their needs. Because not all elderly people are alike in their needs, setting up general criteria for successful ways to locate and house them necessarily overlooks some individual differences. Nevertheless, gerontologists have ideas about specific location, design and services for planned housing.

The Philadelphia Geriatric Center and housing is located in an urban setting familiar to many of its residents, who also may enjoy companionship of like-aged persons. Photo courtesy of U.S. Department of Housing and Urban Development.

Location

One housing expert has identified five special needs of the elderly with respect to a good site location.[10]

1. *Familiarity of neighborhood.* Older persons prefer to stay in neighborhoods where they have spent most of their adult lives. Familiar shopkeepers, streets, and neighbors provide a needed sense of security. Housing for the elderly should be built in neighborhoods that continue to provide the landmarks and settings for positive experiences for potential tenants.

2. *Pedestrian accessibility to key services.* As has been stated already, daily needs should be met by very close facilities, within a block or two. Doctors, churches, a library, may be further but accessible by public transportation. A single church nearby will probably not serve the majority of tenants unless the housing is primarily occupied by a single ethnic group dependent on that church. Sometimes an on-site library can be serviced by a public library.

3. *Safety and security.* Some inner-city sites which might be desirable because of neighborhood familiarity are also less than adequately safe and secure. The problem can be partially solved by locating housing within a part of the neighborhood where owner-occupied residences and estab-

Rural elderly housing can be very satisfactory if a full range of services are available within the housing facility or nearby. Photo courtesy of U.S. Department of Housing and Urban Development.

lished long-term merchants provide stability. High-turnover areas are likely to be high-crime areas.

4. *Environmental barriers.* A busy highway, railroad tracks, hills, and so on, can become barriers to access to nearby facilities. A street that is too wide to cross during a single light can make the desired facility on the other side inaccessible. Sidewalks should be evenly paved and well maintained. An alley or abandoned building can pose a threat to the elderly pedestrian.

5. *Proximity to middle-aged and older neighborhoods.* Even though much has been said about intermingling the elderly and children, most elderly people prefer social contact with others their own age. Shared experiences more easily develop into friendships with like-aged people. Most elderly seem to enjoy observing children at play, as in a schoolyard, but do not care for the noise and activity to become part of their own social environment.

Rural housing for the elderly can be successfully designed if it includes services similar to those found in a suburban or urban neighborhood. For instance, a housing project that includes small stores, barbershops and beauty parlors, a dry cleaning service, snack bar, medical facility, even a church, provides within itself all the major

services required by most prospective tenants. Small rural towns can provide a similar array of services within walking distance of the housing project. Some elderly people do not use locally available services at all. Those who have lived near many services in the past will more likely be users of the same services in their later years.

Suburban locations are not generally desirable because they are strictly residential, and often they do not provide good public transportation. It has been proposed by one housing specialist that suburban shopping centers could become ideal settings for housing for the elderly. The window shopping, people watching, and services provided are features often found in an urban setting.

Urban housing for the elderly is more common than any other locational category, and the greatest need for housing is in urban areas. But not all urban sites are ideal for the development of housing of any type, let alone housing that meets the needs of the elderly. Since many elderly people rely on walking as a main source of transportation, the distance to stores and service facilities is critical. One planner, having researched ideal distances, found that some services should be within three blocks—bus stop (one or two blocks), grocery store, drug store; some facilities could be as far as a mile away—library, movie house; and most fell in between (one-quarter to one-half mile)—church, medical clinic, bank, news-cigar store, restaurant.[11]

Design Features

When housing is planned especially for the elderly, it should include many design features to add safety, security and a sense of well-being. Such considerations are categorized as: design features to be included in the individual unit, those to be included in the overall design of the housing, and those to be included on the exterior, including landscaping details.

Individual Unit Design. The individual unit should have complete privacy, good ventilation, and a cheerful atmosphere. A separate bedroom is desirable, but even in a small efficiency unit the sleeping area can be designated separately by an "L" arrangement. Screening of a small kitchenette is desirable, and an eating area should not only seat four, it should be possible to set it up in more than one space. A generous storage area is needed by most older people as well as display places for knick-knacks, pictures, and plants (a window sill may be wide enough for this). Windows should be easy to work, and they should be low enough to look out of while seated. Heat control and air conditioning should be available in each unit. It should be possible to light every part of the unit. Electrical outlets should be so placed as to eliminate dangling cords. Some luxury features include wall-to-wall carpeting, a full length mirror, and a fold-up ironing board.

The bathroom should be carefully designed. A full-turning radius for a wheelchair is desirable, if not necessary, as well as an outward opening bathroom door. A lifting bar adjacent to the toilet may be needed. The tub should have a seat in it, and a flexible shower head. The side of the tub should be low for easy access. Good lighting, nonskid floors, as well as water temperature controls are basic requirements.

Safety and security needs require a two-way signaling system to a main office from both the living room and bathroom areas. Telephones in more than one place and peepholes in individual unit doors are also desirable. All doorways should have no thresholds.

The kitchen area has special requirements. There should be safety cutoffs for gas. Stove controls should be at the front of the stove, and cabinets should be within reach. Again, good lighting is necessary.

Overall Design Features. Handrails should be available in all halls, stairs or sloping walks. Steps of any kind may prohibit use by many older people, but if they are necessary, they should be few, and they should be clearly marked. Hallways should be short. Nonskid floors should be used throughout, if not wall-to-wall carpeting, and any area rugs must be securely anchored. Orientation within a large housing project can be aided with color variety in hallways and contrasting colors on doors. An institutional look can be avoided with the use of warm colors and textures, color variety, graphics, and pleasing details of interior design.

Tenants love to watch people coming and going in the lobby area, so ample appropriate seating is desirable. Even a community room or lounge might be located within viewing distance of the lobby and entry areas. Hobby and workrooms should be well-equipped, well-lighted, and attractive. The comfort and appearance of a common laundry room should not be overlooked.

If small lounge areas, provided on each

The lounge areas in elderly housing are very important because they provide a setting for daily social contact between individual residents. Photo courtesy of the City of San Luis Obispo Housing Authority.

floor, are included in the design, they should, of course, be comfortable and well-furnished to have any use. Elevators should have slow-closing doors, and be available in nonthreatening hallways. The fewer the tenants sharing a common entrance, the more likely friendships will form.

Exterior and Landscaping. Monitoring of the entry is important for security of the residents. The entryway should be visible from the inside as well. A locked front door can be controlled by individual tenants, but a security guard is a better means of controlling entry.

Tenants like to sit outside and watch people go by. It is therefore desirable to have seating at the entry, at a covered transportation area, and seating throughout the grounds (if any) for all climatic conditions. Garden pathways are desirable, but

they must be smoothly paved and nonthreatening. For instance, low plantings provide security that hedges and large shrubbery do not. Fences, too, should be low enough for protective visibility. The routes to parking areas, clothesline areas, and all entries should be unencumbered by stairs or inclines and must be well lighted.

Planned housing for the elderly should have the aesthetic appeal desirable in all housing. An attractively designed entryway, and the overall use of quality materials can achieve this. Landscaping should be well cared for. The elderly enjoy personalizing exterior space with individual gardens where possible. Even individual porches or balconies can greatly enhance the self-esteem of residents.

Services
Nearly all planned housing for the elderly includes some plan for services. A meal ser-

vice is a fundamental characteristic of congregate housing, however large or small. Housekeeping, transportation, medical and social services may also be included in the housing project.

Meal Services. Some housing includes a meal service that provides for all meals seven days a week. Other housing provides for a lunch or dinner only with other meals prepared within each housing unit in a kitchenette. Still other plans have one hot meal a day available on an optional basis. No doubt meals provide a socializing purpose as well as a nutritional purpose. Older people like to have the opportunity to get out of their rooms and see others as well as be seen by others. Nevertheless, when the elderly have been surveyed regarding the necessity of meal services in their housing, only about a third have been in favor.[12]

Housekeeping   Service. Housekeeping service is desired by those who can afford it. Such a service may include daily maid service, changing and laundering of linens, and general maintenance and repair of the housing unit. Semi-independent elderly probably need such a service because it is very likely that a desire to delegate such chores led to their decision to move into planned housing in the first place.

Transportation   Service. Transportation has become an important aspect of housing for the elderly. Many older people are unable to use public transportation even if it is available within a block or two. If the bus does not come by very often, and if it does not stop very near the point of destination, it is difficult to conveniently plan a trip using this service. Furthermore, merely climbing aboard may be more than some elderly can manage. The door-to-door service of a project-operated bus or van is far more likely to be used by residents regardless of level of competence.

These elderly tenants have created a front porch out of their portion of a housing complex courtyard. It provides an opportunity for people-watching. Photo by author.

Medical Services. On-site medical facilities, in the form of some kind of clinic with regular services of a physician and nurse, are desired by a majority of the elderly in planned housing.[13] Such service provides a sense of security even though older people enjoy an image of living in housing for well elderly, not sick and dependent elderly. The management of housing without on-site medical services often has contact with nearby doctors and assumes supervision of prescriptions.

Social Services. Even though many elderly people would not admit to needing the professional services of a social worker or counselor, such services can be helpful with respect to personal problems. Financial, budget, home management, and le-

Transportation services are very important to many elderly. The persons shown here have been aided in their marketing with a bus provided for their needs by a community agency. Photo courtesy of U.S. Department of Housing and Urban Development.

gal problems may also need the expert advice of others. Whether helping professional staff are provided by public agencies or are hired by the housing management depends on the needs of the residents and their income level. Low-income residents might have negative connotations about social services of any kind.

NURSING HOMES AND THEIR ALTERNATIVES

Even though only a small portion of the elderly live in long-term care facilities, more commonly called nursing homes, the longer people live, the greater the likelihood they may find a nursing home their last residence. The average age of people in nursing homes is eighty-two, and people over eighty have a one-in-two chance of ending their lives there.[14]

Problems with Nursing Homes

Nursing homes have been the focus of much public attention. They have been accused of mistreatment of residents, overcharging, and staffing with underpaid and poorly qualified personnel. States' regulations of nursing homes do vary, and no doubt a family should be wary in selecting one for an aged person.

Nursing homes were at one time considered a residential alternative for people who were unable to live independently in the community because of economic or social reasons, not necessarily health reasons. The federal funds administered by Medicare and Medicaid changed that. Nursing homes have become part of the medical health care system. Two critics of nursing homes say, "The result is a setting that is optimal only for those whose medical problems make them physically or emotionally dependent upon medical assistance but unnecessarily restrictive for vast numbers of nursing home residents capable of greater degrees of independence."[15] Nursing homes receiving federal funds are now closely watched by governmental agencies, congressional committees, and ten regional offices of Long Term Care Standards Enforcement. The focus in government regulations is on the institution, not on the individual nor on the human psychology of recovery.

One major problem with nursing homes and other forms of institutional housing, namely mental hospitals, is that people may be placed in them that are not of such low competence as to need them. The degree of misplacement in institutional housing is unknown, even though research efforts have attempted to determine it. It has been assumed that if the people misplaced in nursing homes were removed into congregate housing, or into private indepen-

Special Types of Housing Financing for the Elderly

Founder's Fee and Life Lease Contracts

Some nonprofit sponsors, frequently church-related groups, finance retirement housing with the help of founder's fees. Paid by the initial occupants (or founders) of the facility, the fee entitles the resident to lifetime use of an apartment or nonhousekeeping unit. In effect, the fees help finance the capital investment to establish the facility and pay off the mortgage. The resident has lifetime security, besides making a contribution to a church or other nonprofit agency.

Besides the payment for life tenancy, there is a monthly charge for maintenance and other services based on operating costs. Arrangements after the initial occupancy vary. Sometimes the new tenant also pays a life-lease fee, somewhat lower than the original occupant's costs; sometimes funds from the secondary tenants are set aside to start another development.

Life-lease or life-contract arrangements usually call for a stipulated sum, based on life-expectancy actuarial tables, that guarantee the older person lifetime occupancy of his/her dwelling unit. An additional monthly charge covers maintenance and services. Some sponsors may return a proportion of the original investment (based on length of stay) if the resident must move out.

Two points need emphasis for both founder's fee and life-lease contracts: Though both guarantee living quarters, they do not provide for ongoing operating services, health plans or other programs; if the resident dies, the apartment reverts to the sponsor, not to the resident's estate. Some sponsors in both plans may make adjustments for those who cannot afford the full costs; conversely, others have escalator clauses in the contracts to cover increasing costs of monthly services.

Life Care

Probably a few homes for the aged and residence-club facilities still offer life-care financing. Based not on life expectancy actuarial tables but projected costs of services, the would-be resident pays an amount equal to the determined costs for total life care, including accommodations, meals, health and personal care.

If the individual has insufficient cash for the projected sum, his/her assets, in an equal amount, become the property of the sponsor. In some instances, total assets, regardless of value, have been appropriated by the sponsors; conversely, other sponsors have continued care of residents living beyond the projected life expectancy.

Relatively few instances of failure have been reported in any of these types of guaranteed life occupancy. However, if you are tempted to try one, be sure to read the fine print in the contract and get an attorney's advice to insure that the sponsor makes good on the commitment. Carefulness now beats losing your lifetime savings and perhaps being homeless.

Reprinted from: The National Council of the Aging, Inc. A Guide for Selection of Retirement Housing (Washington, D.C.) © 1976.

dent housing, then the places thus vacated would or should be taken by the people presently misplaced in mental hospitals.

In the past decade, alternatives to nursing homes have been explored with regard to their effectiveness and their financial and social costs. Each alternative has advantages and disadvantages, which can be perceived differently by individuals, their families, and the sponsoring agencies.

The Family Alternative

It is not known how many low-competency elderly live with families, depending on their relatives to provide complete care. It is generally agreed that it was a far more common practice a hundred years ago than it is today. With housing costs on the rise, it may be that families will now consider caring for a dependent older person whom they would have previously placed in a nursing home. On the other hand, the increased cost of living has brought about an increase in women working outside the home. With no one at home to provide constant daily care, the elderly individual may not be able to get the necessary help within his or her family. The family may provide the living space and hire the assistance of outside people. In any case, the personal costs to the family are high, and the care provided may not necessarily be ideal. The dietary needs, rehabilitation programs, and personal attention that some elderly people may require could easily be unintentionally overlooked in the busy, multigenerational family.

Foster families are a substitute for relatives' care. Since the foster family's motivation for entering into the obligation of caring for an elderly person is an economic one, such an arrangement may not provide the emotional support one would hope. There is a great deal of turnover in the small number of foster care families now in

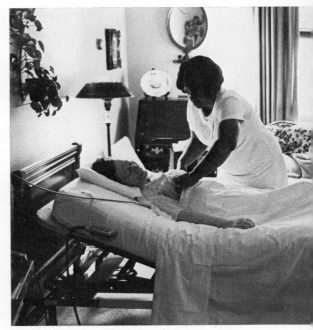

Nursing homes provide the maximum support needed by a few elderly. Alternatives to nursing homes may provide adequate or superior care for those persons not requiring constant medical care. Photo courtesy of U.S. Department of Housing and Urban Development.

use. If payments were increased to these families, stability might also be increased.

Public Service Alternatives

Some communities provide home health services to people who might otherwise be in a nursing home. Medicare payments will cover these services, but they are not yet viewed as a viable alternative to nursing homes. Services are not available everywhere, there are restrictions on eligibility, and physicians may not be in favor. The costs of such care may be as high as nursing home costs, but the benefits to the individual of staying within a known community are undeniable.

Homemaker services are a form of

Geriatric day care centers are settings for companionship and organized activities for individuals who live in housing situations without these benefits. Photo courtesy of U.S. Department of Housing and Urban Development.

nonmedical assistance for elderly people who want to maintain independent living for as long as possible. Homemakers may assist with cooking, cleaning, laundry, ironing, and personal care. Shopping and other chores may also be included. Homemaker services are sometimes combined with home health care provided by visiting professionals. Meals-on-Wheels is a program designed to provide in-home hot meals to the elderly, usually only once a day.

Still another approach to nursing home alternatives is **geriatric day care.** Day care centers for the elderly often have a strong medical orientation. The staff may include nurses, physical therapists, and nutritionists. The daily activities are scheduled to also provide personal care and transportation as well as regular health examinations. Such well-managed day care centers are

few, but they have a positive effect on the physical and mental well-being of those people who have used their service instead of nursing home residence. However, researchers have found that although homemaker and geriatric day care may sustain elderly people's functioning, they are not the answer for all impaired or chronically ill elderly.[16]

In a few places, community care organizations have been set up to identify older people's needs and to provide coordinated services to meet those needs. The programs listed above—homemaker services, in-home health care, meals-on-wheels—may be accompanied by transportation services, telephone reassurance, and medical services.

One of the problems of providing adequate in-home care is that the number of older people in need is not known. The

many rural elderly living in small communities may not have services available, nor may they be willing to use them if they did. Still another problem is that people seek help only when they feel it is a last resort. Families attempting to keep an impaired person in their household may need assistance long before the point when they are looking for an alternative to placement in a nursing home. In the future, the problem will be compounded by the fact that the children of eighty- and ninety-year-olds will themselves be in their sixties or older.[17]

FEDERAL HOUSING PROGRAMS FOR THE ELDERLY

Public housing has been a primary program for meeting the housing needs of the elderly. It has already been noted in chapter 11 that in the 1960s, emphasis was placed on the development of public housing for the elderly. Elderly tenants were less controversial than family tenants, but the shift required design specifications suited to the elderly. By late 1973, approxi-

mately 253,000 housing units had been built for the elderly as public housing.[18]

Often these units are located in buildings designed for the elderly but part of larger housing complexes including families of all ages. Lawton explains that "in other situations, structures, designated for the elderly are interspersed with those serving families; still others variations include the the designation of certain floors in high-rise buildings for the elderly, or of certain units within a floor for the elderly."[19] The units thus designated for the elderly are outfitted with extra grab bars, electric outlets at appropriate heights, and so on. By far the most successful public housing for the elderly, however, has been in projects where they are the only occupants.

Section 202 Housing

The 1959 Housing Act initiated a program for the lending of federal money at low interest rates for the construction of housing

Public housing, shown above and at right, has provided both low-rise and high-rise housing designed for the elderly. Some projects include families as well. Photo courtesy of U.S. Department of Housing and Urban Development.

The elderly residents in this rehabilitated hotel are aided by Section 8 rent supplements so that they pay only 25 percent of their incomes for rent. Photo courtesy of the City of San Luis Obispo Housing Authority

for limited-income elderly and handicapped people. These 3 percent interest rate loans were made to nonprofit organizations. Typical organizations participating in the pro-

gram were churches and synagogues, unions, fraternal organizations, and civic groups organized for this specific purpose. The limited-income elderly and handicapped came to mean people and couples who were above the public housing low-income limits. The rents for 202 housing had to cover administration and maintenance costs as well as the low interest mortgage. Welfare, or even social security-dependent elderly were unable to afford typical rents ($80 to $120 in 1970). Later, when provision for rent supplements helped some people get into elderly 202 housing, their numbers were limited to 20 or 40 percent of any one project.

More 202 housing was built in Florida, California, and in the Northeast. Most midwestern, mountain, and southern states are without much 202 housing. The so-called "retirement" areas seem to have been blessed by both the housing demand and the availability of willing sponsors. The sponsoring organization plays a primary role in housing management, provision of services, activity programs and the like. Curiously, federal policy for 202 tenants was to make them as independent as possible, so on-site meal service, and space for support programs, such as an infirmary, had to be provided by the sponsor without federal funding.

The 202 program was terminated in 1969, then reactivated with the 1974 Hous-

TABLE 13–1 Participation of People over Sixty-five in HUD Rent Subsidy Programs, 1977.

PROGRAM	TOTAL (IN THOUSANDS)	NUMBER OVER 65 (IN THOUSANDS)	PERCENTAGE OF ELDERLY
Public Housing	1,036	342	33.0
Section 202	45	36	80.0
Section 8*	358	180	50.4

*Data includes disabled, handicapped, and people sixty-two and over.

What Are We Doing Wrong?

The need for housing and services for the elderly touches us personally as well as professionally, since most of us have family members who are senior citizens. However, in spite of the fact that we are involved in the problem and can become emotional over it, we cannot seem to find the combination that enables the nonprofit organizations to produce an adequate supply of housing and services for the elderly at prices they can afford.

If we have a good case for our efforts to obtain federal financial assistance for special facilities for the elderly, we obviously are not making an effective presentation to the administration and the Congress.

Why not consider changing the age for the purpose of being eligible for special housing to 70 or 75? This would reduce the number of elderly eligible for special housing by at least one-third. With increased longevity, a good case for such a change can be made.

With an elderly population eligible for special housing reduced to a more manageable size and comprising persons who are more likely to require special facilities, we might find less resistance in seeking special assistance from Congress.

Are we on the right track in our efforts to obtain financial assistance to meet the housing needs of the elderly? Each year we have to fight for every little bit of assistance we get and never have enough to meet our needs.

Is it being realistic to depend so heavily on federal financial assistance to provide housing for the elderly? Should private sources be more heavily involved? Should the community provide more support?

Sponsors of nonprofit housing for the elderly should make a special effort to obtain strong cosponsors. Why shouldn't religious and social welfare organizations begin to look for cosponsors that have great financial

strength and at the same time recognize an obligation to the elderly and the community?

A few years ago, some of the largest corporations in the country were exploring the possibility of building housing for the elderly. Why not revive this interest? Why not use them as cosponsors? Why shouldn't the nation's largest employers share in the problem solving for their retirees? They have used the good years of the elderly; they should help out during the tough ones. This would not change the nonprofit character of the projects, but it would be another way of helping to solve the problem of providing housing and services needs for the elderly.

Excerpted from: Hughes, W. D., "How to Utilize and Improve Federal and State Housing Programs for the Elderly," in A. Greendale and S. F. Knock, Jr., Housing Costs and Housing Needs. © 1976 by Praeger Publishers, Inc. By permission.

---

ing Act. It had produced 45,275 units by 1977, and slightly more than that number were planned for construction. This, however, is a modest level of funding compared to public housing and Section 8 at the same time.[20]

Section 8

Section 8 rent supplements have been used by many elderly people. Since the Section 8 recipient finds the housing of his or her choice, many older people, as well as people of all ages, choose to stay in their present housing, using the rent supplement to provide the difference between what they can afford (25 percent of their income) and the fair market rent for the unit. Of course, the unit must meet HUD program standards, and the landlord must agree to participate. About 35 percent of the recipients are elderly, and their income level is lower on the average than their counterparts renting nonsubsidized units. The proportion of elderly blacks who participate in Section 8 is greater than in the rental population as a whole.[21]

Table 13–1 (page 308) summarizes the benefits of the three major programs affecting housing for the elderly.[22]

SUMMARY

Highly competent elderly people maintain active independent lives. Ideal housing for them provides the challenge appropriate to their capabilities. Other older people require a great deal of support for physical and social needs. A mismatch in housing occurs when highly competent people are in a supportive environment and the reverse, people with low competence are in challenging housing environments without support.

Single-family homes provide a highly challenging and low support environment for the great majority of the elderly. The burdens of ownership, however, may provide special hardships. Property tax benefits are available in one form or another in most states, but maintenance and repairs are often difficult and expensive. Retirement communities may provide single-family residences as well as condominiums and rental units. The built-in recreational and social life with like-aged people is appealing to many.

Very active and independent elderly people may use some form of mobile housing for all or part of their housing needs. Some travel in recreational vehicles for part of the year, using another home base the rest of the time. Others travel all of the time.

Congregate housing meets the needs of those elderly people requiring a supportive environment. Usually dining facilities are available, as well as hobby rooms, lobbies and so on. Older hotels often provide an unplanned form of congregate housing. An emerging trend is for older people to share their homes with outside supportive services taking over where the residents' own cooperative efforts at housekeeping leave off.

Both physical and social impairments can affect the individual's needs for challenge or support. One or more of these can disrupt a stable life and bring about a change of housing environment. Planned housing for the elderly takes these impairments into account. It is desirable to locate housing for the elderly in neighborhoods with supporting services. The housing itself has to be carefully designed regarding physical impairments and the social needs of companionship and security. Meals, housekeeping, transportation, medical and social services may be included in well-planned housing.

The aging process often results in the need for daily health care. The growing number of nursing homes has been the major means of providing housing with built-in health care. Because of their high costs, and their often criticized psychological ill-effects, alternatives to nursing homes have been tried. Families may provide adequate care with or without the help of outside assistance. Foster families are another substitute. Where home health services and homemaker services are available, impaired elderly can remain in the community and get the support they need. Geriatric day care centers are another means of providing needed service while at the same time allowing older people to remain in their homes or with their families.

Of the federal housing programs that have aided the elderly, public housing has benefited the greatest number. Section 202, although specifically designed for housing construction for the elderly, has not resulted in as many recipients as Section 8, a much newer rent supplement program.

Notes

1. Lawton, M. P., *Planning and Managing Housing for the Elderly* (New York: Wiley, 1975), pp. 62–68.
2. Struyk, R. J., and B. J. Soldo, *Improving the Elderly's Housing: A Key to Preserving the Nation's Housing Stock and Neighborhoods.* (Cambridge, Mass.: Ballinger Publishing Company, 1980), p. 79.
3. Gold, S. D., *Property Tax Relief* (Lexington, Mass.: Lexington Books, 1979), p. 55.
4. Ibid., p. 57.
5. Ibid., p. 82.
6. Malozemoff, I. K., J. G. Anderson, and L. V. Rosenbaum, *Housing for the Elderly: Evaluation of the Effectiveness of Congregate Residences* (Boulder, Colo.: Westview Press, 1978).
7. Streib, G. F., "An Alternative Family Form for Older Persons: Need and Social Context," *The Family Coordinator*, 1978, 27(4), p. 416.
8. Lawton, *Planning and Managing*, pp. 59–60.
9. Newman, S., *Housing Adjustments of Older People: A Report of Findings from the First Phase* (Ann Arbor, Mich.: University of Michigan Institute for Social Research, 1975), pp. 50–51.
10. Howell, S. C., "Site Selection and the Elderly," in M. P. Lawton, R. J. Newcomer, and T. O. Byerts, eds., *Community Planning for an Aging Society* (Stroudsburg, Pa: Dowden Hutchison & Ross, 1976).
11. Lawton, *Planning and Managing*, p. 87.
12. Ibid., pp. 107–109.
13. Ibid., p. 110.
14. Tobin, S. S., "The Future Elderly: Needs and Services," *Aging*, 1978, 279–280, p. 23.
15. Wack, J., and J. Rodin, "Nursing Homes for the Aged: The Human Consequences of Legislation-Shaped Environments," *Journal of Social Issues*, 1979, 34(4), p. 8.
16. Wan, T. T. H., W. G. Weissert, and B. B. Livieratos, "Geriatric Day Care and Homemaker Services: An Experimental Study," *Journal of Gerontology*, 1980, 35(2), p. 272.
17. Tobin, "The Future Elderly," p. 25.
18. Lawton, *Planning and Managing*, p. 31.
19. Ibid., p. 34.
20. Struyk & Soldo, op. cit., p. 207.
21. Ibid., p. 233.
22. Ibid., p. 238.

Suggested Readings

Capps, B. J. "Community Care Organizations: An Alternative to Nursing Homes." *Journal of Home Economics*, 1979, 71(3) 40–42.

Carp, F. M. "Environmental Effects upon Mobility of Older People." *Environment and Behavior*, 1980, 12(2) 139–156.

Harbert, A. S. and Wilkinson, C. W. "Growing Old in Rural America." *Aging*, 1979, 291–292, 36–40.

Lawton, M. P. *Planning and Managing Housing for the Elderly*. New York: Wiley, 1975, (chap. 1 "The older person").

Lawton, M. P.; Newcomer, R. J.; and Byerts, T. O., eds. *Community Planning for an Aging Society*. Stroudsburg, Pa.: Dowden Hutchison & Ross, 1976.

The National Council on the Aging, Inc. *A Guide for Selection of Retirement Housing*. Washington, D.C.: Author, 1976.

Rabushka, A. and Jacobs, B. *Old Folks at Home*. New York: Free Press, 1980.

Streib, G. F. and Hilker, M. A. "The Cooperative 'Family': An Alternative Lifestyle for the Elderly." *Alternative Lifestyles*, 1980, 3(2) 167–84.

Struyk, R. J., and Soldo, B. J. *Improving Elderly's Housing: A Key to Preserving the Nation's Housing Stock and Neighborhoods*. Cambridge, Mass.: Ballinger, 1980.

U.S. Department of Housing and Urban Development. *Occasional Papers in Housing and Community Affairs: Housing Options for the Elderly*, Vol. 3. Washington, D.C.: U.S. Government Printing Office, 1978.

Wack, J. and Rodin, J. "Nursing Homes for the Aged: The Human Consequences of Legislation-shaped Environments. *Journal of Social Issues*. 1978, 34(4) 6–21.

Housing and Energy

14

The 1970s witnessed two energy crises, one in 1973 and the other in 1979. On both occasions, fuel shortages brought about long lines at gas stations, higher prices, and public outcry. The headline-making drama of these periods served as a warning signal of the long-range drama, that of shrinking fuel supplies and resulting higher prices affecting the costs of housing of every American family.

Housing is dependent on fuel supplies in many different ways. The construction process itself is an energy consuming process. The making of brick, glass, aluminum, paint, and asphalt roofing, as examples, all

involve high levels of energy consumption, but concrete is the worst offender in this regard. Housing construction is also dependent on transportation. Housing units are built almost entirely out of materials that have been mined, refined, or fabricated— all energy consuming activities—in places other than where they are used. The energy used in transporting, warehousing, handling, and merchandising these materials must be added for a total picture.

Fuel consumption for home heating, water heating, air conditioning, and cooking is the major element in fuel cost increases to the average family. Gas and electricity are the major sources of energy for home consumption. Gas heating accounts for more than half of all homes, oil and kerosene for about 20 percent, and electricity for about 15 percent.[1] More people cook with electricity than with gas, but together they account for less fuel consumption than water heating.

Energy efficiency in homes has become one means of reaching two goals of interest to many Americans: (1) to conserve energy resources; and (2) to reduce their housing costs. Energy efficiency encompasses many aspects of home design and construction and is the subject of the first chapter section. Of particular interest to many energy conservationists is the use of the sun as a limitless and free supply of energy. Solar space and water heating is discussed in the second section. Since the vast majority of home owners are and will be living in existing housing units, the subject of retrofitting an existing house for energy efficiency is discussed in the third section. This is followed by a discussion of earth-sheltered housing.

The chapter ends with two sections that deal with housing and energy issues beyond the scope of an individual housing consumer. The first of these is energy efficient community planning. All residents may benefit when energy efficiency in home design is made part of the community planning of streets and transportation, housing orientation, and the like. Finally, in section six, the federal government's role in housing energy efficiency is examined.

ENERGY-EFFICIENT HOUSING DESIGN AND CONSTRUCTION

Energy is consumed in three major ways: (1) heating the interior space; (2) using gas and/or electricity for water heating, refrigeration, cooking, lighting, appliances, and so on; and (3) sunlight warming roof, walls and penetrating window areas. The largest proportion of energy consumption in winter is for heating the interior.

Energy is lost in two major ways: (1) heat conduction through the exterior shell (roof and walls); and (2) air flow through the house—it comes in cold and leaves warm. In one study of recently built houses meeting minimum standards for insulation, two-thirds of energy loss in the average home was due to conduction, and half of this was through windows alone. Air flow accounted for the other third of energy loss.[2] Energy efficiency, then, refers to both the intake of energy, that is reducing the amount of energy used in heating, cooking, lighting, etc., and the reduction in loss of energy.

It is beyond the scope of this book to detail all the ways that energy can be saved in the home. The heating of water, for instance, can be more energy efficient with insulated tanks and water flow controls. Cooking fuel use can be reduced with careful selection and use of appliances. But the major area in which energy efficiency can be achieved is in home heating and cooling, which can be broken down into the following areas: housing design, insulation, windows and doors, heating systems, and air conditioning.

Housing Design

Energy-efficient housing design must include many aspects affecting the intake of energy and the loss of energy. The most basic factor regarding both is the overall shape and size of a housing unit. The smaller the better, and the more square the better. For the simple reason that less interior space is less costly to heat, smaller houses are more energy efficient. House size as a factor of energy consumption is expressed in cubic feet rather than square feet. Our tradition of thinking of house size in terms of square footage (without concern for ceiling heights) may be outdated. Square shaped houses are generally less appealing than rectangular or other shaped houses, but they offer more enclosure for the

The heat lost by conduction through the exterior shell of the house, the walls, and the roof accounts for a large part of wasted energy in housing. Windows account for the largest portion of this heat loss. Photo courtesy of U.S. Department of Housing and Urban Development.

amount of perimeter. Circular houses, such as geodesic domes, are the most efficient use of perimeter surface for interior enclosure, but they do not appeal to many people, nor are they necessarily efficient in space use.

Since one of the areas of greatest heat loss is the roof, the more enclosed space under one roof, the better. Two-story houses are preferable to one-story houses, and more than two stories are even more efficient. The design trend of opening up one level (or several) to another level, however, may result in excessive heat on an upper level without comfortable steady heat on a lower level. Two principles are involved in this problem. Heat rises, so the bottom of an open interior space, even if not two stories high, is always cooler than an upper portion of the same space. Also, energy efficiency is maximized where rooms can be closed off so that only the space in use is being heated.

The house's exposure and the typical wind velocities affect the airflow problem. Being on the windward side of a housing development can greatly increase the inflow of cold air. Townhouse developments, with their shared walls, have the advantage of exposing only two walls to the airflow. The end units in rows of townhouses have greater energy consumption, generally, than do the ones in the middle.

Insulation

The most critical factor in the exterior surfaces of the house is insulation. Insulation provides the resistance to heat passing through the exterior surface of the house into colder outside air. Some building materials such as plywood, brick and wood siding have naturally insulating qualities, but the standard house wall and roof may be more like heat sieves than heat containers. Therefore, additional insulating material needs to be constructed into these surfaces in order to make them energy efficient.

The ability of a material to insulate, that

Shared walls and two stories are two housing design considerations in achieving energy-efficient housing. Photo by author.

is stop heat flow, is measured as its **R-value.** Materials with high insulating qualities will have a higher R-value than materials with low insulating qualities. The number of inches of insulation thickness is less important than the R-value rating of the chosen material. Materials most often used for insulation are fiberglass, mineral wool, and plastics (polystyrene, polyurethane, and urea-formaldehyde).

The recommended amounts of insulation are based on R-values. The R-value of ceilings should be greater than floors and walls because more heat is lost through the ceiling than through the other surfaces. R-value recommendations have increased in recent years.

If these R-values are desirable, one may wonder if more might be even better. A house can be insulated beyond a point where it pays off. That is, the cost of insulation may not be warranted for the savings in energy consumption. Required amounts of insulation vary depending on general geographical location as well as aspects of the individual house design. For instance, the actual climatic conditions for a given house can be determined by the direction of winds, the slope of land, presence of water, and the natural and man-provided landscaping. Not the least influence is the nearness of other buildings. The "right" amount of insulation for a house in any area is best determined by people who have studied cost effectiveness of different types of insulation in similar houses using the same type of fuel. Where fuel is relatively cheap, added insulation may not pay for itself within a reasonable time period.

Windows and Doors

Houses can be designed in ways to reduce the amount of heat lost through doors and windows. The most fundamental idea in this regard is to reduce the total amount of window area in a house. The windows that are necessary should be arranged to take advantage of the natural heating from the sun. Rooms that are likely to have large window openings for ventilation, view, light and other aesthetic reasons can face the south to optimize their potential for solar heating. North walls are better designed with small windows. Heat zoning is a concept that maximizes these principles of window orientation. The house plan itself is designed around window exposure so that the rooms needing the most windows are arranged on the south and rooms needing the least are arranged on the north.

Windows can have reduced heat loss with double-glazed, or even triple-glazed, windows. Even though these are more expensive than single layers of glass, the insulating effects of air space between two or three layers of glass can reduce energy costs. In severe climates, storm windows provide this kind of insulation. Made of glass or plastic, they provide a seasonal extra window. Besides the heat loss through the glass, there is a great deal of heat loss around the window's frame. Very loose rattling windows may cause extremely high levels of heat loss, whereas tight fitting windows probably do not. Weather stripping

Insulation in exterior walls is important in construction of energy-efficient housing. Photo by author.

and caulking can be of great benefit in reducing the air leakage around the window frame and between parts of the window.

Doors are critical in heat loss. Entries that have double doors (air-lock entries) are an advantage because there is a reduction of cold air entering the already warm house, and of warm air gushing out. The old-fashioned idea of an entry vestibule may make its way back into standard house planning. At the very least, doors should be weather-stripped to prevent heat loss around the door frame.

Heating Systems

The efficiency of heating fuels can be discussed in either of two ways—**combustion efficiency** or **seasonal efficiency.** Combustion efficiency refers to the amount of fuel producing heat when it is on. Modern oil and gas furnaces have about a 75 percent combustion efficiency when they are on. Seasonal efficiency measures the amount of fuel used to heat the house for an entire heating season. Since warm air is lost from the heater even when the system is turned off, the seasonal efficiency may be as low as 50 or 60 percent.[3]

More modern furnaces have a higher combustion efficiency than do older models. Tune-ups are possible on older models, and efficiency can be increased by 5 percent or more which results in substantial dollar savings. The following maintenance procedures increase the combustion efficiency in oil furnaces: cleaning the heat exchanger, flue, and filters; adjusting the air intake for proper amount of air to burn the oil completely; and installing a proper sized nozzle for optimum flue delivery rate. Fewer adjustments can be made on existing gas furnaces, but with either type, an experienced service technician is the best qualified person to do these jobs. Electric heat is efficient, so little if anything can be done to improve it.

This wood supply and butane tank account for the total energy needs other than electricity of a rural family. Their single woodburning stove provides adequate and inexpensive home space heating. Photo by author.

When a furnace is on, a certain amount of lost heat is necessary to carry the products of combustion away from the house. Lost heat when the furnace is turned off can be reduced, but the techniques for accomplishing this have disadvantages as well. Running the furnace continuously is one way. Also, the amount of heat the furnace produces can be reduced, with obvious problems on the coldest days of the year. Drawing air from the outdoors to burn oil and gas in furnaces is more efficient than drawing the needed air from the inside of the house. Some building codes might not permit this alternative.

The excess heat that goes up the flue might be recovered by converting it into usable heat. A flue heat recovery device performs best on the most inefficient furnaces. There are limitations on the amount and placement of the heat that is recovered, and the cost of the devices may outweigh the potential fuel bill savings unless the fuel bills are very high.

Fuel dampers are another means of recovering lost heat. A damper is a circular metal plate that fits within the flue pipe and is linked to the furnace's control system. Dampers can lower fuel bills from 10 to 30 percent.[4] However, there is a controversy over their safety. Governmental agencies do not agree on their usefulness when weighed against their potential hazards. In any case, they, as with all changes in heating systems, should be installed by appropriately qualified technicians.

The installation of a **heat pump** may result in large fuel cost savings in some parts of the country. The heat pump works by using warm outside air and, through a two-stage heat transfer using freon, converting it into heat circulated through a conventional ducting system. The process can be used to cool a house as well. Heat pumps are expensive, and they are best used in areas that have warm winter temperatures. "In areas where the average temperature in winter is approximately 38 degrees, the cost of operating a heat pump is about the same as for oil."[5] Some northern areas might not have advantageous climates nor relatively high fuel costs to warrant the heat-pump alternative. Heat pumps sometimes require an auxiliary heating system.

The use of wood as a fuel has regained popularity after a century of disuse. Fireplaces have been thought of in the past as pleasant, and somewhat luxurious additions to a room's design and atmosphere. In the last few years this attitude has been replaced by some people with the attitude that burning wood can and should be a major source of home heating. The remodelling of fireplaces has resulted. Numerous devices have appeared on the market to increase the heating capacity of the normal fire.

Wood-burning stoves have become very useful to many homeowners. Where an abundant supply of wood is available at a low cost (or for no cost), wood as a major source of fuel for home space heating, cooking, and water heating makes sense. Wood-burning stoves, both of centuries-old design and more modern design, have appeared in great numbers on the marketplace. These stoves may not have heating efficiency (some have about 30 percent) but the shape and wood capacity can be matched to the needs of the users. A large-capacity wood stove placed in a basement with a duct and blower system becomes a wood furnace. These are somewhat expensive and less efficient heating systems when compared to conventional gas, oil or electric furnaces.

Air Conditioning

While it might be natural to assume that keeping the house cool in hot weather is the reverse process of keeping the house warm in cold weather, it is not that simple. Weather conditions can be used to advantage in the summer to help cool the house naturally. If the house stays closed up during the day during the hottest time, the flow of heated air into the house is reduced. Opening up at night allows the cooler air to enter the interior space rapidly. Shade trees, shrubbery and green lawns can help to cool the house, and so can roof overhangs. Concrete and asphalt pavement near the house reflect additional heat. Light colored roofs reflect more heat than darker roofs, keeping the house relatively cooler. Attics should be ventilated to allow hot air to escape.

Air conditioning systems rely on electricity, so the cost of this comfort control appliance depends on the electrical rates within the region. Conservationists encourage the setting of thermostats in hot summer weather at a higher temperature than may be ideal (for example, 80 degrees rather than 65 degrees). The amount of insulation in the house does not affect the efficiency of the cooling system in the same manner it affects the heating system. Insulation put in for heating efficiency will have a bonus effect in the summer, but insulation costs are not justified for air conditioning efficiency alone.

Attic fans meant to circulate the air throughout the whole house might be a substitute for air conditioning in some areas. However, their effectiveness depends on cool breezes coming in from the outside, and they do not offer humidity control. The cost of the fan itself and installation are high but operational costs are low, especially when compared to air conditioners. Smaller fans for single-room use have become fashionable both as a nostalgic design feature and as a space-cooling device.

USING THE SUN

The use of solar energy to heat homes and to heat hot water, as well as swimming pools, has increased in recent years. With the rise in the cost of heating fuels, especially oil, the initial costs of installing solar heating of some type into new housing will be comparatively advantageous.

There are two basic types of solar heating of interior space—active and passive. An active solar system requires mechanical devices, and the passive does not. Passive solar design depends on the architectural design of the house to heat (or cool) its interior space. A hybrid system has some passive design elements combined with some sort of mechanical devices.

Even though sun is free fuel, most solar heating systems rely on a backup conventional system for non-sunny days. The value of the system to the homeowner depends on its initial cost, the size and design of the house, the location, and climate. Photo courtesy of U.S. Department of Housing and Urban Development.

Active Solar Heating

An active solar space heating system begins with **collector panels,** usually on the roof of the house, which heat up either water or air that flows through the tubes within the panels. The air or water then flows into a storage tank of some kind. Heat is drawn out of the storage container when needed. This container is often a large bin of rocks located above or below ground. The storage of water or air is much more easily incorporated into new housing design.

Basically, an active solar heating system is a furnace that uses the sun for fuel. And free fuel it is. But it is also a complex installation of pipes, pumps, fans, ducts, and controls. The entire system can be very expensive. The length of time it takes for the savings in operational costs to compensate for the initial installation depends on many factors—the cost of the equipment, the size of the house, the location, the energy efficiency of the house design, to name the most obvious. A backup heating system if also necessary, so the active solar heating system does not replace another heating system entirely.

The extent to which the backup system, whether oil, gas, electric or wood, must be used depends on the climatic conditions of the house's location, and that, of course, can vary from year to year. Typically, however, a storage tank of hot water or air can heat a home through three or four non-sunny days. If automatic thermostats and controls are part of the system, the switchover to the backup space heating system is no problem for the resident.

Solar hot water heating is accomplished with only a few solar panels, and a smaller, less complicated installation of pipes and controls. The hot water from the panels is simply stored in the hot water tank for use when needed. Again, if the sun does not shine for a few days, the temperature of the hot water in the tank falls to the point where a backup heating system must be used. As the costs of electricity and gas go up, the use of solar energy for hot water heating will become more attractive.

Passive Solar Heating

In the passive design approach, the house itself absorbs the heat from the sun without mechanical aids. The natural means of conduction, radiation and convection, do the job. In a direct gain passive design, the house is oriented so that maximum sun enters the interior space through southern exposure windows. The house should be rectangular with an east-west axis. Clerestory windows and skylights can be helpful in direct gain house designs. The object is to evenly heat the interior space.

The materials used in the house become the heat storage mass. Masonry, adobe, concrete, and stone have high heat holding capacities, so they are used for floors and walls directly absorbing sunlight. As the air in the room cools, the heat thus stored radiates out into the room. Water can be used the same way. Large drums or columns

Solar hot water heating can be adapted to multifamily housing as well as single-family housing. These panels on the flat roof are oriented to the sun even though the building itself is oriented at an angle. Photo courtesy of U.S. Department of Housing and Urban Development.

filled with water will absorb heat during the day and release it at night.

A passive solar design that collects heat in only part of the house is called an indirect gain system. The object is to store the heat in one part and warm the rest of the house by air movement from that part. The same techniques for capturing and holding heat from the sun are used. One form of indirect solar heating is where heat is first absorbed into a masonry wall directly behind south-facing glass and then released into the room.

Greenhouses may be made part of an indirect or a direct gain passive solar heating system. A greenhouse attached to a south wall will gather and store the sun's heat very effectively. It can then provide additional heat for the house through two methods— conduction through the house's wall, and convection through doors and windows. Incidentally, greenhouses can have a cooling effect by allowing hot air to escape through roof openings. A greenhouse is a useful passive system added onto a house with an active system, the combination resulting in a hybrid system.

Whatever the means of heat gathering and storing used in passive solar design, this method of attaining energy efficiency is highly individualistic and still experimental. Passive solar design will not radically change American housing as a whole. Nevertheless, passive solar design demonstrates

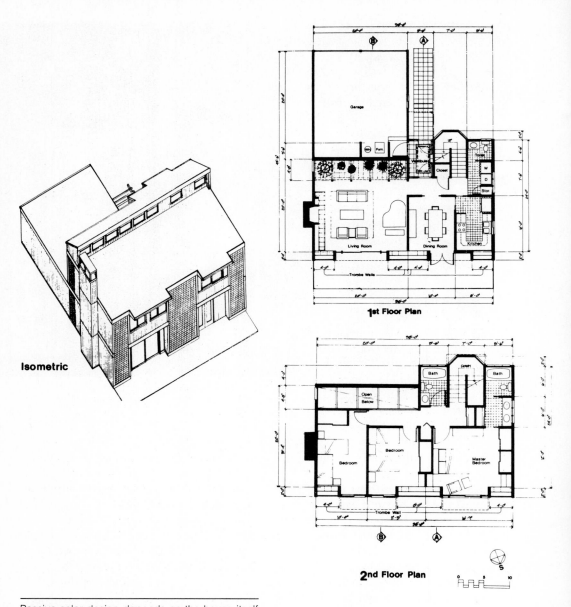

Isometric

1st Floor Plan

2nd Floor Plan

Passive solar design depends on the house itself to collect and store heat. This first-place winner in California's Passive Solar Design Competition uses clerestory windows, a heat-absorbing wall (Trombe wall), southern exposure, and air-lock entry in its design. Photo and plans courtesy of the California State Office of Appropriate Technology.

energy consciousness at its fullest. All houses can be sited to take advantage of this free natural source of heat. All windows can be used for heating as well as air and view. All building materials can be evaluated regarding their heat absorption qualities.

RETROFITTING

New housing construction has become more energy conscious in the past decade. Adequate insulation, double windows, and efficient heating systems, have all been incorporated into thousands of new homes. Since new construction, however well done, accounts for only a small part of the total national housing stock, the major concern in this section is with existing housing.

Retrofitting refers to installation of new materials or equipment into an existing structure. It could be as simple as weather stripping a doorway or as complex as installing an active solar space heating system. In assessing the advantages of retrofitting, and calculating the costs of doing so over time, it is necessary to consider both energy consumption and energy loss.

Energy Consumption

Many home owners have retrofitted their housing with alternative heating systems. The replacement of an oil furnace with a gas furnace is a relatively modest form of retrofitting, however costly it may seem. The decision to do so is based on the savings to be gained in the long run.

To install an active solar heating system is a more complex and more expensive matter. The location of collectors may or may not fit into an existing house's roof design. Even if they do fit, they must be positioned at the appropriate angle to the sun, deter-

Retrofitting an existing house with solar panels may be successful. The panels may (as in this case) or may not fit the roof angle, but they must be positioned to maximize the heat gained from the sun's rays. Photo courtesy of U.S. Department of Housing and Urban Development.

mined by the sun's path from east to west and through the year, winter to summer.

More people are retrofitting for solar hot water heating than for space heating. The principle is the same, except that the hot water from the collectors flows directly into the hot water tank for future use. The initial cost is not so high as for retrofitting for solar space heating for two reasons. The sytem is smaller, and there is no requirement for a large storage tank. Solar panels can be installed on roofs or in backyards to heat hot tubs and swimming pools.

To retrofit a house with a passive solar system might involve major remodeling. There is one relatively simple way, however, to use passive solar heating to cut down on existing heating costs. It is the solar greenhouse. An adequate expanse of south-facing wall, without shade from trees or adjacent buildings, is a must. East or west walls may be used if sufficient sunlight is admitted into the greenhouse's interior space. Any addition of south-facing windows, or of sunlight-capturing skylights, would have passive solar benefits.

Energy Loss

In areas with severe winters, adequate ceiling, floor, and wall insulation can make a critical difference in the amounts of heat lost. The greater the increase in the costs of heating fuel, the greater the advantages in retrofitted insulation. The payback period, that is the length of time in which the retrofitting pays for itself with reduced energy costs, becomes shorter as heating fuel costs increase.

One authority claims that insulation can be overrated as an energy conserving strategy. In houses where some insulation exists, additional insulation may not increase energy efficiency as well as the addition of storm windows, the installation of a heat recovery device in a flue, or even the installation of a solar hot water heater.[6]

More attention should be paid, according to Socolow, to the airflow problem. If a house can completely replace its interior air once or twice an hour, without opening windows and doors, then much energy efficiency can be achieved by closing up the cracks that allow this. Sealants and putty around window frames and doors could help substantially.[7] Storm windows are a fairly inexpensive "retrofit" for a house in a cold climate that does not already have them.

Energy used for other household functions, such as cooking, can also be used as a source of heat. When either hot air or hot water is routed out of the house, its secondary heating function is ignored. Even though no simple method of capturing this lost energy is currently available, it is worthy of designers' attention. Appliances could be designed so that their energy wastes could be used for heating in the winter and funneled off to increase cooling in the summer.

EARTH SHELTERED HOUSING DESIGN

One way of achieving energy efficiency is with an ancient practice of building housing wholly or partially underground. The earth is a natural insulator. During the winter, the earth surrounding some or all of the exterior walls, and perhaps layered on the roof as well, reduces heat loss. During the summer, the earth absorbs heat thus cooling the house without the aid of air conditioning. Some houses have been built mostly above ground but have employed an earth berm (earth piled up against the exterior wall) to take advantage of the earth's insulating qualities.

Housing designed to be partly or mostly underground has to take into consideration many factors in addition to the typical ones related to functional space relationships. An interior environment without natural light and air might be uninhabitable to many persons. The critical factor in earth sheltered housing design is then the size and orientation of windows. Three prototypes of earth sheltered house plans have evolved: the elevational, the atrium, and the penetrational. The elevational type concentrates all window and door openings along one exterior wall, and the other three walls are earth covered. The atrium type uses a central courtyard with the earth covered house surrounding it. The penetrational type uses window openings of various sizes in several locations around the house. These openings penetrate the earth berm to allow light and air into the underground house.

Some earth sheltered houses have incorporated solar heating along with the energy efficiency of underground structures. When the site and orientation allow, passive solar heating can be easily combined with the elevational type of plan and more modestly combined with other types of plans. Solar panels can be used for active solar space heating or water heating. When conventional heating systems are used, their size may be smaller than that needed for the same amount of above-ground interior space, and their efficiency greater since heat loss is reduced.

Two factors might prohibit the building of underground housing in some locations— soil and groundwater. The structure of an earth sheltered house is necessarily heavier than above ground structures, so the bearing capacity of the soil in all types of weather is important. Waterproofing and structural design are affected by the groundwater conditions. A high water table might require structural adjustments that are too costly in relation to the whole project.

The earth sheltered housing built by 1981 was primarily single family dwellings. One might suppose that it was built in remote areas with minimal surrounding development. However, there have been successful earth sheltered housing experiments in standard subdivisions, mixed in with other types of housing. The technology and concern exists to produce multifamily earth sheltered housing as well.

PLANNING AN ENERGY-EFFICIENT COMMUNITY

It is too soon to tell if the rising cost of automobile fuel will alter the housing patterns in and around our cities, but there is well-grounded speculation that it will. Two geographers have related migration patterns to the energy shortage by claiming that the energy shortage can cause unemployment, inflation, and altered consumer spending, and these in turn may prompt families to move (or not to move). For instance, renters may choose to remain renters. "Recent events relating to the energy shortage have affected people's image of their environment and altered their actions, lifestyles, and preferences."[8] Another analyst speculates that the children of the baby boom, ready for single-family house home ownership, may find themselves in the dilemma of wanting a certain type of housing and at the same time facing increasing costs of transportation. The result may be single-family houses built on smaller lots and located closer to work.[9]

Planning an energy efficient community, then, is not only planning for energy efficient housing, but planning for more energy efficient transportation. High-density housing close in to the employment centers of cities accomplishes both goals. The travel distance is reduced, and the increased demand for certain routes of daily commuting may foster an increase in public transportation. Also, more walking and biking can take place. At the same time, higher densities in themselves create energy efficiency. The materials used in construction are reduced, along with the amounts of land development and city services, both housing related energy-consuming activities.

The Davis Example

Davis, California, a community of 33,000 residents, was probably the first town to not only recognize housing and energy problems, but to attempt to do something about them on a community-wide scale. Energy efficiency in housing has become a matter of public policy. Conservation of energy in this community has taken form in increasing pedestrian and bicycle transportation. Bicycle paths have been developed throughout the town, and walking is encouraged by appropriate traffic signals, benches, and shaded landscaping. Bus routes have also expanded. Water conservation and recycling of wastes have been given community attention. It is the measures this community

This rectangular house, oriented to the south as part of Davis, California's energy-efficiency planning can take advantage of solar heating. Photo by author.

has taken toward achieving energy efficient housing development that is of special interest here.

A building code was adopted by the Davis City Council in 1976 that sets energy conservation performance standards for new residential construction. The amount of window area in relation to floor area is limited. The use of unshaded glass is also limited. Since Davis' summer temperatures are exceedingly hot, roofs must be made of light-colored materials to reduce heat absorption. Air conditioning can be eliminated in Davis if windows are protected from direct sunlight, insulation is used, and natural ventilation is incorporated into the housing design.

The street design of Davis has also changed. Narrower streets, lined with shade trees, can be ten degrees cooler than standard-width unshaded streets. Davis requires narrower streets, and street trees. Streets are oriented east and west so that typical rectangular houses have maximum potential for both passive and mechanical solar heating.

A solar house demonstration program was part of the Davis approach. With grant money from HUD, a consulting firm set out to build two prototype houses, both using passive systems. The ambitious goals of the program are briefly stated, and a measure of their impact is the wide adoption of solar housing in Davis:

Solar Dryers

In April, 1977, Davis passed Ordinance No. 876 nullifying regulations that banned the use of clotheslines and establishing requirements for clotheslines in new multi-unit dwellings. The Ordinance states:

The City Council of the city of Davis does hereby ordain as follows:
Section 1. Purpose: It has been determined
(a) Clotheslines are economical and are the most energy efficient method of clothes drying:
(b) Concern for aesthetics has occasionally resulted in subdivision restrictions or landlord rules and regulations banning the construction and use of clotheslines;

(c) Energy required to operate electric and gas clothes-dryers has become increasingly expensive and may in the future become less available; and
(d) The desirability of permitting the use of clotheslines outweighs the aesthetic disadvantages.
Section 2: Section 29-169.1 is hereby added to Chapter 29 of the Code of the City of Davis, 1971, as amended, to read as follows:

Section 29-169.1 Clotheslines:
It shall be unlawful and a nullity to establish any private covenant or restriction which prohibits the use of a clothesline in any residential zone, except that all multi-family

developments (three-family and greater densities) requiring Design Review Commission approval shall require suitable space or facilities except where such space would preclude good project design, to enable residents to dry their clothes using the sun. Such clotheslines shall be convenient to washing facilities and oriented so as to receive sufficient sun to dry clothes throughout the year.

Source: Ridgeway, J., Energy-Efficient Community Planning: A Guide to Saving Energy and Producing Power at the Local Level (Emmaus, Pa.: JG Press, no date), pp. 56–57.

1. Develop an 80- to 90-percent solar heated and a 100-percent naturally cooled dwelling.
2. Reduce the cost by using conventional construction techniques, smaller square footage and efficient solar technology.
3. Use landscaping for solar access in the winter and shading in the summer.
4. Extend and enhance interior spaces with usable outdoor space.
5. Use natural and artificial lighting so that a high quality visual environment is achieved with low energy use.
6. Use high-efficiency appliances, low water-use fixtures, solar hot water heating, and a "solar clothes dryer."
7. Provide full handicapped access to all rooms and services.[10]

Community Strategies

Seattle adopted a strategy of increased densities, improved housing construction, and reduced automobile commuting in 1975. These conservation measures were motivated mainly by a desire to reduce dependence on nuclear power generated electricity. Solar power and wood-burning power to generate electricity were investigated. Seattle set an example of a large city, used to the cheap energy of northwestern hydropower, deciding to change its energy consumption course. The ongoing process is both political and social.

A very different, and very basic, strategy of energy conservation was adopted by Hartford, Connecticut. It is an urban food plan. Community gardens (many of them) are

Builder Planning Solar Community

Picture yourself buying an all-electric home powered by the sun.

With normal use, you've been told, you won't have a utility bill. And if you conserve, you automatically sell any excess energy to the utility—who sends you a check for a change.

Since you are selling electricity, you are considered a small utility by the IRS and you can depreciate your solar roof on your taxes just like the big utilities do.

You are getting an electric car, financed as part of the house like other electric appliances.

After moving in, perhaps you walk out to your car one day and find it won't start. You call General Electric which sends a repairman to your home.

It sounds like a conservationist's dream. And it is.

John F. Long, 60, has been a Phoenix-area home builder for 33 years and he says his recent plans are a "natural evolution" of his firm's conservation research through the years.

His firm has built a solar-powered house with a $260,000 contract from the U.S. Department of Energy, converted three cars to electric power and is seeking funding to build the country's first solar development of 100 homes in north Phoenix.

All these steps are in anticipation of a 22,000-acre development he plans to build 20 miles north of downtown Phoenix on what is now state land.

"I think this will be a showplace and model community for the U.S. and possibly the world," he said of the "planned hometown."

Long hopes for approval to buy some of the land outright, swap acreage for part and lease the rest from the state.

He foresees construction starting in two to three years, with a population of about 30,000 by 1992 and a mature population of 75,000 by 2000.

The community would feature water conservation, with precious rainwater runoff channeled from homes and streets into natural, underground reservoirs for repumping later.

Residents would be able to walk or bicycle along a garden path to nearby schools, stores and offices.

The plans started to emerge May 23 when the solar test house began running on electricity supplied by photovoltaic roof units. Excess electricity generated by the units is fed to utility lines for use elsewhere.

Long's next step was to announce a request for energy department funds to build a subdivision of 100 homes in north Phoenix in fashionable Moon Valley. Model homes are to open by the first part of 1981.

"This will be the first solar-powered development in the United States," Long said.

The option of electric cars financed as part of the 100 homes was the next announcement.

Long said he decided to have his company's chief engineer convert three standard models— the Datsun 310, the Chevy Luv pickup and the Chevrolet Citation—to General Electric motors because the "electric cars"—the ones that look like automobiles—cost $15,000 to $20,000.

"The auto manufacturers have done a heck of a lot of research on safety factors and I thought we might just as well take advantage of that," he said.

His plan would eliminate trips to a car-repair garage.

"We have an arrangement with GE. They will service the motor and controls the same as a refrigerator or washing machine. The service man comes to the home."

He added there would be a 25-year warranty on the GE parts.

The cars will start out as options but Long said he believes they will eventually be part of his home packages. "What were luxuries a few years ago are standard today," he noted.

Long, whose firm has

built thousands of homes in the Phoenix area, said his Moon Valley solar development homes will be aimed at higher incomes, with a price range from $100,000 to $190,000.

He said his firm seriously began considering solar projects after the Arab oil embargo and price hikes in 1974, which made alternate energy sources cost-effective.

But he emphasizes his planned community for north of Phoenix is a "total community" focusing on the quality of life as well as utilizing conservation measures.

This is a 20-year project. When I finish that one, I'll build a larger one," he said.

Source: Los Angeles Times, *Sept. 7, 1980.*
Reprinted by permission of United Press International.

part of the plan along with food-buying clubs, co-op stores, and co-op warehouses. The object is to have more families become self-sufficient in providing most of their food needs, to employ unemployed and underemployed residents, and to reduce the dependence on transportation as an element in food distribution and costs. All of these efforts reduce energy use. The city also has a winterization program to help insulate older homes, a solar marketing group, and an energy auditing program.

Energy audits are the key to a program in Greensboro, North Carolina. The goal is to contact every home owner. The audits provide information about each house's energy efficiency and also make suggestions about what to do. A follow-up contact showed that in the first six months of the program, less than half of the households that had been audited had in fact made insulation or other improvements, but more than that planned to.[11]

When the problems of energy and housing can be solved at the community planning level, energy efficiency can be both easy and cheap. Even so, careful house design and construction remain important, as does individual energy-conserving behavior. Ultimately, the transformation of the nation's housing from largely energy wasteful to largely energy efficient will depend on the decisions and habits of millions of housing consumers.

GOVERNMENT'S ROLE IN ENERGY-EFFICIENT HOUSING

The federal government has fostered energy efficient housing in several ways. The method that most directly affects home owners is a tax incentive to retrofit a house for energy savings. The tax credit available is for two categories of expenditures during the year. The first category is insulation and other energy saving devices (for example, storm windows, weather stripping, furnace improvements) and the second category is for solar, wind, or geothermal installation. For the first category, the credit consists of 15 percent of the first $2,000 spent on appropriate items with an upper limit of $300 per home. Solar, wind or geothermal energy sources get a heftier tax credit—30 percent of the first $2,000 of expenses and 20 percent of the next $8,000 for a maximum of $2,200. These tax credits are available through 1985. Some states have available tax credits similar to those of the federal regulations. The state tax incentive added to the federal incentive can result in a considerable investment saving for energy-conscious home owners.

By late 1978, thirty-two states had enacted mandatory energy standards for housing. These energy codes have been based on performance standards, but there are variations in the language of each state's code and its interpretation by local officials. The current interest in conserving energy in housing has pressured states to develop energy efficiency standards even where no state building code exists. Federal grants made available for developing energy codes in 1975 spurred on the process.

The Energy Conservation and Production Act of 1976 called for the Department of Housing and Urban Development (HUD) to develop federal standards. HUD has worked with the Department of Energy to accomplish this task. The HUD-DOE standard, called the **Building Energy Performance Standard (BEPS),** has not yet been adopted, but its imminent completion has brought about widespread use of state codes to, in effect, beat the deadline after which federal standards would take over. "The odds are that many states will have to make changes, suggesting at the very least, that the headaches and confusion plaguing builders and code officials will persist for some time."[12] State codes that are considered equivalent to the HUD-DOE standard (BEPS) will be left alone, but it is unclear how equivalency will be determined. BEPS, for all the contro-

versy, may eventually change the quality of energy efficiency for new construction by setting down four criteria: (1) the maximum amount of energy consumption a design may permit in any given region; (2) the maximum amount of energy consumption the design of a particular building may permit; (3) the total amount of energy a planned building can be expected to consume once it is built; and (4) the computer program used to calculate the amount of design energy consumption (item 3).[13]

Just as housing codes and building codes have their problems of uniform application and enforcement, so do energy codes. Because energy codes deal with essentially new areas of research and technology, there is no tradition of effective compliance. Furthermore, builders tend to read codes one way, and building inspectors another. Small towns have difficulty enforcing a code written by the state or federal government. Yet another problem is that builders must meet local utility energy efficiency requirements as well as the state or federal requirements.

SUMMARY

Energy efficiency has become an aspect of housing that all of us must consider to some degree or another. Not only is the energy efficient house one that is more economical, it is one that contributes to a national goal of energy conservation. By reducing both the means of energy intake and being much more careful about the loss or wasteful use of energy, we can achieve energy efficiency in our homes.

Size, shape, materials, location and construction affect energy efficient housing design. Insulation is one of the most impor-

tant of these, so the recommended amount of insulation should be determined before making any housing decision. Windows, doors, heating systems, and air conditioning are all features we have taken for granted in the past that now have to be carefully planned for maximum energy efficiency.

The current and increasing interest in solar heating has resulted in a developing solar housing technology. Active solar heating requires expensive mechanical equipment, whereas passive solar heating uses the house's design as a means of capturing heat and releasing it when needed. Solar hot water heating is a relatively modest use of solar technology.

The existing housing stock must be retrofitted for energy efficiency. The addition of insulation, storm windows, caulking and weather stripping, and solar installations can run the gamut in expense from a few hundred to many thousands of dollars. Retrofitting with a greenhouse is one example of passive solar technology adapted to an existing house.

Earth-sheltered housing is gaining acceptance as an energy efficient form of house construction. Several prototypes have evolved, all of them taking advantage of the natural insulating qualities of the earth.

All of the residents of a community benefit when energy efficiency is made part of the planning of streets, transportation, and new housing developments. Davis, California is an example of a comprehensive approach at the community planning level encompassing everything from solar clothes dryers to community-wide bike paths. Other communities have accomplished some energy efficiency with higher density housing, solar programs, energy audits, water recycling, and so on.

The federal government has encouraged energy efficiency through tax incentives. A certain percentage of the cost of retrofitting techniques, such as insulating and a percentage of the cost of solar installations, can be used as a tax credit. Some states have followed the federal example in allowing tax credits to encourage the use of energy saving home improvements.

The implementation of energy codes at the state and federal level has caused much controversy within the housing industry. The exact timetable for adoption, the means of supervision, the fairness of computer evaluations, the adaptability of state and federal mandates to local conditions all remain to be resolved. Despite the arguments, the setting of government regulations for energy conservation will ultimately promote the use of energy efficient building techniques and materials in new housing construction. Complete housing energy efficiency, however, depends on consumer awareness, and a change in attitudes and individual behavior. Housing design will change only if we as consumers want it to change, and energy savings will be substantial only if our daily habits change.

Notes

1. U.S. Bureau of the Census, *Statistical Abstracts of the U.S.*, 100th ed. (Washington, D.C.: U.S. Government Printing Office, 1979), p. 788.
2. Socolow, R. H., "Energy Conservation in Housing; Concepts and Options," in R. W. Burchell and D. Listokin, (eds.), *Future Land Use: Energy, Environmental and Legal constraints* (New Brunswick, N.J.: Rutgers Center for Urban Policy Research, 1975), p. 316.
3. Consumer Reports, *Money-saving Guide to Energy in the Home* (Garden City, N.Y.: Doubleday, 1978), p. 47.
4. Ibid., p. 53.
5. Browne, D., *Alternative Home Heating* (New York: Holt, Rinehart and Winston, 1980), p. 147.
6. Socolow, "Energy Conservation," p. 318.
7. Ibid., p. 319.
8. Henderson, F. M., and M. P. Voilard, "Some Possible Effects of Energy Shortages on Residential Preferences," *The Professional Geographer*, 1975, 27 p. 323.

9. Schafer, R.,"Metropolitan Form and Demographic Change," *Urban Studies*, 1978, *15*, p. 32.
10. Ridgeway, J., *Energy Efficient Community Planning: A Guide to Saving Energy and Producing Power at the Local Level*

11. Ibid., p. 162.
12. "Energy Codes Frustrate Builders," *Professional Builder*, 1978, 43(12), p. 34.
13. "Should Congress Pull the Plug on BEPS?" *Housing*, 1980, 57(5), pp. 47–48.
(Emmaus, Pa.: JG Press, n.d.), p. 52.

Suggested Readings

Anderson, B., and Riordan, M. *The Solar Homebook*. Harrisville, N.H.: Brick House Publishing Co., 1976.

Anderson, C. "Passive Solar Housing: The Other Way to Use the Sun." *Builder*, 1979, 2(31) 43–58.

Browne, D. *Alternative home heating*. New York: Holt, Rinehart and Winston, 1980.

Consumer Reports. *Money-saving Guide to Energy in the Home*. Garden City, N.Y.: Doubleday, 1978.

Farallones Institute. *The Integral Urban House: Self-reliant Living in the City*. San Francisco: Sierra Club Books, 1979.

Journal of Home Economics. 1978, 7 (3), and 1979, 71(4), several articles in each issue related to housing and energy.

McGregor, G. S. "The Davis Program." *Practicing Planner*, 1978 7(4) 33–34.

Mooney, H. A. "The Energy-Efficient Home." *Real Estate Today*, 1980, 13(9) 4–7.

Nadler, A. D. "Planning Aspects of Direct Solar Energy Generation." *Journal of the American Institute of Planners*, 1977, 43 (4) 339–51.

Passive Solar, *Professional Builder*, 1980, 45 (12), 92–103.

Ridgeway, J. *Energy-efficient Community Planning: A Guide to Saving Energy and Producing Power at the Local Level*. Emmaus, Pa.: JG Press, n.d.

Rogers, C. S., and Rogers, R. L. "A House Design for Energy Survival." *Housing and Society*, 1979, 6(2) 88–92.

The Underground Space Center, University of Minnesota. *Earth Sheltered Housing Design: Guidelines, Examples and References*. New York: Van Nostrand Reinhold, 1979.

U.S. Department of Energy. *Passive Design: It's a Natural*. Washington, D.C.: U.S. Government Printing Office, 1980.

Webber, A. "Energy Prospects Require New Planning Considerations in Housing and Community Development Fields." *Journal of Housing*, 1979, 36(5) 253–55.

Housing in Transition

15

There have been many indications throughout this text that housing *is* in transition. Some changes taking place are very obvious such as new ways of financing home ownership; others are more subtle such as the shifts in choices of housing types and locations. This period of transition will lead to a picture of American housing that will be different from the picture we have been familiar with for the past thirty years. It may take yet another thirty years for the picture to become clearly defined. At present, we are only beginning to make out new details and points of focus. The transition process will take us through the present decade and probably the next.

What is the future direction of American housing? One way of answering that question is to examine the movement that is already under way. This chapter will summarize the themes of change and transition which have been identified so far: a growing and shifting population, changing families, changing values, the rising costs of housing, consumerism, the governmental role in housing, and the housing industry.

A GROWING AND SHIFTING POPULATION

We will have many millions more people to house in the remaining years of this century. In a hundred years, our population could double. Whatever statistic is used, however, it is clear that much housing must be added to our existing and deteriorating housing stock.

There is no sign that this nation is making progress towards producing enough housing to meet demand. It is not yet evident whether the slowing of housing production in the late 1970s has created a pent-up demand in the 1980s. If this turns out to be so, housing production will have to be as high throughout the late 1980s as it was in the best years of the 1970s.

If the whole shift in the population is towards an older average age, and if the largest segment of growth will be of older people, what does it mean for our housing future? What kinds of housing should be built to serve this older population? It may be that publicly supported services for the elderly should have more emphasis than production of special types of housing.

The demand for new housing will increase in those regions experiencing increases in population due to migration. The Sunbelt states will gain in population and

Some sections of the country may need to concentrate on maintaining and rehabilitating existing housing stock while other parts of the country will concentrate on providing new housing stock. This could result in a dramatic difference in housing quality between regions of the United States. Photo courtesy of U.S. Department of Housing and Urban Development.

Housing Demand in the '80s and '90s

By the late 1980s, the squeeze will end; the huge age cohorts from the baby boom will be settled in their homes and the new young adults from the reduced birthrate of recent years will demand many fewer new housing units every year. Intelligent economic planning for the next decade requires an awareness that home building toward the end of the century could suffer the economic depression that afflicts education today. Certainly it does not make sense to strain our sinews and distort all our economic priorities now for the purpose of deepening the housing depression of the 1990s. Part of the attractiveness of the current emphasis on rehabbed housing is the likelihood that these homes will want replacement at about the time the housing industry begins to suffer from excess capacity.

Excerpted from: Mayer, M., The Builders: Houses, People, Neighborhoods, Governments, Money (New York: W. W. Norton, 1978), p. 429.

new housing will have to be provided in greater quantities than in regions losing population. It may develop that some sections of the country will concentrate on maintaining and rehabilitating existing housing stock, with relatively little new production, whereas other sections will expand with more new housing than that which now exists. Should this become the case, dramatic differences in the quality of housing stock between regions could develop. By 1990, the whole of the Northeast may be thought of as old, from a housing point of view, whereas the whole of the Southwest may be thought of as new. This dichotomy might only accelerate the migration patterns that brought it about.

As the population as a whole increases, so will the populations of metropolitan areas. The growth problems of huge cities will only worsen. At the same time, many millions of people will prefer to live in what are now small- and moderate-sized communities since our technology is making the choice of workplace less dependent on large city centers. But what is to become of the attractive mid-sized towns of today? Will the pressures of expansion turn them into additional metropolitan areas with all the disadvantages? Perhaps well-planned new communities of considerable size will have another era of creation and, the next time, success.

CHANGING FAMILIES

The nuclear family is not entirely a thing of the past. Housing needs of many nuclear families can still be met with the typical space and features of the single-family detached dwelling in the suburbs. This traditional mainstay of American housing will not disappear nor will the satisfaction it provides for many families. Not only will the present stock of this type of housing be well maintained, it will be increased with new construction. This represents the continuation of well-established family housing needs and the development patterns that meet those needs, but there is also a great deal of change.

How are families changing? Everyone by now is aware of the high divorce rate. An increase of single people living alone, or with other single people, creates housing needs that do not match traditional needs. Even though single-parent families often wish to remain in predivorce housing, or to achieve housing with similar characteristics, their needs are not identical to those of nuclear families.

The impact of women working outside of the home is only just beginning to be felt in housing. All of the assumptions about ideal amounts of space, convenience equipment, desirable location, and available services have to be questioned. What do women working outside of their homes need in their homes to facilitate multifaceted responsibilities? Women can only change their role in the home with the change in role of other members of the family. Not until the family in transition defines its needs can housing in transition satisfactorily meet them.

Along with changing families, the increasing number of elderly people has to be taken into account. It is not yet apparent if most of the elderly will continue to seek independent living in their own homes as they have in the past. It may be that in the future more and more of the elderly will need and want to live with other family members. The doubling up that occurs now with unmarrieds and middle-aged singles might occur among the unrelated elderly, and among family members of different generations.

Families are choosing their own lifestyles. Where in the past family members let their socially prescribed roles dominate their lifestyles, new options are being sought by a great many people. If familism, consumerism, and careerism used to categorize the major lifestyles in our society, they now are challenged by new habits of thinking, new attitudes, new definitions of the quality of life, and new uses of the personal resources of time and energy.

CHANGING VALUES

Values, by definition, are more stable than attitudes, and it is very difficult to document substantial value changes. What appears to be happening with respect to housing values is a perplexing mixture of

The choice of a condominium might achieve the housing values of ownership, privacy, convenience and economy, and aesthetics. Cluster housing also achieves energy efficiency and environmental awareness, two emerging housing values. Photo by author.

persistent values, challenged values, and emerging values.

The persistent values center around the theme of home ownership. Pride of ownership itself dominates these values which also include individualism, privacy, family centrism, comfort and convenience. Economy and aesthetics as housing values also relate to home ownership. None of these traditional housing values are likely to disappear, but they may find alternative forms of expression.

Some traditional housing values are challenged because they have become very difficult for many families to achieve. For instance, if privacy and convenience are primary values, along with home ownership, can all be achieved with the housing choice of a well-located townhouse condominium? Perhaps so. The values of economy and aesthetics might also be achieved.

Attitudes have more flexibility than values, and it may be that attitude changes are leading to value changes. The condominium example will serve. A family may believe that its values would be achieved best by ownership of a single-family suburban house, but its attitudes allow the choice of a townhouse condominium. The housing choice may lead to genuine housing satisfaction. This shift, however slight, may mean a shift in housing values, whether or not readily recognized.

An example of emerging values that are given expression in housing are: conservation of land, of fuel, and of existing housing. Architectural and planning critics have for decades warned the American public that land consumption in the form of endless suburban sprawl is wasteful and unrewarding. It seems some members of that public now agree. Higher density housing developments are one obvious result. The movement, however small, of families moving back to the city is another example

of emerging values. Inner-city location implies use of existing housing and city services as well as conservation of land and the reduction of dependence on fossil fuel for transportation. Government supported rehabilitation and urban homesteading officially sanction this emerging value in conservation.

Values centered on conservation affect individual housing decisions. In the public realm, these translate into a general environmental awareness. Many communities have adopted strategies to limit their growth in order to maintain the character of their communities, maintain clean air, preserve uncrowded streets and public facilities, and so on. Even in communities which have no specific no-growth policies, there may be factions expressing these values when further development is in question.

The trend towards cluster housing and new towns is a form of environmental awareness on the part of both the planners and developers who design them and the housing consumers who choose to live in them. Development is usually placed where it is least destructive to the ecology of the site. Large-scale development can account sensitively for the natural environment of a large area.

It is likely that many states will attempt to preserve their most environmentally sensitive regions, whether coastlines, mountains, waterways, deserts, or other publicly valued areas. Housing development may be viewed as a regional decision rather than a strictly local one. The often destructive patterns of development that have occurred in the past may well be reversed through an increase in public environmental awareness.

A conflict of values is at the heart of a critical issue regarding housing production. Environmental awareness leads to greater governmental control of land use. This, in addition to numerous building codes and normal land development requirements, adds to the construction costs of new housing. At a time when house prices are skyrocketing, and the value of economy is important to many housing consumers, how can additional costs be justified? It isn't clear, however, that the value of personal economy outweighs the public value of environmental awareness.

THE RISING COSTS OF HOUSING

The rising cost of new and existing single-family homes has made headlines in every major publication in the nation. It has become commonplace for house values to double in a few years. Only ten years ago, a house valued at $100,000 was considered extraordinary, and it probably was extraordinary in size, materials used, and details of architecture. Now, first-time buyers are willing and sometimes able to purchase very ordinary houses priced as high or higher.

Rising housing costs can have the effect of spurring interest in home ownership that might not have been there in a different economic climate. The rising value of property is considered a hedge against inflation, and the motivation to invest turns into a fear that if homeownership is not achieved now, it never will be. While not quite panic buying, housing speculation has been a problem in some areas, and no doubt some families have jumped into home ownership before they were ready for it by traditional standards.

The governmental practice of raising interest rates to help slow down inflation has a direct affect on the housing market. When home mortgage money is scarce and available only at high interest rates, prospective home buyers cannot get home loans. Housing production is slowed down. Because fewer houses are being produced, the demand for existing houses increases, thus causing their value to rise, and more buyers are priced out of the market in the process.

Alternative forms of financing have been

The rising costs of housing, particularly dramatic in the past few years, might be spurring interest in homeownership. At the same time, more and more people are finding it difficult to finance a single-family detached home of their dreams. Photo courtesy of Scholz Homes, Toledo, OH.

This multifamily housing might be a prototype of energy-efficient housing of the future. Its orientation insulation, use of windows and attached walls all contribute to reduced energy costs. Photo courtesy of the California State Office of Appropriate Technology.

created to ease the problems for home buyers. When initial house payments can be kept at a minimum, such as is possible in Graduated Payment Mortgages (GPM) and flexible mortgages, the advantage to the housing consumer is obvious. The 1980s will see an increase in alternative forms of mortgaging.

Inflation also has a direct effect on property taxes and maintenance costs. Property taxes have kept pace with inflation in two ways. The costs of providing services which taxes support have risen so that the tax base of a community has had to increase. The value of property on which property taxes are assessed has also increased dramatically. Tax bills are then higher at a time when everything else is higher. The so-called "tax revolt" is a response to inflation, and it will no doubt continue if inflation continues.

The rising costs of fuel for home heating will result in construction that includes energy conservation techniques. Adequate insulation, reduced window areas, house orientation, as well as careful selection of all materials, will improve the efficiency of space heating. Energy costs alone could create a greater acceptance of attached-wall cluster housing.

Should there be widespread adoption of energy codes, there will also be consistent improvement in construction methods to meet the requirements. Although there is some fear that energy codes will increase construction costs, and therefore the selling price of new houses, the long-term savings in energy costs may well compensate for the increase.

Retrofitting existing housing with adequate insulation and better heating meth-

The Ultimate Condominium

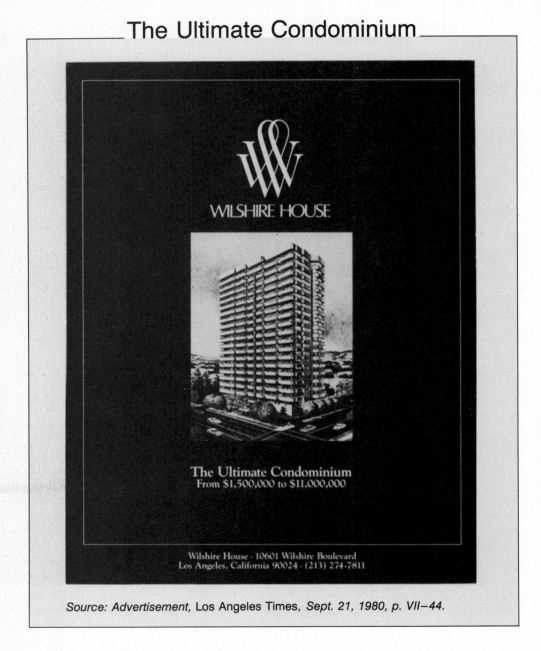

Source: Advertisement, Los Angeles Times, Sept. 21, 1980, p. VII—44.

ods, including solar water and space heating, will probably increase. The economic advantages of retrofitting will probably become more obvious at the same time that retrofitting techniques improve and possibly become less costly. With state and federal tax incentives added to the other financial aspects, more families will choose to cut their monthly fuel bills with retrofitting.

There is an impact of rising energy costs on the kinds of housing choices families make. When transportation costs go up due to fuel shortages, the choice of a location close to the place of employment and to needed services becomes critical. It is too soon to tell if rising costs of energy will reverse traditional suburban expansion by construction of higher-density housing on in-fill sites. If the demand is there, and logically it will be, this type of housing might come to overshadow single-family detached dwellings as the American ideal.

Can the costs of housing be stabilized in the future? No one has any clear-cut suggestions for positive directions toward that goal. Inflation is the critical issue, and until the entire economy is on a more stable path, housing costs will continue to climb at an alarming rate.

CONSUMERISM

The 1970s witnessed a growing activism on the part of consumers with respect to all of their personal spending as well as their public concerns. People demanded product safety, honest advertising, legal recourse, and governmental protection as an integral part of the American economy. This consumerism affected housing in subtle but important ways.

Because housing is such a large investment, consumers have been careful to compare home ownership alternatives. The increase in mobile homes, condominiums, and cooperatives all support a consumer willingness to use these forms of housing to satisfy their housing needs. In many cases, their investment needs are also met. It is probable that condominiums did not gain wide appeal until there was confidence that they had as much potential for increased

value as single-family dwellings. Mobile homes, too, have maintained value or increased in value in recent years, thus dispelling the fear that they were a poor long-term housing investment.

Consumer-oriented developers will use high quality materials that require low maintenance and infrequent repair. They may introduce new materials and construction methods with accompanying consumer education information. Consumers may learn to respond less to the impressive, and sometimes glamorous packaging of housing developments (furnishings and interior design effects of model homes in their richly landscaped settings). Developers could sell houses at a lower cost if these expensive trappings were reduced or eliminated in the selling process. The wise consumer is not dazzled by these effects, but instead is careful to appraise space arrangement, construction, equipment, heating and air conditioning, quality of materials, insulation, and so on.

Cost-conscious consumers may be attracted to smaller lot sizes with reduced street and sidewalk areas in order to find a house for less money. The interest in land conservation can overlap into this kind of consumer demand for energy-saving con- may gain in popularity because it meets a consumer demand for energy saving construction. Paralleling this demand is that of privacy. Developers will learn that cluster housing is more acceptable to housing consumers if it meets their needs for privacy as well as other psychological needs.

The choice of a rental unit by a household is a consumer decision. Where vacancy rates are extremely low, new rental construction minimal, and condominium conversion on the rise, the consumer choice of a truly suitable unit at a fair rent becomes more difficult. It is very important that renters protect themselves with knowl-

An increasing elderly population in the next few decades raises the issue whether we should continue to build elderly housing projects such as this or if we should provide needed services in a way that does not depend on congregate housing production. Photo by author.

edge of tenant-landlord law and that they use that knowledge in the rental agreements they make. Tenants who feel they have been unfairly treated may find tenants' rights groups to be an effective tool toward satisfying their housing needs.

Fair housing is probably the area in which consumers will have to work hardest to make noticeable gains. Fair housing law is difficult to use in specific discrimination cases. Nevertheless, the legal network is there to protect women and blacks and other minority groups often unfairly treated in the housing market. Improvements in legal processes could occur with consumer pressure. Mechanisms should be sought wherein individuals can unite to combat what appears to be an impenetrable system of discrimination.

Educated housing consumers will help form the housing of the future. They will exercise wise judgment in their own housing decisions. They will also help formulate housing policy at all governmental levels by participating in the processes that shape those policies. The political and social environment in which changes occur is, after all, an environment of people. Housing consumers are the people who can and should create an environment to satisfy their needs, lifestyles, and values.

GOVERNMENTAL ROLE

The role of the federal government has been firmly set by its many programs, past and present. There is no reason to believe that some form of rent supplement will not continue in the effort to assist low-income families in their pursuit of decent housing. Public housing will not be abandoned; however, it may not increase much, and some of the existing units are forty years old. The needs of elderly have been well recognized. With the growing numbers of older people, there will be pressure to respond to their particular needs. Programs for the elderly may shift from construction of housing designed specifically for them to provision of adequate facilities and services in existing housing.

It is difficult to imagine that urban problems will become anything but worse. Whether or not the federal government will continue to provide large sums of money for solving the ills of urban life remains to be seen. State governments may well fall heir to this large public responsibility. Localism will probably continue as a political ideal, but it may be impossible to fund and coordinate large-scale programs at city, regional, or state levels. The problems span geographical areas as well as social spheres,

so a federal approach may be the only work-
able one. On the other hand, there is a
growing conservatism regarding governmental control and governmental spending. Perhaps the urban upheavals of the 1960s will
have to be repeated before the American
citizenry is willing to face the complexity of
urban problems. At present, the fear of inflation overshadows any creative efforts at
social problem solving.

Home ownership will continue to be a
dominant federal concern. It may be that
support of home ownership programs will
expand due to pressures by many moderate-
income families denied access to the housing market. When a young family cannot
buy the house it wishes, it feels cheated.
When millions of young families are priced
out of the housing market, they can voice
their collective opinion that something
should be done about it. There are some
beginnings of breakthrough ideas which
would serve this group (not taxing the interest on savings intended for down payments
is one of them). The 1980s may well witness innovative legislation aimed at allowing prospective first-time buyers a chance at
the American dream.

Home ownership will also be supported
by programs that aid the housing industry.
Mortgage market funding and controls may
increase due to pressures from the housing
industry. The developers and builders who
are prevented from building housing that is
certain to sell can lobby for financial support. There is now a pattern of federal support for a steady and healthy housing construction industry, and probably there

Urban problems will continue and may become
worse. Whether or not the solution to them will be
funded at the federal, state or local level, the social ills of many of the nation's urban areas will not
disappear. Photo courtesy of U.S. Department of
Housing and Urban Development.

IE TOWERS

would be little public controversy about expanding the government's role in this regard.

At issue, however, is housing assistance for low-income families. It is doubtful that federal spending for housing will increase, given inflation-fighting policies and a national conservatism. Does this mean, then, that some existing public support for housing low-income families will be diverted to support the needs of moderate-income prospective home buyers? It is possible.

Rental housing is another governmental issue. While rent control has been tried at the local level, it is possible that pressures from desperate tenants, probably organized for this purpose, could bring about rent control at the state or federal level. Tenants' groups in many communities have brought about, in some cases, fairer application of housing codes, management practices, and rent rates. If the number of tenants who have legitimate complaints increases, surely they will be heard, and they may be the stimulus for changes in the way rental housing is financed, taxed, maintained, and regulated.

THE HOUSING INDUSTRY

How will the housing industry respond to the issues already presented? How and where will it build for a growing and older population? How will it design housing for changing families with changing values?

With an atmosphere created by an inflationary economy and conservative politics, it is doubtful that low-income families will receive federal housing assistance to the extent they have in the past. Nevertheless, existing public housing, much of it 20 to 40 years old, should be maintained. Photo courtesy of U.S. Department of Housing and Urban Development.

How will it deal with an increased environmental awareness and the high costs of energy in a consumer-oriented economy? Can it find ways to be less victimized by inflation, and seek ways to combat it? Can it work cooperatively with government at all levels to achieve solutions to obvious housing problems?

There are indications that the housing industry is willing to respond to these changes. The trend toward cluster housing is one example. By planning and constructing housing units that provide adequate space and privacy in such a way that families can adjust their housing values to accept it, the industry has led an unwilling public towards alternative housing solutions. This one type of housing could also be said to respond to the problem of inflation, high energy costs, environmental awareness, and a growing population.

Many builders are constructing better insulated housing that incorporates other energy-saving ideas. New materials are being introduced. While building technology itself shows no signs of significant changes, some builders are willing to experiment and to educate the public about their innovations. The general trend towards more prefabricated components in home building will no doubt continue.

Manufactured housing is gaining in public acceptance partly because it is offering sound construction at a competitive price. This form of housing production will probably account for a larger part of the housing industry in the 1980s. There is clearly an opportunity for manufactured housing to provide much needed new housing in areas that are rapidly growing. There is also a responsibility for the production of well-designed and soundly constructed units to accomplish full consumer satisfaction.

The housing industry complaint that the review and approval process in most communities is too cumbersome and too long may result in streamlining these processes. There may be some building code reforms at the state level which would simplify the local process. When the public realizes that housing costs may be reduced by simpler methods of review, changes could occur.

The housing industry could gain public support by voluntarily serving the housing needs of all income levels. It appears at present that legitimate profit motives can be distorted into an unwillingness to build anything but the most expensive housing possible in a given market. Granted, the buyers of these houses are having their housing needs met. But what about the rest of the public?

Governmental controls at all levels are often made the scapegoat for high housing costs and low production. Yet building codes, zoning controls, subdivision controls, energy codes, and the planning review process are intended to serve the public interest. Can the building industry serve the public interest as effectively and at less cost to the ultimate buyer or renter? A positive answer to that question must come from within the housing industry itself. The industry could deliberately create an atmosphere in which governmental control was unnecessary if it provided a wide range of housing types in desirable locations without harm to the environment.

SUMMARY

The themes summarized in this chapter are briefly restated below:

1. A growing and shifting population may create a demand for new housing in some areas while decreasing demand for new and existing housing in other areas. The increase in the number of elderly people will result in public attention to their special housing needs.

2. Families will increasingly consist of singles, single-parent families, the elderly, and women employed outside the home. These factors will alter the emphasis of housing needs from those of nuclear families to those of changing families.

3. Persistent housing values will find expression in alternative forms of housing; some traditional values may be in conflict with respect to housing decisions; and emerging values based on conservation may accompany traditional values. Environmental awareness may result in a growing acceptance of cluster housing and new town planning.

4. Inflation has brought about a dra-

matic increase in the cost of new and existing housing, interest rates, and property taxes. Rising energy costs may bring about a shift in desired location for housing and an increase in shared-wall housing construction.

5. The trend to consumer awareness is reflected in housing alternatives, and improved construction methods and materials. Renters have a difficult but not impossible task of protecting themselves under tenant-landlord and fair housing law.

6. Many federal government programs will continue, but problems of urban decay, the inability of moderate-income families to own a home, and the declining rental housing supply may spur the creation of new approaches towards solutions at all levels of government.

7. The housing industry may respond to these changes with different types and locations of housing. Leadership within the industry is necessary if it is to produce environmentally sensitive and well-planned housing for all income levels.

Suggested Readings

Breckenfeld, G. "A Decade of Catch-up for Housing." *Fortune*, 1980, *10*(7) 96–105.

Citizens' Advisory Committee on Environmental Quality. *How Will America Grow? A Citizen Guide to Land-Use Planning.* Washington, D.C.: Author, 1976.

Corbett, M. N. *A Better Place to Live: New Designs for Tomorrow's Communities.* Emmaus, PA: Rodale Press, 1981.

Diamond, D. B., Jr. "The Next Housing Crisis." *Real Estate Review*, 1980, *10*(3), 65–71.

Downs, A. "Forum—the Future is

Demographic Change." In R. W. Burchell & D. Listokin, eds. *Future Land Uses: Energy, Environmental and Legal Constraints.* New Brunswick, NJ: Rutgers Center for Urban Policy Research, 1975.

"The 5 & 10 year outlook for housing." *Real Estate Today*, 1980, *13*(8) 4–9.

"The Future of America's Small Towns: Authorities Speak Out." *HUD Challenge*, 1978 *9*(1) 6–8.

"The Future of Urban Housing: Realtors Poll Experts." *HUD Challenge*, 1977, *8*(10) 10–11.

Houstoun, L. O. "Market Trends Reveal

Housing Choices for the 1980s." *Journal of Housing*, 1981, 38(2) 73–79.

Houstoun, L. O. Responding to the 80s: Select Panel Begins Study. *Challenge!*, 1980, 9(8) 4–7.

Muth, R. F. National housing policy. In P. Duignan & A. Rabushka, eds. *The United States in the 1980s.* Palo Alto, CA: Hoover Institution, Stanford University, 1980.

Pratt, J. H., Pratt, J., Moore, S. B., and Moore, W. T. *Environmental Encounters: Experiences in Decision-Making for the Built and Natural Environment.* Dallas: Reverchon Press, 1979.

Glossary

Active solar system. A solar energy heating system that depends on mechanical devices to collect, store, and circulate heat. *See also* Collector panels.

Adjustable rate mortgage (ARM). A mortgage in which the interest fluctuates according to a selected index.

Affordable housing. Housing within the price range of medium income families; that is, income levels within 80 percent to 120 percent of median income of an area.

Amenities. Attractive or desirable natural and man-made features in the housing environment.

Amortization. The monthly payment of principal and interest to fully repay the debt during the term of the mortgage. Amortized mortgages are usually paid in equal monthly payments in which the principal amount is gradually increased as the interest amount is gradually decreased.

Annual percentage rate (APR). The accurate percentage of interest to be paid each year on the true balance of the loan.

Apartment. A set of rooms rented as a housing unit.

Appraisal. An evaluation of the value of property.

Appraised value. An expert opinion about the market value of a piece of real property should it be sold.

Appreciation. Increase in market value.

Areal density. The density (number of housing units per acre) of a specific area such as a city block, census tract, neighborhood, or housing development.

Assessed value. The value placed on a piece of property by local government for purposes of property taxation.

Assumption of mortgage. The buyer of a piece of real property is substituted for the original person (mortgagor) in an existing mortgage agreement and becomes liable for monthly payments upon consent of the lender (mortgagee).

Baby boom. The large increase in the birth rate that lasted from about 1946 to 1961.

Bed-in-a-door type apartments. Apartments designed so that fold-down beds are concealed in closets when not in use.

Binder. *See* Earnest money.

Blight. Deterioration and obsolescence of housing and community facilities. Blighted areas are also called run down areas or slums.

Building code. A set of regulations determined by the local government that establishes minimum construction requirements. Both materials and construction techniques are covered. Traditional codes are based on exact specification whereas some model building codes are based on performance standards.

Building Energy Performance Standards (BEPS). The proposed federal minimum standards for energy efficiency in housing construction.

Building permit. The permit issued by a municipality that allows a builder to proceed with construction.

Bureau of the Census. The department within the U.S. Department of Commerce primarily responsible for collecting information about the nation's population and housing characteristics.

Careerism. A lifestyle in which one or more careers have primary importance in all aspects of life.

Categorical grants. Federal grants given for many specific purposes prior to the enactment of the Community Development Block Grant Program in 1974.

Census data. Information gathered at the time of the census.

Circuit breaker. The name given special tax exemption provisions for people, usually elderly, whose property taxes are excessive in relation to income.

Cleaning deposit. A deposit made by tenants at the time of moving into a rental unit that may be used by the landlord for cleaning costs when the tenant leaves. It must be returned if the unit is left clean.

Closing. The meeting of the parties to a transfer of ownership of a piece of real property. Documents are signed, money changes hands and title to the property is transferred in the presence of lawyers or an escrow officer. *See also* Escrow; Closing costs.

Closing costs. The charges made to both buyers and sellers in the completion of a sales transaction of real property. Typical buyer's closing costs include: recording the deed or the mortgage, title insurance, appraisal, and inspection. Typical seller's closing costs include: cost of abstract of title, real estate commission, and recording the mortgage. Both parties may have to pay attorney's fees, escrow fees, and documentary stamps.

Cloud on the title. A claim or encumbrance which adversely affects the marketability of the title to a piece of property. This could be a judgment or decree which impairs clear title to the land.

Cluster housing. A type of housing development that allows for higher density development of some parts of the land to be balanced by undeveloped parts or open space on other parts of the land. Individual lot sizes are usually reduced in order to gain common open space.

Coastal zones. The land area adjacent to coastlines.

Cognitive mapping. The mental process of identifying one's location in relation to a neighborhood, community, city, or larger region.

Collateral. Property such as stocks, bonds, and savings deposits used as pledges of security for a loan. In a mortgage loan, the borrower pledges the specific piece of real property as security.

Collector panels. The devices designed to collect solar energy. They are usually flat, usually placed on a slant on or in relation to a roof, and are usually used in clusters (for instance 2, 8, 12) to provide sufficient heat.

Combustion efficiency. The efficiency of fuel use calculated while a heating system is turned on. *See also* Seasonal efficiency.

Commission. The fee charged by a broker or real estate agent for selling a piece of property. Standard commissions are 6 or 7 percent of the value of the property. Commissions may be split between two agents, one representing the buyer and the other representing the seller.

The Community Development Block Grant Program. A program in which federal grants are given to local governmental agencies to use in a variety of ways to improve housing and assist in community development.

Community property. All property acquired in the marriage, including real estate, which is jointly owned by husband and wife.

Comprehensive plan. The general policies for planned growth and development of a community usually set forth in text and map form. Comprehensive plans are also called general plans, city plans, and master plans.

Condominium. A form of housing in which there is individual ownership of individual dwelling units and ownership in common with other residents of the facilities and grounds. The commonly owned areas are usually managed by a home owners' association to which all individual owners must belong. *See also* Home Owners' Association; Home owners or maintenance fee.

Condominium conversion. The conversion of existing rental housing, usually multifamily, to condominium ownership. Often extensive alterations and modernization are involved before the units are sold to the previous tenants or other buyers.

Congestion. Overcrowded conditions. The term usually refers to overcrowded streets in which traffic flow is slowed or blocked.

Congregate housing. Housing with a common dining facility in lieu of individual kitchen facilities in each unit. A common form of housing for the elderly.

Consumerism. A lifestyle based on consumption of goods and services.

Contract of Sale. A contract in which the seller agrees to sell and the buyer agrees to buy; price, exact description of the property and date of closing are included with all specific terms and conditions of the sale. Both the seller and the buyer sign the Contract of Sale. Also known as Agreement of Sale, Contract of Purchase, Purchase Agreement or Sales Agreement.

Conventional mortgage. A loan made by a private source of funds, such as a bank or savings and loan institution, without insurance or guaranties provided by any level of government.

Cooperative. A corporation made up of the residents who own stock, not real estate, but who are entitled to live in a housing unit within the structure the corporation owns. Management fees are charged, and the corporation makes decisions regarding policy, management, and maintenance. Also called cooperative housing or simply a co-op.

Crowding. Inadequate space for the occupants of a housing unit. Crowding is often measured in terms of persons per room, but may also be measured by square footage or numbers of bedrooms with respect to ages and sex of occupants.

Custom building. House construction for a specific resident who has determined its design.

Damage deposit. A deposit paid by tenants when moving in. It is held by the landlord to pay for damages made to the rental unit beyond normal wear and tear.

Damper. The draft (air intake) controlling device in a flue.

Decennial years. Those years occuring every ten years. The national census occurs every ten years—1970, 1980, and so on.

Deed. A legal document that is evidence of ownership of real property.

Deed of Trust. A deed given to a third party (such as the lender) until the objectives of the agreement are completed (such as paying off a loan).

Deed restriction. A restriction written into the deed to the property limiting the use of the land.

Default. Failure to pay money due.

Demographic change. A change in the distribution and characteristics of the population.

Density. The number of housing units per acre; the allowable density is determined by the zoning on a given parcel of land.

Density bonus.   An increase in density allowed if certain development conditions are met such as inclusion of housing units for moderate- and low-income families.

Depreciation.   Decrease in market value.

Developer builders.   People whose business involves acquisition of land, readying it for construction, and the actual construction of housing units.

Dinette-type apartment.   A small apartment in which an eating space is incorporated into the living room.

Discretionary funds.   Funds that are allocated at the discretion of the U.S. Department of Housing and Urban Development based on urgency and need.

Disintermediation.   The withdrawal of savings from lending institutions which results in limited resources for home mortgages.

Down payment.   That portion of the sales price of a house paid immediately by the buyer. The remainder is usually mortgaged in one of several ways.

Earnest money.   Also called a binder, it is the deposit made by the buyer to demonstrate serious intent to purchase the property.

Earth sheltered housing design.   Housing that is wholly or partially underground in order to use the earth for insulation.

Easement.   A legal agreement between an owner of real estate and another party who is given access to the property for a specified purpose.

Elderly.   People past middle age. For statistical purposes, at least one member of the household must be over sixty-five for the household to be classified as elderly.

Empty-nesters.   A family in the stage of the life cycle where the children have grown and left home.

Energy audits.   Keeping track of energy usage over a period of time.

Entitlement.   Community Development Block Grant funds that are guaranteed to metropolitan areas and nonmetropolitan areas.

Environmental Impact Statement (EIS).   A detailed report on how a proposed development will affect the natural and man-made environment. The effects of the project are determined with respect to such things as water and air quality, neighborhood and community characteristics, animal life, traffic, as well as to existing scenic, recreational, historic and archaeological sites.

Equity.   The value of the property minus the remaining amount of mortgage owed.

Equity Sharing Mortgage.   An arrangement in which a second party helps with the financing of real property in exchange for a specified portion of the profits when it is sold. Also called Appreciation Participation Mortgage.

Escrow.   In real estate, a third party holds deposits and legal papers concerning the transaction of property from one owner to another. When a house is "in escrow," the completion of the transaction has yet to take place.

Escrow account.   *See* Impound account.

Eviction (evicted).   The legal removal of tenants from a housing unit they occupy.

Exclusionary zoning.   Zoning for large lot sizes, minimum square footage, exclusion of multifamily housing, or exclusion of mobile homes; zoning that allows only housing at a price above the means of moderate- or low-income families.

Fair market rent.   The amount of rent for a housing unit that can fairly be charged in any given housing market. HUD may determine the fair market rent for housing units in certain subsidy programs (Section 8).

Familism.   A lifestyle in which the family and its activities have primary importance in all aspects of life.

Farmers Home Administration (FmHA).   An agency of the U.S. Department of Agriculture that administers programs to aid rural residents.

Federal Home Loan Bank Board (FHLBB). The regulatory agency for savings and loan institutions.

Federal Home Loan Mortgage Corporation (FHLMC) (Freddie Mac). An agency that buys conventional mortgages from private institutions and sells them to large investment clients.

Federal Housing Administration (FHA). A federal agency presently within the U.S. Department of Housing and Urban Development. FHA is known mainly for insuring home mortgages.

Federal National Mortgage Association (FNMA) (Fannie Mae). A government agency that buys and sells FHA mortgages.

Federal Reserve System. The central bank of the United States. The "Fed" controls the flow of money and the fluctuation of interest rates.

Fee simple ownership. Ownership in which no other parties are involved and in which the owner has rights to the space beneath and the air above the specific piece of land.

FHA mortgage. A home loan that is made by a private lender but insured by the Federal Housing Administration.

Fiberglass blanket insulation. Rolls of material consisting of two thin sheets with fiberglass in between and designed to fit between floor joists, wall studs, or roof rafters.

Flexibility clause. A clause that allows for a few skipped payments in a mortgage if paid in due time.

Flexible mortgage. Interest only is paid for a period of time (frequently five years) followed by a fully amortized repayment of the loan for the remaining period of the loan.

FLIP (Flexible Loan Insurance Program). A mortgage arrangement in which a savings account is used to supplement loan payments for the first few years of the mortgage.

Foreclosure. The legal process of dispossessing an owner of real property because of unpaid debt on the mortgage or deed of trust. A forced sale usually occurs.

Foster family. A family that takes responsibility for caring for an unrelated person.

Free-standing new community. A self-sufficient new community (new town) some distance from an existing urban development.

General Warranty Deed. A deed that conveys to the buyer the seller's interest in and title to the property; it also warrants that if the title is defective in any way, the seller is liable.

Geodesic domes. A building system based on the mathematical divisions of a sphere into triangles.

Geriatric day care centers. Day care in a designated facility for elderly people.

Government National Mortgage Association (GNMA) (Ginnie Mae). A government agency that buys and sells mortgages used to finance construction of housing for low- and moderate-income families.

Graduated Payment Mortgage (GPM). A mortgage in which initial payments are low and each year's payments increase at a fixed percentage until they level off to repay the mortgage in a conventional manner. Because the early payments are insufficient to pay all the interest, the loan balance actually increases (negative amortization), and the ultimate payments are thus higher than in a comparable conventional mortgage.

Gridiron method of subdivision. All streets and property lines parallel and perpendicular to one another.

Growth center new town. A smaller new town in a rural area with growth potential.

Heat pump. A heating system using warm outside air.

Heterogeneity. The quality of not being all alike; often used to describe a neighborhood of residents of diverse socioeconomic characteristics.

Highrise. A multifamily housing structure of five or more stories.

Hispanic. Of Spanish origin.

Home builders. Building contractors who build on existing lots.

Homemaker services. Assistance with cooking, cleaning, laundry, and personal care by paid personnel.

Home Owners' Association. The formal organization of all the residents within a housing development for the purpose of managing commonly owned and shared facilities and/ or grounds. In a condominium, the home owners association plays an important role in the management of commonly held property.

Home owners or maintenance fee. The fee charged, usually monthly, to the home owners in a condominium for the management of the commonly owned grounds and facilities.

Home Owners Warranty (HOW). A warranty on new houses which is available from participating builders.

Home range. The territory adjacent to one's residence that is traveled frequently (daily, weekly).

Homogeneity. The quality of being all alike; often used to describe a neighborhood of residents of similar socioeconomic characteristics.

Houseboat. A boat designed to be a residence.

Household. A person or people living together in a housing unit.

Housing Assistance Plan. A plan developed within a community for providing housing assistance for moderate- and low-income families.

Housing code. The minimum requirements all housing units within a municipality must meet before they can be occupied. The requirements include space standards, minimum level of repair, minimum requirements for heat, light, and plumbing, and so on.

Housing start. Each housing unit is counted as part of housing production when excavation for it has begun.

Impound account. A savings account specifically for use in paying annual property taxes and/or hazard insurance. Such an account does not usually earn any interest, but monthly deposits are required as part of the house payment.

Inclusionary zoning. A zoning ordinance that specifies a percentage of housing units to be sold or rented to low- and/or moderate-income families.

Indirect subsidy. Indirect monetary aid benefit.

Infrastructure. The streets, utilities, and provision of services necessary to facilitate development.

In-lieu fees. A fee paid to a municipality instead of participating in a specific program or meeting a specific development requirement.

Inner city. The sections of the city near its center often considered blighted.

Installment land contract. A contract for the purchase of real property in which the seller extends credit to the buyer with specified term of the loan, interest rate, and monthly payments; title is not transferred until the property is paid for in full.

Insulation. The use of nonconducting material to prevent the passage of heat through walls, ceilings, and floors.

Interest. The charge paid for borrowing money.

Joint tenancy. A form of joint ownership in which the surviving party (or parties) inherit the share of ownership of the person who has died.

Junior mortgages. All mortgages on a piece of real property other than the first mortgage.

Kit house. A house erected at the site and made of precut lumber and other structural materials which reduce the need for costly labor in construction.

Land developers. People whose main business is to buy and prepare land for development.

Land use. The use to which land is put, usually categorized in professional planning as residential, commercial, industrial, recreational, or agricultural.

Lease. A legal contract between tenant and landlord effective for a stipulated period of time.

Lien. A claim that one person has on the real property of another person as a security for debt.

Lifestyle. Role emphasis and central life interest of an individual or family.

LHA (Local Public Housing Agency). Local Public Housing Agencies are appointed by a governmental body to administer federal housing assistance programs in its jurisdiction.

Lots. Parcels of land with fixed boundaries.

Lower Income Rental Assistance Program. A federal rent subsidy program; also known as Section 8.

Low-income families. Families whose incomes fall below the level of 80 percent of the median income of a given area. *See also* Very low-income families.

Man-environment relations. An interdisciplinary area of study that is concerned with the interaction between humans and the built environment.

Mansion. A large, imposing private residence.

Masonry. Brick or stone used in construction.

Median income. The income level halfway between the highest and the lowest income levels.

Metropolitan area. An area qualified as a Standard Metropolitan Statistical Area.

Middle class. The social class to which most Americans assign themselves; the class between the wealthy upper class, and the poor or working class.

Midrise. Multifamily housing built with three to five stories.

Migration. A long-range move from one housing or labor market to another.

Mobile home. A manufactured home that can be moved on its own wheels by truck. Mobile homes may be made up of more than one transportable section.

Model Cities Program. A program intended to help solve social, economic, and physical problems at the neighborhood level in selected cities.

Modular. Composed of prefabricated units consisting of at least a floor, wall, and ceiling.

Modular home. A modular home is composed of two or more modular units.

Mortgage. A debt secured by a pledge of real property.

Multifamily housing. Housing designed to accommodate more than two households under one roof, each in a complete and private housing unit.

Negative amortization. A loan in which principal and interest are not amortized at first. The amount of principal owed may be increased in the first few years as is the case in Graduated Payment Mortgages.

Neighborhood. An area of a community in which the residents identify with a certain territory, usually bounded by major streets, often featuring a major facility (school, church, park, and so on), and often similar in architectural and cultural character.

New town. A community planned at the outset to provide residential, commercial, industrial, recreational, educational, and service facilities for an optimum population.

New-town-in-town. A large-scale development including residential, commercial, and recreational facilities within an existing urban environment.

No-growth policies. Policies by a community to slow or inhibit population growth as well as additional development, especially additional housing.

Nonbinding reservation. A reservation for the purchase of a condominium unit not yet constructed.

Nonmetropolitan areas. Areas not classified as Standard Metropolitan Statistical Areas.

Nuclear family. A married couple with at least one child.

Nursing homes. A form of congregate housing for the elderly in which total personal and health care is provided.

On-spec. A house built on speculation; that is, to be sold at a profit to an unknown buyer.

Open-ended mortgage. A clause in a mortgage agreement which allows the borrowing of paid-off principal without prepayment penalty or refinancing charges.

Operation Breakthrough. A program intended to offer support for the design and development of innovative construction materials and techniques to lower the cost of producing housing.

Package mortgage. A mortgage that includes appliances and some furnishings as well as land and buildings.

Passive solar system. A solar energy heating system that depends on the materials and design of the house itself to collect and store heat in its interior space.

Performance Building Code. A building code that specifies how the materials and techniques used in housing construction must perform; that is, a code that sets performance standards rather than specification standards.

Planned unit development (PUD). A zoning classification used in some communities that allows for flexible site development and varying densities within the development, such as medium and high density housing intermixed with open space.

Plywood. A construction material of layers of wood pressed together.

Points. Charges made by lenders to increase their return on money lent for mortgages. One point is 1 percent of the amount of the loan, but the number of points charged varies with economic conditions.

Portable houses. An early form of prefabricated houses.

Prefabricated. Produced in a factory prior to use in housing construction at a particular site.

Prepayment penalty. A charge made by the lender for paying off the principal owed on a mortgage prematurely (prior to the agreed upon term).

Principal. The amount of money borrowed that is still owed at any point throughout the term of the mortgage.

Proximate residences. Individual housing units for elderly people adjacent to family residences.

Public housing. Housing developed under the Low-Income Public Housing Program which assists Local Housing Agencies in constructing, owning, and managing housing for low-income families.

Public Housing Modernization Program. A program designed to finance capital improvements in existing public housing.

Public Housing Operating Subsidies Program. Federal grants to help with operating costs of public housing.

Quitclaim deed. A deed in which one person relinquishes rights to the property to another person without guaranteeing such rights.

Real estate. Land and the improvements on it.

Real estate agent. A person who is licensed by his or her state to bring together parties in a real estate sale. The agent is paid by the seller, but may act on behalf of both buyer and seller. More than one agent (or broker) may be involved in a single sales transaction.

Real estate broker. A person holding a state license to handle sales of real property. The state requirements for a broker's license are more stringent than those for a real estate agent. The broker may belong to the National Association of Real Estate Brokers. *See also* Real estate agent.

Realtor. A real estate broker with membership in the National Association of Real Estate Boards.

Redlining. The practice by some lending institutions and insurance companies of identifying high-risk areas where they refuse to lend mortgage money or to insure property.

Rent. The amount of money paid for the use of property belonging to another person.

Rent control. Regulation, usually at the community level, of the amount of rent that can be charged tenants.

Restrictive condition. A promise to use or not to use the property in a certain way, written so that if the promise is broken the title reverts to the previous owner.

Restrictive covenant. A written promise to use or not to use real property in a certain way.

Retirement community. A large-scale housing development designed to meet the needs of people over a specified age (fifty-five, for example).

Retrofitting. Outfitting existing structures with solar heating.

Reverse Annuity Mortgage (RAM). A form of income for people living in homes with high equities. The recipient (often elderly) continues to live in the home but receives monthly or lump sum payment for a portion of the equity.

Right of survivorship. In a joint ownership, the right of one owner to the share of the other when he or she dies.

Rollover mortgages. A mortgage in which the interest rate is renegotiated after a fixed period of a few years (usually three to five).

Row houses. Three or more attached houses with two or more stories each.

Rural. Any place that is not urban (that is, less than 2500 population).

Rural housing. Any form of housing that exists in nonmetropolitan areas (less than 2500 population).

RV. Recreational vehicle.

R-value. The measurement of the insulating qualities of different materials. The higher the R-value, the more insulation provided.

Satellite new town. A new town dependent on an existing metropolitan area.

Seasonal efficiency. The efficiency of fuel use over an entire season of using a heating system. *See also* Combustion efficiency.

Section 8. Lower-Income Rental Assistance Program.

Section 202 Housing Program. A federal program in which loans are made to nonprofit organizations to develop housing for the elderly and handicapped.

Section 235 Program. A program intended to foster construction of housing for purchase by low- and moderate-income families.

Section 236 Program. A program that offered incentives to build multifamily housing at a cost lower than privately developed multifamily housing.

Section 312. A rehabilitation loan program under Section 312 of the Housing Act of 1964 aimed at salvageable homes in decaying urban neighborhoods.

Section 502. The Farmers Home Administration program that assists rural home owners in a variety of ways.

Security deposit. A deposit made to the landlord by the tenant on occupying a rental unit; it is used for unpaid rent, damage, or cleaning costs and the unused portion (if any) is returned to the tenant on vacating the unit. *See also* Cleaning deposit; Damage deposit.

Self-help housing. Housing constructed by the joint labor of several families, thus saving on the total cost.

Single-family housing. Single family detached houses on individual lots.

Single-room occupancy or SRO hotels. Hotels that rent single rooms to elderly people on an indefinite basis. Where whole families occupy single rooms in old hotels, slum conditions often result.

Slum. An area that is badly deteriorated physically, and is unsanitary, unsafe, poorly serviced by the municipality it is within, and usually overcrowded.

Slum clearance. The removal of buildings from an urban area considered to be a slum.

Social class. Comparative ranking within a society primarily dependent on education, employment, and income.

Social mobility. Movement from one social class to another, usually upwards.

Special warranty deed. A deed that warrants that no claims upon the rights of the seller are being transferred to the buyer.

Specification Building Codes. Building codes that specify exact materials and methods to be used in housing construction.

Speculation. Buying property such as land, at some risk, in the expectation of financial gain at some future date.

Standard Metropolitan Statistical Area (SMSA). Generally, a county that contains at least one city (or twin cities) with a population of 50,000 or more.

Subcontracting. Contracting to have specialized portions of the labor involved in housing construction done by another party.

Subdivision. The process of dividing a parcel of undeveloped land for housing development. This involves the laying out of streets, utilities, individual lots and other components as required by local regulations.

Subsidized housing. Housing which is occupied by families aided by some form of monetary support such as rent subsidy, interest rate subsidy, and so on.

Substandard housing. Unsafe and dilapidated housing, often without plumbing or heating.

Suburbs. Largely residential areas at the outer edges of metropolitan areas.

Sunbelt. Southern and southwestern states, from Florida to California.

Tax rate. The percentage of assessed property value that is charged owners to support local schools and services.

Tax revolt. The term given the popular movement to reduce property taxes or any other form of taxation. The passage of Proposition 13 by referendum in California in 1978 was the first event to signify the strength of negative public opinion about property taxes.

Tenancy by the entirety. A form of joint ownership for married couples in which neither can sell the property without the approval of the spouse.

Tenancy in common. A form of joint ownership in which two or more people own property but each wills it separately from the other(s); that is, there is no right of survivorship.

Tenant. A person who pays rent to occupy or use land.

Tenement house. A multifamily structure built especially to house immigrant families, used extensively in New York City in the nineteeth century.

Tenure. The mode of possessing property, commonly thought of in terms of owning versus renting.

Territoriality. In humans as in animals, the behavior that defines one's territory.

Title company. A company that provides title insurance.

Title insurance. An insurance policy purchased by home buyers to protect them against claims on the property purchased.

Townhouses. *See* Row houses.

Tract housing. Housing designed and built on large tracts of land that is subdivided for this purpose.

Turnkey Program. A program in which private developers construct housing for a Local Public Housing Agency which then purchases it for the use of low-income families.

Urban. Pertaining to a city; however, the U.S. Bureau of the Census classifies any place with more than 2500 residents as urban.

Urban Homesteading Program. A program intended to encourage resettlement in abandoned urban housing and its rehabilitation within a specified period of time.

Urban Renewal Program. A program intended to eliminate slums by replacing them with new development beneficial to the city as a whole.

Usury laws. Laws that prevent charging excessive interest rates for loans. Interest rates considered excessive in the past might be considered normal or economically necessary in the present; usury laws are therefore changing or being eliminated in many states.

Utilities. Services such as gas, electricity, and telephone provided by public utilities to residential areas.

Values. Concepts we have of what is desirable and what ought to be.

VA mortgage. A mortgage which is guaranteed by the Veterans Administration.

Variable Rate Mortgage (VRM). A mortgage with an interest rate that is adjusted over time as economic conditions warrant and as regulations allow.

Very low-income families. Families whose incomes fall below the level of 50 percent of the median income of a given area. *See also* Low-income families.

Vestibule. An entrance hall or room.

Water closets. Toilets.

Well elderly. Elderly people able to maintain independent living.

Wrap-around mortgage. A mortgage in which a second lender makes a new larger loan to the borrower at an interest rate between that on the existing mortgage and that in the market at the time. Also called all-inclusive trust deed.

Zero lot line. A development in which at least one of each house's exterior walls is on the property line.

Zero population growth. A birth rate that replaces the existing population rather than increasing it.

Zoning. The process by which restrictions on land use are determined and enforced.

Index

Numbers in bold face refer to boxes.

Federal taxation policies, 281–282
Fee simple ownership, 195
Female headed households, 33–35
FHA. *See* Federal Housing Administration
FHA mortgage, 145–147, 159, 162, 171, 179
FHLBB. *See* Federal Home Loan Bank Board
FHLMC. *See* Federal Home Loan Mortgage Corporation)
Flexibility clause in a mortgage, 151
Flexible Loan Insurance Program. *See* Flip mortgage
Flexible mortgage, 148
Flip mortgage, 148
Flood insurance, 184
FmHA (*see* Farmers Home Administration)
FNMA (*see* Federal National Mortgage Association)
Foreclosure, 144
Fort Lincoln: A New-Town-in-Town, **242–243**
Foster families for elderly, 304
Founder's fee housing, 303
Freddie Mac. *see* Federal Home Loan Mortgage Association
Free-standing new community, 237
Frieden, B., 56, 61
Fuel dampers, 318

Gans, H. J., 104
Garden homes, 232
General plan. *See* Comprehensive plan
General warranty deed, 195
Geodesic domes, 177–178, 315
Geriatric day care, 305
Ghettos. *See* Black ghettos
The giant gridiron, 4
Ginnie Mae. *See* Government National Mortgage Association
GNMA. *See* Government National Mortgage Association
Good faith estimate of closing costs. *See* Real Estate Settlement Procedures Act
GPM. *See* Graduated Payment Mortgage
Government regulations: affecting the cost of housing, 55, 338; and the housing industry, 345; of nursing homes, 302
Government National Mortgage Association, 284
Government's role in the future, 342–343
Graduated Payment Mortgage, 148, 171, 339
Greenhouses used for solar heating, 321
Greensboro, North Carolina, energy conservation strategies of, 329

Gridiron pattern, 4
Grief syndrome, 136
Growth center new towns, 237
Growth controls, 59. *See also* No growth policies

HAP. *See* Housing Assistance Plan
Hartford, Connecticut, energy conservation strategies, 327–329
Hayward, G. 133
Hazard insurance, 182–184; for condominiums, 173; cost as part of monthly house payment, 150–151; division of in home buying process, 162–163
Health and safety, as housing values, 112
Heat conduction and energy efficient housing, 314. *See also* Insulation
Heat loss, 314, 315
Heating: costs, 181; systems, 317
Heat pump, 318
Heterogeneity, 102–104
HFA. *See* Housing finance agencies
High density housing: in the future, 337; psychological effects of, 130
High density land use, 221
"Highest and Best" Use, The, **223**
Home, as a concept, 133–134
Home buying: deposit, 159; making the decision to buy, 141–143; procedure, 151–158; steps in, 159–163
Home heating, cost of, 339
Home insurance. *see* Hazard insurance
Home maintenance, and social class, 100–101; as a problem for the elderly, 291
Homemaker services for the elderly, 304
Home Mortgage Disclosure Act, 213
Home owners' association, 170, 232; bylaws, 173; fee, 170
Home ownership, 140, 168, 258–260; and social class, 105; and urban renewal, 259–260; as a government concern, 343; as an investment, 168; as a value, 107–108, 337; as forced savings, 188; costs over the term of the mortgage, 146; for the elderly, 291–292; federal support for, 281–282; financial advantages of, 186–189; in rural areas. *See* Section 502; legal aspect of, 194–198; problems of women, 212–213; with land leasing, 164
Home ownership alternatives, 341
Home owners' policies. *See* Hazard insurance
Home Owners Warranty, 198
Home range, 134–135
Home sharing, 293–295

Special warranty deed, 195
Specification standard building code, 200
SRO hotel. *See* Single room occupancy hotel
Stabilizing needs and housing, 119–120
Stage in the life cycle and housing, 76–84;
    and college students, 75; as a factor in
    home buying, 141–142
Standard Metropolitan Statistical Areas, 29
State land use planning, 230–231
State programs for housing assistance, 279–
    281
Steering. *See* Racial steering
Storm windows and energy efficiency, 317; tax
    credit for, 329
Street layout and energy efficiency, 326
Stress *See* Crowding and stress
Subdivisions. *See also* PUDs; The suburban
    ideal
Subdivision controls, 59, 226
Subdivisions of mobile homes, 177
Suburban ideal, the, 10
Suburban Turf: Second Stage Territoriality,
    128
Suburbia as Wasteland, **15**
Suburbs: criticism of, 15; early, 10–11; land
    use in, 4
Substandard housing: in rural areas, 275–
    276. *See also* Housing, national
    characteristics of
Support as a housing need for the elderly,
    289–291
Sun City, Arizona, 292
Sunbelt population growth, 38–39, 334
Sunbelt Growth Phenomenon, The, **39–40**

Taxation of mobile homes, 177
Tax credits for energy conservation, 329
Tax deduction related to home ownership, 281
Tax rate, 184, 186
Tax revolt, 339
Teepees, 92
Tenancy by the entirety, 194
Tenancy in common, 194
Tenant-landlord law, 203–209
Tenants' rights. *See* Rental agreements
Tenements, 7–9
Tenure and housing type: for nuclear families
    with teenagers, 79; for nuclear families with
    young children, 78; for preretirement
    childless couples, 80; for young childless
    couples, 77–78; for young single adults, 76
Termite inspection, 159
Term of the mortgage, 144; effects on monthly
    payment and total cost, 145, 146

Territorialty, 127–128
Time, as a factor in the home building
    process, 51–52
Time shared ownership, 88–89
Title, 160
Title insurance, 195
Toward a Human Architecture, **101**
Townhouses, 232. *See also* Cluster housing
Townships, 4
Transportation and energy efficiency, 325
Transportation service in housing for the
    elderly, 301
Travel trailers, as housing, 90. *See also*
    Mobile housing for the elderly
Tunnard, C., 12
Turnkey public housing, 248, 252

Underground housing. *See* Earth sheltered
    housing design
Uniform Residential Landlord Tenant Act,
    207–209
United States Housing Act of 1937, 248, 249,
    273
Unrelated adults and housing, 82–84
Upper class, 98
Urban Development Corporation. *See* New
    York State Urban Development Corporation
Urban homesteading, 271
Urban housing, 6–10; for the elderly, 298–
    299
Urban problems in the future, 342–343
Urban renewal, 105, 136, 253–258; and
    home ownership, 259–260; criticisms of,
    255, 257–258
URLTA. *See* Uniform Residential Landlord
    Tenant Act
U.S. Department of Housing and Urban
    Development, 210–211, 214–216, 237;
    and energy efficient housing, 329–330;
    HUD guaranteed new communities, 238–
    239; minimum space standards, 130;
    programs in rural areas, 276–277
U.S. government housing policy, 267–268
Usury laws, 194, 284
Utilities costs, 181–182

Value change and housing, 111–112; effects
    in future housing, 336–338
Values, 106; as a factor in home buying, 142;
    as related to life cycle, lifestyle, and social
    class, 113–114. *See also* Housing values
V.A. mortgage, 145–147, 159, 162, 171,
    179
Variable Rate Mortgage, 147